Perfect Vocabulary
한 권으로 끝내는 수능 보카

이상형

연세대학교 교육대학원 영어교육 석사

서울 영일고등학교 교사

저서 : LEADER'S 중학영어(금성출판사) / 교과서 TEACHER'S GUIDE(천재, 금성, 다락원) / 평가문항집 외 다수

제갈문국

동국대학교 통번역 대학원 석사

10년 넘게 영어 교과서 개발 참여

저서 : Oops Diary / Oops Writing Training / Oops Vocabulary(지혜정원) 외 다수

Perfect Vocabulary
한 권으로 끝내는 수능 보카

지은이   이상형, 제갈문국
발행인   정현순

발행처   지혜정원
출판등록   2010년 1월 5일 제313-2010-3호
주소   서울시 광진구 천호대로 109길 59 1층
연락처   TEL. 02.6401.5510 FAX. 02.6280.7379
홈페이지   www.jungwonbook.com

디자인   디자인모노피(주) irasi@hanmail.net
ISBN 978-89-94886-62-6 53740

값 15,800원

어근과 콜로케이션으로 수능 영어 정복하기

Perfect Vocabulary
한 권으로 끝내는 수능 보카

이상형, 제갈문국 지음

머리말

본서 'Perfect Vocabulary 한 권으로 끝내는 수능 보카'는 다년간에 걸친 수학능력 시험, 지역교육지원청 학력평가, 국가수준 학업성취도 평가에 나온 영단어를 심도 있게 분석하여 중고등학생들이 꼭 알아야 할 영단어들을 엄선했으며 여기에 각종 EBS 연계 교재의 고난도 어휘를 포함해 표제어 3500여 개를 수록했다. 제목에 걸맞게 완벽하게 한권으로 시험에 대비할 수 있도록 오랜 기간 심혈을 기울여서 작업하였다. 기본 단어는 물론 고급단어까지 총망라한 본서는 영영 사전적 의미, 동의어, 반의어를 제시하여 단어 암기를 다각도로 할 수 있게 도움을 주고 있으며, 특히 본서에서는 영단어에 대한 예문을 완전한 문장이 아닌 콜로케이션(collocation: 덩어리 학습)으로 제시하여 실질적인 어휘학습을 하는 데 도움이 되게 한 것이 가장 큰 특징이며, 각 단어에 대한 관련 문장들을 언제든지 발화할 수 있도록 유익한 표현들로 엄선하였다.

어휘 속에 숨어 있는 어근풀이, 영영사전적 정의, 동의어/반의어, 콜로케이션이 하나의 덩어리로 되어 있으므로 본서에 제시된 예문을 꼼꼼하게 공부한다면 수학능력시험은 물론 TEPS, TOEIC, TOEFL, IELTS 등을 대비하는 데 큰 도움이 될 것으로 믿는다.

수많은 어휘 책이 시중 서점에 나와 있지만 마땅히 자기 것을 찾지 못한 학생들에게 본서가 영어공부에 대한 작은 희망과 기쁨을 줄 수 있었으면 하는 바람이다.

마지막으로 본서의 출판을 허락한 '지혜정원' 정현순 대표이사님을 비롯한 직원여러분들께 감사함을 전한다.

저자 **이상형, 제갈문국**

차 례

Part I

수능에 꼭 나오는
빈출 어휘 정복

Day 01	**10**	Day 26	**210**
Day 02	**18**	Day 27	**218**
Day 03	**26**	Day 28	**226**
Day 04	**34**	Day 29	**234**
Day 05	**42**	Day 30	**242**
Day 06	**50**	Day 31	**250**
Day 07	**58**	Day 32	**258**
Day 08	**66**	Day 33	**266**
Day 09	**74**	Day 34	**274**
Day 10	**82**	Day 35	**282**
Day 11	**90**	Day 36	**290**
Day 12	**98**	Day 37	**298**
Day 13	**106**	Day 38	**306**
Day 14	**114**	Day 39	**314**
Day 15	**122**	Day 40	**322**
Day 16	**130**	Day 41	**330**
Day 17	**138**	Day 42	**338**
Day 18	**146**	Day 43	**346**
Day 19	**154**	Day 44	**354**
Day 20	**162**	Day 45	**362**
Day 21	**170**	Day 46	**370**
Day 22	**178**	Day 47	**378**
Day 23	**186**	Day 48	**386**
Day 24	**194**	Day 49	**394**
Day 25	**202**	Day 50	**402**

Part II

영어 1등급을 사수하는
고난도 어휘 정복

Day 51	**412**
Day 52	**420**
Day 53	**428**
Day 54	**436**
Day 55	**444**
Day 56	**452**
Day 57	**460**
Day 58	**468**
Day 59	**476**
Day 60	**484**

Part III

영어의 초고수가 되는
어근별 단어 정리

Day 61	**494**
Day 62	**500**
Day 63	**506**
Day 64	**512**
Day 65	**518**
Day 66	**524**
Day 67	**530**

이 책의 활용

01.. 수능에 꼭 나오는 빈출 어휘 정복 / 영어 1등급을 사수하는 고난도 어휘 정복

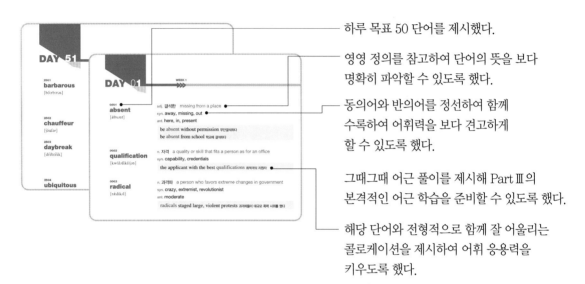

— 하루 목표 50 단어를 제시했다.

— 영영 정의를 참고하여 단어의 뜻을 보다 명확히 파악할 수 있도록 했다.

— 동의어와 반의어를 정선하여 함께 수록하여 어휘력을 보다 견고하게 할 수 있도록 했다.

— 그때그때 어근 풀이를 제시해 Part Ⅲ의 본격적인 어근 학습을 준비할 수 있도록 했다.

— 해당 단어와 전형적으로 함께 잘 어울리는 콜로케이션을 제시하여 어휘 응용력을 키우도록 했다.

02.. 콜로케이션으로 하루 50단어를 내 것으로 확실히 챙긴다

— 주요 어휘를 콜로케이션으로 점검해 보도록 했다. 단어를 기억할 때 콜로케이션으로 함께 기억하는 것은 어휘 확장의 비법이다. 적극 활용하기 바란다.

— 단어의 연번을 두어 정답을 확인하기 용이하도록 했다.

03.. 영어의 초고수가 되는 어근별 단어 정리

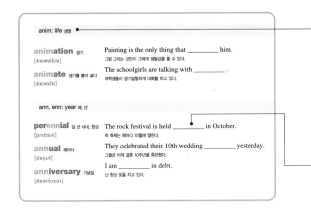

영어의 고급 사용자가 되고자 한다면
어근 학습은 선택이 아닌 필수다.
여기서는 단어 하나를 외우는 것 보다는
원리 파악 즉, 어근 하나에 여러 단어를
연상해 내는 능력을 키우는 것이 목적이다.

모든 단어에 예문을 제시했으며 빈칸
채우기로 바로바로 점검해 볼 수
있도록 했다.

04.. REVIEW TEST로 실력 점검

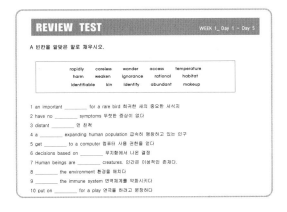

www.jungwonbook.com에서 제공하는
추가 Test를 이용하여 실력을 점검한다.
빈칸 채우기, 4지선다, 퍼즐 등 다양한
형태의 REVIEW TEST로 영단어 학습 후
본인의 실력을 다양한 방법으로 점검해
볼 수 있다.

PART 1

수능에 꼭 나오는
빈출 어휘 정복

하루 50개씩 학습 후 리뷰

0001
absent
[ǽbsənt]

adj. 결석한 missing from a place

syn. away, missing, out

ant. here, in, present

> be absent without permission 무단결석하다
>
> be absent from school 학교에 결석하다

0002
qualification
[kwὰləfikéiʃən]

n. 자격 a quality or skill that fits a person as for an office

syn. capability, credentials

> the applicant with the best qualifications 최적격의 지원자

0003
radical
[rǽdikəl]

n. 과격파 a person who favors extreme changes in government

syn. crazy, extremist, revolutionist

ant. moderate

> radicals staged large, violent protests 과격파들이 대규모 폭력 시위를 했다

0004
calculate
[kǽlkjulèit]

v. 계산하다 to find out how much something will cost, etc. by using numbers

syn. compute, figure, reckon, work out

> calculate the overall costs 전체 비용을 산출하다

0005
sabotage
[sǽbətὰːʒ]

v. 고의로 방해[파괴]하다 to cause the failure of something deliberately

syn. damage, destroy, wreck, undermine

> a deal sabotaged by an angry employee 분노한 직원에 의해 망쳐진 거래

0006
flap
[flæp]

v. 펄럭거리다 to move up and down or back and forth

syn. beat, flop, flutter, whip

> flap in the breeze 바람에 펄럭이다

0007
range
[reindʒ]

n. 범위 a collection of different things or people that are usually similar in some way

syn. variety, selection, assortment,

> a wide range of knowledge 광범위한 지식

0008
calm
[kɑ:m]

v. 진정시키다   to make or become calm
syn. settle, soothe, still, tranquilize
ant. agitate, disquiet, disturb

try to calm her fears 그녀의 공포를 진정시키려 애쓰다

0009
sacrifice
[sǽkrəfàis]

n. 희생   a surrender of something of value as a means of gaining something more desirable
syn. surrender, loss, giving up

make a sacrifice bunt 희생 번트를 대다

0010
raise
[reiz]

v. 올리다   to lift or move something or someone to a higher position
syn. elevate, lift, uphold
ant. drop, lower

raise a monument 비석을 세우다
raise one's hand 손을 들다

0011
race
[reis]

n. 인종   a category of humankind that shares certain distinctive physical traits
syn. people, ethnic group

discriminate on the basis of race 인종 차별을 하다

0012
daring
[dέəriŋ]

adj. 과감한   venturesomely bold in action or thought
syn. brave, bold, adventurous, reckless
ant. unadventurous, unenterprising

ideas that are new and daring 신선하고 과감한 아이디어

0013
cancel
[kǽnsəl]

v. 취소하다   to stop doing or planning to do something
syn. abandon, abort, call off
ant. continue, keep

cancel a magazine subscription 잡지 구독을 취소하다

0014
panic
[pǽnik]

n. 공황   a sudden overpowering fright
syn. fright, horror, fear, scare, terror

get into a panic 공황 상태에 빠져들다
the crowd in a state of panic 공황 상태의 군중

0015
habitual
[həbítʃuəl]

adj. 습관성의   doing something regularly or repeatedly

syn. bred-in-the-bone, chronic

ant. inconstant, infrequent, irregular

habitual drunkards 습관성 주정꾼들

0016
damage
[dǽmidʒ]

n. 피해   physical harm that is done to something or to someone's body

syn. injury, harm, hurt

ant. healing, recovery

cause considerable damage 상당한 피해를 입히다

0017
face-to-face

adj. 얼굴을 마주보고 하는   within each other's sight or presence

syn. direct, person-to-person

met and talked face-to-face 만나서 직접 대화했다

0018
ease
[iːz]

v. 달래다   to free someone from trouble or worry

syn. loosen up, smooth, unclog

ant. complicate

try to ease her of her worries 그녀의 걱정을 덜어주려 애쓰다

0019
babble
[bǽbəl]

v. 지껄이다   to talk foolishly or too much

syn. bumble, chat, chatter

ant. articulate

babble on about sports 스포츠에 관해 계속 지껄이다

0020
sacred
[séikrid]

-cred 믿다

adj. 신성한   very holy

syn. hallowed, holy, untouchable

ant. nonreligious, profane

the sacred pursuit of liberty 신성한 자유의 추구

0021
face
[feis]

v. 마주하다   to stand or sit with your face and body turned toward something

syn. front, look toward

ant. dodge, duck, sidestep

a house facing the park 공원과 마주하고 있는 집

the problems that face us 우리가 직면한 문제들

0022
identical
[aidéntikəl]

adj. 동일한   exactly the same
syn. same
ant. another, different, other

the identical place we stopped before 우리가 전에 멈췄던 바로 그 장소
identical hats 똑같은 모자

0023
paddle
[pǽdl]

v. 물장구치다, 노 젓다   to move the hands or feet about in shallow water
syn. oar

paddled for several hours along the coast 해변을 따라 몇 시간 동안 노를 저었다

0024
object
[ábdʒikt]

n. 사물, 물체   a tangible and visible thing
syn. thing, article, item

bump against some solid object 딱딱한 물체에 부딪히다

0025
ecological
[èkəládʒikəl]

adj. 환경의, 생태의   of or relating to ecology
syn. environmental, green

cause an ecological disaster 생태적 재앙을 일으키다

0026
laboratory
[lǽbərətɔ̀:ri]
-labor 일, 노동

n. 실험실, 연구소   a place equipped for experimental study in a science
   or for testing and analysis

laboratory equipment 실험실 장비

0027
namely
[néimli]

adv. 이른바, 말하자면   that is to say

some groups, namely students and pensioners
몇몇 그룹들, 말하자면 학생들과 연금 수급자들

0028
absolute
[ǽbsəlù:t]

adj. 완전한, 절대적인   very great, or complete
syn. arbitrary, autocratic
ant. limited

absolute nonsense 완전히 터무니없는 소리

0029
ideal
[aidíːəl]

adj. 이상적인   exactly right for a particular purpose, situation, or person
syn. perfect, best, model

an ideal candidate for the job 직무에 최적의 지원자

0030
eager
[íːgər]

adj. 열망하는   very excited and interested

syn. enthusiastic, excited

ant. apathetic, indifferent

the eager faces waiting for her news 그녀의 소식을 열렬히 기다리는 얼굴들

0031
rag
[ræg]

n. 넝마, 헝겊 a piece of old cloth used for cleaning or wiping something

syn. cloth, piece of cloth

the rag trade 의류 산업

0032
habitat
[hǽbətæt]

n. 서식지   the environment in which an animal or plant normally lives or grows

syn. home, environment, surroundings, territory

an important habitat for a rare bird 희귀한 새의 중요한 서식지

0033
identifiable
[aidéntəfàiəbəl]

adj. 식별 가능한   able to be recognized

syn. recognizable, noticeable, discernible

have no identifiable symptoms 뚜렷한 증상이 없다

0034
naive
[nɑːíːv]

adj. 순진한   having or showing a lack of experience or knowledge

syn. ingenuous, innocent

ant. experienced, sophisticated, worldly

a naive belief that all people are good 모든 사람이 선하다는 순진한 믿음

0035
galaxy
[gǽləksi]

n. 은하   any one of the very large groups of stars that make up the universe

syn. star system, solar system

the Andromeda galaxy 안드로메다 은하

0036
neglect
[niglékt]

v. 방치하다   to fail to take care of or to give attention to

syn. bypass, disregard, ignore, overlook

ant. attend to, heed, mind, regard

parents who neglect their children 자녀를 방치하는 부모

0037
label
[léibəl]

v. 라벨을 달다   to put a label on an object

syn. mark, tag, ticket

label the switches so that you don't confuse them
스위치에 라벨을 달아 헷갈리지 않도록 하다

0038
gain
[gein]

v. 얻다   to get something wanted or valued

syn. acquire, get, receive, achieve

ant. decrease, lose

gain an advantage 유리한 고지를 점령하다

0039
facial
[féiʃəl]

adj. 얼굴에 드러나는   of or relating to a person's face

facial expressions 얼굴 표정

0040
dangerous
[déindʒərəs]

adj. 위험한   likely to harm or kill someone, or to damage or destroy something

syn. hazardous, jeopardizing, menacing

ant. harmless, innocent

highly dangerous sport 매우 위험한 스포츠
avoid potentially dangerous situations 잠재적으로 위험한 상황을 피하다

0041
labor
[léibər]

v. 힘쓰다, 고심하다   to work hard in order to achieve something

syn. beaver, dig, drudge, endeavor

ant. idle, ease, let up, slacken

labor for several years as a miner 광부로 몇 년간 노동하다

0042
habit
[hǽbit]

n. 습관   a usual way of behaving

syn. custom, pattern, second nature

healthy eating habits 건강한 식사 습관
get up early from force of habit 습관의 힘으로 일찍 일어나다

0043
kin
[kin]

n. 친척   a person's relatives

syn. blood, clan, folks

ant. nonrelative

distant kin 먼 친척

0044
pack
[pæk]

v. 꾸리다, 채우다   to make into a compact bundle

syn. load, store, bundle

pack a bag/suitcase 가방을 꾸리다

0045
pain
[pein]

n. 고통   a feeling that you have in a part of your body when you are hurt or ill

syn. ache, pang, prick

terrible pains in my stomach 극심한 복통

0046
elder
[éldər]

n. 연장자   one who is older

syn. senior

ant. junior

a child trying to please her elders 어른들에게 재롱부리고 있는 한 아이

0047
mad
[mæd]

adj. 몹시 화난   very angry

syn. angered, fuming, furious

ant. delighted, pleased

mad about the delay 지연에 몹시 화난

0048
object
[əbdʒékt]

v. 반대하다   to disagree with something or oppose something

syn. kick, protest, remonstrate

ant. approve, accept, agree

objected that the statement was misleading 진술이 잘못 되었다고 반대했다

0049
identification
[aidèntəfikéiʃən]

n. 신원 확인, 식별 the act of identifying or the state of being identified

syn. recognition, naming, labelling, distinguishing

an identification card 신분증

need two forms of identification 두 가지 신원 증명 양식이 필요하다

0050
earnestly
[ə́:rnistli]

adv. 열렬히, 진심으로   with sincere intensity

syn. seriously, truly, sincerely, in earnest

ant. jokingly, playfully

she asked earnestly 그녀는 적극적으로 물었다

stared at me earnestly 진지하게 나를 바라봤다

Review

뜻을 써보고 전체 어구의 의미를 생각해 보시오.

01 **cause considerable** damage   예 피해 / 상당한 피해를 입히다.   0016

02 **raise** one's hand   0010

03 **cancel** a magazine subscription   0013

04 **cause** an ecological **disaster**   0025

05 the rag **trade**   0031

06 babble **on about sports**   0019

07 **bump against some solid** object   0024

08 **the applicant with the best** qualifications   0002

09 gain **an advantage**   0038

10 **labor** for several years as a miner   0041

11 facial **expressions**   0039

12 absolute **nonsense**   0028

13 **terrible** pains **in my stomach**   0045

14 **parents who** neglect **their children**   0036

15 mad **about the delay**   0047

16 **a wide** range **of knowledge**   0007

17 **distant** kin   0043

18 **a** naive **belief that all people are good**   0034

19 laboratory **equipment**   0026

20 **a deal** sabotaged **by an angry employee**   0005

0051
wander
[wɑ́ndər]

v. 배회하다   to move or travel about, in, or through without any definite purpose

syn. roam, walk, drift, stroll

wander around the house 집 주변을 서성이다

0052
accelerate
[æksélərèit]

v. 가속하다   to cause something to happen sooner or more quickly

syn. increase, accumulate, snowball

ant. decrease, diminish, dwindle

accelerate economic development 경제 발전을 촉진하다

0053
factor
[fǽktər]

n. 요인   one of several things that influence or cause a situation

syn. element, part, component

ant. whole

price wasn't a factor in the decision 가격은 결정 요인이 아니었다

0054
halfhearted
[hǽfhɑ́ːrtid]

adj. 건성의   lacking heart, spirit, or interest

syn. uneager, unenthusiastic

ant. passionate, hearty, wholehearted

half-hearted applause from the audience 건성으로 치는 관객의 박수

0055
economic
[íːkənɑ́mik]

adj. 경제의, 경제적인   relating to an economy

syn. financial, profitable

ant. unprofitable

economic growth 경제 성장

0056
darken
[dɑ́ːrkən]

v. 어둡게 하다   to make something dark

syn. gloom

ant. brighten, dawn, shine

the skies were darkening 하늘이 어두워지고 있었다

0057
garage sale
[gərɑ́ːʒ seil]

n. (자기집 차고에서 하는) 중고품 염가판매, 거라지 세일 a sale of used furniture, clothing, etc. held at the seller's home

syn. yard sale, tag sale

hold a garage sale 거라지 세일을 열다

0058
handicap
[hǽndikæp]

v. 불리하게 하다   to give someone a disadvantage

syn. clog, cramp, hold back

ant. aid, assist, facilitate, help

be handicapped by their poor level of English
영어 실력이 부족해 불이익을 당하다

0059
abstract
[æbstrǽkt]

adj. 추상적인   based on general ideas or principles rather than specific examples or real events

syn. conceptual, ideal, theoretical

ant. concrete

abstract ideas such as love and hate 사랑과 증오와 같은 추상적 개념

0060
vague
[veig]

adj. 모호한   not clear in meaning

syn. fuzzy, indefinite, unclear

a vague feeling/suspicion 어렴풋한 느낌/의심

0061
wake
[weik]

v. 깨우다   to make someone stop sleeping

syn. awake, awaken, knock up

a cup of coffee will wake me up 커피 한 잔 하면 잠이 깰 것이다

0062
valid
[vǽlid]

adj. 유효한, 타당한   acceptable according to the law

syn. rational, reasonable, logical

ant. irrational, unreasonable, weak

a valid contract 유효한 계약
a valid theory 타당한 이론

0063
yell
[jel]

v. 소리 지르다   to make a sudden, loud cry

syn. howl, screech, shriek

ant. murmur, whisper

yell for help 도와달라고 소리치다

0064
abundant
[əbʌ́ndənt]

adj. 풍부한   existing or available in large quantities

syn. plentiful, ample

ant. minimal, scant, spare

an abundant supply of food 풍부한 식량 공급

0065
panel
[pǽnl]

n. 토론자단, 토론회 a group of people who make decisions or judgments

syn. conference, council, forum, panel discussion

host a panel on free speech 자유 언론에 관한 토론회 사회를 보다

0066
abuse
[əbjúːz]

v. 남용하다, 학대하다 to use something wrongly

syn. ill-treat, ill-use, kick around

abuse a privilege 특권을 남용하다
abuse a child 아이를 학대하다

0067
backward
[bǽkwərd]

adv. 거꾸로 to or toward what is behind

syn. back, rearward

ant. ahead, along, forth, forward

a journey backward in time 과거로의 시간 여행

0068
halfway
[hǽfwèi]

adv. 중간에서, 절반만 in the middle between two points

syn. incomplete, partial

ant. complete, entire, full

halfway through a film 영화의 중간쯤에서

0069
absorb
[əbsɔ́ːrb]

v. 흡수하다, 흡입하다 to take in a gas, liquid, or other substance

syn. drink, soak up, sponge, take up

absorb moisture 습기를 빨아들이다

0070
vacuum
[vǽkjuəm]
-vac 텅 빈

n. 진공 an empty space in which there is no air or other gas

syn. emptiness, space, void

the vacuum of outer space 대기권 밖 우주의 진공

0071
ideology
[àidiálədʒi]

n. 이념, 신조 the set of ideas and beliefs of a group or political party

syn. doctrine, dogma, creed, philosophy

the ideology of a totalitarian society 전체주의 사회의 이념

0072
bacteria
[bæktíəriə]

n. 박테리아, 세균 very small living things that consist of a single cell

syn. microorganisms, viruses, bugs, germs

bacteria can live just about anywhere 박테리아는 거의 어느 곳에서나 서식한다

0073
journalist
[dʒə́:rnəlist]

n. 기자   a writer or editor for a news medium

syn. correspondent, reporter, newshound

an article by a leading sports journalist 잘 나가는 스포츠 기자가 쓴 기사

0074
capability
[kèipəbíləti]

n. 능력, 역량   the ability to do something

syn. qualification, credentials

ant. disability, inability, incapability

increase its manufacturing capability 제조 능력을 상승시키다

0075
landfall
[lǽndfɔ̀:l]

n. (운항 후) 처음 보는 육지   the act of sighting or nearing land, esp from the sea

make a good landfall 예측대로 육지를 발견하다

0076
lack
[læk]

v. 없다, 부족하다   to not have something

syn. miss, want, need, require

time is lacking for an explanation 설명하기에 시간이 부족하다

0077
unambiguous
[ʌ̀næmbíɡjuəs]

adj. 뚜렷한, 모호하지 않은   clearly expressed or understood

syn. apparent, bald-faced, distinct

ant. ambiguous, clouded

an unambiguous message 분명한 메시지

0078
taste
[teist]

v. ~ 맛이 나다, 맛을 보다   to have a particular taste / to sense the flavor of something

syn. flavor, savor, relish, smack

taste the wine 와인 맛을 보다

taste like vinegar 식초 맛이 난다

0079
identify
[aidéntəfài]

v. 신원을 확인하다   to find out who someone is or what something is

syn. distinguish, finger, pinpoint, single out

correctly identify the mushroom 어떤 버섯인지 정확히 식별하다

0080
gas station
[gæs stéiʃən]

n. 주유소   a place where gasoline for vehicles is sold

syn. petrol station, filling station

managed to locate a gas station 어렵사리 주요소를 찾아냈다

0081
observe
[əbzə́ːrv]

v. 관찰하다 to watch and sometimes also listen to someone or something

syn. eye, follow

ant. blink, wink

learn by observing others 다른 사람을 관찰하면서 배우다

0082
narrative
[nǽrətiv]

n. 이야기, (소설 속 사건의) 기술   a story that is told or written

syn. chronicle, chronology, commentary, narration

write a detailed narrative of his life 자기 삶의 이야기를 상세히 쓰다

0083
mandate
[mǽndeit]
-mand 명령하다

v. 의무화하다   to officially demand or require something

syn. dictate, direct, command, order

be mandated by government 정부가 의무화 하다

0084
journey
[dʒə́ːrni]

n. 긴 여행 a going from one place to another usually of some distance

syn. expedition, passage, travel

prepare for a journey 여행 준비를 하다

0085
kindle
[kíndl]

v. 불붙이다, 선동하다   to set alight or start to burn / to stir up

syn. light, start, ignite, fire, spark

kindle a fire using twigs and grass 나뭇가지와 풀을 이용해 불을 붙이다
kindle interest 관심을 유발하다

0086
ecology
[iːkάlədʒi]

v. 생태계, 생태학 the study of the relationships between living organisms and their environment

syn. environment, surroundings, habitat

adjust the ecology to our needs 생태계를 우리의 필요에 맞추다

0087
ultimately
[Áltəmitli]

adv. 궁극적으로   in the end

syn. finally, eventually, in the end, after all

ant. never

be ultimately bound to fail 결국 실패하게 되어 있다

0088
absolutely
[ǽbsəlùːtli]

adv. 절대적으로   in an absolute manner

syn. completely, totally, perfectly

be absolutely certain 완전히 확신하다

0089
manage
[mǽnidʒ]

v. 용케 해내다   to succeed in being able to do something despite obstacles

syn. get through, make out, muddle through

somehow managed to persuade him 용케 그를 설득했다

0090
background
[bǽkgràund]

n. 배경   the scenery or ground behind something

syn. backdrop, ground

ant. foreground

students from very different backgrounds 매우 다른 환경에서 온 학생들

0091
safe
[seif]

n. 안전한   not in danger

syn. secure

ant. susceptible, threatened, vulnerable

live in a perfectly safe neighborhood 아주 안전한 동네에 살다

0092
magical
[mǽdʒikəl]

adj. 마법 같은   very enjoyable, exciting or romantic, in a strange or special way

syn. extraordinary, amazing, outstanding, remarkable

that magical evening we spent together 우리가 함께 보낸 마법 같은 그날 저녁

0093
land
[lænd]

v. 내리다, 착륙하다   to return to the ground or another surface after a flight

syn. anchor, dock, make port

ant. go, leave

landed in a tree 나무에 내려앉았다

0094
badly
[bǽdli]

adv. 몹시, 심각하게   severely or seriously

ant. so-so, tolerably

wanted the job badly 그 일자리를 간절히 원했다

0095
cancer
[kǽnsər]

n. 암   a very serious disease in which cells in one part of the body start to grow in a way that is not normal

syn. tumor

reduce the risk of cancer 암의 위험을 줄이다

0096
facilitate
[fəsílətèit]

v. 용이하게 하다, 촉진하다   to make easier

syn. ease, grease, loosen up, smooth

ant. complicate

> facilitate growth 성장을 촉진하다
>
> facilitate the discussion by asking appropriate questions
> 적절한 질문을 해서 토론을 촉진하다

0097
candidate
[kǽndədèit]

n. 지원자, 후보   someone who is being considered for a job or is competing in an election

syn. applicant, applier, prospect, seeker

> a presidential candidate 대통령 후보

0098
task
[tæsk]

n. 직무, 임무   a piece of work that has been given to someone

syn. assignment, duty, job, chore

> one of my tasks in the morning 내가 아침에 해야 할 임무 중 하나

0099
tap
[tæp]

v. 톡 치다   to strike lightly especially with a slight sound

syn. knock, strike, pat, rap

> tap a pencil on the table 연필로 탁자를 톡 치다

0100
saddle
[sǽdl]

n. 안장   a leather-covered seat that is put on the back of a horse

> put a saddle on a horse 말 위에 안장을 얹다

Review

뜻을 써보고 전체 어구의 의미를 생각해 보시오.

01 a vague suspicion   0060

02 an unambiguous message   0077

03 accelerate economic development   0052

04 students from very different backgrounds   0090

05 increase its manufacturing capability   0074

06 tap a pencil on the table   0099

07 the vacuum of outer space   0070

08 landed in a tree   0093

09 put a saddle on a horse   0100

10 prepare for a journey   0084

11 facilitate growth   0096

12 be absolutely certain   0088

13 learn by observing others   0081

14 be mandated by government   0083

15 reduce the risk of cancer   0095

16 abuse a privilege   0066

17 one of my tasks in the morning   0098

18 abstract ideas such as love and hate   0059

19 yell for help   0063

20 an article by a leading sports journalist   0073

0101
parallel
[pǽrəlèl]

adj. 평행한, 동시 발생의   very similar and often happening at the same time

syn. matching, alike, resembling

ant. different, dissimilar, diverse, unlike

parallel rows of trees 평행하게 늘어선 나무들

0102
paralysis
[pərǽləsis]

n. 마취, 마비   a state of being unable to function, act, or move

ant. mobility, motility, sensation

be in a state of paralysis 마비 상태이다

0103
accompany
[əkʌ́mpəni]
-com 함께

v. 동행하다   to go somewhere with someone

syn. attend, convoy, escort

ant. abandon, desert, ditch, dump, forsake

the pictures that accompany the text 글과 함께 실린 그림들
accompanied their advice with a warning 경고와 함께 충고를 해 주었다

0104
rarely
[rέərli]

adv. 흔치 않게   not very often

syn. infrequently, little, seldom

ant. often

she very rarely complains 그녀는 불평을 거의 하지 않는다

0105
balanced
[bǽlənst]

adj. (무게나 의견이) 균형 잡힌   having weight evenly distributed

syn. unbiased, just, fair, equal

a balanced diet 균형 잡힌 식단

0106
qualify
[kwάləfài]

v. 자격을 갖추다   to have the necessary skill or knowledge to do a particular job or activity

ant. disqualify

qualify to receive financial aid 재정 지원을 받을 자격을 갖추다

0107
saint
[séint]

n. 성인, 성자   a person who is officially recognized by the Christian church as being very holy because of the way he or she lived

syn. holy man

be patient as a saint 성자처럼 참을성이 있다

0108
observer
[əbzɔ́ːrvər]

n. 관찰자, 참관인   a person who sees and notices someone or something

syn. bystander, spectator, onlooker, viewer, watcher

attend their conference as an observer 참관인 자격으로 회의에 참석하다

0109
fade
[feid]

v. 사라지다, 흐려지다   to disappear gradually

syn. disappear, go away, vanish

ant. appear, materialize

a fading memory 사라져가는 기억

the fading light of late afternoon 흐릿해지는 늦은 오후의 빛

0110
rapidly
[rǽpidli]

adv. 빠르게   within a short space of time

syn. quickly, fast, swiftly, briskly, promptly

a rapidly expanding human population 급속히 팽창하고 있는 인구

0111
band
[bænd]

n. 밴드, 단체   a company of people having a common purpose

syn. ensemble, group, orchestra, combo

a band of demonstrators 시위대

0112
accommodate
[əkámədèit]

v. 숙박시키다, 편의를 봐주다   to provide room for someone / to provide what is needed or wanted for someone

syn. fit, hold, take

accommodate 500 guests 투숙객 500명을 수용하다

0113
gather
[gǽðər]

v. 모으다, 모이다   to bring things or people together into a group

syn. accumulate, amass, assemble, collect

ant. disperse, scatter

gathered firewood 땔감을 모았다

0114
handle
[hǽndl]

v. 다루다, 처리하다   to manage or control something with your hands

syn. manage, maneuver, manipulate, cope with

handle a horse 말을 다루다

0115
capacity
[kəpǽsəti]

n. 수용 능력   the ability to hold or contain people or things

syn. volume

ant. incapacity

a large seating capacity 대규모 수용 가능 좌석 수

0116
illness
[ílnis]

n. 병   a condition of being unhealthy in your body or mind

syn. affection, ail, ailment, disease, sickness

found a cure for this illness 이 질병에 대한 치료법을 찾았다

0117
rare
[rɛər]

adj. 흔치 않은, 귀한   seldom occurring or found

syn. priceless, special, unusual

a rare talent 흔치 않은 재능

a rare herb 희귀한 식물

0118
ignore
[ignɔ́ːr]

v. 무시하다   to refuse to take notice of

syn. pay no attention to, neglect, disregard, overlook

ignored the warning signs 경고판을 무시했다

0119
hang
[hæŋ]

v. 매달다   to attach or place something so that it is held up without support from below

syn. dangle, sling, suspend, swing

hang the wash on a clothesline 빨래를 빨래 줄에 걸다

0120
access
[ǽkses]

-cess 가다

n. 입장, 접근 권한   a way of getting near, at, or to something or someone

syn. admission, entry, passage

get access to a computer 컴퓨터 사용 권한을 얻다

0121
daylight
[déilàit]

n. 일광, 주간   the time of day when the sky is light

ant. nightfall, sundown, sunset

let some daylight into the room 방 안으로 햇빛이 들어오게 하다

0122
yield
[jiːld]

v. 1 산출하다 2 포기하다 to produce or bear / to give way, submit, or surrender
syn. 1. produce, crop, harvest
     2. submit, give in, surrender

yielded an abundant harvest 풍족한 수확을 산출했다
face an enemy who would not yield 포기하지 않는 적과 대치하다

0123
accept
[æksépt]
-cept 받다

v. 수락하다 to receive or take something offered
syn. take, have
ant. decline, deny, disapprove, reject

accept an offer 제안을 수락하다

0124
dawn
[dɔːn]

v. 동이 트다 to begin to become light as the sun rises
syn. brighten, lighten

waited for the day to dawn 동이 트기를 기다렸다

0125
salvage
[sǽlvidʒ]

n. 구조 the action of saving property or possessions from being destroyed in a fire, flood, etc.
syn. rescue, saving, recovery

the salvage operation 구조 작전

0126
wasteland
[wéistlæ̀nd]

n. 황무지, 불모지 land where nothing can grow or be built / land that is not usable
syn. barren, desert, desolation

a cultural wasteland 문화적 황무지

0127
capture
[kǽptʃər]

v. 잡다, 체포하다 to catch someone so that they become your prisoner / to catch an animal
syn. catch, arrest, secure, seize

using traps to capture mice 쥐를 잡기 위해 덫을 사용하기

0128
capital
[kǽpitl]
-cap 머리

n. 수도 an important city where the main government of a country, state, etc. is

the capital of the United States 미국의 수도

0129
salary
[sǽləri]

n. 급여 an amount of money that an employee is paid each year

syn. pay, paycheck, payment, wage

a salary of $50,000 a year 연봉 5만 달러

0130
ignorance
[ígnərəns]

n. 무지 lack of knowledge, education, or awareness

syn. unawareness, inexperience, innocence

decisions based on ignorance 무지함에서 나온 결정들

0131
waste
[weist]

n. 낭비 an action or use that results in the unnecessary loss of something valuable

syn. misuse, loss

ways to reduce unnecessary waste 불필요한 낭비를 줄이는 방법들

0132
ecosystem
[í:kousìstəm]

n. 생태계 an ecological community together with its environment, functioning as a unit

the forest ecosystem 산림 생태계

0133
factual
[fǽktʃuəl]

adj. 사실의, 사실에 근거한 limited to, involving, or based on facts

syn. nonfictional, objective, true

ant. fictional

a report filled with factual errors 사실 무근의 오류로 가득한 보고서

0134
economically
[ì:kənámikəli]

adv. 경제적으로 without waste

ant. wastefully

a way to economically heat your house 경제적으로 집에 난방을 갖추는 방법

0135
warrior
[wɔ́(:)riər]

n. 전사, 용사 a person who fights in battles and is known for having courage and skill

syn. fighter, soldier

a proud and brave warrior 자랑스럽고 용맹스런 전사

0136
judge
[dʒʌdʒ]

v. 판단하다, 판결하다 to regard someone as either good or bad

syn. decide, determine, referee

judge people by their appearance 사람을 외모로 판단하다

0137

salute

[səlúːt]

v. 경례하다　to give a sign of respect to a military officer, etc. by moving your right hand to your forehead

syn. greet, welcome, acknowledge

salute the flag 국기에 경례하다

0138

tax

[tæks]

n. 세금　an amount of money that you must pay to the government according to your income, property, goods, etc.

syn. duty, imposition

evade taxes 탈세하다

0139

paradox

[pǽrədàks]

n. 역설, 모순　something that is made up of two opposite things and that seems impossible but is actually true or possible

syn. incongruity, contradiction

a novel full of paradox 역설로 가득한 소설

0140

valuable

[vǽljuːəbəl]

adj. 귀중한, 값비싼　worth a lot of money

syn. precious, premium, priceless

ant. cheap, inexpensive

learned a valuable lesson 귀중한 교훈을 얻었다

0141

panic

[pǽnik]

v. 공황을 일으키다, 공황에 빠지다　to be overcome with extreme fear

syn. shock, spook, startle, terrify

Don't panic. 당황하지 마시오.

0142

technical

[téknikəl]

adj. 전문적인　having special knowledge especially of how machines work or of how a particular kind of work is done

syn. specialized

ant. general

technical language 전문 용어

0143

unattractive

[ʌ̀nətrǽktiv]

-tract 끌다

adj. 매력 없는　not beautiful, interesting, or pleasing

syn. ugly, homely, plain, hideous

an unattractive man 매력 없는 남자

0144
unanimous
[juːnǽnəməs]

adj. 만장일치의   in complete or absolute agreement
ant. disagreeable, discordant, disharmonious

a unanimous decision 만장일치의 결정

0145
value
[vǽljuː]

n. 가치   the amount of money that something is worth
syn. valuation, worth

an increase in the value of the dollar 달러의 가치 상승

0146
daydream
[déidrìːm]

v. 몽상하다   to think pleasant thoughts about your life or future while you are awake
syn. fantasize, dream, imagine

a good place to think, or to daydream 사색하거나 공상하기 좋은 장소

0147
warn
[wɔːrn]

v. 경고하다   to tell someone about possible danger or trouble
syn. advise, alert, caution, forewarn

warned about the difficulties of the job 그 일의 어려움에 대해 경고했다

0148
taxpayer
[tækspéiər]

n. 납세자   someone who pays tax, especially tax on income

the biggest taxpayer 최고액 납세자

0149
tease
[tiːz]

v. 놀리다   to laugh at and criticize in a way that is either friendly and playful
syn. joke, kid, rib

teased me about my voice 내 목소리 때문에 나를 놀렸다

0150
paradise
[pǽrədàis]

n. 천국   a very beautiful, pleasant, or peaceful place that seems to be perfect
syn. utopia, seventh heaven
ant. dystopia, hell

a book lover's paradise 책을 좋아하는 사람들의 천국

Review

뜻을 써보고 전체 어구의 의미를 생각해 보시오.

01 decisions based on ignorance _____ 0130

02 be patient as a saint _____ 0107

03 ignored the warning signs _____ 0118

04 hang the wash on a clothesline _____ 0119

05 qualify to receive financial aid _____ 0106

06 accept an offer _____ 0123

07 evade taxes _____ 0138

08 a unanimous decision _____ 0144

09 found a cure for this illness _____ 0116

10 ways to reduce unnecessary waste _____ 0131

11 using traps to capture mice _____ 0127

12 an increase in the value of the dollar _____ 0145

13 the salvage operation _____ 0125

14 the biggest taxpayer _____ 0148

15 attend their conference as an observer _____ 0108

16 Don't panic. _____ 0141

17 the forest ecosystem _____ 0132

18 a good place to think, or to daydream _____ 0146

19 be in a state of paralysis _____ 0102

20 the pictures that accompany the text _____ 0103

0151
rational
[ræʃənl]

adj. 합리적인, 이성적인   based on facts or reason and not on emotions or feelings

syn. intelligent, reasonable, thinking

human beings are rational creatures 인간은 이성적인 존재다

0152
debate
[dibéit]

v. 토론하다   to discuss something with people whose opinions are different from your own

syn. discuss, question, talk about

ant. disregard, ignore, overlook

the most hotly debated issues today 요즘 가장 열띠게 토론 중인 문제

0153
fair
[fɛər]

adj. 공평한, 공정한   agreeing with what is thought to be right or acceptable

syn. unbiased, impartial, even-handed

a very fair person to do business with 함께 사업을 하기에 매우 공정한 사람

0154
gaze
[geiz]

v. 응시하다, 바라보다   to look long and fixedly

syn. stare, look, view, watch

ant. glance, glimpse

gazed out the window at the snow 창밖의 눈을 바라봤다

0155
hardly
[háːrdli]

adv. 거의 ~아니다   almost not at all

syn. barely, only just, scarcely

could hardly hold the cup 컵을 거의 들 수 없었다

0156
edible
[édəbəl]

adj. 먹을 수 있는   suitable or safe to eat

syn. eatable

ant. inedible, nonedible, uneatable

edible mushrooms 식용 버섯들

0157
technician
[tekníʃən]

n. 기술자, 전문가   a person whose job relates to the practical use of machines or science in industry, medicine, etc.

syn. mechanic, specialist

a computer technician 컴퓨터 기술자

0158
hardship
[háːrdʃìp]

n. 고난, 어려움   something that causes pain, suffering, or loss

syn. adversity, hardness, difficulty

experience a period of financial hardship 경제적 난관의 시기를 겪다

0159
deaf
[def]

adj. 안 들리는   not able to hear

syn. hard of hearing, without hearing

totally deaf since birth 날 때부터 완전히 귀가 먹은

0160
satisfy
[sǽtisfài]

v. 만족시키다   to please someone by giving them something that they want or need

syn. please, indulge, fill, gratify

failed to satisfy audiences 관객을 만족시키지 못했다

0161
faint
[feint]

adj. 희미한, 흐릿한   lacking clarity, brightness, volume, etc.

syn. dim, low, faded

ant. clear, definite

a faint smile on her lips 그녀의 입술에 비친 옅은 미소

0162
technique
[tekníːk]

n. 기술, 기교   a way of doing something by using special knowledge or skill

syn. skill, art, touch, know-how

good piano technique 뛰어난 피아노 치는 기술

0163
dealer
[díːlər]

n. 딜러, 판매업자   a person or firm engaged in commercial purchase and sale

syn. trader, marketer, merchant

a car dealer 자동차 판매업자

0164
gender
[dʒéndər]
-gen 탄생

n. 성별   the state of being male or female

regardless of age, race, or gender 나이, 인종, 성별에 상관없이

0165
mainly
[méinli]

adv. 주로, 대부분   for the most part

syn. chiefly, mostly, largely, generally

be caused mainly by stress 주로 스트레스 때문이다

0166
paralyze
[pǽrəlàiz]

v. 마비시키다   to make a person unable to move or feel all or part of the body

syn. immobilize, freeze, halt

ant. energize

paralyzed the city's transportation system 그 도시의 교통을 마비시켰다

0167
parasitic
[pæ̀rəsítik]

adj. 기생충의, 기생성의 living in or on another animal or plant in order to obtain nourishment

syn. bloodsucking, leechlike

tiny parasitic insects 작은 기생 곤충들

0168
satellite
[sǽtəlàit]

n. 위성   a machine that is sent into space and that moves around the earth, moon, sun, or a planet

syn. spacecraft, space capsule

artificial satellite 인공위성

weather satellite 기상위성

0169
harm
[hɑːrm]

v. 해를 끼치다   to injure physically, morally, or mentally

syn. damage, hurt, ruin

ant. cure, fix, heal, mend, remedy

harm the environment 환경을 해치다

0170
bang
[bæɡ]

v. 쾅 치다   to hit something hard

syn. slam, crash, thump

banged on the window 유리창을 쾅 쳤다

0171
variation
[vɛ̀əriéiʃən]

n. 변형, 차이   a change in the form, position, condition, or amount of something

ant. fixation, stabilization

considerable variation in size and design 크기와 디자인상의 상당한 변형

0172
watchdog
[wátʃdɔ̀(ː)g]

n. 감시자   one that guards against loss, waste, theft, or undesirable practices

syn. overseer, protector

a watchdog agency for consumers 소비자보호 감시 기관

0173
accomplish
[əkámpliʃ]

v. 성취하다   to succeed in doing something

syn. perform, achieve, fulfil

ant. fail

accomplish one's mission 임무를 완수하다

0174
edge
[edʒ]

n. 가장자리   the line or part where an object or area begins or ends

syn. boundary, end, rim, brink

stand close to the edge of the cliff 절벽 끝 가까이에 서다

0175
magnificent
[mægnífəsənt]
-magni 거대한

adj. 웅장한, 황홀한   splendid or impressive in appearance

syn. splendid, striking, grand, impressive

give a magnificent performance 황홀한 공연을 하다

0176
obligated
[ábləgèitid]

adj. 의무감을 느끼는   feeling that you must do something because someone has done something for you

syn. obliged, forced, required, bound

feel obligated to her 그녀에게 의무감을 느끼다

0177
magnify
[mǽgnəfài]
-magni 거대한

v. 확대시키다   to make something seem greater or more important than it is

syn. amplify, inflate, multiply

ant. reduce, lessen, soften

magnified the image 10 times 이미지를 10배 확대시켰다

0178
account
[əkáunt]

v. ~라고 생각하다, 설명하다   to think of something in a specified way

syn. consider, regard, view

account themselves lucky to be alive 자신들이 생존한 것을 행운으로 여기다

couldn't account for the loss 그 손실을 설명할 수 없었다

0179
natal
[néitl]

adj. 탄생의, 타고난   of or relating to birth

syn. natural, built-in

natal instincts 타고난 본능

0180
weaken
[wí:kən]

v. 약화시키다   to make weak

syn. soften

ant. beef up, strengthen

weaken the immune system 면역체계를 약화시키다

0181
partiality
[pὰːrʃiǽləti]

n. 편파적임   an unfair tendency to treat one person, group, or thing better than another

syn. favor, one-sidedness, bias

ant. neutrality, objectivity

the artist's partiality for red 그 화가의 빨간색에 대한 애착

0182
nationwide
[néiʃənwàid]

adj. 전국적인   including or involving all parts of a nation or country

syn. public, national, general, widespread, countrywide

attracted nationwide attention 국가적인 관심을 끌었다

0183
barber
[báːrbər]

n. 이발사   a person whose business is cutting men's hair and shaving or trimming beards

syn. hairdresser, haircutter, stylist

went to the barber to get his hair cut 이발하러 이발사를 찾아갔다

0184
accountant
[əkáuntənt]

n. 회계사   someone whose job is to keep the financial records of a business or person

syn. auditor, book-keeper, bean counter

certified public accountant 공인 회계사(CPA)

tax accountant 세무사

0185
unburden
[ʌnbə́ːrdn]

v. 부담을 덜어주다   to remove a load or burden from

syn. unload, relieve, discharge, lighten

ant. load, pack

unburdened her of the financial worry 그녀의 금전적 근심을 덜어주었다

0186
parental
[pəréntl]

adj. 부모의   of or relating to a parent or parenthood
syn. fatherly, maternal, paternal

parental rights and responsibilities 부모로서의 권리와 책임

0187
weak
[wiːk]

adj. 약한   having little power or force
syn. faint, feeble, frail, languid
ant. mighty, powerful, stout, strong

reply in a weak voice 연약한 목소리로 대답하다

0188
unbearable
[ʌnbɛ́ərəbəl]

adj. 참을 수 없는   too bad, harsh, or extreme to be accepted or endured
syn. insufferable, intolerable, unendurable

unbearable pain 견딜 수 없는 통증

0189
care
[kɛər]

n. 돌봄, 관리   things that are done to keep something in good condition
syn. keeping, control, charge, management, protection

an expert on skin care 피부 관리 전문가

0190
largely
[láːrdʒli]

adv. 주로, 대체로   not completely but mostly
syn. generally, chiefly, mainly, mostly

words largely unknown a decade ago 10년 전에는 대체로 알려지지 않았던 단어들

0191
landscape
[lǽndskèip]

n. 풍경, 지형   an area of land that has a particular quality or appearance
syn. geography, terrain

gaze at the beautiful landscape 아름다운 풍경을 바라보다

0192
objective
[əbdʒéktiv]

adj. 객관적인   based on facts rather than feelings or opinions
syn. experiential, experimental
ant. theoretical, prejudiced, subjective

objective data 객관적인 자료

0193
telegraphic
[tèləgrǽfik]
-graph 쓰다

adj. 전신의, 전보의   of or relating to the telegraph

telegraphic interruption 전신 두절

0194
rate
[reit]

n. 비율, 속도   a quantity or amount considered in relation to or measured against another quantity or amount

syn. degree, standard, scale, proportion

increase at an alarming rate 놀라운 속도로 증가하다

0195
carefree
[kέərfrìː]

adj. 속편한   having no worries or problems

syn. happy-go-lucky, lighthearted, unconcerned

spent a carefree day at the lake 호수에서 근심 없는 하루를 보냈다

0196
career
[kəríər]

n. 직업, 직장생활, 경력   a job or profession that someone does for a long time

syn. occupation, calling, employment

pursue a career in medicine 의료계의 직업 경력을 추구하다

0197
narrow
[nǽrou]

v. 좁히다   to make something smaller in amount or range

syn. restrict, limit, reduce, diminish, constrict

narrow down the choices 선택을 좁혀가다

0198
quality
[kwáləti]

n. 특징, 우수성, 자질   a characteristic or feature that someone or something has

syn. class, grade, rate

have many fine qualities as a statesman 정치가 다운 훌륭한 자질이 다분하다

0199
unaware
[ʌ̀nəwέər]

adj. 모르는   not aware or conscious of

syn. ignorant, oblivious, unsuspecting

ant. informed, knowing, mindful

unaware of the problem 문제를 인지하지 못하고 있는

0200
deadly
[dέdli]

adj. 무시무시한, 치명적인   likely to cause death / extreme or complete

syn. baleful, deathly, fatal

the world's most deadly snake 세계에서 가장 무시무시한 뱀

Review

뜻을 써보고 전체 어구의 의미를 생각해 보시오.

01 experience a period of financial hardship _____ 0158

02 totally deaf since birth _____ 0159

03 paralyzed the city's transportation system _____ 0166

04 tiny parasitic insects _____ 0167

05 give a magnificent performance _____ 0175

06 failed to satisfy audiences _____ 0160

07 harm the environment _____ 0169

08 telegraphic interruption _____ 0193

09 could hardly hold the cup _____ 0155

10 magnified the image 10 times _____ 0177

11 increase at an alarming rate _____ 0194

12 be caused mainly by stress _____ 0165

13 have many fine qualities as a statesman _____ 0198

14 gazed out the window at the snow _____ 0154

15 gaze at the beautiful landscape _____ 0191

16 a computer technician _____ 0157

17 narrow down the choices _____ 0197

18 attracted nationwide attention _____ 0182

19 unbearable pain _____ 0188

20 human beings are rational creatures _____ 0151

0201
participate
[pɑːrtísəpèit]

v. 참여하다, 동참하다 to be involved with others in doing something

syn. partake, share

eager to participate in the city's cultural life
도시 문화생활에 적극 참여하려고 하는

0202
temperament
[témpərəmənt]

n. 기질 the usual attitude, mood, or behavior of a person or animal

syn. nature, temper, disposition

an artistic temperament 예술가적 기질

0203
obscure
[əbskjúər]

adj. 불명료한, 무명의 not clearly expressed, or not easy to understand
/ not well-known

syn. ambiguous

ant. obvious, plain, clear

obscure markings 흐릿한 마킹
an obscure poet 무명 시인

0204
navigate
[nǽvəgèit]

v. 길을 찾다 to find the way to get to a place when you are traveling
in a ship, airplane, car, etc.

syn. pilot, steer

navigate mountain paths in the fog 안개 속에서 산길을 찾아가다

0205
maintain
[meintéin]

-tain 쥐다

v. 유지하다 to continue having or doing something

syn. conserve, keep up, preserve, save

couldn't maintain my composure 평정심을 유지할 수 없었다

0206
react
[riːǽkt]

v. 반응하다 to act in response to another person, a stimulus, etc.

sny. reply, respond

react to the sound 소리에 반응하다

0207
savage
[sǽvidʒ]

adj. 야만적인, 몹시 사나운 not domesticated or under human control

syn. crude, fierce, vicious

ant. civilized

savage beasts 사나운 맹수들

0208
major
[méidʒər]

n. 전공　the main subject studied by a college or university student

his major is sociology 그의 전공은 사회학이다

0209
oblige
[əbláidʒ]

v. 의무적으로 ~하게 하다　to bind or constrain someone to do something by legal, moral, or physical means

syn. compel, force, require, bind

be obliged to pay the minimum wage 의무적으로 최소 임금을 지불해야 한다

0210
lasting
[lǽstiŋ]

adj. 지속되는　continuing to exist or have an effect for a long time

syn. ageless, continuing, dateless

leave a lasting impression 오래 지속되는 인상을 남기다

0211
makeup
[méikʌ̀p]

n. 화장품　substances used to make someone's face look more attractive

syn. cosmetics

put on makeup for a play 연극 하려고 분장을 하다

0212
reach
[riːtʃ]

v. 도달하다　to be able to touch, pick up, or grab something by moving or stretching

syn. arrive, attain, come to

reach the camp before dark 어두워지기 전에 캠프장에 도착하다

0213
variety
[vəráiəti]

n. 여러 가지　a number or collection of different things or people

syn. assortment, multiplicity, diversity

variety store 잡화점

0214
particle
[páːrtikl]

n. 아주 작은 입자　a very small piece of something

syn. bit, crumb

particles of dust 먼지 입자들

0215
naturalistic
[næ̀tʃərəlístik]

adj. 자연주의적인　looking like what appears in nature

syn. lifelike, living, natural

create naturalistic settings for the animals
동물들에게 자연 그대로의 환경을 조성해주다

0216
native
[néitiv]

adj. 1 토박이의 2 타고난 born in a particular place / belonging to a person since birth or childhood
syn. 1 aboriginal
2 inherited, innate

a native German 토박이 독일인
native talents 타고난 재능

0217
obtain
[əbtéin]
-tain 쥐다

v. 획득하다 to gain or get something usually by effort
syn. acquire, attain, gain
ant. forfeit, lose

obtained my parents' permission 부모님의 허락을 받아냈다

0218
ray
[rei]

n. 광선, 빛줄기 an amount of light or heat from the sun
syn. light, radiation

a dazzling ray of light 눈부신 빛줄기

0219
natural
selection

n. 자연 선택, 자연 도태 the process by which organisms that are better suited to their environment than others produce more offspring
syn. survival of the fittest

a product of natural selection 자연 도태의 산물

0220
part
[pɑːrt]

v. 분리시키다, 헤어지다 to separate into two or more parts that move away from each other
syn. divide, fork, separate, spread
ant. join

parted the curtains with one hand 한 손으로 커튼을 열었다

0221
unceasing
[ʌ̀nsíːsiŋ]

adj. 끊임없는 not ceasing or ending
syn. constant, endless, continuing

unceasing efforts 부단한 노력

0222
savings
[séiviŋz]

n. 저축 the amount of money that you have saved especially in a bank over a period of time

syn. provision for a rainy day

use up savings 저축을 탕진하다

0223
imaginative
[imǽdʒənətiv]

adj. 창의적인 having or showing an ability to think of new and interesting ideas

syn. creative, ingenious, innovative

wrote an imaginative story 창의적인 이야기를 썼다

0224
navigator
[nǽvəgèitər]

n. 항해사, 조종사 a person who navigates a ship, an airplane, etc.

syn. mariner, sailor

he acted as a navigator while I drive
내가 운전하는 동안 그가 네비게이터 역할을 했다

0225
careless
[kέərlis]

adj. 부주의한 done, made, or said without enough thought or attention

syn. heedless, incautious, mindless

ant. wary

careless driving 부주의한 운전

0226
uncertain
[ʌnsə́:rtən]

adj. 불확실한 not sure

syn. changeable, unsettled

the origin of the word is uncertain 그 단어의 기원은 불확실하다

0227
various
[vέəriəs]

adj. 다양한 used to refer to several different or many different things, people, etc.

ant. colorless, monotone

a man of various talent 다재다능한 사람

0228
last
[læst]

v. 지속되다 to continue in time

syn. continue, keep, remain

lasted 10 minutes 10분 동안 지속되었다

0229
weary
[wíəri]

adj. 몹시 지친 lacking strength, energy because of a need for rest or sleep

syn. burned-out, exhausted, drained

my weary eyes 나의 지친 눈

0230
cargo
[ká:rgou]

n. 화물 something that is carried from one place to another by boat, airplane, etc.

syn. burden, load, draft, freight

carry a cargo of crude oil 원유 화물을 수송하다

0231
carpenter
[ká:rpəntər]

n. 목수 a person skilled in woodwork, esp in buildings, ships, etc.

syn. joiner, cabinet-maker, woodworker

a carpenter came to fix the bed 목수가 침대를 수리하러 왔다

0232
unchanged
[ʌntʃéindʒd]

adj. 변하지 않은, 그대로의 not altered or different in any way

syn. static, fixed, frozen, stable

remain unchanged 변하지 않은 상태로 있다

0233
imaginary
[imǽdʒənèri]

adj. 상상 속에 있는 existing in the imagination

syn. fictional, made-up, invented

created an imaginary friend to play with 함께 놀 상상 속의 친구를 만들었다

0234
tell
[tel]

v. 구분하다 to recognize something as a result of knowledge, experience, or evidence

you can tell it's a masterpiece 그 작품이 걸작임을 알 수 있을 거야

0235
harmless
[há:rmlis]

adj. 해롭지 않은 not causing harm

syn. hurtless, innocent, inoffensive, safe

a harmless joke 악의 없는 농담

0236
vary
[vέəri]

v. 다양하다, 다르다 to be different or to become different

syn. differ

vary in size 사이즈가 다양하다

0237
accumulate
[əkjúːmjəlèit]

v. 축적하다 to gather or acquire something gradually as time passes
syn. increase, build up, snowball

accumulate a fortune 부를 축적하다

0238
wear
[wεər]

v. 닳다 if something wears or wears thin, it gets thinner or weaker because it has been used a lot
syn. deteriorate, fray, become threadbare

wear thin in places 여기저기 닳아 얇아지다

0239
achieve
[ətʃíːv]

v. 달성하다, 성취하다 to get or reach something by working hard
syn. accomplish, reach, fulfil, gain

achieved a high degree of skill 높은 수준의 기술력에 도달했다

0240
wealth
[welθ]

n. 부, 풍부함 a large amount of money and possessions
syn. fortune, riches, opulence

a nation that has acquired great wealth 엄청난 부를 이룬 나라
offer a wealth of information 풍부한 지식을 제공하다

0241
bark
[bɑːrk]

v. (개가) 짖다 (of a dog) to make its typical loud abrupt cry
syn. howl, snarl, growl

the dog always barks at strangers 그 개는 낯선 사람을 보면 항상 짖는다

0242
bargain
[báːrgən]

n. 흥정, 횡재 something bought or sold at a good price
syn. buy, deal, steal
ant. rip-off

hunt for bargains 값 싼 물건을 찾아다니다

0243
accurate
[ǽkjərit]

adj. 정확한 free from mistakes or errors
syn. correct, exact, on-target

an accurate diagnosis 정확한 진단

0244
last resort
[læst riːsɔ́ːrt]

n. 마지막 수단 the last possible course of action open to one
syn. ace in the hole

use only as a last resort 마지막 수단으로만 사용하다

0245
barely
[béərli]

adv. 간신히, 빠듯하게   hardly or scarcely
syn. marginally, narrowly, lightly

barely escape death 간신히 목숨을 건지다

0246
temperature
[témpərətʃər]

n. 기온   the degree of hotness of a body, substance, or medium
syn. heat

took his temperature 그의 체온을 쟀다

0247
caring
[kέərniŋ]

adj. 다정한, 친절한   feeling or showing care and compassion
syn. compassionate, loving, sensitive, tender, sympathetic

a caring and loving father 다정하고 사랑이 넘치는 아버지

0248
imagination
[imæ̀dʒənéiʃən]

n. 상상력   the ability to think of new things
syn. creativity, inventiveness

have to use our imagination 우리의 상상력을 이용해야 한다

0249
illustrate
[íləstrèit]

v. (예를 들어) 설명하다   to give examples in order to make something easier to understand
syn. demonstrate, exemplify, instance

illustrated his lecture with fun stories 그는 강의에 재미있는 이야기를 곁들였다

0250
harmful
[hάːrmfəl]

adj. 해로운   causing or capable of causing damage or harm
syn. damaging, dangerous, hurtful

be extremely harmful to the environment 환경에 극도로 해롭다

Review

뜻을 써보고 전체 어구의 의미를 생각해 보시오.

01 navigate mountain paths in the fog _____ 0204

02 variety store _____ 0213

03 create naturalistic settings for the animals _____ 0215

04 couldn't maintain my composure _____ 0205

05 careless driving _____ 0225

06 offer a wealth of information _____ 0240

07 be extremely harmful to the environment _____ 0250

08 ① a native German _____ 0216

   ② native talents _____

09 a caring and loving father _____ 0247

10 vary in size _____ 0236

11 took his temperature _____ 0246

12 have to use our imagination _____ 0248

13 wear thin in places _____ 0238

14 a product of natural selection _____ 0219

15 barely escape death _____ 0245

16 a harmless joke _____ 0235

17 he acted as navigator while I drive _____ 0224

18 hunt for bargains _____ 0242

19 remain unchanged _____ 0232

20 unceasing efforts _____ 0221

0251
tense
[tense]

adj. 긴장한, 팽팽한 nervous and not able to relax

syn. uneasy, jumpy, uptight, edgy

a tense meeting 긴장감이 감도는 회의

0252
scare
[skɛər]

v. 겁주다 to cause (someone) to become afraid

syn. frighten, shock, terrify

it scared me to death 그것 때문에 겁나 죽는 줄 알았다

0253
tendency
[téndənsi]

n. 경향 a strong chance that something will happen in a particular way

syn. aptness, proneness, inclination, leaning

have a tendency to avoid arguments 언쟁을 피하려는 경향이 있다

0254
lately
[léitli]

adv. 최근에 in the recent period of time

syn. recently

ant. anciently

saw him lately 최근에 그를 봤다

0255
immediately
[imí:diitli]

adv. 즉시 very quickly and without delay

syn. instantly

ant. slowly, late, tardily

decided to leave immediately 즉시 떠나기로 결심했다

0256
scan
[skæn]

v. 1 훑어보다 2 면밀히 검토하다 to look over or read something quickly
/ to examine by point-by-point or checking

syn. 1 overlook, oversee 2 inspect, scrutinize

scanned it briefly 빠르게 훑어봤다
scanned his face 그의 얼굴을 자세히 살폈다

0257
latitude
[lǽtətjùːd]

n. 위도 distance north or south of the equator measured in degrees
up to 90 degrees

be located at a latitude of 37 degrees north 북위 37도에 위치해 있다

0258
harmonious
[hɑːrmóuniəs]

adj. 조화로운 (esp of colours or sounds) fitting together well

syn. compatible, matching

a harmonious arrangement of colors 조화로운 색상들의 조합

0259
imbalance
[imbǽləns]

n. 불균형   lack of balance

syn. disproportion, lopsidedness

a vitamin imbalance 비타민 불균형

0260
generalist
[dʒénərəlist]

n. 박학다식한 사람, 일반직 직원   a person who is knowledgeable in many fields of study

a generalist profession 일반직 직종

0261
imitate
[ímitèit]

v. 흉내 내다, 모방하다   to make or do something the same way as something else

syn. copy, copycat, mime, mimic

ant. originate

imitated his father's voice 아버지의 목소리를 흉내 냈다

0262
later
[léitər]

adv. 나중에   at a time in the future

syn. afterward

ant. earlier

one week later 일주일 후에

0263
uncomfortable
[ʌnkʌ́mfərtəbəl]

adj. 불편한   feeling physical discomfort

syn. comfortless, discomforting, harsh

an uncomfortable chair 불편한 의자

0264
tend
[tend]

v. 간호하다, 돌보다   to take care of someone or something

tend the wounded 부상자들을 간호하다

tend to the children 아이들을 돌보다

0265
augment
[ɔːgmént]

v. 늘리다, 증대하다   to increase the size or amount of something

syn. amplify, increase, boost

ant. diminish, downsize, dwindle

heavy rains augmented the water supply 폭우가 물 공급량을 늘렸다

0266
tempt
[tempt]

v. 유혹하다 to cause to do or want to do something even though it may be wrong, bad, or unwise

syn. allure, bait, decoy

be tempted to call it quits 그만 끝내고 싶은 유혹을 느끼다

0267
male
[meil]

adj. 남자의 characteristic of boys or men

syn. masculine, manlike, manly

a male nurse 남자 간호사

0268
mandatory
[mǽndətɔːri]
-mand 명령하다

adj. 의무적인 required by a law or rule

syn. compulsory, forced, imperative, required

the mandatory retirement age 법정 은퇴 연령

0269
nearby
[níərbài]

adj. 근처의 not far away

syn. close at hand, within reach, not far away

found it on a nearby table 그것을 가까이에 있는 탁자에서 찾았다

0270
uncommon
[ʌnkámən]
-com 함께

adj. 드문, 흔치 않은 not often found, seen, or experienced

syn. abnormal, extraordinary, exceptional

an uncommon plant 흔치 않은 식물

0271
educational
[èdʒukéiʃənəl]

adj. 교육적인, 교육의 providing knowledge / of or relating to education

syn. instructive, useful, informative

an educational toy 교육적인 장난감

0272
nearly
[níərli]

adv. 거의 almost, or near to a particular amount of time, money, people, or things

syn. closely, near

ant. remotely, distantly

spent nearly four million dollars 거의 400만 달러를 썼다

0273
harmonize
[há:rmənàiz]

v. 조화를 이루다 to be in harmony

syn. agree, blend, chime in

ant. clash, collide, conflict

harmonize with the other people 다른 사람들과 조화를 이루다

0274
faith
[feiθ]

n. 믿음, 신념 a strong feeling of trust or confidence in someone or
　something
syn. confidence, trust, credit, conviction

with a blind faith 맹목적 믿음으로

0275
obvious
[ábviəs]

adj. 명백한 easy to see or notice
syn. clear-cut, apparent, manifest
ant. ambiguous, clouded, unclear

the obvious signs of the disease 질병의 명백한 신호

0276
party
[pá:rti]

n. (소송, 계약 등의) 당사자 a person who is involved in a legal case or contract
syn. person, individual, somebody, someone

the guilty party 가해자
the innocent party 피해자

0277
passion
[pǽʃən]
-passi 고생하다, 느끼다

n. 열정 a strong feeling of enthusiasm or excitement for something
　or about doing something
syn. love, desire, affection

a student with a passion for literature 문학에 열정을 간직한 학생

0278
realize
[rí:əlàiz]

v. 깨닫다 to become conscious or aware of something
syn. ascertain, catch on to, find out

realized the risk that was involved 포함된 위험을 깨달았다

0279
nearsighted
[níərsáitid]

adj. 근시안의 unable to see things that are far away
syn. shortsighted
ant. farsighted

a nearsighted person 근시안인 사람

0280
decay
[dikéi]
-de 하락, 부정

v. 부패하다 to be slowly destroyed by natural processes
syn. break down, corrupt, decompose

the smell of decaying rubbish 부패하는 쓰레기 냄새

0281
editor
[édətər]

n. 편집자　a person whose job is to edit something

syn. compiler, writer, journalist, reviser

worked as a script editor for years 대본 편집자로 몇 년간 일했다

0282
passage
[pǽsidʒ]

n. 통로, 복도　a long, narrow space that connects one place to another

syn. avenue, path, route, way

squeezed through a narrow passage 좁은 통로로 비집고 들어갔다

0283
realist
[ríːəlist]

n. 현실주의자　someone who accepts events and situations as they really are and deals with them in a practical way

syn. pragmatist, positivist

a down-to-earth realist 철저한 현실주의자

0284
realm
[relm]

n. 영역, 범위　an area of activity, interest, or knowledge

syn. area, circle, field, terrain, walk

new discoveries in the realm of medicine 의학 분야의 새 발견들

0285
readily
[rédəli]

adv. 쉽사리, 기꺼이　in a way that shows you are willing to do something

syn. willingly

ant. involuntarily, unwillingly

readily agreed to help us 기꺼이 우리를 돕겠다고 동의했다

0286
fairly
[fɛ́ərli]

adv. 1 상당히　2 공정하게　to some degree or extent but not very or extremely / in a fair way

syn. 1 pretty, quite
　　2 honestly, justifiably, justly

a fairly common disease 꽤 일반적인 질병
treat the children fairly 아이들을 공평하게 대하다

0287
effect
[ifékt]

n. 영향, 효과　a change that results when something is done or happens

syn. aftermath, fruit, outcome, result

ant. cause, reason

the beneficial effects of exercise 운동의 유익한 효과

0288
decade
[dékeid]

n. 십 년 a period of 10 years

the first decade of the 21st century 21세기의 처음 10년

0289
debt
[det]

n. 빚, 부채 an amount of money that you owe to a person, bank, company, etc.

syn. obligation, liability

paid off gambling debts 도박 빚을 갚았다

0290
carton
[kɑ́:rtən]

n. 곽, 통 a light box or container usually made of cardboard or plastic

syn. box, case, pack

a carton of cigarettes 담배 한 보루

0291
scale
[skeil]

n. 저울 either pan or tray of a balance

a set of kitchen scales 부엌 저울 세트

0292
real estate
[rí:əl Istéit]

n. 부동산 property consisting of buildings and land

syn. land

a real estate agent 부동산 중개인

0293
fake
[feik]

v. 꾸며대다, 위조하다 to pretend to have an illness, emotion, etc.

syn. forge, fabricate, counterfeit, falsify, pretend

fake a headache 가짜로 두통이 있다고 하다

0294
scary
[skέəri]

adj. 무서운 causing fear

syn. dreadful, fearsome, frightening

a scary story 무서운 이야기

0295
uncomplaining
[ʌ̀nkəmpléiniŋ]

adj. 불평 없는 willing to deal with a difficult or unpleasant situation without complaining

syn. tolerant, patient

ant. fed up, impatient

willing and uncomplaining helpers 자발적이고 불평 없는 도우미들

0296
tension
[ténʃən]

n. 긴장, 불안 a feeling of nervousness that makes you unable to relax

syn. pressure, strain, stress

ant. comfort

ease the tension with a joke 농담으로 긴장을 풀다

0297
reality
[riǽləti]

n. 현실   the real situation

syn. actuality, case, materiality, fact

ant. fantasy, fiction, illusion

the difference between fiction and reality 허구와 현실의 차이

0298
save
[seiv]

prep. ~외에   other than

syn. apart from, aside from, but, except for

everyone save me is going to the party 나만 빼고 모두들 파티에 갈 것이다

0299
mammal
[mǽməl]

n. 포유류   an animal that is born from its mother's body and drinks its mother's milk as a baby

whales are mammals 고래는 포유류이다

0300
rear
[riər]

v. 키우다   to take care of a young person or animal

syn. bring up, raise, educate, care for

rear cattle 소를 키우다

Review

뜻을 써보고 전체 어구의 의미를 생각해 보시오.

01 ① scanned it briefly _____ 0256

   ② scanned his face _____

02 readily agreed to help us _____ 0285

03 realized the risk that was involved _____ 0278

04 a real estate agent _____ 0292

05 fake a headache _____ 0293

06 worked as a script editor for years _____ 0281

07 the difference between fiction and reality _____ 0297

08 the obvious signs of the disease _____ 0275

09 an uncommon plant _____ 0270

10 be tempted to call it quits _____ 0266

11 heavy rains augmented the water supply _____ 0265

12 a set of kitchen scales _____ 0291

13 whales are mammals _____ 0299

14 a male nurse _____ 0267

15 the beneficial effects of exercise _____ 0287

16 ease the tension with a joke _____ 0296

17 rear cattle _____ 0300

18 willing and uncomplaining helpers _____ 0295

19 an educational toy _____ 0271

20 a student with a passion for literature _____ 0277

DAY 07

0301
haste
[heist]

n. 서두름   great speed in doing something because of limited time
syn. fastness, speed, hurry
ant. slowness

in my haste to escape 도망가려고 서두르다가

0302
impact
[ímpækt]

n. 충돌, (강력한) 영향   the force with which one thing hits another or with which two objects collide
syn. bump, collision, concussion, crash

the environmental impact of tourism 관광이 환경에 미치는 영향

0303
fame
[feim]

n. 명성 the condition of being known or recognized by many people
syn. celebrity, renown
ant. anonymity

gained fame as an actor 배우로서 명성을 얻었다

0304
generate
[dʒénərèit]
-gen 탄생

v. 생성하다   to produce something
syn. bring about, create, produce

generate electricity 전기를 일으키다
generate a lot of revenue 많은 수익을 창출해 내다

0305
occupy
[ákjəpài]

v. 점령하다, 차지하다   to fill or be in
syn. hold, control, dominate, possess

enemy troops occupied the ridge 적군이 능선을 점령했다

0306
necessitate
[nisésətèit]

v. ~을 필요하게 만들다   to make (something) necessary
syn. compel, force, involve, demand, require

necessitate a change of plan 계획 수정이 필요하게 만들다

0307
harness
[háːrnis]

v. 마구를 채우다, (자연력을) 이용하다   to control and use the natural force or power of something
syn. apply, employ, exercise, exploit
ant. ignore, neglect

harness the power of the waterfall 폭포의 힘을 이용하다

0308
launch
[lɔːntʃ]

v. 발진시키다 to throw forward
syn. begin, establish, inaugurate, initiate
ant. close down
launch a new weather satellite 새 기상 위성을 쏘아 올리다

0309
false
[fɔːls]

adj. 거짓의 not real or genuine
syn. incorrect, inexact, invalid
a false statement 거짓 진술

0310
imperfect
[impə́ːrfikt]

adj. 불완전한 having mistakes or problems / not perfect
syn. defective, flawed, faulty
ant. faultless, flawless
an imperfect solution 불완전한 해결안

0311
vastly
[vǽstli]

adv. 엄청나게 to a great degree
syn. hugely, enormously, immensely
be vastly improved 엄청나게 개선되다

0312
necessary
[nésəsèri]

adj. 필요한 needed in order to do something or make something happen
syn. compulsory, forced, imperative, required
unless it's absolutely necessary 꼭 필요하지 않다면

0313
occasion
[əkéiʒən]

n. 경우, 기회, 때 a particular time when something happens
syn. moment, time
did not have occasion to talk with them 그들과 대화할 기회가 없었다

0314
immoral
[imɔ́(ː)rəl]

adj. 비도덕적인 not morally good or right
syn. unethical, unlawful, unrighteous
an immoral and unprincipled decision 비도덕적이고 원칙도 없는 결정

0315
harsh
[hɑːrʃ]

adj. 가혹한, 냉혹한 unpleasant and difficult to accept or experience
syn. bitter, tough, trying
a harsh climate 혹독한 기후

0316
immigrant
[ímigrənt]

n. 이민자　a person who comes to a country to live there

syn. emigrant, incomer

a large immigrant population 많은 이민자 인구

0317
harvest
[háːrvist]

v. 수확하다　to gather a crop

syn. gather, pick, reap

harvest the wheat 밀을 수확하다

0318
generally
[dʒénərəli]

adv. 일반적으로, 대략적으로　in a way that is not detailed or specific

syn. commonly, usually, ordinarily

talked generally about his plans 그의 계획에 대해 대략적으로 말했다

0319
effective
[iféktiv]

adj. 효과적인　producing a result that is wanted

syn. efficient, fruitful, productive

a simple but effective technique 간단하지만 효과적인 기술

0320
falsify
[fɔ́ːlsəfài]

v. 위조하다, 조작하다　to change in order to make people believe something that is not true

syn. bend, color, cook, distort, twist, warp

be caught falsifying financial accounts 은행 계좌를 위조하다가 발각되다

0321
occasional
[əkéiʒənəl]

adj. 이따금의　happening or done sometimes but not often

syn. casual, irregular, unsteady

occasional visitors 가끔 오는 방문객들

0322
neatly
[níːtli]

adv. 단정히　in a tidy and orderly way

syn. tidily, nicely, smartly

a neatly trimmed beard 단정히 깎은 턱수염

0323
impaired
[impέərd]

adj. 손상된　reduced or weakened in strength, quality, etc.

syn. damaged, flawed, faulty, defective

special devices for sight-impaired visitors
시각 장애가 있는 방문객들을 위한 특수 장비들

0324
acoustic
[əkúːstik]

adj. 음향의, 청각의   of or relating to sound or to the sense of hearing
syn. auditory, audile, aural

acoustic wave 음파

0325
generation
[dʒènəréiʃən]
-gen 탄생

n. 세대   a group of people in society who are born and live around the same time
syn. age group, peer group

the previous generation 이전 세대

0326
pastime
[pǽstàim]

n. 취미   an activity or entertainment which makes time pass pleasantly
syn. activity, game, sport, entertainment, leisure, hobby

play cards as a pastime 심심풀이로 카드놀이를 하다

0327
manifest
[mǽnəfèst]

adj. 분명한, 뚜렷한   obvious and easy to notice or understand
syn. obvious, apparent, evident

the program's manifest weaknesses 그 프로그램의 뚜렷한 약점들

0328
pasture
[pǽstʃər]

n. 초원   land covered with grass where sheep, cows, etc. are kept
syn. grassland, grass, meadow

high mountain pastures 고산지대 초원

0329
occupation
[àkjəpéiʃən]

n. 직업   a person's regular work or profession
syn. job, work, calling, business

think about changing occupations 직업을 바꿀까 생각 중이다

0330
manipulate
[mənípjəlèit]
-man 손

v. (손·기계로) 조작하다   to move or control with your hands or by using a machine
syn. exploit, play upon

be manipulated by a computer 컴퓨터로 조작되다

0331
acid
[ǽsid]

adj. (맛이) 신   sour, sharp, or biting to the taste
syn. sour, acidic

an acid flavor 신 맛

0332
weed
[wi:d]

v. 잡초를 뽑다   to remove weeds from an area of land

weed a garden 정원의 잡초를 뽑다

0333
barrier
[bǽriər]

n. 장벽   something such as a fence or natural obstacle that prevents or blocks movement from one place to another

syn. barricade, fence, hedge, wall

a natural barrier between the two countries 두 나라 사이의 자연 장벽

0334
vegetable
[védʒətəbəl]

n. 채소   a part of a plant used as food, for example a potato, bean, or cabbage

eat more fruits and vegetables 과일과 채소를 더 먹다

0335
weightlifting
[wéitliftiŋ]

n. 역도   the sport of lifting heavy weights

weightlifting belt 역도 벨트

0336
barn
[bɑːrn]

n. 헛간, 창고   a large building that is usually bare and plain

syn. shed, outbuilding

a hay barn 건초 헛간

0337
acknowledge
[æknάlidʒ]

v. 인정하다, 알리다   to disclose knowledge of or agreement with

ant. deny

acknowledged their mistake 실수를 인정했다

0338
barren
[bǽrən]

adj. 척박한, 불모의   incapable of producing offspring, seed, or fruit

syn. desolate, empty, desert

a remote and barren island 외딴 불모의 섬

0339
necessarily
[nèsəsérəli]

adv. 반드시, 꼭   used to say that something is necessary and cannot be changed or avoided

syn. inevitably

be not necessarily blamable 반드시 비난할 일은 아니다

0340

weather

[wéðər]

v. 1 기후에 변하다 2 견뎌내다 to expose to the open air I to bear up against and come safely through

syn. 1 toughen, season 2 withstand, survive

be weathered by the sun 햇빛을 쐬어 변색하다

weather a crisis 위기를 견뎌내다

0341

categorize

[kǽtigəràiz]

v. 분류하다 to put into a category

syn. assort, break down, classify

be categorized by type 유형별로 분류되다

0342

decentralize

[diːséntrəlàiz]

-centr 중간

-de 하락, 부정

v. 분권화하다 to reorganize a government, industry, etc. into smaller more autonomous units

syn. disperse, scatter, distribute

ant. centralize

decentralize a museum 박물관을 여러 곳으로 분산시키다

0343

decision

[disíʒən]

n. 결정 a choice that you make about something after thinking about it

syn. conclusion, determination, resolution

ant. hesitation

make a decision 결정하다

0344

deck

[dek]

n. 갑판 a flat surface that forms the main outside floor of a boat or ship

syn. balcony, sundeck, terrace

stood on the deck 갑판 위에 섰다

0345

vast

[væst]

adj. 방대한 very great in size, amount, or extent

syn. astronomical, colossal, enormous

vast knowledge 방대한 지식

0346

cause

[kɔːz]

v. 야기하다, 초래하다 to make something happen or exist

syn. bring about, create, yield, produce

cause an accident 사고를 초래하다

0347
basic
[béisik]

adj. 기본적인, 기초적인   forming or relating to the first or easiest part of something

syn. elementary, beginning, introductory

basic research 기초 조사

0348
acquaintance
[əkwéintəns]

n. 아는 사람   someone who is known but who is not a close friend

syn. associate, neighbor

a casual acquaintance 약간 알고 지내는 사람

0349
cast
[kæst]

v. 던지다   to throw or move something in a forceful way

syn. send out, shoot, throw out

cast dice 주사위를 던지다

0350
efficient
[ifíʃənt]

adj. 효율적인   productive without waste

syn. fruitful, effective, productive

an efficient worker 효율적으로 일하는 직원

Review

뜻을 써보고 전체 어구의 의미를 생각해 보시오.

01 the environmental impact of tourism ⎯⎯⎯⎯⎯⎯⎯ 0302

02 an imperfect solution ⎯⎯⎯⎯⎯⎯⎯ 0310

03 talked generally about his plans ⎯⎯⎯⎯⎯⎯⎯ 0318

04 a harsh climate ⎯⎯⎯⎯⎯⎯⎯ 0315

05 the program's manifest weaknesses ⎯⎯⎯⎯⎯⎯⎯ 0327

06 launch a new weather satellite ⎯⎯⎯⎯⎯⎯⎯ 0308

07 vast knowledge ⎯⎯⎯⎯⎯⎯⎯ 0345

08 be caught falsifying financial accounts ⎯⎯⎯⎯⎯⎯⎯ 0320

09 cause an accident ⎯⎯⎯⎯⎯⎯⎯ 0346

10 basic research ⎯⎯⎯⎯⎯⎯⎯ 0347

11 a casual acquaintance ⎯⎯⎯⎯⎯⎯⎯ 0348

12 the previous generation ⎯⎯⎯⎯⎯⎯⎯ 0325

13 ① be weathered by the sun ⎯⎯⎯⎯⎯⎯⎯ 0340
　　② weather a crisis ⎯⎯⎯⎯⎯⎯⎯

14 decentralize a museum ⎯⎯⎯⎯⎯⎯⎯ 0342

15 harness the power of the waterfall ⎯⎯⎯⎯⎯⎯⎯ 0307

16 cast dice ⎯⎯⎯⎯⎯⎯⎯ 0349

17 be manipulated by a computer ⎯⎯⎯⎯⎯⎯⎯ 0330

18 stood on the deck ⎯⎯⎯⎯⎯⎯⎯ 0344

19 harvest the wheat ⎯⎯⎯⎯⎯⎯⎯ 0317

20 necessitate a change of plan ⎯⎯⎯⎯⎯⎯⎯ 0306

0351
decode
[di:kóud]
-co 함께
-de 하락, 부정

v. 암호를 해독하다　to find or understand the true or hidden meaning of something
syn. break, crack, decipher

decode an ancient inscription 고대 비문을 해독하다

0352
decline
[dikláin]
-de 하락, 부정

v. 1 줄다　2 거절하다　to become lower in amount or less in number l to say that you will not or cannot do something
syn. 1 drop, contract, lower　2 refuse, reject, turn down

decline rapidly 급속도로 감소하다

decline an invitation 초대를 거절하다

0353
battle
[bǽtl]

n. 전투　a fight between large armed forces
syn. fight, war, conflict

the never-ending battle between good and evil 선과 악의 끝없는 전투

0354
effortlessly
[éfərtlisli]

adv. 힘들이지 않고　with ease
syn. freely, handily, smoothly

adapted effortlessly to his new surroundings 새 환경에 쉽게 적응했다

0355
reason
[ri:zn]

n. 이유, 원인　a fact, situation, or intention that explains why something happened or why something is true
syn. cause, grounds, purpose, motive

asked her the reason for her visit 그녀가 방문한 이유를 물었다

0356
patch
[pætʃ]

n. (주변과 다른 작은) 부분　an area that is different from what surrounds it
syn. spot, bit, stretch, scrap, small piece

damp patches on the ceiling 천장에 군데군데 습기 찬 부분들

0357
verbal
[və́:rbəl]

adj. 언어의, 말의　spoken rather than written
syn. spoken, oral, word-of-mouth

a verbal contract 구두 계약

0358
actually
[ǽktʃuəli]

adv. 실제로는　as an actual fact
syn. really, in fact, indeed

we've never actually met 우리는 실제로는 만난 적이 없다

0359

vegetation

[vèdʒətéiʃən]

n. 식물　plants and trees

syn. foliage, green, herbage

the dense vegetation of the jungle 정글의 수북한 식물

0360

acquire

[əkwáiər]

-quire 찾다, 추구하다

v. 얻다, 습득하다　to come to own something

syn. get, win, buy, receive

ant. lose

acquired three new players this year 올해 세 명의 선수를 새로 영입했다

0361

declining

[deklɑ́iniŋ]

-de 하락

adj. 줄어드는, 약해지는　becoming less or worse

syn. descending, drooping

ant. unbending, upright

a declining industry 하락세의 산업

0362

terrify

[térəfài]

v. 겁먹게 하다　to cause someone to be extremely afraid

syn. fright, horrify, panic, scare, shock

his violence terrified her 그의 폭력에 그녀는 겁먹었다

0363

vehicle

[víːikəl]

n. 탈것　a machine that is used to carry people or goods from one place to another

syn. motor vehicle, means of transport

cars, trucks, and other vehicles 차, 트럭, 그리고 다른 탈것들

0364

farewell

[fɛ̀ərwél]

n. 작별　an act of leaving

syn. goodbye, parting, departure, adieu

a farewell party 송별회

0365

absently

[ǽbsəntli]

adv. 멍하니　in an absent-minded or preoccupied manner

syn. distractedly, dreamily, vacantly, blankly

gazed absently into the street 멍하니 거리를 응시했다

0366
narration
[næréiʃən]

n. 내레이션 the act or process of telling a story or describing what happens

syn. story, narrative, commentary

do narrations for documentaries 다큐멘터리 내레이션을 하다

0367
gathering
[gǽðəriŋ]

n. 모임 an occasion when people come together as a group

syn. assembly, group, crowd, meeting, get-together

a gathering of political leaders 정치 지도자들 모임

0368
uncomplicated
[ʌnkámpləkèitid]
-plic 접다

adj. 복잡하지 않은 easy to understand, do, or use

syn. simple, easy, direct, unsophisticated

an uncomplicated, straightforward person 단순하고 단도직입적인 사람

0369
terms
[təːrmz]

n. 관계 mutual relationship or standing

syn. relationship

be on good terms 좋은 관계로 지내다

0370
reason
[ríːzən]

v. 판단하다, 추론하다 to form a particular judgment about a situation after carefully considering the facts

syn. deduce, conclude, work out, solve, resolve, infer

the human ability to reason 인간의 판단하는 능력

0371
cell
[sel]

n. 세포, 작은 칸 any one of the very small parts that together form all living things

syn. unit, section

the cells of a honeycomb 벌집의 칸

0372
celebrity
[səlébrəti]

n. 유명인 a famous person

syn. star, superstar, big name, dignitary

literary and artistic celebrities 문학 및 예술 분야 저명인사들

0373
basis
[béisis]

n. 기반, 기초　something from which another thing develops or can develop

syn. base, bottom, foundation, ground, root

provide the basis for future negotiations 앞으로의 협상을 위한 토대를 제공하다

0374
terminate
[tə́:rmənèit]
-term 경계

v. 끝내다　to cause something to end

syn. close out, complete, finish, wrap up

terminate a treaty 조약을 해제하다

0375
basin
[béisən]

n. (큰 강의) 유역　any partially enclosed or sheltered area where vessels may be moored or docked

syn. valley, hollow, gorge, ravine

the Amazon Basin 아마존 유역

0376
unconditional
[ʌ̀nkəndíʃənəl]

adj. 무조건의　without conditions or limitations

syn. absolute, full, complete

an unconditional surrender 무조건 항복

0377
headquarters
[hédkwɔ̀:rtərz]

n. 본사, 본부　the place where a company or organization has its main offices

syn. head office, base, nerve centre

the headquarters of the United Nations 유엔 본부

0378
implement
[ímpləmənt]

v. 시행하다　to begin to do or use something, such as a plan

syn. administer, apply, execute, enforce

ant. neglect

implement the committee's decisions 위원회의 결정사항을 시행하다

0379
veil
[veil]

v. 베일로 가리다　to hide or partly hide something

syn. cover, curtain, disguise

ant. expose, reveal, show, uncover

be veiled by clouds 구름에 가려지다

0380
heal
[hi:l]

v. 치유하다, 낫다   to make someone healthy or well again
syn. cure, fix, mend

heal a wound 상처를 치유하다

0381
manned
[mænd]

adj. 유인의   carrying or done by a person

put a manned spacecraft in orbit 유인 우주선을 궤도에 올리다

0382
manipulative
[mənípjələ̀itiv]
-man 손

adj. 능수능란한   tending to negotiate, control, or influence skilfully
syn. scheming, calculating, cunning

he was sly, selfish, and manipulative 그는 교활하고, 이기적이고, 능수능란했다

0383
leak
[li:k]

v. 새다   to let something such as a liquid or gas in or out through a
hole in a surface
syn. drip, trickle, ooze

confidential information leaked out 비밀 정보가 새나갔다

0384
layer
[léiər]

n. 층, 겹   an amount of something that is spread over an area
syn. covering, film, coat, blanket

several layers of clothing 여러 겹의 옷

0385
healing
[hí:liŋ]

adj. 치유의   of or relating to recovery
syn. curing, mending

the healing process 치유의 과정

0386
scenery
[sí:nəri]

n. 풍경   the natural features of a landscape
syn. landscape, view, surroundings, outlook

enjoy the scenery 풍경을 감상하다

0387
implied
[impláid]

adj. 함축적인   not directly expressed
syn. suggested, unspoken, implicit

an implied criticism 함축적인 비평

0388

genetics

[dʒinétiks]

-gen 탄생

n. 유전학   the scientific study of how genes control the characteristics of plants and animals

applied genetics 응용 유전학

0389

hateful

[héitfəl]

adj. 악의에 찬   full of hate

syn. malicious

ant. benevolent, loving

a hateful look 증오에 찬 표정

0390

gene

[dʒiːn]

-gen 탄생

n. 유전자   a part of a cell that controls or influences the appearance, growth, etc.

the genes that regulate cell division 세포분할을 통제하는 유전자

0391

acquisition

[ӕkwəzíʃən]

n. 습득   the act of acquiring or gaining possession

syn. acquiring, gaining

theories of child language acquisition 아동 언어 습득 이론

0392

head

[hed]

v. 향해가다   to go in a specified direction or toward a specified place

headed back to the office 사무실로 돌아왔다

0393

fast

[fæst]

n. 금식   a period of time when you eat no food or very little food, often for religious reasons

syn. fasting, diet

a fast day 금식일

0394

genetic

[dʒinétik]

-gen 탄생

adj. 유전의, 유전자의   of, relating to, or involving genes

syn. hereditary

be caused by a genetic defect 유전자 결함이 원인이 되다

0395

effort

[éfərt]

n. 노력   a serious attempt to do something

syn. labor, pains, sweat

a job requiring time and effort 시간과 노력을 요하는 직업

0396
scent
[sent]

n. 냄새, 향기   a pleasant smell that is produced by something

syn. aroma, balm

ant. stench, stink

a keen scent 강한 향기

0397
scatter
[skǽtər]

v. 흩어뜨리다   to cause things to separate and go in different directions

syn. disperse

ant. assemble, cluster, collect

scattered the books on the table 탁자 위의 책들을 흩어뜨렸다

0398
reasonable
[ríːzənəbəl]

adj. 타당한, 합리적인   fair and sensible

syn. rational, logical, sensible, sound

ant. irrational, illogical, incoherent

a reasonable theory 타당한 이론

a reasonable price 공정한 가격

0399
rapid
[rǽpid]

adj. 빠른   happening in a short amount of time

syn. swift, fleet, speedy

ant. slow

a rapid growth 빠른 성장

0400
pat
[pæt]

v. 톡톡 치다   to strike lightly with a flat instrument

syn. caress, pet, stroke

gently patted the dog's head 개의 머리를 부드럽게 토닥거렸다

Review

뜻을 써보고 전체 어구의 의미를 생각해 보시오.

01 asked her the reason for her visit   0355

02 acquired three new players this year   0360

03 do narrations for documentaries   0366

04 be on good terms   0369

05 an unconditional surrender   0376

06 the genes that regulate cell division   0390

07 an implied criticism   0387

08 be caused by a genetic defect   0394

09 an uncomplicated, straightforward person   0368

10 gently patted the dog's head   0400

11 a hateful look   0389

12 the cells of a honeycomb   0371

13 applied genetics   0388

14 damp patches on the ceiling   0356

15 a farewell party   0364

16 a reasonable price   0398

17 decode an ancient inscription   0351

18 the Amazon Basin   0375

19 ① decline rapidly   0352

    ② decline an invitation

20 we've never actually met   0358

0401
receive
[risí:v]
-ceive 받다

v. 받다   to get or be given something

syn. get, accept, be given

received a letter from her 그녀로부터 편지를 한 통 받았다

0402
bearable
[bέərəbəl]

adj. 견딜 만한   possible to bear

syn. tolerable, sustainable, endurable

the medication made it bearable 약 때문에 견딜만했다

0403
unfit
[ʌnfít]

adj. 부적합한   not having the necessary qualities, skills, mental health, etc.

syn. unsuitable, inadequate, inappropriate, useless

be unfit for human habitation 사람이 거주하기에는 부적합하다

0404
central
[séntrəl]
-centr 중간

adj. 중앙의   in the middle of something

syn. inner, middle, mid

live in central London 런던 중심부에 살다

0405
testimony
[téstəmòuni]

n. 증언   a declaration of truth or fact

syn. evidence, information, statement, witness

call a person in testimony 아무를 증인으로 부르다

0406
addictive
[ədíktiv]

adj. 중독성 있는   causing a strong and harmful need to regularly have or do something

syn. habit-forming, compelling, compulsive

an addictive drug 중독성 있는 약
the addictive thrill of surfing 중독성 있는 파도타기의 스릴

0407
adapt
[ədǽpt]
-apt 적합

v. 적합하게 하다, 변경하다   to change something to make it more suitable for a new use or situation

syn. adjust, tailor

a specially adapted car 특별히 변형한 차

74

0408
welfare
[wélfὲər]

n. 복지, 행복, 번영 the state of being happy, healthy, or successful
syn. good, interest, well-being

social welfare 사회 복지

0409
patiently
[péiʃəntli]

adv. 참을성 있게 in such a way as to endure trying circumstances with even temper

people waiting patiently in line 줄서서 참을성 있게 기다리는 사람들

0410
wetland
[wétlænd]

n. 습지, 늪지 an area of land that is covered with shallow water
syn. bog, marshland, moor, swampland

protect the wetlands from development 습지를 개발로부터 보호하다

0411
recall
[rikɔ́:l]

v. 회상하다 to remember something from the past
syn. flash back, remember, recollect
ant. forget

recalled seeing her somewhere before 그녀를 어디선가 본 것을 기억해냈다

0412
centralize
[séntrəlàiz]
-centr 중간

v. 집중시키다 to draw or move something towards a centre
syn. concentrate, unify, unite
ant. decentralize

centralize all the data in one file 자료를 하나의 파일로 통합하다

0413
beat
[bi:t]

v. 치다, 두드리다 to hit repeatedly
syn. hit, strike, knock, punch

beat a drum 드럼을 치다

0414
unfair
[ʌ̀nfέər]

adj. 불공평한 treating people in a way that favors some over others
syn. biased, prejudiced, unjust, one-sided, partial

unfair dismissal 부당 해고

0415
unfamiliar
[ʌ̀nfəmíljər]

adj. 낯선 not known or experienced
syn. strange, new, unknown, unaccustomed

an unfamiliar place 낯선 장소

0416
well-being
[wélbíːiŋ]

n. 행복, 안녕, 복지   the state of being happy, healthy, or successful
syn. welfare, comfort, happiness, prosperity
ant. ill-being

material well-being 물질적 행복

0417
certainly
[sə́ːrtənli]

adv. 확실히   without doubt
syn. assuredly, indeed, clearly, definitely

he certainly rides very well 그는 확실히 정말 잘 탄다

0418
decrease
[dikriːs]
-de 하락

v. 감소하다   to become less
syn. drop, decline, lessen, contract
ant. escalate, expand, increase

decreased significantly 대폭 감소했다

0419
verdict
[və́ːrdikt]
-dict 말하다

n. 판결   the decision made by a jury in a trial
syn. diagnosis, judgment, resolution, decision

reached a guilty verdict 유죄 판결을 내렸다

0420
beam
[biːm]

v. 빛을 발하다   to send out beams of light or energy
syn. shine, radiate, ray

the sun beamed its light 태양이 빛을 내비쳤다

0421
well-defined
[wéldifáind]

adj. 잘 정의된   clearly shown or explained
syn. straightforward, clear-cut

a set of well-defined tasks 잘 정돈된 일련의 업무

0422
vibrate
[váibreit]

v. 떨다, 진동하다   to move back and forth or from side to side with very short, quick movements
syn. quiver, shudder, shake

vibrate to the beat of the music 음악 소리에 진동하다

0423
receptive
[riséptiv]
-cept 받다

adj. 수용적인   willing to listen to or accept ideas, suggestions, etc.
syn. open, open-minded
ant. narrow-minded, unreceptive

a receptive audience 잘 받아들이는 청중

0424
century
[séntʃuri]

n. 백 년, 세기   a period of 100 years

celebrate the beginning of the 21st century 21세기의 시작을 축하하다

0425
whatever
[hwatévər]

pron. 무엇이건   no matter what / regardless of what

take whatever you want 원하는 건 뭐든 가져라

0426
add
[æd]

v. 더하다   to put something with another thing or group of things

ant. remove, subtract, take off

add some new flowers to the garden 정원에 새 꽃을 더 심다

0427
decorate
[dékərèit]

v. 장식하다   to make more attractive by adding ornament, color, etc.

syn. adorn, array, beautify, ornament

enjoy decorating the Christmas tree 크리스마스 트리 장식을 즐기다

0428
vertical
[və́:rtikəl]

adj. 수직의   positioned up and down rather than from side to side

syn. upright, erect

ant. horizontal

a shirt with vertical stripes 수직 줄무늬 셔츠

0429
theft
[θeft]

n. 도둑질, 절도   the act or crime of stealing

syn. robbery, stealing

pardon theft 절도를 눈감아 주다

0430
deem
[di:m]

v. ~로 여기다   to think of something in a particular way

syn. conceive, consider, believe

deemed it wise to go slow 천천히 가는 것이 현명하다고 여겼다

0431
patient
[péiʃənt]

n. 환자   a person who receives medical care or treatment

syn. sick person, sufferer

cancer patients 암 환자들

0432
bear
[bɛər]

v. ~한 특성을 갖다, 간직하다   to seem to be a particular kind of thing or to have particular qualities

syn. display, have, show, hold, carry, possess, exhibit

bear no relation to the facts 사실과 관련이 전혀 없다

0433
unanticipated
[ʌnæntísəpèitid]

adj. 예상치 못한   not expected or anticipated

syn. abrupt, sudden, unexpected, unforeseen

unanticipated side effects 예상치 못한 부작용

0434
scholarly
[skálərli]

adj. 학술적인, 학구적인   connected with scholars or with the formal study of a subject

syn. intellectual, learned

a scholarly approach 학문적 접근

0435
deed
[di:d]

n. 행위   something that is done

syn. feat, stunt, trick

a hero's daring deeds 영웅의 용감한 행위

0436
uncut
[ʌnkʌ́t]

adj. 무삭제의   not shortened or edited

the film's uncut version 그 영화의 무삭제판

0437
arctic
[á:rktik]

adj. 북극의   of or relating to the North Pole or the region around it

ant. antarctic

an arctic expedition 북극 탐험

0438
territory
[térətɔ̀:ri]
-terr 땅

n. 지역, 영토   an area of land that belongs to or is controlled by a government

syn. district, area, land, region

disputed territory 분쟁 중인 영토

0439
school
[sku:l]

v. 떼 지어 헤엄쳐 다니다   to swim or feed in a school

bluefish are schooling 푸른 물고기들이 떼 지어 헤엄치고 있다

0440
unconscious
[ʌnkánʃəs]

adj. 의식을 잃은   not awake especially because of an injury, drug, etc.

syn. senseless

ant. conscious, alert, awake

be unconscious for three days 3일 동안 의식을 잃다

78

0441
occur
[əkə́:r]

v. 발생하다　to happen, especially unexpectedly
syn. happen, take place, come about

the accident occurred at noon 사건은 정오에 발생했다

0442
unfiltered
[ʌ̀nfíltərd]

adj. 걸러지지 않은　not having been passed through a filter

unfiltered news sources 여과되지 않은 뉴스 자료

0443
nectar
[néktər]

n. 과일 즙　a thick juice that comes from some fruits

peach nectar 복숭아 즙

0444
recent
[ríːsnt]

adj. 최근의　happening or starting a short time ago
syn. not long past, just gone

a recent study 최근의 연구

0445
patience
[péiʃəns]

n. 참을성　the ability to wait for a long time without becoming angry or upset
syn. tolerance
ant. impatience

lose patience 참을성을 잃다

0446
elaborate
[ilǽbərət]
-labor 일, 노동

adj. 정교한, 공들인　made or done with great care or with much detail
syn. complicated, detailed, sophisticated

made elaborate preparations 세심한 준비를 했다

0447
odd
[ɑd]

adj. 이상한　strange or unusual
syn. strange, unusual, different

a really odd sense of humor 정말 이상한 유머 감각

0448
path
[pæθ]

n. 길　a track that is made by people or animals walking over the ground
syn. line, pathway, route

a winding path through the woods 숲으로 난 꾸불꾸불한 길

79

0449
terse
[təːrs]

adj. 무뚝뚝한   brief and direct in a way that may seem rude or unfriendly

syn. brief, crisp, curt

ant. wordy

terse reply 무뚝뚝한 대꾸

0450
negative
[négətiv]

adj. 부정적인   expressing disagreement or criticism

syn. pessimistic, cynical, unwilling

ant. accepting, agreeable, approving

a negative response 부정적인 반응

Review

뜻을 써보고 전체 어구의 의미를 생각해 보시오.

01 an unfamiliar place _____ 0415

02 enjoy decorating the Christmas tree _____ 0427

03 bear no relation to the facts _____ 0432

04 the sun beamed its light _____ 0420

05 people waiting patiently in line _____ 0409

06 take whatever you want _____ 0425

07 a hero's daring deeds _____ 0435

08 a negative response _____ 0450

09 terse reply _____ 0449

10 bluefish are schooling _____ 0439

11 he certainly rides very well _____ 0417

12 an addictive drug _____ 0406

13 decreased significantly _____ 0418

14 an arctic expedition _____ 0437

15 add some new flowers to the garden _____ 0426

16 a winding path through the woods _____ 0448

17 the accident occurred at noon _____ 0441

18 lose patience _____ 0445

19 a really odd sense of humor _____ 0447

20 the medication made it bearable _____ 0402

0451
theory
[θíəri]

n. 이론   an idea or set of ideas that is intended to explain facts or events

syn. hypothesis, proposition, supposition, thesis

ant. fact, knowledge

a widely accepted scientific theory 널리 인정받는 과학 이론

0452
scout
[skaut]

v. 정찰하다   to explore an area to obtain information as about an enemy

syn. check out, watch, survey, observe, spy, probe

a military scouting party 군 정찰대

0453
underdeveloped
[ʌndərdivéləpt]

adj. 저개발의   not developed to a normal size or strength / having many poor people and few industries

syn. developing, third-world

underdeveloped nations 저개발 국가들

0454
fatigue
[fətíːg]

n. 피로   the state of being very tired

syn. burnout, collapse, exhaustion, tiredness, weariness

ant. refreshment

be overcome by fatigue 피로에 녹초가 되다

0455
genre
[ʒáːnrə]

n. 장르   a particular type or category of literature or art

syn. type, kind, class

a classic of the mystery genre 미스터리 장르의 고전

0456
offender
[əféndər]

n. 위반자, 범법자   a person who has committed a crime

syn. criminal, convict, lawbreaker

a young offender institution 소년원

0457
heartland
[háːrtlæ̀nd]

n. 심장지대   the core or most vital area

syn. center, stronghold

the industrial heartland of Korea 한국 산업의 심장지대

0458
fatality
[feitǽləti]

n. 사망자　a death caused by an accident, war, violence, or disease

syn. casualty, loss, prey, victim

caused one fatality and several injuries
한 명의 사망자와 여러 명의 부상자를 유발했다

0459
genius
[dʒíːnjəs]
-gen 탄생

n. 천재　a very smart or talented person

syn. brain, intellect, wizard

ant. blockhead, dodo, dummy

great scientific geniuses 위대한 과학 천재들

0460
import
[impɔ́ːrt]

v. 수입하다　to bring a product into a country to be sold

syn. bring in, buy in, ship in

a dealer who imports cars 자동차 수입업자

0461
nervous
[nɔ́ːrvəs]

adj. 긴장된　often or easily becoming worried and afraid about what might happen

syn. anxious, tense, jumpy

ant. calm, collected, cool, easy, relaxed

be a little nervous of change 변화에 약간 긴장되다

0462
undeniable
[ʌ̀ndináiəbəl]
-de 부정

adj. 확실한　clearly true

syn. certain, evident, undoubted

an undeniable fact 확실한 사실

0463
therapy
[θérəpi]

n. 치료　the treatment of physical or mental illnesses

syn. remedy, cure

needed intensive therapy 집중 치료가 필요했다

0464
impose
[impóuz]
-im 내부

v. 부과하다　to establish or apply by authority

syn. charge, enforce

impose a fine 벌금을 부과하다

0465
martial art
[mά:rʃəl ɑ:rt]

n. 무술　any one of several forms of fighting and self-defense that are widely practiced as sports

a self-defense martial art 호신술

0466
paradigm
[pǽrədaim]

n. 전형적인 예　a model or pattern for something that may be copied

syn. model, example

a paradigm for students to copy 학생들이 배워야할 전형적인 예

0467
legitimate
[lidʒítəmit]

-leg 법

adj. 정당한, 타당한　fair or reasonable

syn. reasonable, just, correct, sensible, valid

a legitimate excuse for being late 지각에 대한 타당한 이유

0468
negotiation
[nigòuʃiéiʃən]

n. 협상　a formal discussion between people who are trying to reach an agreement

syn. compromise, give-and-take, concession

be skilled at negotiation 협상에 능하다

0469
manufacture
[mὰnjəfǽktʃər]

-man 손

v. 제조하다　to make something usually in large amounts by using machines

syn. make, produce

materials used in manufacturing cars 자동차 제조에 쓰이는 재료들

0470
lessen
[lésn]

v. 감소하다, 줄이다　to become less or to cause something to become less

syn. diminish, decrease, reduce

ant. expand, increase, raise

lessen the pain 통증을 완화시키다

0471
marine
[mərí:n]

adj. 해양의　relating to the sea and creatures that live in it

syn. maritime, oceanic

marine ecology 해양 생태계

0472
offend
[əfénd]

v. 해를 가하다   to cause a person to feel hurt, angry, or upset by something said or done

ant. comply with, conform to, follow

be offended by the criticism 비평에 상처를 받다

0473
scrapbook
[skrǽpbùk]

n. 스크랩북   a book in which you save pictures, articles, or other material

syn. collection

a scrapbook of all the articles I wrote 내가 쓴 기사를 모두 모아 놓은 스크랩북

0474
nerve
[nəːrv]

n. 용기   courage that allows you to do something that is dangerous or difficult

syn. bravery, courage, spirit

had the nerve to ask her out 용기 있게 그녀에게 데이트 신청을 했다

0475
theme
[θiːm]

n. 주제, 테마   a particular subject or issue that is discussed often or repeatedly

popular themes in children's books 어린이 책에서 인기 있는 주제들

0476
negligence
[néɡlidʒəns]

n. 부주의, 태만, 과실   lack of normal care or attention

syn. carelessness

ant. carefulness, caution

negligence in carrying out safety procedures 안전 절차 수행에 태만함

0477
theorize
[θíːəràiz]

v. 가설을 세우다   to think of or suggest ideas about what is possibly true or real

syn. speculate, conjecture, hypothesize

theorize about what may have caused the fire
무엇이 화재를 일으켰을지 가설을 세우다

0478
legislation
[lèdʒisléiʃən]

n. 입법, 법률제정, 법률   the action or process of making laws

syn. lawmaking, regulation, enactment

draft legislation 법률을 입안하다

0479
undergo
[ʌ̀ndərgóu]

v. 겪다 to experience or endure something

syn. experience, go through

undergo a dramatic change of feelings 급격한 감정 변화를 겪다

0480
undermine
[ʌ̀ndərmáin]

v. 약화시키다 to make weaker or less effective usually in a secret or gradual way

syn. damage, weaken, threaten, hurt, injure, impair

be undermined by a series of failures 계속된 실패로 약화되다

0481
underpin
[ʌ̀ndərpín]

v. 지지하다 to strengthen or support something from below

syn. sustain, support, uphold

a wall underpinned by metal beams 철제 기둥으로 버티고 있는 벽

0482
recognize
[rékəgnàiz]

v. 인지하다, 인정하다 to know and remember because of previous knowledge or experience

syn. appreciate, apprehend, assimilate

ant. miss

recognized the odor at once 그 냄새를 즉시 알아차렸다

0483
election
[ilékʃən]

n. 선거 the act or process of choosing someone for a public office by voting

syn. vote, poll, ballot

election campaigns 선거 운동

0484
impress
[imprés]

v. 깊은 인상을 주다 to produce a vivid impression of

syn. move, strike, touch, affect

his honesty impressed us 그의 정직함이 깊은 인상을 주었다

0485
length
[leŋkθ]

n. 길이 the distance from one end of something to the other end

syn. distance, reach, measure, extent, span

10 meters in length 길이 10미터

0486
recite
[risáit]

v. 낭송하다   to read out loud or say from memory usually for an audience

syn. narrate, tell, recount

recited the poem 시를 낭송했다

0487
offensive
[əfénsiv]

adj. 불쾌한   causing someone to feel hurt, angry, or upset

syn. insulting, rude, abusive, embarrassing, annoying

made some offensive remarks 다소 불쾌한 말을 했다

0488
general
[dʒénərəl]

adj. 포괄적인   affecting all the people or things in a group

syn. common, overall, universal

ant. individual, particular

a general introduction to the subject 주제에 대한 포괄적인 소개

0489
pause
[pɔːz]

v. (잠시) 멈추다   to stop temporarily

syn. stop briefly, delay, hesitate, break

paused briefly to look at the scenery 경치를 보려고 잠시 멈추었다

0490
implication
[ìmpləkéiʃən]
-plic 접다

n. 함축된 의미   something that is suggested without being said directly

syn. suggestion, hint, inference

the implication of your silence 당신의 침묵의 의미

0491
impractical
[imprǽktikəl]

adj. 비실용적인   not easy to do or use

syn. unserviceable, unusable, unworkable, useless

ant. useful, functional

clothes that are attractive but impractical 예쁘지만 비실용적인 옷들

0492
healthy
[hélθi]

adj. 건강한   physically strong and not ill / helping you to stay physically strong and not ill

syn. well, sound, fit, strong

a healthy baby 건강한 아기
a healthy lifestyle 건강한 생활 습관

0493
impression
[impréʃən]
-press 밀다

n. 인상　the effect that something or someone has on a person's thoughts or feelings

syn. effect, influence, impact

made a favorable impression 호의적 인상을 심어줬다

first impression 첫인상

0494
gentle
[dʒéntl]

adj. 상냥한, 부드러운　having a mild or kindly nature or character

syn. kind, loving, peaceful, soft, quiet, pacific, tender

a quiet and gentle man 조용하고 상냥한 남자

0495
recess
[ríːses]
-cess 가다

n. 휴식 시간　a short period of time during the school day when children can play

syn. break, rest, holiday

play outside at recess 쉬는 시간에 나가서 놀다

0496
margin
[máːrdʒin]

n. 여백, 범위　an edge or rim, and the area immediately adjacent to it

syn. edge, side, limit, border

a book with wide margins 끝 여백이 넓은 책

margin of error 오차 범위

0497
elect
[ilékt]

v. 선출하다　to select someone for a position, job, etc. by voting

syn. choose, handpick, name, single out

elected her class president 그녀를 회장으로 선출했다

0498
paved
[peivd]

adj. (길이) 포장된　covered with a firm surface suitable for travel

a paved road 포장도로

0499
fatal
[féitl]

adj. 치명적인　causing death

syn. destructive, disastrous, unfortunate

a fatal attraction to gambling 도박으로의 치명적 이끌림

0500
elastic
[ilǽstik]

adj. 탄력적인　able to be changed

syn. bouncy, flexible, resilient

ant. inflexible, rigid, stiff

an elastic headband 신축성 있는 머리띠

an elastic schedule 탄력적인 스케줄

Review

뜻을 써보고 전체 어구의 의미를 생각해 보시오.

01 materials used in manufacturing cars _____ 0469

02 a fatal attraction to gambling _____ 0499

03 lessen the pain _____ 0470

04 play outside at recess _____ 0495

05 the industrial heartland of Korea _____ 0457

06 theorize about what may have caused the fire _____ 0477

07 a paved road _____ 0498

08 a classic of the mystery genre _____ 0455

09 an elastic headband _____ 0500

10 elected her class president _____ 0497

11 the implication of your silence _____ 0490

12 a self-defense martial art _____ 0465

13 first impression _____ 0493

14 paused briefly to look at the scenery _____ 0489

15 a legitimate excuse for being late _____ 0467

16 had the nerve to ask her out _____ 0474

17 his honesty impressed us _____ 0484

18 be overcome by fatigue _____ 0454

19 a dealer who imports cars _____ 0460

20 be offended by the criticism _____ 0472

0501
marvel
[máːrvəl]
-mar 놀라다, 보다

n. 경이로움 someone or something that is extremely good, skillful, etc.
syn. wonder, miracle, phenomenon
the marvels of nature 자연의 경이로운 것들

0502
nest
[nest]

n. 둥지, 보금자리 the place where a bird lays its eggs and takes care of its young
syn. hotbed, den, breeding-ground
build a nest 둥지를 짓다

0503
fault
[fɔːlt]

n. 실수, 결점 a problem or bad part that prevents something from being perfect
syn. mistake, slip, error, offence, blunder
ant. merit, virtue
committed too many faults to win 이기기 위해 너무 많은 잘못을 범했다

0504
admit
[ædmít]

v. 인정하다 to concede as true or valid
syn. acknowledge, agree, allow, concede
ant. deny
admitted making a mistake 실수 한 것을 인정했다

0505
favor
[féivər]

v. 찬성하다, 지지하다 to approve of or support something
syn. support, like, back
favored the idea 그 아이디어에 찬성했다

0506
neural
[njúərəl]

adj. 신경계통의 of or relating to a nerve or the nervous system
suffer from a neural disorder 신경 계통 병을 앓다

0507
mass
[mæs]

n. 무리 a large body of persons in a group
syn. crowd, group, body, pack
a mass of spectators 구경꾼 무리

0508
genuine
[dʒénjuin]
-gen 탄생

adj. 진실한, 진심 어린 sincere and honest
syn. heartfelt, earnest
a deep and genuine love

0509
lifeguard
[láifgà:rd]

n. 인명 구조원　a usually expert swimmer employed to safeguard other swimmers

lifeguard's high chair 인명 구조원의 높은 의자

0510
admire
[ædmáiər]

v. 존경하다, 감탄하다　to feel respect or approval for someone or something

syn. appreciate, consider, esteem, respect

admired his dedication 그의 헌신에 존경심을 가졌다
admired the scenery 경치에 감탄했다

0511
admirable
[ǽdmərəbəl]

adj. 감탄스러운　deserving to be admired

syn. applaudable, commendable, creditable

an admirable achievement 감탄할 만한 성과

0512
massive
[mǽsiv]

adj. 막대한, 거대한　very large in amount or degree

syn. huge, great, enormous

a massive amount of money 거액의 돈

0513
lifelong
[láiflɔ̀(:)ŋ]

adj. 평생 동안의　continuing or lasting through a person's life

syn. long-lasting, permanent, lifetime

had a lifelong love of nature 평생 자연을 사랑했다

0514
masterpiece
[mǽstərpì:s]

n. 걸작, 대작　a great book, painting, piece of music, movie, etc.

syn. masterwork

be recognized as a masterpiece 걸작으로 인정받다

0515
offer
[ɔ́(:)fər]

v. 1 제공하다 2 제의하다　to provide or supply something / to say that you are willing to do something

syn. 1 provide, present, furnish
2 propose, suggest

offer money as compensation 보상으로 돈을 제공하다
be offered a job 일자리를 제의 받다

0516
challenging
[tʃǽlindʒiŋ]

adj. 어려운   difficult in a way that is usually interesting or enjoyable

syn. backbreaking, hard, demanding, difficult

ant. easy, effortless

found the job challenging and fun 일이 어렵고도 재미있었다

0517
defect
[difékt]

-de 하락, 부정

n. 결점   something that causes weakness or failure

syn. fault, flaw, imperfection

two worst character defects 두 가지 최악의 성격 결함

0518
net
[net]

adj. 총, 전체의   after everything is completed

syn. final, closing, ultimate

net earnings 총 수익

0519
defeat
[difít]

v. 이기다   to overcome in a contest or competition

syn. beat, crush, overwhelm

ant. lose

defeat the opposing team 상대 팀을 이기다

0520
beloved
[bilʌ́vid]

adj. 사랑받는   very much loved

syn. darling, cherished, dear

a beloved public figure 사랑받는 공인

0521
lifetime
[láiftàim]

n. 일평생   the time during which a person is alive

syn. life span, life

a lifetime spent traveling the world 세계 여행에 보낸 일평생

0522
favorite
[féivərit]

n. 선호하는 것   a person or a thing that is liked more than others

syn. darling, pet, preference

that movie is my favorite 그 영화는 내가 제일 좋아하는 것이다

0523
beforehand
[bifɔ́:rhænd]

adv. 전에   at an earlier or previous time

syn. in advance, before, earlier

came an hour beforehand 한 시간 전에 왔다

0524
electronic
[ilèktránik]

adj. 전자기기의 produced by the use of electronic equipment

electronic banking 인터넷 뱅킹

0525
imprint
[imprint]

v. 새기다, 찍다 to establish firmly

syn. engrave, print, stamp, impress

a picture imprinted in my memory 내 기억에 각인된 모습

0526
geology
[dʒìːáləitʃi]

n. 지질학 a science that studies rocks, layers of soil, etc.

marine geology 해양지질학

0527
liberal
[líbərəl]

adj. 개방된, 자유로운 willing to understand and respect other people's ideas, opinions, and feelings

syn. easy-going, unbiased, broad-minded, unprejudiced

a liberal view 개방된 견해

0528
license
[láisəns]

v. 허가하다 to give official permission to someone to do or use something

syn. permit, commission, enable, sanction, allow

be licensed to sell liquor 술을 팔도록 허가 받다

0529
behave
[bihéiv]

v. 1 행동하다 2 바르게 행동하다 to act in a particular way / to act in an acceptable way

syn. 1 act, react
2 be polite, act correctly

behaved like a child 어린애처럼 행동했다

she told me to behave 그녀는 내게 똑바로 행동하라고 했다

0530
challenge
[tʃǽlindʒ]

v. 저지하다, 반박하다 to question the action or authority of someone

syn. contest, dispute, question

ant. accept, believe, embrace, swallow

the police challenged the stranger 경찰들이 그 이방인을 막아섰다

0531
electricity
[ilèktrísəti]

n. 전기   a form of energy that is carried through wires and is used to operate machines, lights, etc.

an old building with no electricity 전기가 들어오지 않는 낡은 집

0532
certificate
[sərtífəkit]

n. 자격증   a document that is official proof that you have finished school or a course of training

syn. document, licence, warrant, voucher, diploma

earn the teaching certificate 교사 자격증을 따다

0533
behavior
[bihéivjər]

n. 행동, 태도   the way a person or animal acts or behaves

syn. conduct, actions, bearing, attitude

study the behavior of elephants 코끼리들의 행동을 연구하다

0534
improve
[imprú:v]

v. 개선하다   to make something better

syn. enhance, enrich, upgrade

ant. worsen

improved sales 매출을 증가시켰다

0535
imprudent
[imprú:dənt]

adj. 둔한   not wise or sensible

syn. tactless, undiplomatic, unwise

ant. advisable, discreet, tactful, wise

an imprudent investor 둔한 투자자

0536
elegant
[éləgənt]

adj. 우아한   graceful and attractive

syn. classy, graceful, majestic, refined

ant. unstylish

the most elegant First Lady 가장 우아한 영부인

0537
heated
[hí:tid]

adj. 과열된   marked by excited or angry feelings

syn. excited, frenzied, hyperactive

ant. chilled, cool

a heated discussion 과열된 토론

0538
faulty
[fɔ́:lti]

adj. 결함 있는   having a mistake, fault, or weakness
syn. amiss, defective, flawed, imperfect
ant. perfect

faulty wiring 하자 있는 배선

0539
impressive
[imprésiv]
-press 밀다

adj. 인상적인   making a good impression
syn. impactful, moving, touching

have an impressive vocabulary 인상 깊은 어휘력을 가지고 있다

0540
favorable
[féivərəbəl]

adj. 호의적인   showing approval
syn. approving, friendly, good, positive
ant. disapproving, negative

a favorable reply 긍정적인 답변
a favorable wind 순풍

0541
additional
[ədíʃənəl]

adj. 추가의   more than is usual or expected
syn. added, another, else

additional information 추가 정보

0542
adolescence
[æ̀dəlésəns]

n. 사춘기   the period of life when a child develops into an adult
syn. teens, youth, minority

struggled through his adolescence 사춘기에 방황했다

0543
favoritism
[féivəritìzəm]

n. 편애   the practice of giving special treatment to a person or group
syn. bias, preference

show favoritism 편애하다

0544
lie
[lai]
-lay -lain

v. 눕다   to be or to stay at rest in a horizontal position
syn. rest, sprawl, stretch out

lie motionless 꼼짝 않고 누워있다

0545
heavily
[hévili]

adv. 심하게, 아주 많이 to a great degree
syn. greatly, immensely
ant. little, negligibly, slightly

drank and smoked heavily for years 여러 해 동안 심하게 술 마시고 담배 폈다

0546
element
[éləmənt]

n. 요소 a particular part of something such as a situation or activity
syn. building block, factor, ingredient
ant. whole

an essential element of a democracy 민주주의의 필수 요소

0547
unexpected
[ʌ̀nikspéktid]

adj. 예상치 못한 not expected
syn. abrupt, sudden, unanticipated
ant. anticipated, foreseen

an unexpected turn of events 예상치 못한 일의 발생

0548
adequate
[ǽdikwit]

adj. 충분한 enough for some need or requirement
syn. satisfactory, serviceable, tolerable
ant. deficient, lacking

get adequate water 충분한 물을 확보하다

0549
geographical
[dʒì:əgrǽfikəl]

adj. 지리학의, 지리적인 of or relating to geography

geographical location 지리적 위치

0550
imprison
[imprizn]
-in 내부

v. 투옥하다, 감금하다 to put someone in prison
syn. confine, incarcerate, lock up
ant. discharge, free, liberate, release

be imprisoned for murder 살인죄로 투옥되다

96

Review

뜻을 써보고 전체 어구의 의미를 생각해 보시오.

01 defeat the opposing team _____ 0519

02 favored the idea _____ 0505

03 show favoritism _____ 0543

04 a mass of spectators _____ 0507

05 improved sales _____ 0534

06 additional information _____ 0541

07 admired his dedication _____ 0511

08 drank and smoked heavily for years _____ 0545

09 lie motionless _____ 0544

10 a deep and genuine love _____ 0508

11 a lifetime spent traveling the world _____ 0521

12 an imprudent investor _____ 0535

13 two worst character defects _____ 0517

14 came an hour beforehand _____ 0523

15 ① behaved like a child _____ 0529
　 ② she told me to behave _____

16 the most elegant First Lady _____ 0536

17 ① be offered a job _____ 0515
　 ② offer money as compensation _____

18 electronic banking _____ 0524

19 committed too many faults to win _____ 0503

20 the marvels of nature _____ 0501

0551
reconstruction
[rìːkənstrʌ́kʃən]
-struct 세우다

n. 재건 the act or process of building something that was damaged or destroyed again

syn. rebuilding, reform, restoration

the reconstruction of postwar Europe 전후 유럽 재건

0552
adversity
[ædvə́ːrsəti]

n. 역경 a difficult situation or condition

syn. misfortune, mischance, tragedy

ant. fortune, luck, serendipity

showed courage in the face of adversity 역경에 맞서 용기를 보여줬다

0553
scrutiny
[skrúːtəni]

n. 정밀조사 the act of carefully examining something especially in a critical way

syn. audit, check, checkup, examination

the close scrutiny of data 자료 정밀 조사

0554
sculpture
[skʌ́lptʃər]

n. 조각 a piece of art that is made by carving or molding clay, stone, metal, etc.

syn. statue, figure, model

collect modern sculpture 현대 조각품들을 수집하다

0555
biased
[báiəst]

adj. 편향된 having or showing an unfair tendency to believe that some people, ideas, etc. are better than others

syn. partial, one-sided, prejudiced

ant. equal, neutral, nonpartisan, objective

biased press reports 편향된 언론 보도

0556
scratch
[skrætʃ]

v. 긁다 to rub your skin with something sharp especially in order to stop an itch

syn. rub, scrape

scratched my back for me 나의 등을 긁어 주었다
scratch a match 성냥을 긋다

0557
charity
[tʃǽrəti]

n. 자선　the act of giving money, food, or other kinds of help to people who are poor, sick, etc.

syn. donations, help, relief

a charity show 자선 쇼

0558
adventurous
[ædvéntʃərəs]

adj. 1 위험한　2 모험심 많은　full of danger and excitement / not afraid to do new and dangerous or exciting things

syn. 1 adventuresome
　　2 bold, audacious, daring

an adventurous journey 위험한 여행
adventurous travelers 모험심 많은 여행자들

0559
sea level
[si: lévəl]

n. 해수면　the average height of the sea's surface

70 meters above sea level 해발 70미터

0560
record
[rékərd]
-cord 심장

adj. 기록적인　best or most remarkable among other similar things

a record rainfall 기록적인 호우

0561
thought
[θɔːt]

n. 생각　something that you think of

syn. reflection, study, consideration

abandoned all thoughts of going home 집에 가겠다는 생각을 모두 버렸다

0562
thick
[θik]

adj. 두꺼운　having a large distance between the top and bottom or front and back surfaces

syn. chunky, fat

ant. skinny, slender, slim, thin

a thick layer of ice 두꺼운 얼음 층

0563
charm
[tʃɑːrm]

n. 매력　an attractive quality

syn. attraction, appeal, fascination

have many charms 매력이 많다

0564
charitable
[tʃǽrətəbəl]

adj. 자선의   done or designed to help people who are poor, sick, etc.

syn. beneficent, benevolent, humanitarian

charitable fund 자선기금

0565
understandable
[ʌ̀ndərstǽndəbəl]

adj. 이해할 만한   normal and reasonable in a particular situation

syn. acceptable, justifiable, reasonable

an understandable mistake 이해가 되는 실수

0566
underprivileged
[ʌ̀ndərprívəlidʒd]

adj. 소외받는   having less money, education, etc. than the other people in a society

syn. disadvantaged, deprived

ant. advantaged, privileged

underprivileged sections of the community 사회 소외 구역

0567
defend
[difénd]

v. 방어하다   to fight in order to keep something safe

syn. cover, fend, guard, protect, shield

ant. assail, assault, attack

successfully defended their championship 챔피언 자리를 성공적으로 지켜냈다

0568
deficient
[difíʃənt]
-de 하락, 부정

adj. 부족한   not having enough of something that is important or necessary

syn. lacking, wanting, needing, short, inadequate

a diet deficient in calcium 칼슘이 부족한 식단

0569
thief
[θiːf]

n. 도둑   a person who steals something from another

syn. robber, crook, burglar, stealer

a petty thief 좀도둑

0570
seasoned
[síːzənd]

adj. 경험 많은   experienced in a particular activity or job

syn. experienced, veteran, mature, practised

a seasoned performer 노련한 연기자

0571

deficiency

[difíʃənsi]

-de 하락, 부정

n. 결핍 a lack of something that your body needs

syn. lack, shortage, scarcity

ant. abundance, adequacy, wealth

anaemia caused by iron deficiency 철분 부족으로 오는 빈혈

0572

adult

[ədʌ́lt]

n. 어른, 성인 a fully grown person or animal

syn. grown-up

appeal both to children and to adults 아이들과 성인들에게 모두 인기 있다

0573

defy

[difái]

-de 하락, 부정

v. 거부하다, 대항하다 to refuse to obey something or someone

syn. disobey, mock, rebel

ant. comply with, conform to, obey

defy one's parents 부모님께 반항하다

0574

reconsider

[rì:kənsídər]

v. 재고하다 to consider again especially with a view to changing or reversing

syn. rethink, review

ant. uphold

refused to reconsider her decision 결정을 재고하기를 거부했다

0575

payment

[péimənt]

n. 지급, 급료 the act of giving money for something

syn. wages, fee, reward

require payment in advance 선 지급을 요구하다

0576

recommend

[rèkəménd]

-mend 지시하다

v. 추천하다 to advise as the best course or choice

syn. advocate, suggest, endorse

recommended him for the position 그를 그 자리에 추천했다

0577

charge

[tʃɑ:rdʒ]

v. 1 충전하다 2 기소하다 to give an amount of electricity to something / to accuse someone officially of committing a crime

syn. 1 fill, load

2 accuse, indict

charge the car's battery 자동차 배터리를 충전하다

charged him with armed robbery 무장 강도죄로 기소했다

0578
bilingual
[bailíŋgwəl]

adj. 이중 언어 사용의   able to speak and understand two languages

bilingual in English and Korean 영어와 한국어, 이중 언어를 사용하는

0579
advertise
[ǽdvərtàiz]

v. 광고하다, 알리다   to make the public aware of something that is being sold

syn. publicize, promote

began to advertise on the radio 라디오 광고를 시작했다

0580
peasant
[pézənt]

n. 소작농   a poor farmer or farm worker who has low social status

syn. countryman

treated us like a bunch of peasants 우리를 시골뜨기들 취급했다

0581
advent
[ǽdvent]

n. 도래, 출현   the introduction of a new product, idea, custom, etc.

syn. coming, approach, appearance, arrival

the advent of computers 컴퓨터의 출현

0582
benefit
[bénəfit]
-bene 좋음

n. 이점, 혜택   a good or helpful result or effect

syn. profit, gain, advantage

a benefit of museum membership 박물관 회원의 혜택

0583
characteristic
[kæ̀riktərístik]

n. 특징   a special quality or trait that makes a person, thing, or group different from others

syn. quality, specific, stamp, touch, trait

physical characteristics 신체적 특징들

0584
beverage
[bévəridʒ]

n. 음료수   something you can drink

syn. drink, quencher, refreshment

alcoholic beverages 알코올 음료

0585
pay
[pei]

v. 지불하다   to give in return for goods or service

syn. reward, compensate

pay wages 월급을 지급하다

pay by the hour 시간제로 지급하다

0586
advance
[ədvǽns]

v. 나아가다   to move forward

syn. progress, proceed, go ahead

advanced slowly down the street 거리로 천천히 나아갔다

0587
bend
[bend]

v. 구부리다   to use force to cause something to become curved

syn. arch, bow, crook, curve

ant. straighten, unbend, uncurl

bend a wire into a circle 철사를 둥글게 구부리다

0588
adopt
[ədápt]
-opt 바라다

v. 입양하다   to take a child of other parents legally as your own child

syn. raise, nurse, mother, rear, foster

decided to adopt a child 아이를 입양하기로 결정했다

0589
undervalue
[ʌndərvǽljuː]

v. 과소평가하다   to place too low a value on something

syn. underrate, underestimate

ant. overestimate, overrate, overvalue

be undervalued as a poet 시인으로서 저평가되다

0590
advantage
[ədvǽntidʒ]

n. 유리한 점, 이점   something that helps to make someone or something better or more likely to succeed than others

syn. high ground, inside track

ant. disadvantage, drawback, handicap

the advantages of living in a small town 작은 마을에 사는 것의 장점들

0591
official
[əfíʃəl]

adj. 공식적인   used about things that are decided by a government

syn. authorized, approved, formal

the country's official language 그 나라의 공식 언어

0592
adrift
[ədríft]

adv. 표류하여   floating on the water without being tied to anything or controlled by anyone

syn. afloat, cast off, unanchored

a boat adrift on the sea 바다에 표류 중인 보트

0593
elevation
[èləvéiʃən]

n. 상승, 증가   an act or result of lifting or raising someone or something
syn. ascent

charted the elevations in his temperature 그의 체온 상승을 표로 작성했다

0594
besides
[bisáidz]

adv. 게다가   in addition to something

other languages besides English and French 영어와 프랑스어 외에 다른 언어들

0595
ongoing
[ángòuiŋ]

adj. 계속 진행 중인   being actually in process
syn. in progress, continuing, current, growing

an ongoing debate over the issue 그 문제에 관해 계속 진행 중인 토론

0596
peaceful
[píːsfəl]

adj. 평화로운   quiet and calm
syn. pacific

settle the conflict by peaceful means 평화적인 방법으로 갈등을 안정시키다

0597
bet
[bet]

v. 내기하다   to risk losing something such as money if your guess about what will happen is wrong
syn. gamble

bet 100,000 won on the game 그 게임에 십 만원 걸었다

0598
pedestrian
[pədéstriən]
-ped 발

n. 보행자   a person who is walking in a city, along a road, etc.
syn. walker, foot-traveller

a group of pedestrians 한 무리의 보행자들

0599
undertake
[ʌndərtéik]

v. 떠맡다, 수행하다   to begin or attempt something
syn. shoulder, take over, assume

the lawyer who undertook the case 그 사건을 맡은 변호사

0600
one-sided
[wʌnsáidid]

adj. 1 편파적인 2 일방적인   showing only one opinion or point of view / led or controlled by one of the two people or groups involved
syn. 1 biased, prejudiced 2 unbalanced, ill-matched

a one-sided view 편파적인 관점
a one-sided match 일방적인 경기

Review

뜻을 써보고 전체 어구의 의미를 생각해 보시오.

0570
01 a seasoned performer

0557
02 a charity show

0577
03 ① charge the car's battery

   ② charged him with armed robbery

0586
04 advanced slowly down the street

0583
05 physical characteristics

0590
06 the advantages of living in a small town

0596
07 settle the conflict by peaceful means

0555
08 biased press reports

0572
09 appeal both to children and to adults

0597
10 bet 100,000 won on the game

0568
11 a diet deficient in calcium

0574
12 refused to reconsider her decision

0581
13 the advent of computers

0567
14 successfully defended their championship

0551
15 the reconstruction of postwar Europe

0592
16 a boat adrift on the sea

0552
17 showed courage in the face of adversity

0580
18 treated us like a bunch of peasants

0569
19 a petty thief

0554
20 collect modern sculpture

0601
eliminate
[ilímənèit]

v. 제거하다   to get rid of something that is not wanted or needed
syn. close out, rule out, shut out
ant. admit, include

eliminate the causes of the epidemic 그 전염병의 원인을 제거하다

0602
glance
[ɡlæns]

n. 힐끗 봄   a quick look
syn. glimpse, peek, peep

gave me a quick glance 나를 힐끗 봤다

0603
threaten
[θrétn]

v. 위협하다   to tell someone that you might or you will cause them harm, especially in order to make them do something
syn. menace

threatened him with a gun 총으로 그를 위협했다

0604
charming
[tʃá:rmiŋ]

adj. 매혹적인   very attractive and pleasant
syn. appealing, attractive

a book with charming illustrations 멋진 삽화들이 있는 책

0605
biography
[baiáɡrəfi]
-bio 생명
-graphy 쓰다

n. 전기   the story of a real person's life written by someone other than that person
syn. memoir

a new biography of Abraham Lincoln 아브라함 링컨의 새 전기

0606
inaccurate
[inǽkjərit]

adj. 부정확한   having a mistake or error
syn. false, incorrect, inexact
ant. correct, errorless, exact, precise

an inaccurate translation 부정확한 번역

0607
advocacy
[ǽdvəkəsi]
-voc 부름, 소리

n. 옹호, 지지   strong public support for something
syn. recommendation, support

strenuous advocacy of the right 줄기찬 권리의 주장

0608
feature
[fíːtʃər]

n. 특징, 기능 an interesting or important part, quality, ability, etc.

syn. character, property, quality, specific

new safety features 새 안전 기능들

0609
gesture
[dʒéstʃər]
-gest 나르다

n. 몸짓 a movement of your body that shows or emphasizes an idea or a feeling

syn. sign, signal

a dramatic gesture 과장된 몸짓

0610
pen
[pen]

v. 쓰다 to write something such as a letter, a book, etc. especially using a pen

syn. write down, draft, compose

penned a letter 편지를 썼다

0611
undesirable
[ʌndizáiərəbəl]

adj. 바람직하지 못한, 해로운 bad, harmful, or unpleasant

syn. unwanted, unwelcome

some undesirable side effects 해로운 부작용들

0612
section
[sékʃən]

n. 한 부분, 칸 a part cut off or separated from the main body of something

syn. part, piece, portion, division

the frozen food section 냉동식품 칸

0613
rectangular
[rektǽŋgjələr]
-rect 올바름

adj. 직사각형의 shaped like a rectangle

a rectangular table 직사각형의 탁자

0614
geometry
[dʒiːámətri]

n. 기하학, 기하학적 구조 a branch of mathematics that deals with points, lines, angles, surfaces, and solids

syn. figure, form, shape

the geometry of a spider's web 거미줄의 기하학적 구조

0615
elite
[ilíːt]

n. 상류층   the people who have the most wealth and status in a society

syn. cream, upper class

ant. proletarians

the elites of wealth and power 부와 권력의 상류층

0616
secretly
[sikríːtli]

adv. 비밀리에   in secret

syn. covertly

record secretly 비밀리에 기록하다

0617
inaudible
[inɔ́ːdəbəl]
-aud 듣다

adj. 안 들리는   not loud enough to be heard

syn. unheard, out of earshot

inaudible comments 들리지 않는 코멘트

0618
recycling
[riːsáikliŋ]

n. 재활용   the act of processing used materials into new products for further use

syn. reprocess, reuse

recycling bin 재활용 용기

0619
undeserved
[ʌndizə́ːrvd]

adj. 자격이 없는, 억울한   if something is undeserved, you get it although you should not, because you have not done anything to deserve or to cause it

syn. unjust

an undeserved blame 누명

0620
inactive
[inǽktiv]

adj. 비활동적인   not taking part in physical activity or exercise

syn. lazy, passive, slow

physically inactive people 신체적으로 비활동적인 사람들

0621
bind
[baind]

v. 묶다   to tie or wrap something with rope, string, etc.

syn. tie, unite, join, wrap

bind the hair 머리카락을 묶다

0622
cheap
[tʃiːp]

adj. 값싼   not costing a lot of money

syn. affordable

ant. costly, dear, deluxe, expensive

a good cheap hotel 저렴하고 좋은 호텔

0623
inborn
[ínbɔ́ːrn]

adj. 천부적인   existing from the time someone is born

syn. built-in, innate, inherent

an inborn talent for music 음악에의 천부적 재능

0624
advised
[ædváizd]

adj. 신중한, 숙고한

syn. deliberate, calculated, considered

an ill-advised remarks 무분별한 말

0625
undifferentiated
[ʌ̀ndifərénʃièitid]

adj. 차별되지 않는   not having any distinguishing features

society as an undifferentiated whole 차별 없는 전체로서의 사회

0626
impulsive
[impʌ́lsiv]

adj. 충동적인   doing things or tending to do things suddenly and without careful thought

syn. compulsive

made an impulsive decision 충동적인 결정을 했다

0627
chart
[tʃɑːrt]

v. 지도[도표]를 그리다   to make a map of an area

syn. plot, map out, sketch, draft

charted the coastline 해안 지도를 그렸다

0628
undeveloped
[ʌ̀ndivéləpt]

adj. 미발달의   not fully grown

undeveloped limbs 미발달한 수족

0629
material
[mətíəriəl]

n. 재료, 물질   a substance from which something is made or can be made

syn. stuff, things, articles, items

sticky material 끈적끈적한 물질

0630
secure
[sikjúər]

adj. 안전한   protected from danger or harm

syn. safe, protected, shielded

ant. insecure

enter a secure area 안전한 구역으로 들어가다

0631
chase
[tʃeis]

v. 쫓다   to follow rapidly

syn. follow, track, hunt, run after

chased the suspect 혐의자를 쫓았다

0632
opponent
[əpóunənt]

n. 상대편   a person, team, group, etc. that is competing against another in a contest

syn. adversary, foe, rival

a formidable opponent 위협적인 상대

0633
peer
[piər]

n. 또래, 동료   a person who belongs to the same age group or social group as someone else

syn. fellow, contemporary

peer pressure 또래들이 주는 압박

0634
threat
[θret]

n. 위협   a statement saying you will be harmed if you do not do what someone wants you to do

syn. menace

ignored their threats 그들의 위협을 무시했다

0635
elusive
[ilú:siv]

adj. 종잡을 수 없는   hard to find or capture

syn. evasive, slippery

an elusive thought 종잡을 수 없는 생각

0636
fear
[fiər]

v. 두려워하다, 걱정하다   to be afraid of something

syn. bother, worry, sweat

feared to go out at night 밤에 외출하는 것을 두려워했다

0637
given
[gívən]

adj. 주어진 specific or previously stated
syn. specified, particular, specific

at a given time 주어진 시간에

0638
neutral
[njú:trəl]

adj. 중립의 not supporting either side of an argument, fight, war, etc.
syn. unbiased, impartial
ant. allied, confederate

a neutral nation 중립국가

0639
recover
[rikʌ́vər]

v. 회복하다 to become healthy after an illness or injury
syn. get back, regain

recovered consciousness in the hospital 병원에서 의식을 회복했다

0640
elliptical
[ilíptikəl]

adj. 타원형의 shaped like a flattened circle
syn. oval, egg-shaped

an elliptical orbit 타원형의 궤도

0641
recreational
[rèkriéiʃənəl]

adj. 오락의 done for enjoyment

recreational facilities 오락시설

0642
peel
[pi:l]

v. 껍질을 벗기다 to remove the skin from a fruit, vegetable, etc.
syn. shell, skin

peel an orange 오렌지 껍질을 벗기다

0643
secondary
[sékəndèri]

adj. 2차적인, 부차적인 not as important or valuable as something else
syn. minor, lesser, lower, inferior, unimportant

winning is secondary 이기는 것은 2차적인 문제다

0644
operate
[ápərèit]

v. 조작하다, 운전하다 to use and control something
syn. handle, run, work

a license to operate a motor vehicle 자동차 운전면허증

0645
operagoer
[ápərəgòuər]

n. 오페라 보러가는 사람   someone who attends operas

first-time operagoers 처음 오페라 구경을 간 사람들

0646
three-dimensional
[θríːdiménʃənəl]

adj. 삼차원의, 입체적인   having, or seeming to have, length, depth, and height

syn. lifelike, living, naturalistic

a three-dimensional model of the bridge 입체 다리 모형

0647
materialistic
[mətíəriəlístik]

adj. 물질주의의   attaching a lot of importance to money and material possessions

syn. consumerist

lead a materialistic lifestyle 물질을 추구하는 삶을 살다

0648
opportunity
[àpərtʃúːnəti]

n. 기회   an amount of time or a situation in which something can be done

syn. chance, occasion

have an opportunity to ask questions 질문할 기회를 갖다

0649
peninsula
[pənínsjulə]

n. 반도   a piece of land that is almost entirely surrounded by water and is attached to a larger land area

syn. foreland, headland

divided Korean peninsula 분단된 한반도

0650
open-ended
[óupənéndid]

adj. 미확정의   not ending in a certain way or on a certain date

an open-ended question 주관식 질문

Review

뜻을 써보고 전체 어구의 의미를 생각해 보시오.

01 at a given time   0637

02 peer pressure   0633

03 a dramatic gesture   0609

04 recreational facilities   0641

05 winning is secondary   0643

06 a neutral nation   0638

07 a good cheap hotel   0622

08 have an opportunity to ask questions   0648

09 first-time operagoers   0645

10 an elusive thought   0635

11 a license to operate a motor vehicle   0644

12 an open-ended question   0650

13 a book with charming illustrations   0604

14 peel an orange   0642

15 society as an undifferentiated whole   0625

16 a three-dimensional model of the bridge   0646

17 threatened him with a gun   0603

18 an undeserved blame   0619

19 the frozen food section   0612

20 inaudible comments   0617

0651
fertile
[fə́:rtl]

adj. 비옥한 producing many plants or crops
syn. fruitful, productive
ant. barren, dead

fertile land 비옥한 땅

0652
fence
[fens]

n. 담장 a structure made of wood, metal, etc. that surrounds a piece of land
syn. barricade, barrier, hedge, wall

put up a fence 담장을 세우다

0653
reduce
[ridʒú:s]

v. 줄이다, 낮추다 to make something smaller in size, amount, number, etc.
syn. lessen, cut, lower

reduce taxes 세금을 줄이다

0654
tickle
[tíkəl]

v. 간지럼 태우다 to move your fingers gently over someone's body in order to make them laugh

tickled my nose 내 코를 간질였다

0655
including
[inklú:diŋ]
-clud 닫다

prep. 포함된 used for mentioning that someone or something is part of a particular group or amount
syn. containing, with, counting, plus

not including tax 세금 별도

0656
degrade
[digréid]
-de 하락, 부정

v. 1 멸시하다 2 질을 떨어뜨리다 to treat poorly and without respect / to make the quality of something worse
syn. 1 disgrace, humiliate 2 reduce, lower, downgrade

felt degraded by their remarks 그들의 말에 모욕감을 느꼈다
degrade the image quality 사진의 질을 떨어뜨리다

0657
seedling
[sí:dliŋ]

n. 묘목 a young plant that is grown from seed

transplant a seedling 묘종을 옮겨 심다

0658
degree
[digríː]

n. 1 정도, 단계 2 학위 a stage in a scale of relative amount or intensity / a course of study at a university, or the qualification that you get after completing the course

a high degree of stress 고도의 스트레스
a master's degree in English literature 영문학 석사 학위

0659
opposite
[ápəzit]

adj. 반대의 as different as possible from something else
syn. facing, other, opposing
ant. alike, analogous, like, similar

they ran in opposite directions 그들은 반대 방향으로 뛰었다

0660
reflect
[riflékt]
-flec 구부러지다

v. 보이다, 반영하다 to show or express
syn. image, mirror

be reflected in the water 물에 반영되다

0661
perfect
[pərfékt]

v. 완성하다, 개선하다 to make something good, perfect or better
syn. complete, finalize, finish, polish
ant. worsen

perfect a painting 그림을 완성하다

0662
embrace
[embréis]
-em 내부, 안

v. 수용하다, 포옹하다 to accept something readily or gladly
syn. accept, support, welcome
ant. exclude, leave out

embrace democracy 민주주의를 수용하다

0663
height
[hait]

n. 높이, 키 a measurement of how tall a person or thing is
syn. tallness, stature, highness

a woman of average height 평균 키의 여자

0664
feed
[fiːd]
-fed -fed

v. 먹이다 to give food to someone or something
syn. cater for, provide for, nourish

fed the horses with apples 말들에게 사과를 먹였다

0665
reference
[réfərəns]

n. 참조   the act of looking at or in something for information

the reference section of the library 도서관의 참고서적 섹션

0666
emerge
[imə́:rdʒ]

v. 나타나다, 알려지다   to rise or appear from a hidden or unknown place or condition

syn. come up, arise, surface

new problems emerged 새로운 문제가 떠올랐다

0667
thrilling
[θríliŋ]

adj. 매우 흥분되는   very exciting or stimulating

syn. exciting, gripping, hair-raising

a thrilling 4-3 victory 짜릿한 4대3 승리

0668
incidental
[ìnsədéntl]

adj. 부수적으로 발생하는   happening as a minor part or result of something else

syn. casual, accidental

ant. certain, planned, fixed

a incidental part of the job 그 일에 부수적으로 발생하는 일

0669
include
[inklú:d]
-clud 닫다

v. 포함하다   to have something as part of a group or total

syn. contain, embrace, encompass

ant. exclude

be included in the tour package 여행 패키지에 포함되어 있다

0670
perceive
[pərsí:v]
-ceive 받다

v. 인지하다   to notice or become aware of something

syn. feel, scent, see, sense

ant. miss

perceived threats 위협을 알아챘다

0671
definitely
[défənitli]
-fin 끝

adj. 틀림없이   in a definite manner

syn. certainly, absolutely

definitely remember 확실히 기억난다

0672
refined
[rifáind]

adj. 정제된, 세련된   improved to be more precise or exact
syn. improved, advanced
refined and elegant works of art 세련되고 우아한 예술 작품

0673
mature
[mətʃúər]

adj. 성숙한   having or showing the mental and emotional qualities of an adult
syn. matured, ripe, ripened
ant. adolescent, green, immature, juvenile
was mature enough to live on his own 혼자 살 수 있을 만큼 자랐다

0674
incorporate
[inkɔ́ːrpərèit]
-corp 신체

v. 흡수하다, 통합하다   to include something as part of something else
syn. absorb, integrate
ant. break down, break up, separate
incorporate the latest safety features 최신 안전 기능을 포함하다

0675
helpless
[hélplis]

adj. 무력한   unable to do something to make a situation, task, etc. better or easier
syn. defenseless, vulnerable
lay helpless on the floor 바닥에 무력하게 누워있었다

0676
throughout
[θruːáut]

prep. ~동안 내내   during an entire situation or period of time
syn. all through
it troubled her throughout her life 그것은 평생 그녀를 괴롭혔다

0677
matter
[mǽtər]

v. 중요하다   to be of consequence or importance
syn. be important, make a difference, count
it matters a lot to me 그건 나에겐 매우 중요하다

0678
tie
[tai]

adj. 묶다   to fasten or be fastened with string, thread, etc.
syn. bind, knot
tied him to a chair 그를 의자에 묶었다

0679
incentive
[inséntiv]

n. 인센티브, 장려책   something that encourages a person to do something or to work harder

syn. motive, encouragement, bait

offer incentives to foreign investors 해외 투자자들에게 인센티브를 제공하다

0680
securely
[sikjúərli]

adv. 단단히   tied, fastened, etc. tightly, especially in order to make something safe

syn. firmly

fastened my seatbelt securely 안전벨트를 꽉 멨다

0681
opposed
[əpóuzd]

adj. ~에 반대하는   not agreeing with or approving of something or someone

syn. against, anti, hostile

be opposed to the war 전쟁에 반대하다

0682
emergency
[imə́:rdʒənsi]

n. 위급상황   an unexpected and usually dangerous situation that calls for immediate action

syn. crisis

declared a state of emergency 위급상황을 선포했다

0683
undress
[ʌndrés]

v. 옷을 벗다   to take your clothes off

syn. disrobe, strip, unclothe

undressed and got into the water 옷을 벗고 물로 들어갔다

0684
maxim
[mǽksim]

n. 격언   a well-known phrase that expresses a general truth about life or a rule about behavior

syn. saying, proverb

a common maxim 흔한 격언

0685
undoubtedly
[ʌndáutidli]

adv. 의심의 여지 없이   certainly or definitely

he is undoubtedly talented 그는 확실히 재능이 있다

0686

unease
[ʌníːz]

n. 불안, 근심   a feeling of worry or slight fear about something

syn. anxiety, uneasiness, worry

felt a growing sense of unease 불안감이 커지는 것을 느꼈다

0687

advocate
[ǽdvəkit]

-voc 부름, 소리

n. 옹호자   a person who argues for or supports a cause or policy

syn. supporter, backer

a passionate advocate of civil rights 열성적인 시민권 옹호자

0688

perceptual
[pəːrséptjuəl]

-cept 받다

adj. 지각력의   of or relating to perception

perceptual skills 지각 능력

0689

gleam
[gliːm]

v. 밝게 빛나다   to shine brightly

syn. flash, glimmer, glint

a light gleamed in the distance 멀리서 불빛이 비쳤다

0690

embarrassing
[imbǽrəsiŋ]

adj. 당황스럽게 하는   causing one to feel confusion or self-consciousness

syn. humiliating

asked such embarrassing questions 정말 당황스럽게 하는 질문들을 했다

0691

global
[glóubəl]

adj. 국제적인   including or affecting the whole world

syn. worldwide, world, international, universal

global changes in climate 기후의 국제적 변화

0692

maximize
[mǽksəmàiz]

v. 최대한 활용하다   to make as high or great as possible

syn. optimize

rearrange the furniture to maximize the space
공간을 최대한 활용하려고 가구를 재배치하다

0693

oppose
[əpóuz]

v. 반대하다   to disagree with or disapprove of something

syn. resist, repel, withstand

ant. succumb, surrender, yield

oppose the death penalty 사형 제도를 반대하다

0694
security
[sikjúəriti]

n. 안전   the state of being protected or safe from harm

syn. guard, protection, safeguard

ant. danger

provide adequate security 충분한 안전을 제공하다

0695
female
[fí:meil]

n. 여자   a woman or a girl

there were more males than females 여자보다 남자가 많았다

0696
embarrassed
[imbǽrəst]

adj. 당황스러운   feeling confusion or self-consciousness

syn. ashamed, uncomfortable

felt embarrassed and humiliated 당황스럽고 모욕감을 느꼈다

0697
emerging
[imə́:rdʒiŋ]

adj. 최근 나타나는   coming into being or to notice

an emerging industry 신흥 산업

0698
unequal
[ʌní:kwəl]

adj. 부당한, 불공정한   not the same in a way that is unfair

syn. unbalanced, unfair

an unequal contest 불공정한 대회

0699
feelings
[fí:liŋz]

n. 감정, 느낌, 생각   someone's feelings are their thoughts, emotions, and attitudes

hurt my feelings 내 감정을 상하게 했다

0700
define
[difáin]

v. 정의하다   to explain the meaning of a word, phrase, etc.

syn. describe, characterize, explain

a term that is difficult to define 정의하기 어려운 용어

Review

뜻을 써보고 전체 어구의 의미를 생각해 보시오.

01 definitely remember   0671

02 it troubled her throughout her life   0676

03 felt embarrassed and humiliated   0696

04 a woman of average height   0663

05 provide adequate security   0694

06 a passionate advocate of civil rights   0687

07 was mature enough to live on his own   0673

08 declared a state of emergency   0682

09 perceived threats   0670

10 there were more males than females   0695

11 new problems emerged   0666

12 an unequal contest   0698

13 an incidental part of the job   0668

14 an emerging industry   0697

15 a term that is difficult to define   0700

16 asked such embarrassing questions   0690

17 perfect a painting   0661

18 he is undoubtedly talented   0685

19 ① a high degree of stress   0658

   ② a master's degree in English literature

20 fertile land   0651

0701
perfume
[pə́:rfju:m]

n. 향수　a liquid substance that you put on your body in small amounts in order to smell pleasant

syn. scent, essence

a bottle of expensive perfume 비싼 향수 한 병

0702
glow
[glou]

v. 은은히 빛나다　to shine with low light and heat but usually without flame

syn. blaze, burn

the coals glowed in the fireplace 석탄이 화로에서 빛나고 있었다

0703
fiction
[fíkʃən]

n. 소설, 허구　written stories about people and events that are not real

syn. fable, fantasy

ant. fact, materiality, reality

distinguish fact from fiction 사실과 허구를 구분하다

0704
incorrect
[ìnkərékt]
-rect 올바름

adj. 틀린　wrong, or not accurate or true

syn. mistaken, wrong

ant. correct, right

an incorrect answer 틀린 답

0705
emotion
[imóuʃən]

n. 감정, 정서　a strong feeling such as love, anger, joy, hate, or fear

syn. feeling, passion, sentiment

betray one's emotion 감정을 표출하다

0706
chef
[ʃef]

n. 주방장, 요리사　a professional cook who usually is in charge of a kitchen in a restaurant

syn. cook

a chef at a five-star restaurant 5성급 호텔의 주방장

0707
increase
[inkríːs]

v. 증가하다, 증가시키다　to become larger or greater in size, amount, number, etc.

syn. enlarge, escalate, expand, extend

ant. decrease

increase one's wealth substantially 부를 상당히 증가시키다

0708
chemical
[kémikəl]

adj. 화학적인   of or relating to chemistry

chemical reactions 화학 반응

0709
emit
[imít]

-mit 전송하다

v. 내뿜다   to send light, energy, etc. out from a source

syn. cast, discharge, exhale

ant. absorb, inhale

chimneys emitting thick, black smoke 짙은 검은 연기를 내뿜는 굴뚝들

0710
delay
[diléi]

n. 지체, 연기   a situation in which something happens later than it should

syn. holdback, holdup, wait

ant. haste, rush

get started without delay 지체 없이 출발하다

0711
fierce
[fiərs]

adj. 격렬한   very strong or intense

syn. grim, savage, vicious

ant. gentle, mild

a fierce argument 격렬한 논쟁

0712
incredible
[inkrédəbəl]

-cred 믿다

adj. 믿을 수 없는, 놀라운   difficult or impossible to believe

syn. unbelievable, unthinkable

incredible skills 놀라운 기술들

0713
increasingly
[inkríːsiŋli]

adv. 점점 더   more and more

grew increasingly hopeless 점점 더 희망이 없어졌다

0714
performance
[pərfɔ́ːrməns]

n. 성과, 수행   the act of doing a job, an activity, etc.

syn. achievement

an annual performance assessment 연간 성과 평가

0715
gloomy
[glúːmi]

adj. 어두운, 우울한   causing feelings of sadness

syn. black, bleak, cheerless

ant. bright, cheerful, festive

gloomy weather 우중충한 날씨

0716
option
[ápʃən]
-opt 바라다

n. 선택, 선택권   the opportunity or ability to choose something or to choose between two or more things

syn. choice, alternative, selection

didn't have many options open 고를 수 있는 선택권이 그리 많지 않았다

0717
glory
[glɔ́:ri]

n. 영광, 영예   something that is a source of great pride

syn. celebrity, fame, renown, repute

ant. disgrace, dishonor

restore the company to its former glory 과거의 영광에 이르도록 회사를 재건하다

0718
meaningful
[mí:niŋfəl]

adj. 의미 깊은   having a clear meaning

syn. significant, suggestive

produce meaningful results 의미 깊은 결과를 내다

0719
reflection
[riflékʃən]
-flec 구부러지다

n. 반영, 반사   an image that is seen in a mirror or on a shiny surface

syn. mirror image

look at one's reflection in the mirror 거울에 비친 자신의 모습을 보다

0720
delicious
[dilíʃəs]

adj. 아주 맛있는   very appealing to the senses, esp to the taste or smell

syn. tasty, yummy

serve a delicious banquet 진수성찬을 베풀다

0721
refuel
[ri:fjú:əl]

v. 재급유하다   to provide with additional fuel

refueled the airplane 비행기의 연료를 다시 채웠다

0722
optimal
[áptəməl]
-opt 바라다

adj. 최상의, 최적의   most desirable or satisfactory

under optimal conditions 최적의 환경에서

0723
goal
[goul]

n. 목표   something that you are trying to do or achieve

syn. aim, end, target, purpose

share a common goal 공동의 목표를 공유하다

0724
cherish
[tʃériʃ]

v. 소중히 여기다   to feel or show great love for someone or something
syn. adore, love, worship

a book cherished by many 많은 이들에게 사랑받는 책

0725
optimism
[áptəmìzəm]
-opt 바라다

n. 낙관   a feeling or belief that good things will happen in the future
ant. pessimism

blind optimism 맹목적 낙관

0726
deliberate
[dilíbərəit]

adj. 의도적인   done or said in a way that is planned or intended
syn. intentional, calculated, considered
ant. casual, unadvised

a deliberate attempt to humiliate him 그에게 모욕을 주려는 의도적인 시도

0727
festive
[féstiv]

adj. 축제 분위기의   of, relating to, or suitable for a feast or festival
syn. merry, jolly, gleeful

be in a festive mood 축제 분위기이다

0728
emission
[imíʃən]

n. 배출   the act of sending out something such as energy or gas from a source
syn. giving off, release

the emission of greenhouse gases 온실 가스 배출

0729
emotional
[imóuʃənəl]

adj. 정서의, 감정적인   relating to emotions / likely to show or express emotion

emotional stress 정서적 스트레스
become very emotional 매우 감정적으로 되다

0730
orchard
[ɔ́ːrtʃərd]

n. 과수원   a place where people grow fruit trees

a cherry orchard 체리 과수원

0731
affection
[əfékʃən]

n. 애착, 보살핌   a feeling of liking and caring for someone or something
syn. love, attachment, passion

great affection for the country 나라에 대한 강한 애착

0732
means
[miːnz]

n. 수단 a method for doing or achieving something

syn. method, way, course

an effective means 효과적인 방법

0733
seed
[siːd]

n. 씨, 씨앗 a small object produced by a plant from which a new plant can grow

a packet of sunflower seeds 해바라기 씨앗 한 봉지

0734
score
[skɔːr]

v. 득점하다 get points, goals, runs, etc., in a game or contest

syn. gain, win

ant. lose

scored four points 4점 득점했다

0735
field
[fiːld]

n. 들판, 밭 an open area of land without trees or buildings

syn. clearing, ground

huge fields of barley 거대한 보리 밭

0736
fiber
[fáibər]

n. 섬유질 plant material that cannot be digested but that helps you to digest other food

syn. thread, strand

wood fiber 나무 섬유

0737
delightful
[diláitfəl]

adj. 매우 기쁜 very pleasant or attractive

syn. pleasant, pleasing, charming

a delightful party 매우 즐거운 파티

0738
mayor
[méiər]

n. 시장 an official who is elected to be the head of the government of a city or town

the mayor of New York 뉴욕시 시장

0739
period
[píəriəd]

n. 기간 a length of time during which a series of events or an action takes place or is completed

syn. time, term, season, space

during the period of adolescence 청소년 기간 동안

0740
perform
[pərfɔ́ːrm]

v. 수행하다, 실시하다   to do an action or activity that usually requires training or skill

syn. accomplish, achieve, carry out

had to perform surgery immediately 즉시 수술을 실시해야 했다

0741
perception
[pərsépʃən]
-cept 받다

n. 지각, 자각   the way you think about or understand someone or something

syn. discernment, insight, wisdom

visual perception 시각적 지각

0742
reform
[riːfɔ́ːrm]
-form 형성하다

v. 개혁하다, 개선하다   to improve a situation by correcting things that are wrong or unfair

syn. improve, better, correct, restore

must be radically reformed 전면적인 개혁이 필요하다

0743
imagine
[imǽdʒin]

v. 상상하다 to think of or create something that is not real in your mind

syn. dream, fancy, visualize

imagine a world without poverty or war 빈곤도 전쟁도 없는 세상을 상상하다

0744
opposition
[ɑ̀pəzíʃən]

n. 반대, 항의   actions or opinions that show that you disagree with or disapprove of someone or something

syn. defiance, resistance

face strong opposition 강한 저항에 직면하다

0745
affective
[əféktiv]

adj. 정서적인   relating to the emotions or to someone's moods

syn. emotional

an affective disorder 정서 장애

0746
orbit
[ɔ́ːrbit]

n. 궤도   a circular path

syn. path, course, track, cycle

the earth's orbit around the sun 태양 주위의 지구의 궤도

0747

periodically

[pìəriádikəli]

adv. 주기적으로   at regular intervals of time

circulate periodically 주기적으로 순환하다

0748

affect

[əfékt]

v. 영향을 미치다   to produce an effect upon

syn. influence, impact

decisions which affect our lives 우리의 삶에 영향을 미치는 결정들

0749

check-up

[tʃékʌp]

n. 검진   an examination of a person made by a doctor to make sure the person is healthy

syn. check, inspection, examination

go for a checkup every year 해마다 검진을 받으러 가다

0750

cheer

[tʃiər]

v. 응원하다   to shout with joy, approval, or enthusiasm

syn. applaud, acclaim

the crowd cheered him 군중들이 그를 응원했다

128

Review

뜻을 써보고 전체 어구의 의미를 생각해 보시오.

01 a deliberate attempt to humiliate him _____ 0726

02 a book cherished by many _____ 0724

03 had to perform surgery immediately _____ 0740

04 be in a festive mood _____ 0727

05 huge fields of barley _____ 0735

06 must be radically reformed _____ 0742

07 blind optimism _____ 0725

08 go for a checkup every year _____ 0749

09 the crowd cheered him _____ 0750

10 circulate periodically _____ 0747

11 the earth's orbit around the sun _____ 0746

12 the emission of greenhouse gases _____ 0728

13 decisions which affect our lives _____ 0748

14 great affection for the country _____ 0731

15 face strong opposition _____ 0744

16 the mayor of New York _____ 0738

17 an affective disorder _____ 0745

18 get started without delay _____ 0710

19 gloomy weather _____ 0715

20 restore the company to its former glory _____ 0717

DAY 16

0751
blank
[blæŋk]

adj. 빈   without any writing, marks, or pictures
syn. empty, vacant

a blank sheet of paper 빈 종이

0752
aggressive
[əgrésiv]

adj. 공격적인   using forceful methods to succeed or to do something
syn. assertive, enterprising, fierce

started to get aggressive 공격적으로 변하기 시작했다

0753
seemingly
[síːmiŋli]

adv. 외견상으로는   appearing to have a particular quality, when this may or may not be true
syn. apparently, outwardly, on the surface

seemingly unrelated bits of information 외견상으로는 상관없어 보이는 정보들

0754
permit
[pəːrmít]

v. 허용하다   to allow something to happen
syn. green-light, allow

permit access to records 기록 열람을 허용하다

0755
circular
[sə́ːrkjələr]

adj. 원형의, 순환하는   shaped like a circle or part of a circle / moving or going around in a circle
syn. roundabout
ant. straight, straightforward

a circular staircase 나선형 계단
a circular tour of the city 도시 순회 관광

0756
childhood
[tʃáildhùd]

n. 어린 시절   the period of time when a person is a child
syn. springtime, youth
ant. adulthood

had a happy childhood 행복한 유년 시절을 보냈다

0757
emphasis
[émfəsis]

n. 강조   special attention or importance
syn. accent, accentuation, stress

placed emphasis on practical work 실무를 강조했다

0758
chew
[tʃuː]

v. 씹다   to bite food several times before swallowing it
syn. chaw, nibble

chew gum in class 수업 중에 껌을 씹다

0759
persistent
[pəːrsístənt]
-sist 서다

adj. 끈질긴, 집요한   continuing to do something in a determined way
syn. dogged, insistent, patient
ant. quitting, surrendering, yielding

a persistent salesman 끈질긴 판매원

0760
chief
[tʃiːf]

adj. 가장 중요한   main or most important
syn. cardinal, central, foremost
ant. last, least

the chief cause of poverty 빈곤의 가장 중요한 원인

0761
affirm
[əfə́ːrm]

v. 단언하다   to say that something is true in a confident way
syn. declare, insist, claim
ant. deny

affirmed his innocence 그가 결백하다고 단언했다

0762
age
[eidʒ]

v. 노화하다   to become old or older
syn. mature, develop, grow

the population is aging 인구가 고령화되어 가고 있다

0763
seize
[siːz]

v. 꽉 잡다   to get or take something in a forceful, sudden, or violent way
syn. behold, catch
ant. miss

seized her by the arm 그녀의 팔을 꽉 잡았다

0764
chill
[tʃil]

n. 한기   a cold feeling
syn. coldness, bite, nip

a chill in the autumn air 가을 공기 중의 한기

0765
agent
[éidʒənt]

n. 대리인, 중개상   a person who does business for another person
syn. broker, worker

a travel agent 여행사 직원

0766
chore
[tʃɔːr]

n. 허드렛일   a small routine task, esp a domestic one
syn. assignment, duty, job, task

household chores 집안 허드렛일

0767
bitter
[bítər]

adj. 혹독한, 매서운   felt or experienced in a strong and unpleasant way
syn. severe, intense

bitter cold 혹독한 추위

0768
chronic
[kránik]
-chron 시간

adj. 만성적인   continuing or occurring again and again for a long time
syn. habitual, confirmed
ant. intermittent, occasional

chronic indigestion 만성 소화불량

0769
empirical
[empírikəl]

adj. 경험에 의거한, 실증적인   based on testing or experience
syn. experiential, experimental, objective
ant. theoretical

an empirical study 실증적 연구

0770
empathetic
[èmpəθétik]
-em 내부, 안
-path 고생하다, 느끼다

adj. 감정이입의, 동정심 많은   able to understand how someone feels because you can imagine what it is like to be them
syn. compassionate, sympathetic, understanding
ant. cold-blooded

an empathetic listener 이해심 많게 잘 들어주는 사람

0771
independent
[ìndipéndənt]
-pend 매달다

adj. 독립적인   not depending on other people for money
syn. self-reliant

a very independent person 매우 독립적인 사람

0772
demand
[diménd]
-mand 명령하다

v. 요구하다   to say in a very firm way that you want something
syn. request, ask for

demanded a refund 환불을 요구했다

0773
indicate
[índikèit]

v. 가리키다, 암시하다 to show that something exists or is true
syn. show, suggest, reveal
indicate a serious condition 심각한 생태를 암시하다

0774
emphasize
[émfəsàiz]

v. 강조하다 to give special attention to something
syn. accent, highlight
emphasize the point 요점을 강조하다

0775
empire
[émpaiər]

n. 제국 a group of countries ruled by an emperor or empress
the Roman empire 로마제국

0776
employer
[emplɔ́iər]

n. 고용주 a person, company, or organization that employs people
employer-employee relations 고용주와 고용인 관계

0777
circulate
[sə́:rkjəlèit]

v. 순환시키다 to cause something to go or spread from one person
or place to another
syn. spread
circulate a rumor 소문을 퍼뜨리다

0778
personality
[pə̀:rsənǽləti]

n. 개성 the set of emotional qualities, ways of behaving, etc., that
makes a person different from other people
syn. character, disposition, individuality
have different personalities 다른 개성을 가지고 있다

0779
indeed
[indí:d]

adv. 확실히 without any question
syn. assuredly, certainly, clearly
you can indeed do better than that 너는 확실히 그것보다는 잘 할 수 있다

0780
finally
[fáinəli]
-fin 끝

adv. 마침내 after a long delay
syn. eventually, at last, in the end
finally arrived home 마침내 집에 도착했다

0781
timepiece
[táimpìːs]

n. 시계   a clock or watch

attach a pendulum to a timepiece 시계에 추를 달다

0782
incur
[inkə́ːr]

v. 자초하다   to cause yourself to have or experience something unpleasant or unwanted

syn. experience, suffer, earn

incurred huge losses 큰 손실을 자초했다

0783
seem
[siːm]

v. ~인 듯하다   to appear to be something, or to appear to have a particular quality

syn. feel, look, sound

seemed like a good idea 좋은 아이디어 같았다

0784
employ
[emplɔ́i]

-em 내부, 안

v. 고용하다   to use or get the services of someone to do a particular job

syn. hire

employ someone to manage production 생산 관리를 위해 사람을 고용하다

0785
tight
[tait]

adj. 꼭 끼는   fitting very close to your body

syn. close-fitting

tight jeans 꼭 끼는 바지

0786
deluxe
[dəlúks]

adj. 호화로운, 사치스런   of better quality and usually more expensive than the usual ones of its kind

syn. luxurious, lavish

articles deluxe 사치품

0787
delivery
[dilívəri]

n. 배달   the act of taking something to a person or place

syn. handing over, transfer, distribution

a delivery service 배달 서비스

0788
independently
[ìndipéndəntli]

-pend 매달다

adv. 독립적으로   on one's own

syn. separately, alone, solo

act independently 독자적으로 행동하다

0789
segment
[ségmənt]

n. 부분, 조각   a separate part of anything

syn. portion, section, part

ant. whole, sum, total

eight equal segments 여덟 개의 동일한 조각들

0790
tiny
[táini]

adj. 아주 작은   extremely small

syn. atomic, minute

ant. astronomical, cosmic

a tiny town 아주 작은 마을

0791
figure
[fígjər]

n. 인물, 유명인   a prominent personality

syn. big name, dignitary

a political figure 정치적 인물

0792
age group

n. 연령대   people born at a particular time

a book for kids in the 5-7 age group 5-7세 나이대 아이들을 위한 책

0793
filter
[fíltər]

v. 여과하다   to pass something, such as a gas or liquid through a filter to remove something unwanted

syn. screen

sunglasses that filter ultraviolet light 자외선을 차단하는 선글라스

0794
chop
[tʃɑp]

v. 썰다, 다지다   to cut into or sever usually by repeated blows of a sharp instrument

syn. cut, sever

chop up an onion 양파를 다지다

0795
seek
[si:k]
-sought -sought

v. 구하다, 찾다   to search for someone or something

syn. pursue, quest, search, look for

seek advice 조언을 구하다

0796
refuse
[rifjúːz]

v. 거절하다   to say that you will not accept something, such as a gift or offer

syn. decline, reject

ant. grant, permit

refuse a gift 선물을 거절하다

0797
timber
[tímbər]

n. 목재   trees that are grown in order to produce wood

syn. wood, logs

a timber cottage 통나무 오두막 집

0798
personal
[pə́ːrsənəl]

adj. 개인적인   belonging or relating to a particular person

syn. individual, personalized, private

ant. public, shared, universal

my personal opinion 나의 개인적 의견

0799
indifference
[indífərəns]

n. 무관심   lack of interest or sympathy

syn. apathy

ant. concern, interest, regard

public indifference to racial discrimination 인종 차별에 대한 대중의 무관심

0800
regarding
[rigáːrdiŋ]

prep. ~에 관해서는   concerning a particular subject

syn. concerning, on, about

had little to say regarding the accident 그 사건에 관해서는 할 말이 거의 없었다

Review

뜻을 써보고 전체 어구의 의미를 생각해 보시오.

01 incurred huge losses _____ 0782

02 bitter cold _____ 0767

03 seized her by the arm _____ 0763

04 chronic indigestion _____ 0768

05 articles deluxe _____ 0786

06 an empirical study _____ 0769

07 the chief cause of poverty _____ 0760

08 act independently _____ 0788

09 chop up an onion _____ 0794

10 a travel agent _____ 0765

11 a political figure _____ 0791

12 demanded a refund _____ 0772

13 employer-employee relations _____ 0776

14 employ someone to manage production _____ 0784

15 a tiny town _____ 0790

16 my personal opinion _____ 0798

17 seemingly unrelated bits of information _____ 0753

18 permit access to records _____ 0754

19 circulate a rumor _____ 0777

20 a blank sheet of paper _____ 0751

0801
claim
[kleim]

v. 주장하다 to say that something is true when some people may say it is not true

syn. declare, insist

ant. deny

claimed **the inheritance** 상속권을 주장했다

0802
individual
[ìndəvídʒuəl]

n. 개인 a single person

an odd-looking individual 이상하게 생긴 사람

0803
regret
[rigrét]

v. 후회하다 to feel sad or sorry about something that you did or did not do

syn. deplore, lament, repent

regret **one's mistakes** 실수를 후회하다

0804
dense
[dens]

adj. 빽빽한, 밀집한 having parts that are close together

syn. compact, crowded, close, thick

a dense **forest** 빽빽한 숲

0805
medical
[médikəl]

adj. 의료의 of or relating to the treatment of diseases and injuries

a medical **student** 의대 학생

0806
persuade
[pə:rswéid]

v. 설득하다 to cause someone to do something by asking, arguing, or giving reasons

syn. talk someone into, urge, advise

persuaded **him to go back to school** 그를 학교로 돌아가도록 설득했다

0807
indoors
[indɔ́:rz]

adv. 실내에서 in or into a building

worked indoors **all afternoon** 오후 내내 실내에서 일했다

0808
regulate
[régjəlèit]

v. 규제하다, 통제하다 to make rules or laws that control something

syn. govern, rule

regulate **foreign trade** 해외 무역을 규제하다

0809
mechanical
[məkǽnikəl]

adj. 기계로 작동되는　of or relating to machinery

syn. automatic, robotic

mechanical parts 기계 부품

0810
self-control
[sélfkəntróul]

n. 자기 통제　the ability to exercise restraint or control over one's feelings, emotions, reactions, etc.

syn. willpower, restraint, self-discipline

showed self-control 자기 통제를 보여주었다

0811
persuasive
[pərswéisiv]

adj. 설득력 있는　able to cause people to do or believe something

syn. compelling, conclusive, convincing

a persuasive argument 설득력 있는 주장

0812
personally
[pə́:rsənəli]

adv. 직접, 몸소　used to say that something was done by a particuar person and not by someone else

syn. face-to-face

blamed me personally 나를 직접대고 비난했다

0813
sense
[sens]

v. 감지하다, 눈치 채다　to understand or be aware of something without being told about it or having evidence that it is true

syn. perceive, scent, feel

ant. miss

sense movement 움직임을 감지하다

0814
employment
[emplɔ́imənt]
-em 내부, 안

n. 고용　the condition of having a paid job

terms and conditions of employment 고용의 기간 및 조건

0815
agency
[éidʒənsi]

n. 대행사　a business that provides a particular service

an advertising agency 광고 대행사

0816
clarity
[klǽrəti]

n. 명료성　the quality of being easily understood

syn. clearness

ant. cloudiness, opacity

clarity of thought 사고의 명료함

0817
pest
[pest]

n. 해충   an animal or insect that causes problems for people especially by damaging crops

syn. plague

mice and other household pests 쥐와 다른 가정 해충들

0818
sensibility
[sènsəbíləti]

n. 감수성   the ability to experience deep emotions, especially as a reaction to literature or art

syn. intuition, appreciation, delicacy

her fine poetic sensibility 그녀의 세련된 시적 감수성

0819
medicine
[médəsən]

n. 약   a substance that is used in treating disease or relieving pain and that is usually in the form of a pill or a liquid

syn. drug, medication

forgot to take his medicine 약 먹는 것을 깜빡했다

0820
demonstrate
[démənstrèit]
-demo 사람

v. 예를 들어 입증하다[설명하다]   to prove something by showing examples of it

syn. prove, show

demonstrated the correct procedure 올바른 절차를 예를 들어 설명했다

0821
finance
[finǽns]

v. 자금을 조달하다   to provide money for something or someone

syn. fund

financed him to study abroad 그가 해외에서 공부하도록 자금을 댔다

0822
civilization
[sìvəlizéiʃən]

n. 문명   the condition that exists when people have developed effective ways of organizing a society and care about art, science, etc.

syn. culture, life, lifestyle, society

study ancient Greek civilization 고대 그리스 문명을 연구하다

0823
regular
[régjələr]

adj. 규칙적인   happening over and over again at the same time or in the same way

syn. periodic, repeated

ant. inconstant, infrequent, irregular

hold regular meetings 정기적으로 회의를 열다

0824
demanding
[dimǽndiŋ]

adj. 까다로운, 요구가 많은   requiring much time, attention, or effort

syn. burdensome, challenging

demanding customers 까다로운 고객

0825
selfless
[sélflis]

adj. 이타적인   having or showing great concern for other people and little or no concern for yourself

syn. unselfish, generous, altruistic

selfless devotion to their work 이타적인 업무에의 헌신

0826
indifferent
[indífərənt]

adj. 무관심한   not interested in or concerned about something

syn. unconcerned, uncurious, uninterested

be indifferent to money 돈에 무관심하다

0827
empower
[empáuər]
-em 내부, 안

v. 권한을 주다   to give power to someone

syn. accredit, enable

ant. disqualify

empowered him to act on her behalf 그가 그녀 대신 활동하도록 권한을 줬다

0828
denial
[dináiəl]
-de 하락, 부정

n. 부인   a statement saying that something is not true or real

syn. refusal, rejection, turndown

ant. approval

issued a flat denial 아니라고 딱 잡아뗐다

0829
mediate
[mí:dièit]
-medi 중간

v. 중재하다   to try to end a disagreement between two people or groups

syn. intercede, interpose, intervene

ant. overlook

mediate the dispute 분쟁을 중재하다

0830
circumstance
[sɔ́:rkəmstæns]

n. 상황, 전후 사정   a fact or condition that affects a situation

syn. condition, situation

rapid change in economic circumstance 경제 상황의 빠른 변화

0831
register
[rédʒəstər]

v. 등록하다   to record information about something in a book or system of public records
syn. list, enroll

register a new car 새 차를 등록하다

0832
agreement
[əgríːmənt]

n. 합의   the act of agreeing
syn. accord, unison
ant. conflict, disagreement

wide agreement on this issue 이 문제에 관한 폭넓은 합의

0833
deprivation
[dèprəvéiʃən]
-de 하락, 부정

n. 결핍, 박탈   the state of not having something that people need
syn. loss
ant. gain

sleep deprivation 수면 부족

0834
seldom
[séldəm]

adv. 거의 ~않는   not often
syn. rarely
ant. often

we seldom see each other 우리는 서로 자주 안 만난다

0835
senior
[síːjər]

n. 연장자   a person who is older than another person
syn. elder
ant. junior

four years my senior 나보다 4살 손위

0836
sensible
[sénsəbəl]

adj. 분별 있는, 센스 있는   having or showing good sense or judgment
syn. discernible

gave me some sensible advice 내게 센스 있는 조언을 해주었다

0837
regularly
[régjələrli]

adv. 규칙적으로   on a regular basis

go to church regularly 교회에 규칙적으로 가다

142

0838
rehabilitate
[rìːhəbílətèit]

v. 재활 치료를 하다 to bring back to a normal, healthy condition after an illness, injury, drug problem, etc.

syn. redeem, regenerate, reform

rehabilitate drug addicts 마약 중독 환자들을 재활 치료하다

0839
mechanism
[mékənìzəm]

n. 기계 장치, 메커니즘 a mechanical part or group of parts having a particular function

syn. system, structure

a camera's shutter mechanism 카메라 셔터의 기계 장치

0840
tire
[taiər]

v. 지치다 to become weary

syn. exhaust, drain, fatigue

he still tires easily 그는 아직도 쉽게 지친다

0841
measure
[méʒər]

v. 측정하다 to find out the size, length, or amount of something

syn. gauge, scale, span

an instrument for measuring air pressure 기압을 측정하는 도구

0842
region
[ríːdʒən]

n. 지역 a large area of land whose politics, geography, or culture is different from other areas

syn. area, district

eastern jungle region 동부 밀림 지역

0843
perspective
[pəːrspéktiv]

n. 관점 a way of thinking about something

from a historical perspective 역사적 관점에서

0844
regional
[ríːdʒənəl]

adj. 지방 특유의 relating to or typical of a particular area of a country or the world

syn. provincial

a regional accent 지방 특유의 억양

0845
select
[silékt]

v. 선택하다 to choose someone or something from a group

syn. elect, handpick, choose

select 12 applicants 12명의 지원자를 선택했다

0846
aid
[eid]

v. 돕다   to provide what is useful or necessary

syn. help, assist, back

ant. hinder

a home run that was aided by the wind 바람의 도움을 받은 홈런

0847
agricultural
[æ̀grikʌ́ltʃərəl]

adj. 농업의   of, relating to, or used in farming or agriculture

syn. farming

agricultural product 농산품

0848
self-made
[sélfméid]

adj. 자수성가한   made rich and successful by your own efforts

a self-made man 자수성가한 남자

0849
personalize
[pə́:rsənəlàiz]

v. 개인의 필요에 맞추다   to change or design something for a particular person

syn. individualize, personify

be personalized to the client's needs 고객의 요구에 맞춰지다

0850
measurable
[méʒərəbəl]

adj. 주목할 만한   large or important enough to have an effect that can be seen or felt

syn. significant, distinct

measurable improvements 주목할 만한 진전

Review

뜻을 써보고 전체 어구의 의미를 생각해 보시오.

01 register a new car   0831

02 sleep deprivation   0833

03 her fine poetic sensibility   0818

04 forgot to take his medicine   0819

05 gave me some sensible advice   0836

06 mice and other household pests   0817

07 selfless devotion to their work   0825

08 he still tires easily   0840

09 mediate the dispute   0829

10 a regional accent   0844

11 empowered him to act on her behalf   0827

12 go to church regularly   0837

13 agricultural product   0847

14 terms and conditions of employment   0814

15 measurable improvements   0850

16 blamed me personally   0812

17 an instrument for measuring air pressure   0841

18 an odd-looking individual   0802

19 sense movement   0813

20 regret one's mistakes   0803

0851
depict
[dipíkt]

v. 묘사하다, 표현하다   to describe someone or something using words, a story, etc.
syn. describe, present, represent, detail, outline
a mural depicting a famous battle 유명한 전투를 묘사하는 벽화

0852
alive
[əláiv]

adj. 살아 있는   having life
syn. breathing, live, living
ant. breathless, cold, dead
managed to stay alive 가까스로 살아 있었다

0853
depress
[diprés]
-press 밀다

v. 우울하게 하다   to make someone feel sad
syn. sadden
ant. brighten
be depressed by the loss 상실감에 우울했다

0854
rehearsal
[rihə́:rsəl]

n. 예행연습, 리허설   an event at which a person or group practices an activity in order to prepare for a public performance
syn. practice, trial
was 15 minutes late to rehearsal 리허설에 15분 늦었다

0855
separate
[sépərèit]

v. 분리시키다   to cause two or more people or things to stop being together, joined, or connected
syn. break up, decouple
ant. join, link, unify, unite
separate mail 우편물을 분리하다

0856
related
[riléitid]

adj. 관련 있는   connected in some way
syn. affiliated, akin, allied
ant. unrelated
ancient history and other related subjects 고대 역사와 그 외 관련 주제들

0857
amaze
[əméiz]

v. 놀라게 하다   to surprise and sometimes confuse someone very much
syn. surprise, astonish, astound
amazed audiences 관객을 놀라게 했다

0858
amuse
[əmjúːz]

v. 즐겁게 하다   to make someone laugh or smile
syn. entertain

amuse the child with a story 이야기로 아이를 즐겁게 해주다

0859
reject
[ridʒékt]

v. 거절하다   to refuse to believe, accept, or consider something
syn. decline, refuse, deny

rejected the suggestion 제안을 거절했다

0860
philosophy
[filásəfi]

n. 철학   the study of ideas about knowledge, truth, the nature and meaning of life, etc.
syn. thought, reason, wisdom

a professor of philosophy 철학 교수

0861
reinforce
[rìːinfɔ́ːrs]

v. 강화하다, 보강하다   to make an idea, belief, or feeling stronger
syn. back, bolster, support

reinforce racial stereotypes 인종에 대한 편견을 강화하다

0862
serious
[síəriəs]

adj. 심각한   having an important or dangerous possible result
syn. grave, bad, critical

cause a serious injury 심각한 부상을 입히다

0863
sensitive
[sénsətiv]

adj. 예민한, 민감한   easily upset by the things that people think or say about you
syn. delicate, keen
ant. invulnerable, unexposed

be very sensitive to criticism 비평에 매우 예민하다

0864
amazing
[əméiziŋ]

adj. 놀라운   causing great surprise or wonder
syn. surprising, astonishing, astounding

have an amazing ability 놀라운 능력을 가지고 있다

0865
clingy
[klíŋi]

adj. 들러붙는   tending to stick to another thing

long clingy skirts 달라붙는 긴 치마

0866
alternative
[ɔ:ltə́:rnətiv]
-alter 다른

n. 대안   something that can be chosen instead of something else
syn. choice, option

offered no alternative 대안을 전혀 제시하지 않았다

0867
climate
[kláimit]

n. 기후   the usual weather conditions in a particular place or region
syn. atmosphere, air

the humid climate of Malaysia 말레이시아의 후덥지근한 기후

0868
depth
[depθ]

n. 깊이   the distance from the top to the bottom of something
syn. deepness

the depth of a hole 구덩이의 깊이

0869
altitude
[ǽltətjù:d]

n. 고도   the height of a place or thing above sea level
syn. height, summit, peak, elevation

a jet cruising at an altitude of 2km 고도 2,000미터로 날고 있는 제트기

0870
client
[kláiənt]

n. 의뢰인, 고객   someone who gets services or advice from a professional person, company, or organization
syn. customer

a meeting with an important client 중요한 의뢰인과의 만남

0871
amount
[əmáunt]

n. 양, 액수   a quantity of something
syn. quantity, quantum, volume

have an enormous amount of energy 엄청난 양의 에너지를 가지고 있다

0872
memory
[méməri]

n. 기억력   the power or process of remembering what has been learned
syn. ability to remember

have a selective memory 선택적인 기억력을 가지고 있다

0873
depressed
[diprést]

adj. 우울한   feeling sad
syn. sad, unhappy, moody, gloomy

felt lonely and depressed 외롭고 우울했다

0874
depart
[dipá:rt]

v. 떠나다 to leave a place especially to start a journey

ant. arrive, come, show up, turn up

be scheduled to depart tomorrow 내일 떠나기로 예정되어 있다

0875
department
[dipá:rtmənt]

n. 부서 one of the major parts of a company, organization, government, or school

syn. division

sales department 영업부

0876
clipping
[klípiŋ]

n. 오려낸 것 something that has been cut out of a newspaper or magazine

syn. cutting

a newspaper clipping 신문에서 오려 낸 기사

0877
sermon
[sə́:rmən]

n. 설교 a speech about a moral or religious subject that is usually given by a religious leader

syn. preaching, speech

preach a sermon 설교하다

0878
enact
[enǽkt]

v. (법을) 제정하다 to make a bill or other legislation officially become part of the law

syn. constitute, pass, legislate

enact a law 법을 제정하다

0879
firm
[fə:rm]

adj. 단단한, 확고한 fairly hard or solid

syn. solid, stout, strong

ant. weak

a soft but firm voice 부드럽지만 단호한 목소리

0880
alternate
[ɔ́:ltərnit]
-alter 다른

adj. 번갈아 일어나는 happening or coming one after another, in a regular pattern

syn. interchanging, every other, rotating

a day of alternate sunshine and rain 비가 왔다 해가 났다 하는 날

0881
classical
[klǽsikəl]

adj. 고전적인, (음악이) 클래식의　of a kind that has been respected for a long time

classical **music** 고전 음악

0882
dependent
[dipéndənt]
-pend 매달다

adj. 의존적인　needing someone or something else for support, help, etc.

ant. independent

dependent children 부양하고 있는 아이들

0883
clean
[kli:n]

v. 청소하다　to make something clean

syn. cleanse, wash, sweep, dust

she **cleaned** and her husband cooked 그녀는 청소를 하고 남편은 요리를 했다

0884
petroleum
[pitróuliəm]

n. 석유　a kind of oil that comes from below the ground and that is the source of gasoline and other products

process **petroleum** 석유를 정제하다

0885
deposit
[dipázit]

v. 예금하다　to put money in a bank account

syn. bank

ant. withdraw

deposited over 3 million won 300만원 넘게 예금했다

0886
phenomenon
[finámənàn]
-phenomena pl.

n. 현상　an event or situation that can be seen to happen or exist

natural **phenomena like earthquakes** 지진과 같은 자연 현상들

0887
industry
[índəstri]

n. 산업, 공업　a group of businesses that provide a particular product or service

syn. business

niche **industry** 틈새 산업

0888
first aid
[fə́:rstéid]

n. 응급 처치　emergency treatment given to a sick or injured person

syn. emergency care

gave him **first aid for his sprained ankle** 발목을 삔 그에게 응급처치를 했다

150

0889
classify
[klǽsəfài]

v. 분류하다　to arrange people or things into groups based on ways that they are alike

syn. assort, break down, categorize

classify books by subject 책을 주제별로 분류하다

0890
empty
[émpti]

adj. 텅 빈　containing nothing

syn. blank, vacant

ant. full

empty shelves 텅 빈 선반

0891
melt
[melt]

v. 녹다　to change or to cause something to change from a solid to a liquid usually because of heat

syn. dissolve

the sugar melted in the coffee 설탕이 커피에 녹았다

0892
allow
[əláu]

v. 허용하다, 허락하다　to permit someone to have or do something

syn. green-light, permit

ant. ban, forbid, prohibit

allow an hour for lunch 점심시간으로 한 시간을 허용하다

0893
meditation
[mèdətéiʃən]

n. 명상　the act or process of spending time in quiet thought

syn. contemplation

spent the morning in meditation 오전을 명상을 하며 보냈다

0894
induce
[indʒúːs]

v. 유도하다　to cause someone or something to do something

syn. cause, invoke

induce people to eat more fruit 사람들이 과일을 더 먹도록 유도하다

0895
pesticide
[péstəsàid]
-cide 죽이다

n. 살충제, 농약　a chemical that is used to kill animals or insects that damage plants or crops

syn. insectcide

crops sprayed with pesticide 농약을 뿌린 작물

0896
deny
[dinái]
-de 허락, 부정

v. 부정하다, 거부하다   to say that something is not true

syn. reject

ant. acknowledge, admit, allow

deny an allegation 혐의를 부정하다

0897
enable
[enéibəl]

v. ~할 수 있게 하다   to make someone or something able to do or to be something

syn. allow, empower, let, permit

ant. prevent

training that enables people to earn a living
사람들이 생계를 꾸릴 수 있도록 해주는 훈련

0898
encounter
[enkáuntər]

v. (문제에) 직면하다   to have or experience problems, difficulties, etc.

syn. stumble upon

ant. avoid, dodge, duck, elude

encounter difficulties 어려움에 직면하다

0899
classic
[klǽsik]

adj. 일류의, 최고 수준의   used to say that something has come to be considered one of the best of its kind

classic literary works 최고의 문학 작품들

0900
aisle
[ail]

n. 통로   a passage where people walk through a store, market, etc.

syn. hallway

an aisle seat 통로 쪽 자리

Review

뜻을 써보고 전체 어구의 의미를 생각해 보시오.

01 the depth of a hole _____ 0868

02 preach a sermon _____ 0877

03 a professor of philosophy _____ 0860

04 enact a law _____ 0878

05 dependent children _____ 0882

06 separate mail _____ 0855

07 crops sprayed with pesticide _____ 0895

08 be scheduled to depart tomorrow _____ 0874

09 spent the morning in meditation _____ 0893

10 long clingy skirts _____ 0865

11 process petroleum _____ 0884

12 deposited over 3 million won _____ 0885

13 a mural depicting a famous battle _____ 0851

14 amazed audiences _____ 0857

15 reinforce racial stereotypes _____ 0861

16 ancient history and other related subjects _____ 0856

17 have an enormous amount of energy _____ 0871

18 offered no alternative _____ 0866

19 be depressed by the loss _____ 0853

20 cause a serious injury _____ 0862

0901
endow
[endáu]

v. 기부하다　to give money to a school, hospital, or other institution

syn. finance, fund, pay for

endow a scholarship 장학금을 기부하다

0902
desirable
[dizáiərəbəl]

adj. 바람직한　having good or pleasing qualities

syn. advantageous, useful, valuable

ant. inadvisable

a desirable place to live 거주하기에 바람직한 곳

0903
coastal
[kóustəl]

adj. 해안의, 연안의　in the sea or on the land near the coast

syn. seaside

the coastal path 연안의 오솔길

0904
physical
[fízikəl]

adj. 신체의, 육체의　relating to the body of a person instead of the mind

syn. bodily, corporal

physical and emotional health 신체적 그리고 정서적 건강

0905
pile
[pail]

v. 쌓다　to heap in abundance

syn. load, stuff, heap, stack

piled potatoes on his plate 그의 접시에 감자를 쌓아 올렸다

0906
fit¹
[fit]

n. 발작, 경련　a sudden strong emotion that you cannot control

smashed the plate in a fit of rage 격노하여 접시를 박살냈다

0907
serve
[sə:rv]

v. 기여하다, 도움이 되다　to be useful or helpful for a particular purpose or reason

will serve its purpose 그 용도에 유용할 것이다

0908
inexcusable
[ìnikskjú:zəbəl]

adj. 용서받을 수 없는　too bad or wrong to be excused or ignored

syn. unforgivable, unjustifiable

ant. excusable

inexcusable rudeness 용서받을 수 없는 무례함

0909
several
[sévərəl]

adj. 여럿의, 몇몇의   more than two but not very many
syn. some, a few

arrived several hours ago 몇 시간 전에 도착했다

0910
servant
[sə́:rvənt]

n. 하인, 종   a person who is hired to do household or personal duties such as cleaning and cooking
syn. maid, helper

servant girl 하녀

0911
mental
[méntl]

adj. 정신의   of or relating to the mind
syn. spiritual, intellectual

mental health 정신 건강

0912
severance
[sévərəns]

n. 고용 종료, 해고   the act of ending someone's employment

a severance pay 퇴직금

0913
relative
[rélətiv]

adj. 상대적인, 상대성의   having a particular quality when compared with something else
syn. comparative
ant. absolute, complete, perfect

the relative merits of both approaches 두 가지 접근법의 상대적 장점들

0914
session
[séʃən]

n. (특정) 기간, 시간   a period of time that is used to do a particular activity
syn. period, stretch, time

a recording session 녹음 기간

0915
physics
[fíziks]

n. 물리학   a science that deals with matter and energy and the way they act on each other in heat, light, electricity, and sound

the impact of Einstein on modern physics 현대 물리학에 끼친 아인슈타인의 영향

0916
inexpensive
[ìnikspénsiv]

adj. 비싸지 않은   low in price
syn. affordable, cheap, low-end
ant. costly, dear, deluxe, expensive

a relatively inexpensive hotel 비교적 저렴한 호텔

0917
photography
[fətágrəfi]
-graphy 쓰다

n. 사진 찍기, 사진 촬영 기법   the art, process, or job of taking pictures with a camera

studied both film and still photography 영화와 사진을 공부했다

0918
coal
[koul]

n. 석탄   a black or brownish-black hard substance within the earth that is used as a fuel

a coal mine 탄광

0919
inequality
[ìnikwálǝti]

n. 불평등   an unfair situation in which some people have more rights or better opportunities than other people

syn. disparity, difference

the problem of inequality 불평등의 문제

0920
mention
[ménʃǝn]

v. 언급하다   to talk about, write about, or refer to something or someone especially in a brief way

syn. cite, drop, refer to

didn't mention her all evening 저녁 내내 그녀에 대한 언급은 없었다

0921
encyclopedia
[ensàikloupí:diǝ]

n. 백과사전   a reference resource which provides information about many different subjects or about one particular subject

online encyclopedia 온라인 백과사전

0922
description
[diskrípʃǝn]
-script 쓰다

n. 서술, 묘사   a statement that tells you how something or someone looks, sounds, etc.

syn. definition, depiction

a writer with a gift of description 묘사의 재능을 타고난 작가

0923
endurance
[indʒúǝrǝns]

n. 인내심   the ability to do something difficult for a long time

syn. duration, persistence

a marathon runner's endurance 마라톤 주자의 인내심

0924
anger
[ǽŋgǝr]

n. 화, 분노   a strong feeling of being upset or annoyed because of something wrong or bad

syn. outrage, wrath

couldn't hide my anger 나의 분노를 숨길 수 없었다

0925
clue
[kluː]

n. 단서   something that helps a person find something, understand something, or solve a mystery or puzzle

syn. hint, cue, indication

had no clue what he meant 그가 의미하는 바를 전혀 몰랐다

0926
desire
[dizaiər]

v. 갈망하다   to want or wish for something

syn. die for, covet, crave

desire success 성공을 갈망하다

0927
descent¹
[disént]
-de 하락

n. 내려오기   the act of moving down to a lower place or position

syn. dip, dive, plunge

ant. ascent

the plane made a sudden descent 비행기가 급강하했다

0928
descent²
[disént]
-de 하락

n. 혈통   the origin of your parents or other older members of your family

syn. origin, ancestry, lineage

they're all of Irish descent 그들은 모두 아일랜드 혈통이다

0929
coast
[koust]

n. 해안   the land along or near a sea or ocean

syn. shore, beach, seaside

a pretty stretch of coast 아름답게 뻗은 해안

0930
maddening
[mǽdniŋ]

adj. 미치게 하는   making you feel very angry

syn. irritating, annoying, disturbing

maddening delays 몹시 화나게 하는 연착

0931
endure
[endʒúər]

v. 견디다   to experience pain or suffering for a long time

syn. suffer, sustain, undergo

ant. cease, end

endured great pain 엄청난 고통을 견뎌냈다

0932
despair
[dispέər]
-de 하락, 부정

n. 절망   the feeling of no longer having any hope

syn. hopelessness

ant. hope, hopefulness

finally gave up in despair 결국 자포자기해서 포기했다

0933
desert
[dizə́:rt]
-de 하락, 부정

v. 버리고 떠나다 to go away from a place

syn. leave, abandon

desert a town 마을을 버리고 떠나다

0934
inefficient
[ìnifíʃənt]

adj. 비효율적인 not capable of producing desired results without wasting materials, time, or energy

syn. ineffective

an inefficient use of fuel 비효율적인 연료 사용

0935
endangered
[endéindʒər]

adj. 멸종위기에 처한 being or relating to an endangered species

syn. vulnerable, exposed

save endangered animals 멸종위기에 처한 동물들을 구하다

0936
analyze
[ǽnəlàiz]

v. 분석하다 to study something closely and carefully

syn. anatomize, break down

be analyzed by computer 컴퓨터로 분석되다

0937
ancestor
[ǽnsestər]

n. 조상 a person who was in someone's family in past times

ant. descendant

the ancestor of the modern horse 오늘날 말의 조상

0938
shade
[ʃeid]

n. 그늘 an area of slight darkness that is produced when something blocks the light of the sun

sat in the shade of a willow tree 버드나무 그늘 아래 앉았다

0939
anatomy
[ənǽtəmi]

n. 해부학 the study of the structure of living things

syn. analysis, dismemberment, dissection

take a class on anatomy 해부학 수업을 듣다

0940
severe
[sivíər]

adj. 심각한 very bad, serious, or unpleasant

syn. serious, critical

caused severe damage 심각한 피해를 유발했다

0941
sew
[sou]

v. 바느질하다 to make or repair something such as a piece of clothing by using a needle and thread

syn. stitch

ant. unsew

sewed a patch onto his sleeve 팔꿈치에 헝겊조각을 꿰맸다

0942
ancient
[éinʃənt]

adj. 고대의, 아주 오래된 very old

syn. aged, old

an ancient pine tree 아주 오래된 소나무

0943
close
[klous]
-clos 닫다

adj. 가까운 near in space

syn. nearby

stood close together 가까이 함께 서 있었다

0944
sewer
[sjúːər]

n. 하수도 an underground pipe or passage that carries sewage

syn. gutter

clear the sewer 하수도를 뚫다

0945
inevitable
[inévitəbəl]

adj. 불가피한 incapable of being avoided or evaded

ant. avoidable, evadable

an inevitable accident 불가피한 사고

0946
fit²
[fit]

v. 사이즈가 맞다 to be the right size and shape for someone or something

syn. suit, meet, match

the suit fits him perfectly 정장이 그에게 완벽히 맞다

0947
endeavor
[endévər]

v. 노력하다, 애쓰다 to seriously or continually try to do something

syn. strain, strive, struggle, sweat

endeavor to finish the race 경주를 끝내려고 애쓰다

0948
describe
[diskráib]
-scribe 쓰다

v. 묘사하다, 설명하다 to give details about what someone or something is like

syn. explain, express, illustrate

described **my feelings** 내 감정을 설명했다

0949
firsthand
[fə́:rsthǽnd]

adj. 직접의 coming directly from actually experiencing or seeing something

syn. direct, immediate

ant. indirect, secondhand

a firsthand **account of the war** 직접 경험한 전쟁에 대한 설명

0950
encourage
[enkə́:ridʒ]

v. 설득하다, 권장하다 to make someone more determined, hopeful, or confident

syn. inspire, cheer up

ant. discourage, dishearten

encouraged **him to go back to school** 그를 학교로 돌아가도록 설득했다

Review

뜻을 써보고 전체 어구의 의미를 생각해 보시오.

01 will serve its purpose _____ 0907

02 had no clue what he meant _____ 0925

03 they're all of Irish descent _____ 0928

04 servant girl _____ 0910

05 a pretty stretch of coast _____ 0929

06 save endangered animals _____ 0935

07 encouraged him to go back to school _____ 0950

08 the coastal path _____ 0903

09 a marathon runner's endurance _____ 0923

10 take a class on anatomy _____ 0939

11 online encyclopedia _____ 0921

12 a writer with a gift of description _____ 0922

13 caused severe damage _____ 0940

14 finally gave up in despair _____ 0932

15 endow a scholarship _____ 0901

16 the problem of inequality _____ 0919

17 endured great pain _____ 0931

18 physical and emotional health _____ 0904

19 mental health _____ 0911

20 smashed the plate in a fit of rage _____ 0906

DAY 20

0951
destination
[dèstənéiʃən]

n. 목적지, 도착지   a place to which a person is going or something is being sent

reached their destination 그들의 목적지에 도착했다

0952
shadow
[ʃǽdou]

n. 그림자   an area of darkness created when a source of light is blocked

a long shadow across the lawn 잔디밭을 가로지르는 긴 그림자

0953
destruction
[distrʌ́kʃən]
-struct 세우다

n. 파괴   the act or process of damaging something so badly that it no longer exists or cannot be repaired
syn. demolition
ant. construction, erection

the destruction of the environment 환경의 파괴

0954
coincidental
[kouìnsədéntl]
-co 함께

adj. 우연히 발생한   happening or existing by chance and not because of being planned
syn. accidental, unintentional

a coincidental resemblance 우연히 닮음

0955
collective
[kəléktiv]
-co 함께

adj. 집단의, 단체의   shared or done by a group of people
syn. collaborative, combined, common
ant. exclusive, individual, one-man

a collective decision to go on strike 파업 한다는 집단의 결정

0956
colleague
[kάliːg]
-co 함께

n. 동료   a person who works with you
syn. coworker

a colleague of mine from the office 사무실 동료 중 한 명

0957
cocoon
[kəkúːn]

n. 고치, 보호막   a covering usually made of silk which some insects make around themselves to protect them while they grow
syn. armor, capsule, shell

a protective cocoon of bodyguards 경호원들의 보호막

0958

desperate

[déspərit]

-de 하락, 부정

adj. 절망적인   very sad and upset because of having little or no hope

syn. hopeless

ant. hopeful, optimistic

desperate cries for help 절망적인 도움 요청

0959

announce

[ənáuns]

v. 공표하다   to make something known in a public or formal way

syn. declare, publicize, publish, release

announced a cut in taxes 세금 감축을 공표했다

0960

cognitive

[kágnətiv]

adj. 인지의   of, relating to, or involving conscious mental activities

a child's cognitive development 아동의 인지 발달

0961

enhance

[enhǽns]

v. 향상시키다   to improve something, or to make it more attractive or more valuable

syn. improve, refine, upgrade

ant. worsen

enhance the residents' quality of life 거주민들의 삶의 질을 향상시키다

0962

inferior

[infíəriər]

adj. 열악한, 열등한   low or lower in quality

syn. lower

ant. higher, superior, upper

always felt inferior to his older brother 형에게 늘 열등감을 느꼈다

0963

despite

[dispáit]

-de 하락, 부정

prep. ~에도 불구하고   without being prevented by something

syn. in spite of, in the face of, regardless of

played despite an injury 부상에도 불구하고 경기를 뛰었다

0964

shame

[ʃeim]

n. 죄책감, 후회   a feeling of guilt, regret, or sadness that you have because you know you have done something wrong

syn. regret, remorse, guilt

felt shame for his lies 거짓말 한 것이 부끄러웠다

0965
enlargement
[enlɑ́:rdʒmənt]

n. 확대, 확장 the act of making something larger or of becoming larger

syn. expansion, increase

enlargement of the company's offices 회사 사무실 확장

0966
destroy
[distrɔ́i]
-de 하락, 부정

v. 파괴하다 to damage something so badly that it cannot be repaired

syn. ruin, break down

ant. build, construct, erect

an earthquake destroyed the town 지진이 그 마을을 파괴했다

0967
pitiful
[pítifəl]

adj. 불쌍한, 가엾은 looking or sounding so unhappy that you feel sympathy and sadness

syn. pathetic, distressing, miserable

a pitiful sight 가엾은 광경

0968
plain
[plein]

adj. 장식이 없는 having no pattern or decoration

syn. simple, unadorned, undecorated

plain black shoes 장식 없는 검은 구두

0969
pitfall
[pítfɔ́:l]

n. 함정, 곤란 a danger or problem that is hidden or not obvious at first

syn. booby trap, catch-22

the pitfalls of running a business 사업 운영의 난관들

0970
infant
[ínfənt]

n. 유아 a very young child

syn. child, baby

ant. adult, grown-up

an infant school 유치원

0971
engrave
[engréiv]

v. 새기다, 명심하다 to cut or carve lines, letters, designs, etc. onto or into a hard surface

syn. etch, inscribe

a trophy engraved with the winner's name 우승자의 이름이 새겨진 트로피

164

0972
pitch
[pitʃ]

v. 힘껏 던지다　to throw something using a lot of force

syn. throw, launch, cast

pitched the trash into the bin 쓰레기를 쓰레기통에 던졌다

0973
relevance
[rélǝvǝns]

n. 관련성, 타당성　relation to the matter at hand

syn. connection

have no relevance 전혀 관련성이 없다

0974
enforce
[enfɔ́ːrs]

v. (법률 등을) 집행하다, 시행하다　to make a law, rule, etc. active or effective

syn. administer, apply, execute, implement

enforce laws 법을 집행하다

0975
fixed
[fikst]

adj. 고정된　placed or attached in a way that does not move easily

syn. set, settled, stable

ant. alterable, changeable, elastic

a small mirror fixed to the wall 벽에 고정된 작은 거울

0976
sharp
[ʃɑːrp]

adj. 날카로운　having a thin edge that is able to cut things or a fine point that is able to make a hole in things

syn. edgy, keen

ant. blunt, dull

a sharp knife 날카로운 칼

0977
relaxed
[rilǽkst]

adj. 느긋한, 여유 있는　calm and free from stress, worry, or anxiety

syn. easy, casual, leisurely

a relaxed atmosphere 여유로운 분위기

0978
planet
[plǽnǝt]

n. 행성　a large, round object in space that travels around a star

the planets of our solar system 태양계의 행성들

0979
infect
[infékt]

v. 감염시키다　to cause someone or something to become sick or affected by disease

syn. contaminate, transmit disease to

avoid infecting other people 다른 사람 감염시키는 것을 피하다

0980
shameless
[ʃéimlis]

adj. 뻔뻔한 having or showing no shame
syn. unabashed, unashamed, unblushing
shameless behavior 부끄러움을 모르는 태도

0981
engage
[engéidʒ]

v. 고용하다 to start to employ someone or use their services
syn. employ, commission, hire
engaged a new sales director 새 영업 부장을 고용했다

0982
shave
[ʃeiv]

v. 면도하다 to cut off hair, wool, a beard, etc. very close to the skin
syn. trim, cut, crop
cut myself shaving 면도하다가 베었다

0983
collect
[kəlékt]
-co 함께

v. 모으다, 수집하다 to get things from different places and bring them together
syn. gather
ant. scatter
collect stamps 우표를 수집하다

0984
annoyance
[ənɔ́iəns]

n. 짜증, 성가심 the feeling of being annoyed
syn. disturbance, vexation
ant. delight, pleasure
expressed annoyance at the slow service 늦은 서비스에 대해 짜증을 표현했다

0985
reliable
[riláiəbəl]

adj. 믿음직한 able to be trusted to do or provide what is needed
syn. dependable, trustworthy
ant. unreliable
reliable information 믿을 수 있는 정보

0986
shape
[ʃeip]

n. 형체, 형태 the form or outline of an object
syn. form
a cake in the shape of a Christmas tree 크리스마스 트리 형태의 케이크

0987
disease
[dizíːz]

n. 질병 an illness that affects a person, animal, or plant
syn. illness, sickness, ailment
ant. health, wellness

a disease of the mind 마음의 병

0988
sharply
[ʃáːrpli]

adv. 급격히 suddenly and by a large amount

interest rates have fallen sharply 이자율이 급격히 떨어졌다

0989
relieved
[rilíːvd]

adj. 안도하는 happy and relaxed because something bad has not happened or because a bad situation has ended
syn. glad, happy, pleased

she sounded relieved 그녀는 안도하는 것 같았다

0990
reliant
[riláiənt]

adj. 의존적인 needing someone or something for help, support, etc.
syn. dependent, relying

become reliant upon technology 과학기술에 의지하게 되다

0991
energetic
[ènərdʒétik]

adj. 정열적인 having or showing a lot of energy
syn. dynamic, vigorous
ant. dull, listless, sluggish

an energetic personality 정열적인 성격

0992
release
[rilíːz]

v. 풀어주다 to set someone or something free
syn. unleash, unlock, let go
ant. constrain, hold

release hostages 인질을 풀어주다

0993
share
[ʃɛər]

v. 나누다, 공유하다 to have or use something with others
syn. divide, split

shared the money equally 돈을 똑같이 나눴다

0994
plank
[plæŋk]

n. 널빤지   a long, thick board that is used especially in building something

syn. board, timber

a wooden plank 나무판자 하나

0995
flat
[flæt]

adj. 평평한   having a smooth, level, or even surface

syn. even

flat ground 평평한 땅

0996
fix
[fiks]

v. 고정하다   to attach something in such a way that it will not move

syn. stick, attach

ant. detach, undo

fixed his eyes on the horizon 눈을 수평선에 고정했다

0997
pirate
[páiərət]

n. 해적   someone who attacks and steals from a ship at sea

syn. freebooter, rover

a pirate boat 해적선

0998
pioneer
[pàiəníər]

n. 개척자, 선구자   a person who helps create or develop new ideas, methods, etc.

syn. founder, leader, developer, innovator

the pioneer spirit 개척자 정신

0999
infer
[infɔ́:r]

v. 추론하다, 추리하다   to form an opinion from evidence

syn. deduce, derive, reason

infer a conclusion 결론을 추리하다

1000
enemy
[énəmi]

n. 적   someone who is opposed to someone else and tries to do them harm

syn. adversary, antagonist, foe, opponent

ant. friend

alcohol was his greatest enemy 술은 그의 가장 큰 적이었다

Review

뜻을 써보고 전체 어구의 의미를 생각해 보시오.

01 played despite an injury _____ 0963

02 plain black shoes _____ 0968

03 pitched the trash into the bin _____ 0972

04 the planets of our solar system _____ 0978

05 enforce laws _____ 0974

06 infer a conclusion _____ 0999

07 flat ground _____ 0995

08 a pirate boat _____ 0997

09 the pioneer spirit _____ 0998

10 the pitfalls of running a business _____ 0969

11 collect stamps _____ 0983

12 release hostages _____ 0992

13 a long shadow across the lawn _____ 0952

14 reliable information _____ 0985

15 interest rates have fallen sharply _____ 0988

16 have no relevance _____ 0973

17 avoid infecting other people _____ 0979

18 a child's cognitive development _____ 0960

19 always felt inferior to his older brother _____ 0962

20 a coincidental resemblance _____ 0954

DAY 21

1001
plateau
[plætóu]

n. 고원　a large flat area of land that is higher than other areas of land that surround it

syn. tableland

a plateau covering hundreds of miles 수백 마일에 달하는 고원

1002
ensue
[ensú:]

v. 잇따르다, 결과로 발생하다　to happen as a result

syn. follow, result

problems that ensue from food shortages 식량부족에 따른 문제들

1003
comfort
[kʌ́mfərt]

v. 위로하다　to cause someone to feel less worried, upset, frightened, etc.

syn. cheer, soothe

ant. distress, trouble

comforted her heartbroken friend 상심한 그녀의 친구를 위로해줬다

1004
flesh
[fleʃ]

n. 살, 피부　the soft parts of the body of an animal or person

syn. meat

the dog's teeth sank into my flesh 그 개의 이빨이 내 살로 깊숙이 박혔다

1005
combine
[kəmbáin]
-com 함께

v. 결합하다　to join together

syn. join together, link, connect, merge

combine two companies 두 회사를 합병하다

1006
detailed
[dí:teild]
-tail 자르다

adj. 자세한　including many details

syn. elaborate, particular, thorough

ant. summary

very detailed instructions 매우 자세한 지시사항

1007
reluctant
[rilʌ́ktənt]

adj. 내키지 않는　not willing or eager to do something

syn. hesitant, unwilling

be reluctant to get involved 개입하고 싶어 하지 않다

1008
combat
[kámbæt]

v. 예방 조치를 하다 to do something in order to try to stop something bad from happening or a bad situation from becoming worse

syn. fight, battle against

measures to combat crime 범죄를 막기 위한 조치

1009
remote
[rimóut]

adj. 먼, 외딴 far away

syn. distant, far

the remote past 먼 과거

1010
detect
[ditékt]

v. 탐지하다, 감지하다 to discover or notice the presence of something that is hidden or hard to see, hear, taste, etc.

syn. discover, find, reveal

detect alcohol in the blood 혈중 알코올을 탐지하다

1011
flexible
[fléksəbəl]
-flex 구부러지다

adj. 휠 수 있는, 유연한 capable of bending or being bent

syn. changeable, elastic

ant. established, fixed

flexible branches swaying in the breeze 바람에 흔들거리는 유연한 나뭇가지들

1012
comment
[kámənt]

v. 논평하다, 견해를 밝히다 to make a statement about someone or something

syn. remark

refused to comment 언급을 회피했다

1013
detail
[dí:teil]
-tail 자르다

n. 세부사항 the small parts of something

syn. item, particular, point

every detail of the wedding 결혼식의 모든 세부사항들

1014
shift
[ʃift]

n. 바꿈, 변화 a change in position or direction

syn. change, switch

a shift away from tradition 전통으로부터의 변화

1015
command
[kəmǽnd]
-mand 명령하다

v. 명령하다   to give someone an order
syn. direct, instruct, order, tell
commanded us to leave 우리에게 떠나라고 명령했다

1016
remind
[rimáind]

v. 상기시키다   to make someone think about something again
syn. make you remember
you remind me of your father 너는 너의 아버지를 떠올리게 한다

1017
enroll
[enróul]

v. 등록하다, 가입하다   to become a member or participant
syn. list, register
we enrolled in the history course 우리는 역사 수업을 수강 신청했다

1018
shiny
[ʃáini]

adj. 빛나는   having a smooth, shining, bright appearance
syn. brilliant, glowing
ant. dim, dull
shiny new shoes 밝게 빛나는 새 구두

1019
inflow
[ínflòu]

n. 유입   a flow or movement of something into a place, organization, etc.
syn. influx
ant. outflow, outpouring
an inflow of funds 자금의 유입

1020
plot
[plɑt]

v. 모의하다   to plan secretly to do something usually illegal or harmful
syn. plan, scheme
plot a coup 쿠데타를 모의하다

1021
plant
[plænt]

v. 심다   to put a seed, flower, or plant in the ground to grow
syn. seed, sow
plant seeds 씨앗을 심다

1022
inflame
[infléim]

v. 격앙시키다, 부채질하다   to make a situation worse by making people more angry or excited
syn. intensify, worsen, fan
inflamed an already dangerous situation 이미 위험한 상황을 악화시켰다

1023
remodel
[ri:mádl]

v. 개조하다　to change the structure, shape, or appearance of something

syn. alter, modify, remake

remodeled the kitchen 부엌을 개조했다

1024
remember
[rimémbər]

v. 기억하다　to have or keep an image or idea in your mind of something or someone from the past

syn. recall, recollect, reminisce

ant. forget

remember the old days 지난날들을 기억하다

1025
please
[pli:z]

v. 기쁘게 하다　to make someone happy or satisfied

syn. satisfy

ant. displease

be pleased by her decision 그녀의 결정으로 기뻐하다

1026
shelf
[ʃelf]

n. 선반　a flat board which is attached to a wall, frame, etc. and on which objects can be placed

syn. rack, bookshelf, mantelpiece

don't have much shelf space 선반 공간이 많지 않다

1027
plantation
[plæntéiʃən]

n. 대규모 농장　a large farm where crops such as tea, coffee, cotton, and sugar are grown

a sugar plantation 사탕수수 농장

1028
religious
[rilídʒəs]

adj. 신앙심 있는　believing in a god or a group of gods and following the rules of a religion

syn. devotional, sacred, spiritual

ant. profane, secular

a religious person 신앙심 있는 사람

1029
shore
[ʃɔːr]

n. 해안, 물가　the land bordering a usually large body of water

syn. beach, coast

managed to swim to the shore 가까스로 해안까지 헤엄쳐 갔다

1030
ensure
[enʃúər]

v. 보장하다   to make something sure, certain, or safe

syn. assure, guarantee, insure

ensure secrecy 비밀을 보장하다

1031
detached
[ditǽtʃt]

adj. 1 분리된   2 사심 없는   separate from another part or thing / not influenced by emotions or personal interest

syn. 1 separate, free, disconnected   2 objective, neutral, impartial

a detached house 단독주택
a detached observer 사심 없는 관찰자

1032
comfortable
[kʌ́mfərtəbl]

adj. 편안한   not causing any physically unpleasant feelings

syn. cozy, snug, soft

ant. uncomfortable

a comfortable chair 편한 의자

1033
colonist
[kálənist]

n. 식민지 이주자   someone who settles in a new colony

syn. pioneer, settler

British colonists settled the area 영국인 식민지 이주자들이 그곳에 정착했다

1034
shortage
[ʃɔ́ːrtidʒ]

n. 부족, 결핍   a lack of something that you need or want

syn. lack, deficiency, undersupply

ant. plenty, sufficiency, wealth

a shortage of clean water 깨끗한 물의 부족

1035
plenty
[plénti]

n. 풍족함   a large number or amount

syn. abundance

ant. deficiency

had plenty of time to finish the job 그 일을 끝내는 데 충분한 시간이 있었다

1036
remindful
[rimáindfəl]

adj. ~을 잊지 않고 있는   tending to remind

a man remindful of his duties 직무를 잊지 않고 있는 사람

1037
enterprise
[éntərpràiz]

n. 기업   a business organization
syn. business, company, firm

small and medium-sized enterprises 중소기업들

1038
shoot
[ʃuːt]

v. 총을 쏘다   to fire a gun
syn. open fire on, blast

be ordered not to shoot 총을 쏘지 말라는 명령을 받다

1039
infinite
[ínfənit]
-fin 끝

adj. 무한의   having no limits
syn. boundless, endless, limitless
ant. finite, limited

infinite space 끝이 없는 우주

1040
colonize
[kálənàiz]

v. 식민지로 만들다   to take control of another country by going to live there or by sending people to live there
syn. settle, people, populate

colonize an island 섬에 사람을 이주시키다

1041
remain
[riméin]

v. 남다   to be left when the other parts are gone or have been used
syn. stay, continue, go on

remain single 독신으로 남다

1042
shelter
[ʃéltər]

n. 은신처, 주거지   a place that provides food and protection for people or animals that need assistance
syn. refuge, haven, sanctuary

made a shelter from branches 나뭇가지로 은신처를 만들었다

1043
flavor
[fléivər]

n. 향, 맛   a particular type of taste
syn. taste, aroma

a dish with unusual flavor 독특한 맛의 음식

1044
shield
[ʃiːld]

n. 보호막   something that defends or protects someone or something
syn. guard, protection, screen

provide a shield against nuclear attack 핵 공격에 대한 보호막을 제공하다

175

1045
entail
[entéil]

v. 수반하다   to have something as a part, step, or result
syn. include, involve
ant. exclude

entail considerable expense 상당한 액수의 비용을 수반하다

1046
remains
[iméinz]

n. 남은 것   the parts of something that are left after the rest has been destroyed or has disappeared
syn. remnants, leftovers

the remains of the evening meal 저녁 식사 후 남은 음식

1047
flatter
[flǽtər]

v. 아부하다   to praise someone in a way that is not sincere
syn. overpraise

the portrait flatters him 초상화가 실물보다 잘 나왔다

1048
plump
[plʌmp]

adj. 통통한   having a full, rounded shape
syn. chubby, round
ant. lean, skinny, slender

pinched his plump cheeks 그의 통통한 볼을 꼬집었다

1049
remark
[rimá:rk]

v. 언급하다   to make a statement about someone or something
syn. comment

make a remark 한마디 하다

1050
enrich
[enrítʃ]

v. 풍요롭게 하다, 가치를 높이다   to make someone rich or richer / to improve the quality of something
syn. enhance, improve, upgrade
ant. worsen

the experience will enrich your life 그 경험은 너의 삶을 풍족하게 해줄 것이다

Review

뜻을 써보고 전체 어구의 의미를 생각해 보시오.

01 you remind me of your father _____ 1016

02 be reluctant to get involved _____ 1007

03 the remains of the evening meal _____ 1046

04 ① a detached house _____ 1031

　② a detached observer _____

05 the experience will enrich your life _____ 1050

06 the portrait flatters him _____ 1047

07 a comfortable chair _____ 1032

08 the remote past _____ 1009

09 detect alcohol in the blood _____ 1010

10 don't have much shelf space _____ 1026

11 colonize an island _____ 1040

12 had plenty of time to finish the job _____ 1035

13 infinite space _____ 1039

14 shiny new shoes _____ 1018

15 a sugar plantation _____ 1027

16 ensure secrecy _____ 1030

17 managed to swim to the shore _____ 1029

18 a plateau covering hundreds of miles _____ 1001

19 plant seeds _____ 1021

20 every detail of the wedding _____ 1013

DAY 22

1051
remove
[rimúːv]

v. 제거하다   to move or take something away from a place
syn. erase, eliminate

a good way to remove stains 얼룩을 제거하는 좋은 방법

1052
communal
[kəmjúːnəl]
-com 함께

adj. 공동의, 공용의   shared or used by members of a group or community
syn. common, shared, public

a communal kitchen 공용 부엌

1053
enthusiastic
[enθúːziǽstik]

adj. 열성적인   feeling or showing strong excitement about something
syn. anxious, ardent
ant. indifferent, uneager

received an enthusiastic welcome 열렬히 환영 받았다

1054
deterioration
[ditìəriəréiʃən]
-de 하락, 부정

n. 악화   the act or process of becoming worse
syn. worsening
ant. improvement, recovery

the gradual deterioration of the weather 점차적인 기상 악화

1055
develop
[divéləp]

v. 현상하다   to make a photograph out of a photographic film, using chemicals

have the film developed 필름을 현상시키다

1056
detergent
[ditə́ːrdʒənt]

n. 세제   a liquid or powder used for washing clothes or dishes
syn. cleanser, cleaner, soap

dissolve detergent in water 물에 세제를 풀다

1057
flip
[flip]

v. 홱 튀기다   to turn something over by throwing it up in the air with a quick movement
syn. toss, fling

flip a coin 동전을 튀기다

1058
point
[pɔint]

v. 가리키다   to show someone where to look by moving your finger in a particular direction

syn. aim, direct

pointed her finger at the door 손가락으로 문을 가리켰다

1059
inform
[infɔ́ːrm]

v. 알리다   to give information to someone

syn. let someone know, notify

inform a prisoner of his rights 수감자에게 그의 권리를 알리다

1060
commute
[kəmjúːt]

v. 통근하다   to travel regularly to and from a place and especially between where you live and where you work

syn. travel

commute to work every day by train 매일 기차를 타고 통근하다

1061
shrink
[ʃriŋk]
-shrank -shrunk

v. 줄다, 수축하다   to become smaller in amount, size, or value

syn. compress, contract

ant. expand, swell

the sweater shrank 스웨터가 줄었다

1062
community
[kəmjúːnəti]
-com 함께

n. 주민, 지역사회, 공동체   a group of people who live in the same area such as a city, town, or neighborhood

syn. neighborhood

the farming community 농경 공동체

1063
silent
[sáilənt]

adj. 조용한   not speaking or making noise

syn. dumb, mute, speechless

the audience fell silent 관객이 조용해졌다

1064
portray
[pɔːrtréi]

v. 묘사하다, 나타내다   to describe someone or something in a particular way

syn. describe, sketch

portrayed himself as a victim 자신을 피해자로 묘사했다

1065
common
[kámən]

adj. 공동의, 공공의　belonging to or shared by two or more people or groups

syn. shared, collective

work for the common good 공공의 이익을 위한 일

1066
shortly
[ʃɔ́ːrtli]

adv. 곧　in or within a short time

syn. briefly

shortly after sunset 일몰 후 곧

1067
pop
[pɑp]

v. (펑하고) 터지다　to suddenly break open or come away from something often with a short, loud noise

syn. blow, burst, go off

the buttons popped off my sweater 스웨터의 단추들이 톡톡 떨어졌다

1068
side effect
[saíd ifèkt]

n. 부작용　an often harmful and unwanted effect of a drug or chemical that occurs along with the desired effect

cause side effects 부작용을 일으키다

1069
informal
[infɔ́ːrməl]

adj. 비격식의　having a friendly and relaxed quality

syn. irregular, unceremonious

ant. formal

an informal meeting 비공식 모임

1070
portrait
[pɔ́ːrtrit]

n. 초상화, 인물사진　a painting, drawing, or photograph of a person that usually only includes the person's head and shoulders

a self portrait 자화상

1071
commonality
[kàmənǽləti]
-com 함께

n. 유사성　the fact of sharing features or qualities

syn. similarity

share important commonalities 중요한 유사성을 공유하다

1072
similar
[símələr]
-simul 같음

adj. 유사한　almost the same as someone or something else

syn. akin, resembling, matching

got remarkably similar results 놀랍도록 유사한 결과가 나왔다

1073
commoner
[kámənər]

n. 평민, 서민   a person who is not a member of the nobility

a prince who married a commoner 평민과 결혼한 왕자

1074
simplicity
[simplísəti]

n. 간단함, 평이함   the state or quality of being plain or not fancy or complicated

syn. plainness, unsophistication

the simplicity of the music 그 음악의 단순성

1075
poet
[póuit]

n. 시인   a person who writes poems

syn. bard

a lyric poet 서정시인

1076
sighting
[sáitiŋ]

n. 목격   an occasion when you see something unusual or something that you have been looking for

unconfirmed sightings of UFOs 확인되지 않은 UFO 목격담들

1077
significance
[signífikəns]

n. 중요성   the quality of being important

syn. importance

ant. slightness, smallness, triviality

religious significance 종교적 의의

1078
commonly
[kámənli]

adv. 흔히, 보통   usually or frequently

commonly used words 상용어

1079
policy
[páləsi]

n. 정책, 방침   a plan of action adopted or pursued by an individual, government, party, business, etc.

syn. plan, scheme

marketing policy 판매 정책

1080
simultaneous
[sàiməltéiniəs]
-simul 같음

adj. 동시에 발생하는   happening or done at the same time

syn. coincident, synchronic

simultaneous interpretation 동시통역

181

1081

influential

[ìnfluénʃəl]

-flu 흐르다

adj. 영향력 있는 having the power to cause changes

syn. authoritative, forceful, weighty

ant. powerless, unimportant, weak

the most influential people 가장 영향력 있는 사람들

1082

signature

[sígnətʃər]

n. 서명 a person's name written in that person's handwriting

falsify a signature 서명을 위조하다

1083

commercial

[kəmə́:rʃəl]

adj. 상업의, 영리 목적의 related to or used in the buying and selling of goods and services

a commercial school 실업계 학교

1084

determine

[ditə́:rmin]

-term 경계

v. 결정하다 to officially decide something

syn. decide

determine which is right 어느 것이 옳은지 결정하다

1085

sincere

[sinsíər]

adj. 진심어린 having or showing true feelings that are expressed in an honest way

syn. heartfelt

ant. affected, artificial, false

sincere sympathy 진심어린 동정심

1086

polish

[páliʃ]

v. 광내다 to make something smooth and shiny by rubbing it

syn. varnish, wax, glaze

polished my shoes 구두 광을 냈다

1087

pollution

[pəlú:ʃən]

n. 오염 the action or process of making land, water, air, etc. dirty and not safe

syn. contamination, dirtying

cause pollution of the air and water 공기와 물의 오염을 유발하다

1088

signal

[sígnl]

n. 신호 an event or act which shows that something exists or that gives information about something

syn. sign, gesture, indication

a danger signal 위험 신호

182

1089
commitment
[kəmítmənt]
-com 함께

n. 헌신, 약속　the attitude of someone who works very hard to do or support something

syn. dedication, devotion, faith

ant. disloyalty

show commitment 헌신적인 태도를 보이다

1090
simplify
[símpləfài]

v. 간소화하다　to make something easier to do or understand

syn. streamline

ant. complicate

simplify the process 절차를 간소화하다

1091
popular
[pápjələr]

adj. 인기 있는, 대중적인　liked or enjoyed by many people

syn. well-liked, liked, favored

a popular guy in school 학교에서 인기 있는 친구

1092
pole
[poul]

n. 막대기, 장대　a long slender usually cylindrical object as a length of wood

syn. rod, post, staff

a ski pole 스키 폴

1093
shoulder
[ʃóuldər]

v. 책임지다, 떠맡다　to deal with or accept something as your responsibility or duty

syn. take over, undertake, assume

shoulder the blame for the failure 실패에 대한 비난을 떠맡다

1094
committee
[kəmíti]
-com 함께

n. 위원회　a group of people who are chosen to do a particular job or to make decisions about something

syn. commission, panel

assemble a committee 위원회를 소집하다

1095
sink
[siŋk]
-sank -sunk

v. 가라앉다, 빠지다　to go down below the surface of water, mud, etc.

syn. descend, lower, go down

my foot sank into the deep mud 내 발이 진흙 깊숙이 빠졌다

1096
shorten
[ʃɔ́ːrtn]

v. 줄이다, 단축하다　to make something shorter
syn. abridge, curtail
ant. elongate, extend, lengthen

shorten a skirt 스커트 길이를 줄이다

1097
shrug
[ʃrʌg]

v. 어깨를 들썩하다　to raise and lower your shoulders usually to show that you do not know or care about something

he shrugged his shoulders 그는 어깨를 들썩했다

1098
poem
[póuim]

n. 시　a piece of writing that usually has figurative language and that is written in separate lines that often have a repeated rhythm and sometimes rhyme
syn. lyric, song, verse

wrote a poem about the wind 바람에 관한 시를 썼다

1099
politician
[pàlitíʃən]

n. 정치인　someone who is active in government usually as an elected official

a bloated politician 거만한 정치인

1100
influence
[ínfluəns]
-flu 흐르다

v. 영향을 끼치다　to affect or change someone or something in an indirect but usually important way
syn. impact, impress

the weather influence people's behavior 날씨가 사람들의 행동에 영향을 끼친다

Review

뜻을 써보고 전체 어구의 의미를 생각해 보시오.

01 **have the film** developed 1055

02 determine **which is right** 1084

03 **work for the** common **good** 1066

04 **the** simplicity **of the music** 1074

05 **a lyric** poet 1075

06 **a self** portrait 1070

07 **the buttons** popped **off my sweater** 1067

08 **religious** significance 1077

09 simplify **the process** 1090

10 **share important** commonalities 1071

11 **falsify a** signature 1082

12 **a ski** pole 1092

13 **assemble a** committee 1094

14 simultaneous **interpretation** 1080

15 inform **a prisoner of his rights** 1059

16 **marketing** policy 1079

17 **the audience fell** silent 1063

18 **got remarkably** similar **results** 1072

19 **received an** enthusiastic **welcome** 1053

20 **the sweater** shrank 1061

DAY 23

1101
complimentary
[kàmpləméntəri]

adj. 1 칭찬의 2 무료의 expressing praise or admiration for someone / given for free
syn. 1 admiring, applauding 2 free, donated

a complimentary remark 칭찬의 말
complimentary tickets 무료 제공 티켓

1102
slight
[slait]

adj. 약간의 very small in degree or amount
syn. small, minor, insignificant
ant. mighty, powerful

a slight wound 가벼운 상처

1103
component
[kəmpóunənt]
-com 함께

n. 부품, 구성 요소 one of the parts of something such as a system or mixture
syn. building block, element, factor

the car component industry 자동차 부품 산업

1104
complementary
[kàmpləméntəri]

adj. 상호 보완적인 completing something else or making it better
syn. supplementary

complementary cooperation 상호 보완적인 협력

1105
skilled
[skild]

adj. 숙련된, 능숙한 having the training, knowledge, and experience that is needed to do something
syn. proficient, skillful
ant. amateurish, inexperienced

a very skilled and talented writer 숙련되고 재능 있는 작가

1106
competence
[kámpətəns]

n. 능숙함 the ability to do something in a satisfactory or effective way
syn. capability, ability

the competence of the government 정부의 능력

1107
composer
[kəmpóuzər]

n. 작곡가 a person who writes music

a classical composer like Beethoven 베토벤 같은 고전 음악 작곡가

186

1108
situate
[sítʃuèit]

v. 위치시키다   to place someone or something in a particular location

syn. position, place

situated the new office building near the airport
새 사무실 건물을 공항 근처에 위치시켰다

1109
devoted
[divóutid]

adj. 헌신적인   having strong love or loyalty for something or someone

syn. dedicated, loving, committed, loyal

a devoted fan 헌신적인 팬

1110
compensation
[kàmpənséiʃən]

n. 보상, 보상금   something that is done or given to make up for damage, trouble, etc.

syn. damages, payment

claim compensation 보상금을 요구하다

1111
diabetes
[dàiəbí:tis]

n. 당뇨병   a serious disease in which there is too much sugar in your blood

suffer from diabetes 당뇨병을 앓다

1112
competent
[kámpətənt]

adj. 능숙한   able to do something well or well enough to meet a standard

syn. able, skilled, capable

ant. unqualified, incompetent

a competent teacher 유능한 교사

1113
compliment
[kámpləmənt]

v. 칭찬하다, 축하하다   to say nice things about someone or something

syn. congratulate

ant. tease

complimented her on her election victory 그녀의 당선을 축하해 주었다

1114
diagnose
[dáiəgnòus]

v. 진단하다   to recognize a disease, illness, etc. by examining someone

syn. identify, determine, pinpoint

diagnosed the patient 환자를 진단했다

1115

snap

[snæp]

v. 툭 꺾다[치다]   to break quickly with a short, sharp sound

syn. pop, click, crackle

fish snapping at the bait 미끼를 툭툭 치는 물고기

1116

compensate

[kámpənsèit]

v. 보상하다, 배상하다   to pay someone money because they have suffered an injury or loss

syn. repay, refund, reimburse

compensate the victims for their loss 피해자에게 손실 보상을 하다

1117

flood

[flʌd]

v. 범람하다   to become covered or filled with water

syn. overflow

ant. drain

the valley flooded 계곡 물이 넘쳤다

1118

complete

[kəmplí:t]

v. 완성하다   to finish something by adding the parts that are missing

syn. finalize, perfect, polish

ant. begin, open, start

complete a painting 그림을 완성하다

1119

site

[sait]

n. 장소, 현장   the place where something is, was, or will be located

syn. location, place, spot

the site of the accident 사고 현장

1120

complicated

[kámpləkèitid]

-plic 접다

adj. 복잡한   hard to understand, explain, or deal with / having many parts or steps

syn. complex, sophisticated, tangled

ant. plain, simple

a complicated issue 복잡한 문제

1121

compare

[kəmpέər]

-com 함께

v. 비교하다, 비슷하다 to say that something is similar to something else

syn. assimilate, equate, liken

ant. contrast

nothing compares to you 그 무엇도 너 만한 것이 없다

1122
complain
[kəmpléin]

v. 불평하다   to say something that expresses annoyance or unhappiness

syn. grumble

complain about the weather 날씨에 대해 불평하다

1123
slope
[sloup]

n. 경사면, 경사지   ground that slants downward or upward

syn. slant, ramp

a steep slope 가파른 경사면

1124
compel
[kəmpél]
-pel 몰다

v. 강요하다   to force someone to do something

syn. force, drive, impel

felt compelled to resign 사퇴할 수밖에 없을 것 같았다

1125
bank
[bæŋk]

n. 둑, 제방   land along the side of a river or lake

the river bank 강 둑

1126
slide
[slaid]
-slid -slid

v. 미끄러지다, 미끄러트리다   to move smoothly along a surface

syn. slip, snake

slid the paper under the door 종이를 문 아래로 밀어 넣었다

1127
photographer
[fətágrəfər]
-graph 쓰다

n. 사진사, 사진작가   a person who takes photographs especially as a job

syn. lensman, shooter, shutterbug

a fashion photographer 패션 사진작가

1128
depression
[dipréʃən]
-press 밀다

n. 우울증   a state of feeling sad

syn. recession, slump

undergo treatment for severe depression 심한 우울증으로 치료를 받다

1129
biology
[baiálədʒi]
-bio 생명

n. 생물학   the scientific study of living things

a degree in biology 생물학 학위

1130
comparative
[kəmpǽrətiv]
-com 함께

adj. 비교의, 비교적인　involving the act of looking at the ways that things are alike or different
syn. relative

comparative linguistics 비교 언어학

1131
script
[skript]

n. 대본　the written text of a stage play, screenplay, or broadcast
syn. manuscript, lines, text

a film script 영화 대본

1132
compete
[kəmpíːt]
-com 함께

v. 경쟁하다　to try to be better or more successful than someone or something else
syn. contend, fight, rival, contest

compete with others for a prize 상을 타려고 다른 사람들과 경쟁하다

1133
competitive
[kəmpétətiv]

adj. 1 경쟁력 있는　2 경쟁심 강한　as good as or better than others of the same kind / always trying to be more successful than other people

be competitive in today's job market 오늘날의 구직 시장에서 경쟁력을 갖추다
a competitive player 경쟁심이 강한 선수

1134
slum
[slʌm]

n. 빈민가　an area of a city where poor people live and the buildings are in bad condition
syn. ghetto

urban slums 도시 빈민가

1135
affective
[əféktiv]

adj. 정서상의　relating to, arising from, or influencing feelings or emotions

affective disorders 정서 장애

1136
comparable
[kámpərəbəl]
-com 함께

adj. 비슷한, 비교할 만한　fairly similar to another thing, so that it is reasonable to compare them
syn. resembling, similar, parallel

be in a comparable financial situation 비슷한 재정적 상황에 놓여 있다

1137
skeptical
[sképtikəl]

adj. 회의적인 having or expressing doubt about something such as a claim or statement

syn. suspicious, unbelieving

he looked skeptical 그는 믿지 않는 것 같았다

1138
compose
[kəmpóuz]

v. 작곡하다, 글을 창작하다 to create and write a piece of music or writing

syn. create, write, produce

compose a poem 시를 쓰다

1139
shine
[ʃain]

v. 빛나다 to give off light

syn. beam, radiate

shine brightly 밝게 빛나다

1140
so-called
[sóukɔ́:ld]

adj. 소위, 이른바 (used to indicate the name that is commonly or usually used for something)

syn. alleged, supposed

the so-called black box 소위 블랙박스라는 것

1141
dialect
[dáiəlèkt]

n. 방언, 사투리 a way of speaking a language that is used only in a particular area or by a particular group

syn. jargon

speak in dialect 사투리로 말하다

1142
sled
[sled]

n. 썰매 a small vehicle used for sliding over snow, often used by children or in some sports

sled dog 썰매 끄는 개

1143
float
[flout]

v. 둥둥 뜨다 to be carried along by moving water or air

syn. drift, waft

ant. sink

yellow leaves floated down 노란 나뭇잎들이 떠내려갔다

1144
soak
[souk]

v. 흠뻑 젖게 하다   to make someone or something very wet with water or another liquid
syn. drench, drown

be soaked by the rain 비에 흠뻑 젖다

1145
complex
[kəmpléks]

adj. 복잡한   consisting of many different parts and often difficult to understand
syn. complicated, mixed
ant. plain, simple

a highly complex process 매우 복잡한 절차

1146
device
[diváis]

n. 장비, 기계   an object, machine, or piece of equipment that has been made for some special purpose
syn. tool, instrument

electronic devices 전자 기기들

1147
skyrocket
[skáirɑ̀kit]

v. 치솟다   to increase quickly to a very high level or amount
syn. soar, zoom
ant. nose-dive, plummet, plunge, slump

prices are skyrocketing 가격이 치솟고 있다

1148
companion
[kəmpǽnjən]
-com 함께

n. 동료, 동반자   someone who is with you
syn. friend, partner, ally, colleague

a travelling companion 여행 동료

1149
devote
[divóut]

v. 헌신하다   to spend a lot of time or effort doing something
syn. dedicate, give, commit

devoted most of his time to his painting 그의 거의 모든 시간을 그림에 바쳤다

1150
compact
[kəmpǽkt]

adj. 작고 촘촘한, 다부진   using little space and having parts that are close together
syn. closely packed, compressed

a compact body 다부진 몸

Review

뜻을 써보고 전체 어구의 의미를 생각해 보시오.

01 a classical composer like Beethoven _____ 1107

02 fish snapping at the bait _____ 1115

03 a steep slope _____ 1123

04 slid the paper under the door _____ 1126

05 undergo treatment for severe depression _____ 1128

06 speak in dialect _____ 1141

07 urban slums _____ 1134

08 the so-called black box _____ 1140

09 affective disorders _____ 1135

10 devoted most of his time to his painting _____ 1149

11 suffer from diabetes _____ 1111

12 compete with others for a prize _____ 1132

13 yellow leaves floated down _____ 1143

14 compensate the victims for their loss _____ 1116

15 be soaked by the rain _____ 1144

16 the competence of the government _____ 1106

17 shine brightly _____ 1139

18 electronic devices _____ 1146

19 the car component industry _____ 1103

20 compose a poem _____ 1138

DAY 24

1151
agreeable
[əgríːəbəl]

adj. 유쾌한, 쾌활한 conforming to your own liking or feelings or nature
syn. pleasant, amiable, friendly

have an agreeable conversation 유쾌한 대화를 나누다

1152
replace
[ripléis]

v. 제자리에 놓다, 되돌리다 to substitute a person or thing for
syn. displace, reinstate, restore

replace the old 기존의 것을 대체하다

1153
rust
[rʌst]

n. 녹 reddish brown surface formed on iron

gather rust 녹슬다
with a rust-proof coating 녹 방지 코팅으로

1154
rude
[ruːd]

adj. 무례한, 거친 socially incorrect in behavior
syn. impolite, impudent

a rude comment 무례한 말 [논평]

1155
rotation
[routéiʃən]

n. 회전, 교대, 순환, 차례 the act of rotating as if on an axis
syn. turning, spinning, alternation

by rotation 차례로, 교대로

1156
rival
[ráivəl]

n. 경쟁자, 라이벌 the contestant you hope to defeat
syn. challenger, competitor, contender

a strong rival 강력한 라이벌

1157
rhyme
[raim]

n. 운, 시 correspondence in the sounds of two or more lines
syn. poem, verse, song

a poem written in rhyme 운율에 맞게 쓴 시

1158
productivity
[pròudʌktívəti]

n. 생산성, 생산력, 다산, 풍요 the quality of being productive or having the power to produce

labor productivity 노동 생산성

1159
proceed
[prousíːd]

v. 나아가다, 가다, 진행하다 to move ahead / travel onward in time or space
syn. continue, go on, carry on

proceed according to plan 계획대로 진행하다

1160
multiple
[mʌ́ltəpəl]

adj. 복합의, 복식의, 다양한 having or involving or consisting of more than one part or entity or individual

syn. many, manifold, plural, numerous, several

cause multiple side effects 다양한 부작용을 불러일으키다

1161
solve
[salv]

v. 해결하다, 풀다, 해독하다 to find the solution to or understand the meaning of

syn. resolve, settle, work out

solve the problem of waste disposal 쓰레기 처리 문제를 해결하다

1162
solitary
[sálitèri]
-sol 홀로

adj. 고독한, 쓸쓸한, 유일한 characterized by or preferring solitude

syn. lonely, seclude, only

a solitary life 고독한 삶

1163
statement
[stéitmənt]

n. 성명, 담화문, 진술 a message that is stated or declared

syn. announcement

issued an official statement 공식 발표를 했다

1164
stimulate
[stímjəlèit]

v. 자극하다, 촉진하다 to act as a stimulant

syn. inspire, encourage

ant. deter, stifle

stimulate discussion among students 학생들 간 토론을 활발하게 하다
stimulate trade 무역을 촉진하다

1165
storage
[stɔ́:ridʒ]

n. 저장, 보관 the act of storing something

syn. accumulation, reserve, reservoir

food storage facilities 식품 저장 시설

1166
tolerance
[tálərəns]

n. 관용, 인내 the power or capacity of an organism to tolerate unfavorable environmental conditions

syn. acceptance, respect, endurance

ant. intolerance

have no tolerance for jokes of any kind 어떤 종류의 농담도 용인하지 않다

1167
trace
[treis]

v. 추적하다, 발견하다 to follow, discover, or ascertain the course of development of something

syn. pursue, track, trail

trace deer 사슴을 추적하다

1168
unit
[júːnit]

n. 단위, 단위체 any division of quantity accepted as a standard of measurement or exchange

syn. part, portion, element, component

a unit price 단가

1169
unlock
[ʌnlák]

v. 자물쇠를 열다, 열다, 누설하다 to open the lock of

syn. open, reveal

unlock the mystery of the placebo effect 플라시보 효과의 신비를 밝히다

1170
victim
[víktim]

n. 희생자, 만만한 사람 an unfortunate person who suffers from some adverse circumstance

syn. casualty, game, sufferer, prey, fatality

a victim of circumstance 환경의 희생자 (처한 환경의 영향을 받은 범죄자 · 부랑아 등)

1171
process
[práses]
-cess 가다

n. 진행, 경과, 과정 a particular course of action intended to achieve a result

syn. procedure, operation

the process of growth 성장의 과정

1172
hold
[hould]

v. 1 열다, 주최하다 2 보유하다, 잡다 to organize or be responsible for / to have or keep in your hand, arms, etc.

syn. 1 preside over, conduct 2 clench, clutch, grip

the Festival will be held in this city 그 축제가 이 도시에서 열린다

hold the ladder steady 사다리를 꽉 잡다

1173
expectation
[èkspektéiʃən]

n. 예상, 기대 belief about the future

syn. outlook, prospect

without much expectation 많은 기대를 하지 않고

1174
exaggerate
[igzǽdʒərèit]

v. 과장하다, 침소봉대하다   to enlarge beyond bounds or the truth

syn. overstate, magnify, amplify

the economic benefits of casinos are greatly exaggerated
카지노의 경제적인 이익은 굉장히 과장되었다

1175
dysfunctional
[disfʌ́ŋkʃənəl]

adj. 기능장애의, 역기능의   dysfunctional relationships do not work normally and are not happy or successful

syn. nonadaptive

children from dysfunctional families 결손 가정 출신의 아동들

1176
drive
[draiv]

v. 몰다, 쫓아버리다   to force into or from an action or state, either physically or metaphorically

she drives me crazy 그녀 때문에 미치겠다

1177
dull
[dʌl]

adj. 지루한, 침체한 lacking in liveliness or animation

syn. subdued, slow, boring, tedious

trade is dull 불경기이다

1178
dozen
[dʌ́zn]

n. 다스, 12개 a group of 12 people or things

syn. twelve

in dozens 다스로, 한 다스씩

1179
divide
[diváid]

v. 나누다, 분할하다   to separate into parts or portions

syn. split, separate

the U.S. is divided into 50 states 미국은 50개의 주로 나뉜다

1180
distribution
[dìstrəbjúːʃən]
-dis 멀어짐

n. 유통, 분배   the act of delivering something to a store or business / the way that something is divided or spread out

syn. dispersion, spread, dispensation, division

illegal distribution of music and movies 음악과 영화의 불법 유통
the distribution of wealth 부의 분배

1181
multitasking
[mʌltitǽskiŋ]

n. 다중작업, 동시에 여러 가지 일을 할 수 있는 능력　the ability that can do a lot of work simultaneously

develop a smooth conversation manner and multitasking skills
원만한 화술과 많은 일들을 한꺼번에 처리하는 기술을 발전시키다

1182
moisture
[mɔ́istʃər]

n. 습기, 수분　wetness caused by water

syn. dampness, humidity, moistness

the moisture in the air 공기 중의 습기

1183
praise
[preiz]

n. 칭찬　an expression of approval and commendation

syn. applause, cheering, compliment

in return for praise 칭찬에 대한 보답으로

1184
predator
[prédətər]

n. 약탈자, 포식자, 육식동물　someone who attacks in search of booty

be attacked by predators 포식자들에게 공격을 받다

1185
priceless
[práislis]

adj. 값을 매길 수 없는, 대단히 중요한　very valuable

syn. invaluable, precious

ant. worthless

the value of the emerald is priceless 그 에메랄드의 가치는 값으로 매길 수 없다

1186
resell
[ri:sél]

v. 되팔다　to sell again after having bought it

syn. sell again

resell stocks 주식을 되팔다

1187
rescue
[réskju:]

v. 구조하다, 구하다　to free from harm or evil

syn. recover, save

ant. abandon

rescue up to six people at a time 한 번에 6명까지 구하다

1188
reproduce
[rì:prədjú:s]

v. 재생하다, 복제하다, 복사하다　to make a copy or equivalent of

syn. duplicate, copy, imitate

reproduce a severed branch 잘려나간 가지를 재생하다

reproduce in facsimile 원본대로 복사하다

1189
repair
[ripɛ́ə:r]

v. 고치다, 수리하다   to restore by replacing a part or putting together what is torn or broken

syn. mend, fix, restore

repaired her TV set TV를 고쳤다

1190
self-esteem
[sélfistí:m]

n. 자아 존중감, 자긍심   a feeling of pride in yourself

syn. selfpride

develop higher self-esteem 더 높은 자아 존중감을 발달시키다

1191
disturb
[distə́:rb]
-dis 멀어짐, 부정

v. 방해하다, 혼란시키다   to destroy the peace or tranquility of

syn. upset, trouble, interrupt

the noise disturbed my concentration 소음 때문에 집중하는데 방해가 됐다

1192
collaboration
[kəlǽbəréiʃən]
-co 함께

n. 협력, 협동   act of working jointly

syn. cooperation

work in collaboration 협업하다

1193
compost
[kámpoust]
-com 함께

n. 혼합물, 퇴비   a mixture of decaying vegetation and manure

compost heap 퇴비더미

1194
comprehend
[kàmprihénd]
-com 함께

v. 1 이해하다, 파악하다   2 포함하다   to get the meaning of something / to include in scope

syn. 1 understand   2 include, cover, embrace

read and comprehend the story 이야기를 읽고 이해하다

science comprehends many disciplines 과학에는 여러 분야가 있다

1195
by-product
[baiprádəkt]

n. 부산물, 부차적 결과 a secondary and sometimes unexpected consequence

syn. spin-off, offshoot

produce dangerous by-products 유해한 부산물들을 만들어내다

1196
atom
[ǽtəm]

n. 원자, 극소량　the smallest component of an element having the chemical properties of the element

syn. molecule, particle

the splitting of the atom 원자의 분열

1197
aural
[ɔ́:rəl]

adj. 귀의, 청각의　of or pertaining to hearing or the ear

improve aural perception 청각이 좋아지다

1198
attach
[ətǽtʃ]

v. 부착하다, 첨부하다, 붙이다, 애착심을 갖게 하다　to cause to be attached

syn. fasten, append, affix, tack, pin

ant. detach

the spider's thread attached to the window sill 창틀에 붙은 거미줄

1199
merciful
[mə́:rsifəl]

adj. 자비로운, 인정 많은　treating people with kindness and forgiveness

syn. benevolent, compassionate, humane, sympathetic

be merciful to the weak 약자에게 인정이 많다

1200
intervention
[ìntərvénʃən]

n. 개입, 간섭, 신의 중재　the act of intervening

syn. interference, interruption, mediation

armed intervention 무력 개입

Review

뜻을 써보고 전체 어구의 의미를 생각해 보시오.

01 improve aural perception _____ 1197

02 cause multiple side effects _____ 1160

03 food storage facilities _____ 1165

04 replace the old _____ 1152

05 be merciful to the weak _____ 1199

06 a poem written in rhyme _____ 1157

07 ① read and comprehend the story _____ 1194

　　② science comprehends many disciplines _____

08 reproduce in facsimile _____ 1188

09 develop higher self-esteem _____ 1190

10 work in collaboration _____ 1192

11 a victim of circumstance _____ 1170

12 trace deer _____ 1167

13 unlock the mystery of the placebo effect _____ 1169

14 trade is dull _____ 1177

15 she drives me crazy _____ 1176

16 solve the problem of waste disposal _____ 1161

17 labor productivity _____ 1158

18 without much expectation _____ 1173

19 in dozens _____ 1178

20 be attacked by predators _____ 1184

DAY 25

1201
retirement
[ritáiərmənt]

n. 은퇴, 은거, 퇴직　the state of being retired from one's business or occupation

syn. retreat, withdrawal

announce one's retirement 은퇴를 발표하다

1202
trim
[trim]

v. 손질하다　to remove the edges from and cut down to the desired size

syn. crop, shave

trim one's beard 턱수염을 가지런히 깎다

1203
stunning
[stʌ́niŋ]

adj. 기절할 만큼 놀라운, 멋진　very surprising or shocking

syn. astonishing, amazing

a stunning view of the lake 그 호수의 굉장히 멋진 광경

1204
retouch
[ri:tʌ́tʃ]

v. 손질하다, 수정하다　to rework in order to improve

syn. touch up, fix, repair, mend

retouch a photograph 사진을 수정하다

1205
subset
[sʌ́bsèt]
-sub 아래의

n. 부분 집합, 일부분　a set whose members are members of another set

a subset of total spending 총 비용의 일부분

1206
return
[ritə́:rn]

v. (원래대로) 되돌아가다, 돌려주다　to come back

syn. come back, reappear, replace

return to one's old habit 본래의 습관으로 돌아가다

1207
turmoil
[tə́:rmɔil]

n. 소란, 소동, 혼란, 불안　a violent disturbance

syn. agitation, unrest

ant. order

emotional turmoil 정서 불안

1208
substandard
[sʌ̀bstǽndərd]
-sub 아래의

adj. 표준 이하의, 규격 이하의　falling short of some prescribed norm

syn. inferior, second-rate

ant. standard, adequate

substandard goods 수준 이하의 제품

1209
quotation
[kwoʊtéiʃən]

n. 인용, 인용구 a short note recognizing a source of information or of a quoted passage

syn. citation, cite, acknowledgment, credit, reference, mention

illustrated his point with a quotation 인용하여 그의 요점을 설명했다

1210
revalidate
[ri:vǽlədèit]

v. 재확인하다, 갱신하다 to reconfirm[renew] something

syn. reconfirm

proposals to revalidate doctors regularly
의사들을 정기적으로 재허가 하자는 제안서

1211
curious
[kjúəriəs]

adj. 호기심 있는, 진기한, 기묘한 beyond or deviating from the usual or expected; eager to investigate

syn. prying, snoopy

ant. apathetic, indifferent

be curious about the film 그 영화가 궁금하다

1212
bumpy
[bʌ́mpi]

adj. 울퉁불퉁한, 덜컹덜컹하는 causing or characterized by jolts and irregular movements

syn. rough, rocky

ant. smooth

a bumpy country road 울퉁불퉁한 시골길

1213
cultivation
[kʌ̀ltəvéiʃən]

n. 경작, 재배 production of food by preparing the land to grow crops

syn. breeding

the cultivation of oysters 굴 양식

1214
breeze
[bri:z]

n. 산들바람, 미풍 a slight wind

a cool breeze blew by 시원한 산들바람이 불어왔다

1215
cuisine
[kwizí:n]

n. 요리, 요리법, 조리 the practice or manner of preparing food or the food so prepared

syn. culinary art, recipe

a mouthwatering cuisine 군침이 도는 요리

1216
complacent
[kəmpléisənt]
-plac 기쁘게 하다

adj. 현실에 안주하는, 자기만족의　contented to a fault with oneself or one's actions

syn. selfsatisfied, unconcerned

a dangerously complacent attitude 위험할 정도로 현실에 안주하는 태도

1217
comprehension
[kàmprihénʃən]

n. 이해, 이해력　ability to understand

syn. understanding, realization

be beyond one's comprehension 이해하기 어렵다

1218
conformity
[kənfɔ́:rməti]
-con 함께

n. 따름, 순응　correspondence in form or appearance

syn. uniformity, accord, harmony

ant. disparity, discord

be against global conformity 세계적 획일화에 반대하다

1219
cone
[koun]

n. 원뿔체, 원뿔꼴　any cone-shaped artifact

begin selling ice cream in waffle cones 와플 콘에 아이스크림을 팔기 시작하다

1220
wingspan
[wíŋspæn]

n. 날개길이　the distance from the tip of one of a pair of wings to that of the other

syn. wingspread

their wingspan can be almost 3 meters 날개폭은 거의 3m이다

1221
zealous
[zéləs]

adj. 열심인, 열광적인　feeling or showing strong and energetic support for a person, cause, etc.

syn. avid, enthusiastic, fervent

a zealous supporter 열렬한 지지자

1222
revolt
[rivóult]

n. 반란, 반역, 폭동　organized opposition to authority

syn. uprising, rebellion, mutiny

repress a revolt 반란을 진압하다

1223
uphold
[ʌphóuld]

v. 지지하다　to keep or maintain in unaltered condition

syn. defend, justify, support, maintain

cannot uphold such conduct 그런 행위는 지지할 수 없다

1224
revolution
[rèvəlúːʃən]

n. 혁명　a drastic and far-reaching change in ways of thinking and behaving

syn. revolt, rebellion, takeover

start a political revolution 정치 개혁을 시작하다

1225
wrap
[ræp]

v. 포장하다, 싸다, 마치다　to arrange or fold as a cover or protection

wrap up the two-day schedule 이틀간의 일정을 마치다

1226
withdraw
[wiðdrɔ́ː]

v. 1 철회하다 2 돈을 인출하다　to pull back or move away / to remove money from a bank account

syn. 1 back away, retreat　2 take out, extract, draw out

withdraw one's eyes from a scene 어떤 광경에서 눈을 돌리다

withdraw savings from an account 계좌에서 예금을 찾다

1227
revolutionize
[rèvəlúːʃənàiz]

v. 혁신을 일으키다　to change radically

syn. change, transform

revolutionize the world 세계를 변혁시키다

1228
preserve
[prizɔ́ːrv]

v. 유지하다, 보존하다　to keep or maintain in unaltered condition

syn. keep, maintain, guard, safeguard, conserve

ant. waste, abolish

preserve historical monuments 사적을 보존하다

1229
premonitory
[primánitɔ̀ːri]
-mon 경고

adj. 예고[전조]의　warning of future misfortune

syn. precursory

a premonitory advice 전조격의 충고

1230
reward
[riwɔ́ːrd]

n. 보수, 포상　a recompense for worthy acts or retribution for wrongdoing

syn. compensation, payment

offered a reward for his capture 그의 체포에 대해 포상을 내렸다

1231
escape
[iskéip]

v. 달아나다, 탈출하다   to run away from confinement
syn. flee, dodge

escape from a prison 교도소를 탈출하다

1232
reply
[riplái]

v. 대답하다, 응전하다   to react verbally
syn. answer, respond

reply to a question 질문에 답하다

1233
submerge
[səbmə́:rdʒ]
-sub 아래의

v. 물속에 잠그다   to sink below the surface
syn. immerse, plunge

submerge the pen point in the ink 펜촉을 잉크에 담그다

1234
represent
[rèprizént]

v. 대표하다   to act or speak officially for someone or something
syn. act for, speak for

represented his country at the meeting 회의에서 그의 국가를 대표했다

1235
establish
[istǽbliʃ]
-sta 서다

v. 설립하다, 설치하다   to set up or found
syn. install, organize

establish a university 대학을 설립하다

1236
drag
[dræg]

v. 끌고 가다, 질질 끌다   to draw slowly or heavily

dragged the chair over to the window 창 쪽으로 의자를 끌고 갔다
the debate has dragged on for good 논쟁은 끝없이 계속됐다

1237
draw
[drɔː]

v. 1 당기다, 이끌다 2 그리다   to cause to move by pulling / to make a mark or lines on a surface
syn. 1 pull, drag, haul 2 sketch, outline

draw a conclusion 결론을 이끌어내다
draw a line 선을 긋다

1238
customer
[kʌ́stəmər]

n. 손님, 고객   someone who pays for goods or services
syn. client

a regular customer 단골고객

1239
cue
[kju:]

n. 신호, 단서　an actor's line that immediately precedes and serves as a reminder for some action or speech

syn. hint, suggestion, sign, signal, clue

give a cue to start 시작 신호를 보내다

1240
budget
[bʌ́dʒit]

n. 예산, 재정　a sum of money allocated for a particular purpose

syn. funds, allowance

a large budget deficit 엄청난 재정 적자

1241
vote
[vout]

v. 투표하다　to cast a vote

the right to vote 투표[선거]권

1242
twofold
[túːfòuld]

adj. 두 배의, 이중적인　having more than one decidedly dissimilar aspects or qualities

syn. double, dual, doubled

a twofold increase 두 배의 증가

1243
oxygen
[ɑ́ksidʒən]

n. 산소　a chemical that is found in the air, that has no color, taste, or smell, and that is necessary for life

an oxygen breathing apparatus 산소 흡입기

1244
virtue
[vɔ́ːrtʃuː]

n. 미덕, 장점　the quality of doing what is right and avoiding what is wrong

syn. uprightness, integrity, honor

kindness is a virtue 친절은 하나의 미덕이다

1245
wholehearted
[hóulháːrtid]

adj. 전심의, 성심성의의　with unconditional and enthusiastic devotion

syn. sincere

wholehearted support 전폭적인 지지

1246
automobile
[ɔ́ːtəməbìːl]

n. 자동차　a motor vehicle with four wheels

syn. car, auto, machine, motorcar

the automobile industry 자동차 산업

207

1247
audience
[ɔ́:diəns]
-aud 듣다

n. 관객, 청중   a gathering of spectators or listeners at a performance

syn. gathering, spectators

the audience applauded 청중은 박수갈채를 보냈다

1248
awkward
[ɔ́:kwərd]

adj. 어색한, 서투른   causing inconvenience

syn. ungraceful, clumsy

feel awkward 어색해하다

due to their awkward English 그들의 서투른 영어 때문에

1249
backfire
[bǽkfàiər]

v. 역효과를 낳다   to come back to the originator of an action with an undesired effect

syn. backlash, recoil, boomerang

the strategy had backfired 그 전략은 역효과를 가져왔다

1250
consequently
[kánsikwəntli]
-sequ 뒤따르다

adv. 결과적으로   because of the reason given

syn. so, therefore, hence, accordingly

taxes were lowered, and consequently complaints were fewer
세금을 낮추자, 결과적으로 불평이 줄었다

Review

뜻을 써보고 전체 어구의 의미를 생각해 보시오.

01 escape from a prison _____ 1231

02 a zealous supporter _____ 1221

03 begin selling ice cream in waffle cones _____ 1219

04 cannot uphold such conduct _____ 1223

05 a large budget deficit _____ 1240

06 revolutionize the world _____ 1227

07 the audience applauded _____ 1247

08 their wingspan can be almost 3 meters _____ 1220

09 start a political revolution _____ 1224

10 wholehearted support _____ 1245

11 be against global conformity _____ 1218

12 a cool breeze blew by _____ 1214

13 ① draw a conclusion _____ 1237
　　② draw a line _____

14 wrap up the two-day schedule _____ 1225

15 a dangerously complacent attitude _____ 1216

16 kindness is a virtue _____ 1244

17 retouch a photograph _____ 1204

18 announce one's retirement _____ 1201

19 an oxygen breathing apparatus _____ 1243

20 a regular customer _____ 1238

DAY 26

1251
retina
[rétənə]

n. (눈의) 망막   the innermost light-sensitive membrane covering the back wall of the eyeball

contact the retina 망막에 닿다

1252
stubborn
[stʌ́bərn]

adj. 완고한, 끈질긴   tenaciously unwilling
syn. inflexible, unyielding

he's very stubborn 그는 매우 완고하다

1253
awesome
[ɔ́:səm]

adj. 굉장한, 멋진   inspiring awe or admiration or wonder
syn. impressive

that new car is totally awesome 저 차는 단연 최고다

1254
pursuit
[pərsú:t]

n. 추구, 수행   the act of pursuing in an effort to overtake or capture
syn. chase, pursual, following

the pursuit of happiness 행복의 추구
the pursuit of plan 계획의 수행

1255
overlap
[òuvərlǽp]

v. 겹치다, 일치하다   to coincide partially or wholly
syn. overlay, overlie, overhang

a fish's scales overlap each other 물고기의 비늘은 서로 겹쳐져 있다

1256
structure
[strʌ́ktʃər]
-struct 세우다

n. 구조, 건물   a thing constructed
syn. building

the economic structure of Korea 한국의 경제 구조

1257
problematic
[prɑ̀bləmǽtik]

adj. 문제가 되는   open to doubt or debate
syn. debatable, knotty, tough

the problematic situation 문제가 되는 상황

1258
visible
[vízəbəl]
-vis 보다

adj. 눈에 보이는, 명백한, 뚜렷한   capable of being seen / open to easy view
syn. perceptible, observable, perceivable

visible stars 눈에 보이는 별

1259
stuff
[stʌf]

n. 재료, 원료, 물자   the tangible substance that goes into the makeup of a physical object

syn. fabric, material, substance

building stuff 건축 자재

1260
vomit
[vámit]

v. 토하다, 게우다   to eject the contents of the stomach through the mouth

syn. throw up

the patient was vomiting blood 그 환자는 피를 토하고 있었다

1261
string
[striŋ]

n. 줄, 실, 일련   a lightweight cord

syn. cord, strand, thread, sequence, series

a string of violent attacks 일련의 폭력행위

1262
vital
[váitl]
-vit 생명

adj. 생명의, 치명적인, 중요한   urgently needed

syn. critical, lifesustaining

play a vital role in our society 우리 사회에서 필수적인 역할을 한다

1263
youth
[ju:θ]

n. 젊은이, 젊은 혈기   a young person

syn. boy

ant. adult, grown-up

youth unemployment 청년 실업

1264
striking
[stráikiŋ]

adj. 현저한, 두드러진   sensational in appearance or thrilling in effect

syn. attractive, dazzling, stunning

a striking idea 멋있는 생각

a striking feature 두드러진 특징

1265
unfocused
[ʌnfóukəst]

adj. 초점이 맞지 않는   not being in or brought into focus

syn. dispersed

ant. focused

unfocused questions 목적이 불분명한 질문

1266
twist
[twist]

v. 왜곡하다, 비틀다 to bend or turn something in order to change its shape

syn. twine, wind, bend, curl

ant. unwind, straighten

twist and alter the definition 정의를 왜곡하다

1267
ownership
[óunərʃìp]

n. 소유자임, 소유권 the relation of an owner to the thing possessed

syn. possession, title, entitlement

state ownership 국가 소유, 국유(國有)

1268
strive
[straiv]

v. 노력하다, 애쓰다, 싸우다 to attempt by employing effort

syn. attempt, endeavor, labor, struggle

strive against fate 운명에 맞서 싸우다

1269
curiosity
[kjùəriásəti]

n. 호기심 a state in which you want to learn more about something

syn. wonder, oddity, peculiarity

ant. apathy

curiosity killed the cat 지나친 호기심은 금물

1270
original
[ərídʒənəl]

adj. 최초의, 독창적인 preceding all others in time or being as first made or performed

syn. creative, innovative, inventive

a highly original design 매우 독창적인 디자인

1271
suspicion
[səspíʃən]

n. 의심 an impression that something might be the case

syn. disbelief, distrust, doubt,

ant. trust

harbor a suspicion 의심을 품다

1272
loss
[lɔ(:)s]

n. 손실, 실패 something that is lost

syn. damage

ant. gain

the loss of health 건강의 상실

1273
survive
[sərváiv]
-sur 초과하여
-viv 생명

v. 생존하다, 살아남다, ~보다 오래 살다　to continue to live through hardship or adversity / to live longer than
syn. exist, live, subsist, continue, outlast, outlive

survive without the air conditioner 에어컨 없이 생존하다
he survived his children 그는 자기 자식들보다 오래 살았다

1274
twinkle
[twíŋkəl]

v. 반짝이다　to shine intermittently with a sparkling light
syn. flicker, glimmer, glitter

twinkled like stars in the sky 그것들은 하늘의 별처럼 반짝였다

1275
sympathize
[símpəθàiz]
-path 고생하다, 느끼다

v. 동정하다, 측은히 여기다　to share the feelings of
syn. empathize, pity

sympathize with a person 아무에게 동정하다

1276
typically
[típikəli]

adv. 전형적으로, 일반적으로　in a typical manner
syn. normally, generally, usually

typically live in open spaces 전형적으로 열린 공간에서 산다

1277
unintended
[ʌninténdid]

adj. 의도하지 않은　not deliberate
syn. unintentional, unplanned
ant. intended, planned

an unintended suicide goal 의도되지 않은 자책골

1278
surpass
[sərpǽs]
-sur 초과하여

v. ~보다 낫다, ~을 능가하다　to distinguish oneself
syn. exceed, outclass, outdo, transcend
ant. fail

surpass the world record 세계 기록을 뛰어넘다

1279
worthwhile
[wə́ːrθhwáil]

adj. 보람이 있는, 시간을 들일만한　sufficiently valuable to justify the investment of time or interest
syn. rewarding, beneficial, productive
ant. pointless

a worthwhile book 읽을 만한 책

1280
swift
[swift]

adj. 날랜, 빠른 moving very fast

syn. brisk, fast, fleet

ant. slow

come up with swift measures 신속한 조치를 취하다

1281
sturdy
[stə́:rdi]

adj. 튼튼한, 건장한 having rugged physical strength

syn. firm, secure, solid, strong, stout

ant. flimsy, frail

sturdy young athletes 튼튼한 젊은 운동선수들

1282
condition
[kəndíʃən]

n. 조건, 상태, 환경 a state at a particular time

syn. circumstance, state

deal with various weather conditions 다양한 날씨 상황에 대처하다

1283
conscience
[kánʃəns]

n. 양심 a feeling that something you have done is morally wrong

syn. ethics, morals, sense of right and wrong

telling a lie goes against my conscience 거짓말을 하는 것은 내 양심에 어긋난다

1284
subject
[sʌ́bdʒikt]

n. 1 주제 2 학과 the subject matter of a conversation or discussion / branch of knowledge

syn. matter, theme, topic

investigate a subject 어떤 주제를 조사하다
fail two subjects 두 과목에서 실패하다

1285
exist
[igzíst]

v. 존재하다, 살다 to have an existence

syn. be, live

mars is too dry for life to exist 화성은 생명체가 살기에는 너무 건조하다

1286
symptom
[símptəm]

n. 징후, 증상 a change in the body or mind which indicates that a disease is present

syn. evidence, feature, indication

headache is a symptom of many diseases 두통은 여러 질병의 증상이다
symptoms of an inner turmoil 내분의 징후

1287
luxury
[lʌ́kʃəri]

n. 사치, 사치품　something that is an indulgence rather than a necessity

syn. high living, wealth, richness, well-being

live in luxury 호화롭게 살다

1288
sympathy
[símpəθi]

n. 동정, 헤아림　an inclination to support or be loyal to or to agree with an opinion

syn. compassion, empathy, pity

have[feel] sympathy for the poor 가난한 사람들에게 동정심을 갖다

1289
lower
[lóuər]

v. 낮추다, 내려가다　to move something or somebody to a lower position

syn. take down, let down, get down, bring down

lower the expectations 기대를 낮추다

1290
trip
[trip]

v. 발이 걸려 넘어지다, 헛디디다　to miss a step and fall or nearly fall

syn. stumble, topple, tumble

trip over the root of a tree 나무 뿌리에 걸려 넘어지다

1291
primary
[práimèri]
-prim 처음의

adj. 1 첫째의, 주요한 2 초기의　most important / happening or coming first

syn. 1 cardinal, chief, dominant　2 earliest, beginning

my primary goals in life 내 인생의 주요 목표
the primary stage of civilization 문명의 초기 단계

1292
stare
[stɛər]

v. 응시하다, 빤히 보다　to look at with fixed eyes

syn. eye, goggle, watch

stare a person up and down 아무를 빤히 위아래로 훑어보다

1293
present
[prézənt]

adj. 출석한, 현재의　being or existing in a specified place

syn. in attendance

ant. absent, away, missing

be present at the wedding 그 결혼식에 참석하다

1294
start
[stɑ:rt]

v. 출발하다, 시작하다 to take the first step or steps in carrying out an action

syn. begin, commence, depart

ant. end, finish, stop

the show starts at eight 쇼는 여덟시에 시작한다

1295
respect
[rispékt]
-spect 보다

n. 1 존경 2 관점 the condition of being honored / a particular way of thinking about or looking at something

syn. 1 regard, honor, recognition 2 point, matter, aspect

show respect 존경심을 표현하다
in all respects 모든 점에서

1296
respondent
[rispándənt]
-spond 약속

n. 응답자 someone who responds

syn. answerer

60% of the respondents agreed with the suggestion
그 응답자들 중 60%가 그 제안에 동의했다

1297
previous
[prí:viəs]
-pre 이전의

adj. 앞의, 이전의 just preceding something else in time or order

syn. earlier, prior

a previous engagement 선약

1298
status
[stéitəs]

n. 지위, 자격, 신분 the relative position or standing of things or especially persons in a society

syn. position, rank

marital status 결혼 여부

1299
respected
[rispéktid]

adj. 훌륭한, 평판이 좋은, 존경받는 receiving deferential regard

syn. admired, honored

a well-known and respected figure 유명하고 존경받는 인물

1300
unsuspecting
[ʌnsəspéktiŋ]

adj. 생각지도 못한, 의심하지 않는 not suspicious

syn. unsuspicious, trusting

deceiving the unsuspecting public 의심하지 않던 대중들을 속이기

Review

뜻을 써보고 전체 어구의 의미를 생각해 보시오.

01 survive without the air conditioner 　　　　　　　　　　　　　　　　1273

02 trip over the root of a tree 　　　　　　　　　　　　　　　　1290

03 a previous engagement 　　　　　　　　　　　　　　　　297

04 telling a lie goes against my conscience 　　　　　　　　　　　　　　　　1283

05 stare a person up and down 　　　　　　　　　　　　　　　　1292

06 marital status 　　　　　　　　　　　　　　　　1298

07 mars is too dry for life to exist 　　　　　　　　　　　　　　　　1285

08 lower the expectations 　　　　　　　　　　　　　　　　1289

09 visible stars 　　　　　　　　　　　　　　　　1258

10 live in luxury 　　　　　　　　　　　　　　　　1287

11 deal with various weather conditions 　　　　　　　　　　　　　　　　1282

12 sympathize with a person 　　　　　　　　　　　　　　　　1275

13 the economic structure of Korea 　　　　　　　　　　　　　　　　1256

14 symptoms of an inner turmoil 　　　　　　　　　　　　　　　　1286

15 the problematic situation 　　　　　　　　　　　　　　　　1257

16 twist and alter the definition 　　　　　　　　　　　　　　　　1266

17 strive against fate 　　　　　　　　　　　　　　　　1268

18 unfocused questions 　　　　　　　　　　　　　　　　1265

19 typically live in open spaces 　　　　　　　　　　　　　　　　1276

20 harbor a suspicion 　　　　　　　　　　　　　　　　1271

DAY 27

1301
representation
[rèprizentéiʃən]

n. 표현, 묘사   a presentation to the mind in the form of an idea or image
syn. depiction, illustration, image, symbol

a theatrical representation 연극의 상연

1302
quit
[kwit]

v. 그만두다, 떠나다   to give up
syn. discontinue, stop, cease, give up

quit a job 일을 그만두다

1303
request
[rikwést]
-quest 찾다, 추구하다

n. 요구, 요청   a formal message requesting something that is submitted to an authority
syn. call, inquiry

a storm of ad requests 쇄도하는 광고요청

1304
punish
[pʌ́niʃ]
-pun 처벌하다

v. 벌하다, 응징하다   to impose a penalty on / to inflict punishment on
syn. penalize

punish people who violate social rules 사회 규칙을 위반하는 사람을 벌하다

1305
reproduction
[rìːprədʌ́kʃən]

n. 재생, 복제, 번식   the process of generating offspring
syn. duplication, copy, remake

wildlife reproduction and vegetation growth 야생동물의 번식과 초목의 성장

1306
publicity
[pʌblísəti]
-publicist
n. 정치평론가, 홍보담당자

n. 홍보, 광고   a message issued in behalf of some product or cause or idea or person or institution
syn. promotion

a publicity campaign 공보[선전] 활동

1307
rob
[rab]

v. ~에서 훔치다, 강탈하다   to take something away by force or without the consent of the owner
syn. burglarize, cheat, loot

rob a person of his money 아무에게서 돈을 빼앗다
rob an empty house 빈 집을 털다

1308
plight
[plait]

n. 곤경, 어려움   a situation from which extrication is difficult especially an unpleasant or trying one
syn. predicament, difficulty, dilemma, pinch

the plight of the unemployed 실직자들의 곤경

1309
righteous
[ráitʃəs]

adj. 올바른, 정직한   characterized by or proceeding from accepted standards of morality or justice

syn. moral, virtuous, ethical

ant. immoral

righteous behavior 올바른 태도

1310
own
[oun]

v. 소유하다, 지배하다   to have ownership or possession of

syn. possess, have, hold

own three houses in Jejudo 제주도에 집 3채를 소유하고 있다

1311
ridiculous
[ridíkjələs]

adj. 우스운, 어리석은, 터무니없는   extremely silly or unreasonable

syn. absurd, foolish, laughable

ant. sensible

a ridiculous scheme 어처구니없는 계획

1312
still
[stil]

adj. 정지된, 소리 나지 않는   not in physical motion

syn. inactive, motionless, static

in a still photo 정지된 사진 속에서

1313
rot
[rɑt]

v. 썩다   to break down

syn. decompose, decay

the smell of rotting garbage 쓰레기 썩는 냄새

1314
merchant
[mɔ́:rtʃənt]

n. 상인, 무역상인   someone who buys and sells goods especially in large amounts

syn. dealer, retailer, salesman

a wholesale merchant 도매상

1315
rush
[rʌʃ]

v. 돌진하다, 급습하다   to move fast

syn. dash, hasten, hurry, race

rush to the scene 현장으로 달려가다

1316
migration
[maigréiʃən]

n. 이주, 이동   the movement of persons from one country or locality to another

syn. emigration, nomadism, relocation

seasonal migration (사람 · 동물의) 계절에 따른 이주[이동]

1317
respond
[rispánd]
-spond 약속

v. 응답하다, 응수하다   to show a response or a reaction to something

syn. react, answer

ant. question

respond to an insult with a blow 모욕에 대해 일격을 가하여 응수하다

1318
loosen
[lú:sən]

v. 풀다, 늦추다   to make something less tight or firm

syn. ease, relax, slacken

ant. tighten

loosened her belt for comfort 몸을 편하게 하기 위해 벨트를 풀었다

1319
restrain
[ri:stréin]

v. 제지하다, 금하다, 구속하다   to hold back

syn. bridle, check, control, curb

restrain a child from doing mischief 아이에게 장난을 못하게 하다
restrain one's anger 분노를 참다

1320
loom
[lu:m]

v. 불쑥 나타나다   to come into view indistinctly

a ferry loomed up in the fog 나룻배가 안개 속에서 불쑥 나타났다

1321
rural
[rúərəl]

adj. 시골의, 지방의   of or relating to the country, country people or life, or agriculture

syn. rustic, agricultural

ant. urban, cosmopolitan

a rural community 농촌

1322
lightning
[láitniŋ]

n. 번개   the flashes of light that are produced in the sky during a storm

a flash of lightning 번개 한 번 치는 것

1323
run
[rʌn]

v. 운영하다, 경영하다   to organize or be in charge of an activity, business, organization, or country

syn. be in charge of, own, head

ran a restaurant in Busan 부산에서 식당을 운영했다

1324
lift
[lift]

v. 1 들어 올리다 2 폐지하다   to raise from a lower to a higher position / to remove a rule or a law that says that something is not allowed

syn. 1 raise, pick up, hoist 2 revoke, end, remove

lifted the phone 전화기를 들었다
lift a tariff 관세를 폐지하다

1325
rub
[rʌb]

v. 문지르다, 쓰다듬다, 바르다   to move over something with pressure

syn. spread, apply, press, scrub

rub some ointment on the mosquito bites 모기 물린 데 연고를 바르다

1326
sympathetic
[sìmpəθétik]

adj. 동정적인, 인정 많은   feeling or showing concern about someone who is in a bad situation

syn. compassionate, warm, friendly, supportive

a sympathetic listener 동정심을 갖고 들어주는 사람

1327
knowledgeable
[nɑ́lidʒəbəl]

adj. 지식이 있는, 정통한   highly educated

syn. well-informed, acquainted

be very knowledgeable about the subject 그 주제에 대해 아주 잘 안다

1328
sprint
[sprint]

v. 전속력으로 달리다, 역주하다   to run very fast, usually for a short distance

syn. dash, rush

sprinted at full speed for one minute 전속력으로 1분간 역주했다

1329
justify
[dʒʌ́stəfài]
-jus 법, 정의

v. 정당화하다, 변명하다   to provide or be a good reason for something

syn. excuse

the end justifies the means 목적은 수단을 정당화 한다

1330
sprout
[spraut]

v. 싹이 트다, 발육[성장]하다   to produce new leaves, buds, etc.

syn. bud, shoot

new leaves sprouting from the trees 나무들에서 싹이 돋아나고 있는 새 잎들

1331
ivory
[áivəri]

n. 상아, 상아색   a hard white substance that forms the tusks of elephants and other animals

syn. tusk

a ban on the ivory trade 상아 무역 금지령

1332
spell
[spel]

v. 철자를 말하다[쓰다]   to form a word by writing or naming the letters in order

spell the word 그 단어 철자를 말하다

1333
irritation
[ìrətéiʃən]

n. 안달, 초조   the psychological state of being irritated or annoyed

syn. annoyance, provocation

feel a rising irritation 점점 안달 나다

1334
issue
[íʃuː]

n. 1 문제, 쟁점   2 발행, 호   something that people are talking about, thinking about, etc. / the version of a newspaper, magazine, etc.

syn. 1 topic, matter, problem   2 edition, printing, copy

current issues 현재의 문제들
the May issue of a magazine 잡지의 5월호

1335
stable
[stéibl]

adj. 안정된, 견고한, 지속적인   resistant to change of position or condition

syn. fixed, secure

ant. unstable, flimsy

stable foundations 견고한 토대

1336
invite
[inváit]

v. 초청하다, 초대하다   to call for someone to one's house

syn. ask, ask for

invited us to dinner 우리를 저녁 식사에 초대했다
invite questions 질문할 기회를 주다

1337
stake
[steik]

n. 1 말뚝 2 내기 밑천, 투자지분 a pole or stake set up to mark something

syn. 1 pole, stick 2 bet, interest, share

drive in a stake 말뚝을 박다
have a 76% stake in Kookmin Bank 국민은행에 76%의 지분이 있다

1338
investment
[invéstmənt]

n. 투자 the act of investing

encourage foreign investment 해외 투자를 장려하다

1339
substitute
[sʌ́bstitjùːt]
-stit 서다
-sub 아래의

v. 대체하다, 교체하다 to put or use someone or something in place of someone or something else

syn. exchange, switch, fill in

be substituted in the second 후반전에 교체되다

1340
instrument
[ínstrəmənt]

n. 악기, 도구, 기구, 수단 a device that requires skill for proper use

syn. tool, means, device, equipment

musical instrument 악기
an instrument of study 연구의 수단

1341
substantial
[səbstǽnʃəl]

adj. 상당한, 실질적인 large in amount, size, or number

syn. abundant, considerable

ant. meager, trivial

a substantial change 상당한 변화

1342
floppy
[flápi]

adj. 헐렁한, 축 늘어진, 유연한 hanging limply

syn. droopy, sagging

a dog with floppy ears 귀가 축 늘어진 개

1343
suburb
[sʌ́bəːrb]
-sub 아래의

n. 교외, 근교 a residential district located on the outskirts of a city

syn. outskirts

a suburb of London 런던 교외

1344
follow-up
[fálouʌ̀p]

n. 후속, 뒤를 따름　an activity that continues something that has already begun

take follow-up measures 후속조치를 취하다

1345
symbolic
[simbálik]

adj. 상징주의적인　relating to or using or proceeding by means of symbols

syn. characteristic, indicative, representative

one of Korea's symbolic places 한국의 상징적 장소 중 하나

1346
supervise
[súːpərvàiz]
-vis 보다

v. 지도하다, 감독하다, 감시하다　to watch and direct

syn. oversee

supervise building work 건설 공사를 감독하다

1347
forbid
[fərbíd]

v. 금하다　to command against

syn. prohibit, ban

forbid a person wine 아무에게 술을 금하다

1348
suit
[suːt]

n. 1 소송　2 정장　a claim or complaint that someone makes in a court of law / a set of clothes made from the same cloth, usually a jacket with trousers or a skirt

syn. 1 lawsuit, petition, plea　2 outfit

drop the patent suit 특허소송을 취하다
a business suit 비즈니스 정장

1349
extreme
[ikstríːm]

adj. 극도의, 지나친　of the greatest possible degree or extent or intensity

syn. utmost, ultimate

extreme measures 강경책

1350
sweep
[swiːp]
-sweeping a. 압도적인

v. 청소하다, 휩쓸다　to sweep across or over

syn. brush, broom, brush, tidy up

sweep up the leaves 낙엽을 쓸어버리다

Review

뜻을 써보고 전체 어구의 의미를 생각해 보시오.

01 encourage foreign investment _____ 1338

02 in a still photo _____ 1312

03 sweep up the leaves _____ 1350

04 the plight of the unemployed _____ 1308

05 a ridiculous scheme _____ 1311

06 rub some ointment on the mosquito bites _____ 1325

07 the smell of rotting garbage _____ 1313

08 supervise building work _____ 1346

09 ① drop the patent suit _____ 1348

   ② a business suit _____

10 rob a person of his money _____ 1307

11 a wholesale merchant _____ 1314

12 new leaves sprouting from the trees _____ 1330

13 respond to an insult with a blow _____ 1317

14 extreme measures _____ 1349

15 loosened her belt for comfort _____ 1318

16 the end justifies the means _____ 1329

17 righteous behavior _____ 1309

18 seasonal migration _____ 1316

19 invite questions _____ 1336

20 musical instrument _____ 1340

DAY 28

1351
worth
[wəːrθ]

prep. ~의 가치가 있는   worthy of being treated in a particular way

an actor worth several million dollars 수백만 달러의 가치가 있는 배우

1352
correctly
[kəréktli]
-rect 올바름

adv. 바르게, 정확하게   in an accurate manner

syn. right, aright

pronounce a word correctly 단어를 정확하게 발음하다

1353
article
[áːrtikl]

n. 기사, 논문   a piece of writing about a particular subject that is included in a magazine, newspaper, etc.

syn. essay, composition

read an article about Internet addiction 인터넷 중독에 대한 기사를 읽다

1354
disrupt
[disrʌ́pt]
-dis 멀어짐, 부정
-rupt 망치다

v. 방해하다, 혼란시키다   to make a break in

syn. interrupt, interfere

it disrupts all metabolic pathways 그것은 모든 신진대사 경로를 방해한다

1355
frequency
[fríːkwənsi]

n. 주파수, 빈번함 the number of occurrences within a given time period

use radio frequencies 라디오 주파수를 사용하다
decrease in frequency 빈도수가 줄다

1356
creation
[kriːéiʃən]

n. 창조, 창출   the human act of creating

syn. birth, nativity, formation

wealth creation 부의 창출

1357
heritage
[héritidʒ]
-heri 상속

n. 상속, 유산   practices that are handed down from the past by tradition

syn. legacy

Korea's rich cultural heritage 스페인의 풍부한 문화유산

1358
sorrow
[sárou]

n. 슬픔, 비애   a feeling of sadness or grief caused especially by the loss of someone or something

syn. anguish, grief

a life filled with joys and sorrows 기쁨과 슬픔으로 가득한 삶

1359
bottom
[bátəm]

n. 밑바닥, 근본　the lowest part, point, or level of something
syn. underside, undersurface, buttocks

at the bottom of each page 각 페이지 맨 아래 부분에

1360
utility
[ju:tíləti]
-pl. 유용한 것, 공공시설

n. 유용, 유익　the quality of being of practical use / the service provided by a public utility
syn. usefulness, convenience, advantage

pay the public utility bills 공공요금을 지불하다

1361
blend
[blend]

v. 섞다, 혼합하다　to combine into one / to blend or harmonize
syn. mix, merge, mingle

blend mayonnaise with other ingredients 마요네즈를 다른 재료와 섞다

1362
golden
[góuldən]

adj. 금빛의, 귀중한, 행복한　having the deep slightly brownish color of gold / very happy and successful
syn. precious, splendid, superb

golden days 황금기

1363
intrude
[intrú:d]

v. 침입하다, 간섭하다　to enter uninvited
syn. invade, interfere, interrupt

intrude our territorial waters 우리의 영해를 침범하다

1364
unnecessary
[ʌnnésəsèri]

adj. 불필요한, 쓸모없는　not necessary
syn. useless, unneeded

without feeling any unnecessary stress 불필요한 스트레스를 받지 않고

1365
freeze
[fri:z]

v. 얼다, 얼게 하다　to stop moving or become immobilized
syn. chill, harden, solidify
ant. thaw

it's freezing 몹시 춥다

1366
cramped
[kræmpt]

adj. 비좁고 갑갑한　constricted in size

live in a cramped little apartment 비좁은 아파트에 살다

1367
euphemism
[jú:fəmìzəm]

n. 완곡어법   a mild or pleasant word or phrase that is used instead of one that is unpleasant or offensive

employ a euphemism 완곡한 표현을 쓰다

1368
guest
[ɡest]

n. 손님, 특별손님   a visitor to whom hospitality is extended

syn. visitor, invitee

a guest of honor (만찬회 등의) 주빈

1369
contaminate
[kəntǽmənèit]
-con 함께

v. 오염시키다   to make impure

syn. pollute, foul

automobile fumes contaminate the air 자동차의 배기가스는 공기를 오염시킨다

1370
modify
[mádəfài]

v. 변경하다, 조절하다   to change some parts of something while not changing other parts

syn. alter, change, transform

modify a contract 계약을 변경하다

1371
criticism
[krítisìzəm]

n. 비평, 비판능력   disapproval expressed by pointing out faults or shortcomings

syn. judgement, critique

attract criticism 비판을 초래하다

1372
frighten
[fráitn]

v. 두려워하게 하다   to cause someone to become afraid

syn. scare, alarm, terrify, shock

frighten a cat away 고양이를 놀래어 쫓아 버리다

1373
instinct
[ínstiŋkt]

n. 본능, 직관   inborn pattern of behavior often responsive to specific stimuli

syn. intuition, feeling, impulse

women's instincts 여성의 직감

1374
credibility
[krèdəbíləti]
-cred 믿다

n. 신용, 신빙성   the quality of being believable or trustworthy

syn. reliability, trustworthiness, credibleness

establish the national credibility 국가의 신뢰도를 다지다

1375
misplace
[mispléis]

v. 잘못 두다   to place something where one cannot find it again

please don't misplace it 잃어버리지 않게 잘 간수하세요

1376
logical
[ládʒikəl]

adj. 논리적인, 논리상의   capable of or reflecting the capability for correct and valid reasoning

syn. clear, rational, coherent

a logical result 논리적인 결과

1377
gut
[gʌt]
-pl. 용기, 배짱

n. 장, 창자   the internal organs of an animal

syn. intestine, bowel

the large[small] gut 대[소]장

1378
visual
[víʒuəl]
-vis 보다

adj. 시각의, 눈에 보이는   relating to or using sight

syn. optical, visible, observable

the visual nerve 시신경

1379
whenever
[ʰwenévər]

conj. ~할 때마다   at any time when

whenever he made a presentation 그가 프레젠테이션을 할 때마다

1380
create
[kriːéit]

v. 만들다, 창조하다   to make or cause to be or to become

syn. originate, make, cause

create a lot of problems 많은 문제들을 유발하다

1381
florist
[flɔ́(ː)rist]

n. 화초 재배자, 꽃장수   someone who grows and sells flowers

work with a florist 꽃집에서 일하다

1382
injure
[índʒər]

v. 상처를 입히다   to cause injuries or bodily harm to

syn. harm

she fell and injured herself 그녀는 넘어져 다쳤다

1383
millennium
[miléniəm]
-enn 해, 년

n. 천년간, 황금시대   a span of a thousand years

in the beginning of the millennium 새 천 년이 시작할 때에

1384
origin
[ɔ́:rədʒin]

n. 기원　the place where something begins, where it springs into being

syn. beginning, derivation, root, source

the origin of civilization 문명의 기원

1385
transformation
[trænsfərméiʃən]
-form 형성하다
-trans 가로질러

n. 변형, 변화　a change into someone or something completely different

syn. change, evolution

an economic transformation 경제적 변화
undergo a complete transformation 완전한 탈바꿈 과정을 겪다

1386
practically
[prǽktikəli]

adv. 실제적으로, 실용적으로　in a practical manner

syn. almost, nearly

practically guarantees success 사실상 성공을 보장하다

1387
appliance
[əpláiəns]

n. 기구, 장치, 장비　a device or control that is very useful for a particular job

syn. apparatus, device, machine

from bottles to electric appliances 병에서 전기기구까지

1388
contract
[kántrækt]
-con 함께
-tract 끌다

v. 1 계약하다　2 수축하다　to engage by written agreement / to become smaller

syn. 1 make a deal　2 reduce, shorten

contract an alliance with Russia 러시아와 동맹을 맺다
the hot metal contracted as it cooled 뜨거운 철이 식자 수축했다

1389
govern
[ɡʌ́vərn]

v. 통치하다, 다스리다, 운영하다　to control and manage an area, city, or country and its people

syn. regulate, regularize, order

govern a public enterprise 공공 기업을 운용하다

1390
transmit
[trænsmít]
-mit 전송하다
-trans 가로질러

v. 보내다, 전송하다, (병을) 옮기다　to transfer to another

syn. convey, deliver, dispatch

signals transmitted from a satellite 위성에서 전송된 신호
transmit one's illness 병을 옮기다

1391
apply
[əplái]

v. 1 적용하다[되다] 2 지원하다, 신청하다   to have an effect on or to concern a particular person, group, or situation / to ask formally for something usually in writing

syn. 1 fit, suit 2 request, seek, appeal

the way does not apply to the case 그 방법은 이 경우에 맞지 않다
apply for a job 일자리에 응모하다

1392
correspond
[kɔ̀:rəspánd]
-co 함께
-spond 약속

v. 일치하다, 부합하다   to be compatible, similar or consistent

syn. agree, harmonize, accord, match

correspond roughly 대략 일치하다

1393
draft
[dræft]

n. 초안, 입안   a document ordering the payment of money

syn. sketch

a draft of the contract 계약서 초안

1394
correspondence
[kɔ̀:rəspándəns]
-co 함께
-spond 약속

n. 서신교환, 대응, 연락   the activity of writing letters or e-mails to someone

online correspondence can be monitored 온라인 편지는 감시될 수도 있다

1395
annoying
[ənɔ́iiŋ]

adj. 성가신, 귀찮은   causing irritation or annoyance

syn. bothersome, irritating

annoying questions 성가신 질문들

1396
summit
[sʌ́mit]

n. 정상, 꼭대기   the highest level or degree attainable

syn. apex, crest, crown

a summit conference 수뇌[정상] 회담

1397
following
[fálouiŋ]

adj. 다음의, 그 뒤에 오는   coming next

syn. coming, next, succeeding

ant. precedent, previous

in the following year 그 다음 해에

1398
pursue
[pərsú:]

v. 뒤쫓다, 추구하다　to follow and try to catch or capture something /
to try to get or do something over a period of time
syn. follow

pursue a robber 강도를 뒤쫓다
pursue pleasure 쾌락을 추구하다

1399
question
[kwéstʃən]

v. 묻다, 신문하다, 의문으로 여기다　to pose a series of questions to
syn. interrogate

question a suspect 용의자를 신문하다

1400
stillness
[stílnis]

n. 고요함, 정적　a state of no motion or movement

in the stillness of the lab
실습실의 고요함 속에서

Review

뜻을 써보고 전체 어구의 의미를 생각해 보시오.

01 please don't misplace it _____ 1375

02 ① the way does not apply to the case _____ 1391

  ② apply for a job _____

03 correspond roughly _____ 1392

04 question a suspect _____ 1399

05 automobile fumes contaminate the air _____ 1369

06 pursue a robber _____ 1398

07 wealth creation _____ 1356

08 the origin of civilization _____ 1384

09 pronounce a word correctly _____ 1352

10 it disrupts all metabolic pathways _____ 1354

11 employ a euphemism _____ 1367

12 a life filled with joys and sorrows _____ 1358

13 modify a contract _____ 1370

14 in the beginning of the millennium _____ 1383

15 in the following year _____ 1397

16 frighten a cat away _____ 1372

17 intrude our territorial waters _____ 1363

18 without feeling any unnecessary stress _____ 1364

19 women's instincts _____ 1373

20 govern a public enterprise _____ 1389

1401
breathe
[briːð]
-breath n. 숨

v. 숨을 쉬다   to move air into and out of your lungs
syn. take a breath, respire

breathed deeply before speaking again 다시 말을 하기 전에 심호흡을 했다

1402
fur
[fəːr]

n. 모피, 부드러운 털   the hairy coat of an animal
syn. pelt

wear fur coats 털 코트를 입다

1403
consideration
[kənsìdəréiʃən]

n. 고려, 고려의 대상   the process of giving careful thought to something
syn. thinking, reflection

give a serious consideration 심각하게 고려하다

1404
infrequent
[infríːkwənt]

adj. 희귀한, 드문   not occurring regularly or at short intervals
syn. scarce, scant, sparse

infrequent visits 드문 방문

1405
nevertheless
[nèvərðəlés]

adv. 그럼에도 불구하고   despite anything to the contrary
syn. nonetheless

a predictable, but nevertheless funny, story 뻔하지만, 그래도, 재미있는 이야기

1406
crooked
[krúkid]

adj. 구부러진, 부정직한   not straight or aligned
syn. curled, curling, curved

crooked country roads 구불구불한 시골길

1407
likewise
[láikwàiz]

adv. 똑같이, 비슷하게   in the same way
syn. similarly, as well

watch him and do likewise 그가 하는 것을 보고 똑같이 해라

1408
order
[ɔ́ːrdər]

n. 1 명령   2 질서   a command given by a superior / a situation in which everything is well organized or arranged
syn. 1 command, mandate   2 harmony, regularity

an order, not a request 요청이 아닌 명령
in alphabetical order 알파벳 순(順)으로

1409
attractive
[ətrǽktiv]
-tract 끌다

adj. 매력적인 pleasing to the eye or mind especially through beauty or charm

syn. inviting, appealing

make it a very attractive place to work 일하기에 매우 매력적인 곳으로 만들다

1410
cupboard
[kʌ́bərd]

n. 찬장 a small room or cabinet used for storage space

syn. closet

a pot is next to the cupboard 찬장 옆에 냄비가 있다

1411
install
[instɔ́:l]

v. 설치하다, 장착하다 to set up for use

syn. put in, set up

install CCTVs on the corridors 복도에 CCTV를 설치하다

1412
counter
[káuntər]

v. 반대하다, 억제하다 to take action in order to oppose or stop something or reduce its negative effects

syn. block, resist

caffeine is known to counter tiredness
카페인은 피로를 억제하는 것으로 알려져 있다

1413
overwhelming
[òuvərhwélmiŋ]

adj. 압도적인, 불가항력적인 so strong as to be irresistible

syn. crushing, stunning, severe, overpowering

an overwhelming disaster 불가항력적 재해
an overwhelming victory 압도적 승리

1414
misuse
[misjú:z]

v. 잘못 사용하다, 남용하다 to use incorrectly

syn. abuse

misuse robots 로봇을 잘못 사용하다
misuse one's power 권력을 남용하다

1415
pure
[pjuər]

adj. 순수한, 순전한, 완전한 not mixed with anything else

syn. faultless, innocent

ant. tainted, mixed

a work of pure genius 완전한 천재의 작품
pure gold 순금

1416
surprise
[sərpráiz]

v. 깜짝 놀라게 하다　to cause to be surprised

syn. astonish, astound, shock, startle

nothing surprises him 어떤 것도 그를 놀라게 하지 못한다

1417
conceal
[kənsíːl]
-con 함께

v. 숨기다, 비밀로 하다　to prevent from being seen or discovered

syn. hide, mask, camouflage

try to conceal the scandal 스캔들을 감추려고 애쓰다

1418
wound
[wuːnd]

n. 부상, 상처　an injury to living tissue

syn. injury, hurt, sore, cut

a knife wound 칼에 베인 상처

1419
assert
[əsə́ːrt]

v. 단언하다, 주장하다　to state firmly that something is true

syn. affirm, declare, state

assert one's rights 자신의 권리를 주장하다

1420
consistency
[əsə́ːrt]
-con 함께
-sist 서다

n. 일관성　the property of holding together and retaining its shape

syn. coherence

his statements lacked consistency 그의 진술은 일관성이 부족했다

1421
hopeless
[hóuplis]

adj. 절망적인　without hope because there seems to be no possibility of comfort or success

syn. despairing, despondent, desperate

for a moment I felt hopeless 잠시 동안 나는 절망감을 느꼈다

1422
mist
[mist]

n. 안개, 흐릿함　a thin fog with condensation near the ground

syn. haze, fog

a thick mist 짙은 안개

1423
probe
[proub]

v. 탐침으로 찾다, 면밀히 조사하다　to look into or examine something carefully

syn. dig into, explore, research

unmanned vehicles probed space 무인 우주선이 우주를 탐사했다

1424
corresponding
[kɔ̀:rəspándiŋ]
-co 함께
-spond 약속

adj. 상응하는, 같은   similar especially in position or purpose

syn. matching, parallel

in the corresponding period of last year 작년 같은 기간에 있어서

1425
exchange
[ikstʃéindʒ]

v. 교환하다, 환전하다   to give to, and receive from, one another

syn. change, interchange

exchange prisoners 포로를 교환하다

1426
mode
[moud]

n. 모드, 형태, 양식   how something is done or how it happens

syn. manner, way, method

a mode of energy 에너지의 한 형태

all modes of reading are not equal 독서 방식은 모두 동일한 것이 아니다

1427
conceive
[kənsí:v]
-con 함께
-ceive 받다

v. 1 생각하다, 고안하다   2 임신하다   to have the idea for / to become pregnant

syn. 1 imagine, envisage 2 become pregnant

a badly conceived design 엉터리로 고안된 디자인

conceive a child 아기를 임신하다

1428
author
[ɔ́:θər]

n. 저자, 작품, 장본인   a person who has written a book or who writes many books

syn. writer

remember the name of the author 그 저자의 이름을 기억해내다

1429
greenery
[grí:nəri]

n. 푸른 잎, 푸른 나무   green foliage

syn. verdure

be decorated with flowers and greenery 꽃과 식물들로 꾸며져 있다

1430
branch
[bræntʃ]

n. 나무 가지, 지점   a division of some larger or more complex organization

syn. subdivision

an overseas branch 해외지점

1431
dwelling
[dwéliŋ]

n. 집, 주소   housing that someone is living in
syn. home, domicile

built a modest dwelling near the pond 연못 근처에 적당한 집 한 채를 지었다

1432
intellectual
[ìntəléktʃuəl]

adj. 지적인, 지능적인   of or associated with or requiring the use of the mind
syn. intelligent, rational

people with intellectual disabilities 지적 장애인들

1433
contribution
[kàntrəbjúːʃən]

n. 기부, 기고, 기여   something that you do that helps to achieve something or to make it successful
syn. charity, donation

make a contribution to charity 자선단체에 기부하다

1434
mount
[maunt]

v. 타다, 탑재하다   to go up or advance
syn. climb

mount a platform 등단(登壇)하다
mount on a horse 말을 타다

1435
intensity
[inténsəti]
-tens 뻗다

n. 강렬함, 집중   the amount of energy transmitted
syn. concentration, strength

gather intensity 격렬함을 더하다
the degree of intensity 강도

1436
foster
[fɔ́(ː)stər]

v. 양육하다, 촉진하다   to help something grow or develop
syn. raise, bring up, nurture, promote

foster competitiveness 경쟁력을 키우다
foster company morale 직원들의 사기를 진작시키다

1437
conceit
[kənsíːt]

n. 자부심, 자만   feelings of excessive pride
syn. pride, arrogance

be full of conceit 자만심을 꽉 차 있다

1438
probability
[pràbəbíləti]

n. 확률, 있음직함 a measure of how likely it is that some event will occur

syn. chance

determine the probability of a particular event
특정한 사건이 일어날 확률을 판단하다

1439
attract
[ətrǽkt]
-tract 끌다

v. 끌다, 매혹하다 to direct toward itself or oneself by means of some psychological power or physical attributes

syn. pull, draw, appeal

attract tourists and make money 관광객을 유치하고 돈을 벌다

1440
blindness
[bláindnis]

n. 맹목, 무분별 the state of being blind or lacking sight

syn. recklessness, ignorance

love is blindness 사랑은 맹목이다

1441
grab
[grǽb]

v. 움켜잡다 to quickly take and hold something with your hand or arms

syn. catch, take hold of

he grabbed me by the arm 그가 내 팔을 붙잡았다

1442
application
[æ̀plikéiʃən]

n. 적용, 신청, 지원 an act of applying

the application of a theory to a case 이론을 사례에 적용시키기
the application of medicine to a wound 상처에 약을 바르기

1443
equilibrium
[ì:kwəlíbriəm]

n. 균형, 평정 a state in which opposing forces or actions are balanced

syn. balance, stability, steadiness

lose one's equilibrium 마음의 평정을 잃다

1444
injury
[índʒəri]

n. 상해, 손상, 부상 any physical damage to the body caused by violence or accident or fracture, etc.

syn. hurt, harm

finish the event without an injury 부상 없이 경기를 끝내다

1445
minority
[minɔ́:riti]
-min 작은, 소형의

n. 소수파 a group of people who differ racially or politically from a larger group of which it is a part

a minority party 소수당

1446
appreciate
[əprí:ʃièit]

v. 1 평가하다, 이해하다   2 감사하다   to understand the worth or importante of something / to be grateful for something

syn. 1 acknowledge, recognize 2 thank, cherish

appreciate the dangers of a situation 사태가 위험함을 알아채다
I appreciate your help 도와주셔서 감사합니다

1447
originate
[ərídʒənèit]

v. 시작하다, 생기다   to come into existence

syn. arise, rise, develop, spring up

Mocha originated from Yemen 모카는 예멘에서 유래되었다

1448
blurred
[blə:rd]

adj. 선명하지 않은, 흐릿해진   indistinct or hazy in outline

syn. bleary, blurry, foggy, fuzzy

a blurred photo 흐릿한 사진

1449
supreme
[səprí:m]

adj. 최고의, 최상의, 가장 중요한   final or last in your life or progress

syn. ultimate

ant. inferior, mediocre

a supreme work of art 최고의 예술작품

1450
practice
[prǽktis]

n. 실행, 연습, 습관   a customary way of operation or behavior

syn. exercise, drill, practise

a harmful practice 해로운 습관
a writing practice 쓰기 연습

Review

뜻을 써보고 전체 어구의 의미를 생각해 보시오.

01 make it a very attractive place to work   1409

02 nothing surprises him   1416

03 a knife wound   1418

04 people with intellectual disabilities   1432

05 infrequent visits   1404

06 try to conceal the scandal   1417

07 the application of a theory to a case   1442

08 a predictable, but nevertheless funny, story   1405

09 exchange prisoners   1425

10 a writing practice   1450

11 ① a badly conceived design   1427
　 ② conceive a child

12 wear fur coats   1402

13 attract tourists and make money   1439

14 assert one's rights   1419

15 be decorated with flowers and greenery   1429

16 watch him and do likewise   1407

17 breathed deeply before speaking again   1401

18 a thick mist   1422

19 an overwhelming disaster   1413

20 pure gold   1415

DAY 30

1451
block
[blɑk]

v. 막다, 방해하다 to be placed in front of something so that people or things cannot pass through

syn. barricade, blockade, stop

block the sun 해를 가리다

1452
concentrate
[kánsəntrèit]
-con 함께
-centr 중간

v. (정신을) 집중하다 to direct one's attention on something

syn. center, focus

concentrate upon a problem 어떤 문제에 전념하다

1453
annoyed
[ənɔ́id]

adj. 짜증난 feeling slightly angry or impatient

syn. irritated, pissed off

an annoyed driver 짜증난 운전자

1454
virtual
[və́:rtʃuəl]

adj. 1 거의 ~와 다름없는 2 가상의 almost the same as the thing that is mentioned / created by computers, or appearing on computers or the Internet

a virtual defeat 사실상의 패배
virtual reality 가상현실

1455
confine
[kənfáin]
-fin 끝

v. 국한하다, 제한하다 to place limits on

syn. restrict, restrain

confine a talk to ten minutes 대화를 10분으로 제한하다

1456
prevailing
[privéiliŋ]

adj. 널리 보급되어 있는, 지배적인 most frequent or common

syn. dominant

the prevailing speculations 지배적인 견해

1457
social
[sóuʃəl]

adj. 사회의, 사교적인 relating to human society and its members

syn. group, communal, collective

social reforms 사회개혁

1458
overseas
[óuvərsíːz]

adv. 해외에서, 해외로 가는   beyond or across the sea
syn. abroad

lived overseas for a time 한동안 해외에 거주했다

1459
consequence
[kánsikwèns]
-sequ 뒤따르다

n. 결과, 중대성   something that happens as a result of a particular action or set of conditions
syn. result, effect, outcome

lead to undesirable consequences 원하지 않는 결과로 이어지다

1460
display
[displéi]

v. 보이다, 표현하다   to show or express something
syn. exhibit, express

display the artistic talents 예술적 재능을 선보이다

1461
minimal
[mínəməl]

adj. 최소의, 극미한   the least possible
syn. minimum, smallest, slightest

dishes with minimal fat 최소한의 지방이 든 음식

1462
solitude
[sálitʃùːd]
-sol 홀로

n. 고독, 외로움   a state of social isolation
syn. seclusion, privacy, retirement

in solitude 홀로, 외로이

1463
current
[kə́ːrənt]

adj. 현재의, 지금의   occurring in or belonging to the present time
syn. present

current law 현행법

1464
guess
[ges]

n. 추측, 추정   a message expressing an opinion based on incomplete evidence
syn. estimate, conjecture, assumption

take a guess 추측하다

1465
sparkling
[spáːrkliŋ]

adj. 반짝이는   shining with brilliant points of light like stars
syn. glittering

the sparkling waters of the lake 반짝거리는 호수의 물
sparkling eyes 반짝이는 눈

1466
crowded
[kráudid]

adj. 붐비는, 혼잡한   overfilled or compacted or concentrated
syn. packed

a crowded theater 만원인 극장

1467
livelihood
[láivlihùd]

n. 생계, 살림   the financial means whereby one lives
syn. bread and butter, living

earn a livelihood by writing 문필로 생계를 세우다

1468
messy
[mési]

adj. 어질러진, 더러운   dirty and disorderly
syn. untidy, tangled

messy hair 엉망인 머리

1469
survey
[sə:rvéi]

n. 조사, 연구, 평가   a detailed critical inspection
syn. analysis, examination, investigation

according to a recent survey 최근 조사에 따르면

1470
predict
[pridíkt]
-pre 이전의
-dict 말하다

v. 예언하다, 예보하다, 예측하다   to make a prediction about
syn. foretell, anticipate

predict the results 결과를 예측하다

1471
conclusion
[kənklú:ʒən]
-con 함께
-clus 닫다

n. 결론, 종료   a position or opinion or judgment reached after consideration
syn. outcome, result

come to the conclusion 결론에 도달하다

1472
merchandise
[mə́:rtʃəndàiz]

n. 상품, 제품   commodities offered for sale

focusing on merchandise exportation 상품 수출에 초점을 맞추기

1473
universe
[júːnəvə̀:rs]

n. 우주, 세계   all of space and everything in it
syn. cosmos

the origin of the universe 우주의 기원

1474
locate
[loukéit]

v. 1 ~의 위치를 알아내다 2 ~에 위치를 정하다   to discover the location of / to determine the place of

a country located in the middle of Europe 유럽의 중앙에 위치한 나라
locate an office in Paris 파리에 사무실을 두다

1475
confirm
[kənfə́:rm]
-con 함께

v. 확증하다, 확인하다   to establish or strengthen as with new evidence or facts

syn. assure, verify, prove

confirm a reservation 예약을 확정하다

1476
properly
[prápərli]

adv. 적당하게, 제대로   in the right manner

breathe properly 제대로 호흡하다

1477
noisy
[nɔ́izi]

adj. 떠들썩한, 시끄러운   full of loud and nonmusical sounds

syn. loud, clamorous, lively

a noisy cafeteria 시끄러운 식당

1478
solid
[sálid]
-sol 홀로

adj. 고체의, 탄탄한, 훌륭한   hard or firm, with a fixed shape, and not a liquid or gas

display solid performances 탄탄한 경기력을 보여주다
create solid results 좋은 결과를 내다

1479
organization
[ɔ̀:rgənəzéiʃən]

n. 조직, 조직체   a group of people who work together

syn. association, corporation

through a nonprofit organization 비영리 재단을 통하여

1480
wholly
[hóulli]

adv. 완전히   to a complete degree or to the full or entire extent

syn. entirely, completely, totally

few men are wholly bad 완전히 나쁜 사람은 거의 없다

1481
transparent
[trænspɛ́ərənt]
-trans 가로질러

adj. 투명한, 명료한 able to be seen through / easy to notice or understand

syn. clear, crystal, lucid
ant. murky, vague

a transparent plastic container 투명한 플라스틱 용기

1482
unless
[ənlés]

conj. ~하지 않으면 (used to say that something will happen or be true if something else does not happen or is not true)

syn. if ~ not

unless you go, I won't go 네가 안 가면 나도 안 갈 거야

1483
wholesale
[hóulsèil]

adv. 도매의, 대량의 at a wholesale price

syn. in large quantities

buy food wholesale 대량으로 음식을 사다

1484
transport
[trænspɔ́ːrt]
-port 문
-trans 가로질러

v. 운송하다, 수송하다 to carry someone or something from one place to another

syn. carry, ship, deliver

the cost of transporting goods 상품의 운송비용

1485
inland
[ínlənd]

adj. 내륙의, 국내의 situated away from an area's coast or border

inland transportation 국내수송

1486
tip
[tip]

v. 기울다 to move into a sloping position, so that one end or side is higher than the other, or to make something do this

syn. tilt

his head tipped to one side 그의 머리가 한 쪽으로 기울었다

1487
approach
[əpróutʃ]

v. 접근하다, 다가가다 to move towards

syn. access

approach completion 완성에 가깝다

1488
surface
[sə́ːrfis]

n. 표면, 외면, 외부 an outside part or layer of something

syn. covering, exterior, outside

an uneven road surface 고르지 않은 도로 표면

1489
inner
[ínər]

adj. 내면, 내부의, 내적인 located inward

syn. inside, interior, internal

develop inner beauty 내면의 아름다움을 가꾸다

1490
board
[bɔːrd]

n. 1 보드, 판자 2 위원회, 이사회 a long, thin, flat piece of wood / a committee having supervisory powers

nailed some boards over the broken window 깨진 창에 판자를 못 박았다
board of directors 이사회

1491
sophisticated
[səfístəkèitid]

adj. 세련된, 정교한, 복잡한 highly developed and complex
syn. cultured, refined, complicated
ant. simple

a sophisticated design 세련된 디자인

1492
blood pressure
[blʌ́d préʃər]
-press 밀다

n. 혈압 the pressure of the circulating blood against the walls of the blood vessels

suffer from high blood pressure 고혈압으로 고통을 겪다

1493
continue
[kəntínjuː]

v. 계속하다, 지속시키다 to continue a certain state, condition, or activity
syn. go on, proceed

continued to work into the night 밤까지 계속해서 일을 했다

1494
swap
[swɑp]

v. 물물 교환하다 to give something to someone and receive something in return
syn. exchange, switch

swap jokes 농담을 주고받다

1495
extraordinary
[ikstrɔ́ːrdənèri]

adj. 대단한, 터무니없는 beyond what is ordinary or usual
syn. unusual, amazing, marvelous

an extraordinary achievement 대단한 업적

1496
insignificant
[ìnsignífikənt]

adj. 미미한, 하찮은 small or unimportant
syn. inconsequential, inessential, unimportant, petty

lost an insignificant amount of money 몇 푼 안 되는 돈을 분실했다

1497

unfortunately

[ʌnfɔ́ːrtʃənitli]

adv. 불행히도   by bad luck

syn. unluckily, regrettably

unfortunately it rained all day 불행히도 하루 종일 비가 왔다

1498

lock

[lɑk]

v. 자물쇠를 채우다   to fasten with a lock

syn. bolt, padlock, hook, clamp

lock the bike to the fence 자전거를 울타리에 잠그다

lock the door 문을 잠그다

1499

focus

[fóukəs]

v. 초점을 맞추다, 주목하다   to direct one's attention on something

syn. concentrate, center, rivet

focus on one's studies 공부에 집중하다

1500

credible

[krédəbəl]

-cred 믿다

adj. 신용할 수 있는, 확실한   capable of being believed

syn. reliable, believable, trustworthy

credible information 믿을 수 있는 정보

Review

뜻을 써보고 전체 어구의 의미를 생각해 보시오.

01 **develop** inner **beauty** 1489

02 **lost an** insignificant **amount of money** 1496

03 credible **information** 1500

04 **focus on one's studies** 1499

05 **block the sun** 1451

06 **an** extraordinary **achievement** 1495

07 swap **jokes** 1494

08 unless **you go, I won't go** 1482

09 **a** transparent **plastic container** 1481

10 concentrate **upon a problem** 1452

11 messy **hair** 1468

12 **focusing on** merchandise **exportation** 1472

13 **create** solid **results** 1478

14 **breathe** properly 1476

15 **the** prevailing **speculations** 1456

16 predict **the results** 1470

17 **a** sophisticated **design** 1491

18 **his head** tipped **to one side** 1486

19 current **law** 1463

20 inland **transportation** 1485

DAY 31

1501
novel
[návəl]
-nov 새로운

adj. 신기한, 참신한 original and of a kind not seen before
syn. strange, new

a novel idea 신기한 생각
a dress of novel design 참신한 디자인의 드레스

1502
soil
[sɔil]

n. 토양, 흙, 땅 the upper layer of earth
syn. earth, land, ground

a rich soil 기름진 땅

1503
quarter
[kwɔ́:rtər]

n. 4분의 1 one of four equal parts

a quarter after 4 o'clock 4시 15분

1504
union
[jú:njən]

n. 결합, 합일, 조합 an organization of employees formed to bargain with the employer

spiritual union 정신적 결합
union gives strength 단결은 힘이다

1505
outing
[áutiŋ]

n. 소풍, 외출 a journey taken for pleasure
syn. excursion, pleasant trip

go for an outing 소풍 가다

1506
brilliant
[bríljənt]

adj. 1 빛나는 2 멋진 flashing with light / very impressive or successful
syn. radiant, shining, splendid

brilliant jewels 빛나는 보석
a brilliant achievement 훌륭한 업적

1507
concern
[kənsə́:rn]

v. ~에 관계하다, 관심이 있다 to be relevant to
syn. involve, affect, interest

to whom it may concern 관계자에게

1508
violation
[vàiəléiʃən]

n. 위반, 방해 an act that disregards an agreement or a right
syn. misdemeanor, infringement

a traffic violation 교통위반

1509
posted
[póustid]

adj. 공지한　publicly announced

syn. updated

the posted speed limit 공지된 속도제한
keep me posted 나한테 계속 알려줘

1510
critical
[krítikəl]

adj. 1 비판적인　2 매우 중요한　expressing an opinion when you think something is wrong or bad / very important

syn. 1 judgmental　2 crucial

a critical attitude 비판적 태도
a critical factor 매우 중요한 요소

1511
sociable
[sóuʃəbəl]

adj. 사교적인, 붙임성 있는　inclined to companionship with others

syn. social, outgoing, gregarious, friendly

a sociable gathering 사교 모임

1512
critic
[krítik]

n. 비평가, 평론가　a person who is professionally engaged in the analysis and interpretation

syn. judge, expert

a music critic 음악 비평가

1513
junk
[dʒʌŋk]

n. 쓰레기, 잡동사니　the remains of something that has been destroyed or broken up

syn. rubbish, trash, debris

all that old junk in the attic 다락방에 있는 쓸모없는 물건들

1514
automatically
[ɔ̀:təmǽtikəli]

adv. 자동적으로, 저절로　as the result of a situation or action, and without your having to do anything more

the door opened automatically 문이 저절로 열렸다

1515
specialist
[spéʃəlist]

n. 전문가　an expert who is devoted to one occupation or branch of learning

syn. authority, expert, master

a wildlife specialist 야생동물 전문가

1516
limited
[límitid]

adj. 제한된, 한정된　small in range or scope
syn. restricted, controlled, restrained

with the limited resources available 이용 가능한 제한된 자원으로

1517
insistent
[insístənt]
-sist 서다

adj. 주장[고집]하는, 집요한　repetitive and persistent
syn. persistent

an insistent demand 끈질긴 요구

1518
conditional
[kəndíʃənəl]

adj. 조건부의, 부분적인　imposing or depending on or containing a condition
syn. indefinite, uncertain, limited

a conditional contract 조건부 계약

1519
midwife
[mídwàif]

n. 산파　a woman skilled in aiding the delivery of babies

act as midwife 산파로서의 역할을 하다

1520
blunt
[blʌnt]

adj. 무딘, 퉁명스러운　having a broad or rounded end
syn. dull, thick

a blunt refusal 쌀쌀맞은 거절
a blunt knife 무딘 칼

1521
bounce
[bauns]

v. 되튀다　to spring back
syn. bound

bounce a ball 공을 튀기다

1522
distinction
[distíŋkʃən]
-dis 멀어짐, 부정

n. 차별, 구별　a difference that you can see, hear, smell, feel, etc.
syn. characteristic, difference, particularity

without distinction 차별 없이
gain[win] distinction 이름을 떨치다

1523
flour
[flauər]

n. 밀가루, 가루　fine powdery foodstuff obtained by grinding

coat the meat with flour 고기에 밀가루를 입히다

1524
kinship
[kínʃip]

n. 친족관계   a close connection marked by community of interests or similarity in nature or character
syn. affinity, family relationship

the ties of kinship 친족 관계

1525
entire
[entáiər]
-en 내부, 안

adj. 전체의, 내내   not lacking or leaving out any part
syn. complete, whole, total

in the entire Korea 한국 전체에서

1526
aspiration
[æ̀spəréiʃən]
-spir 숨 쉬다

n. 열망, 포부   a will to succeed; a cherished desire
syn. hope, desire, ambition

aspirations of fame 명예욕

1527
goods
[ɡudz]

n. 재산, 물건   items for sale
syn. merchandise, possessions

competing goods 경쟁 상품
buy or sell goods and services 재화와 용역을 사고팔다

1528
informed
[infɔ́ːrmd]

adj. 1 정보에 근거한   2 많이 알고 있는, 정통한   based on information / having information
syn. 1 well-founded 2 educated

an informed guess 자세한 정보에 근거한 추측
informed sources 정통한 소식통

1529
herb
[həːrb]

n. 허브, 약초   a plant lacking a permanent woody stem

beneficial herbs 이로운 약초

1530
conference
[kánfərəns]
-con 함께

n. 회담, 협의, 회의   a large formal meeting where a lot of people discuss important matters
syn. meeting, seminar, assembly

hold a conference 회의[협의회]를 열다

1531
bond
[bɔnd]
-con 함께

n. 유대, 묶는 것　something that unites two or more people or groups, such as love, or a shared interest or idea
syn. band, bind, bracelet

the bond between nations 국가 간의 유대

1532
diligence
[dílədʒəns]

n. 근면, 성실　the attitude or behaviour of someone who works very hard and very carefully
syn. industry, effort

with diligence 근면하게

1533
hesitate
[hézətèit]
-hesitant adj. 주저하는

v. 주저하다, 망설이다　to pause or hold back in uncertainty or unwillingness
syn. pause, delay, lag, waver

hesitated to take the offer 제의를 수락할지 망설였다

1534
innovation
[ìnouvéiʃən]
-nov 새로운

n. 혁신　a creation resulting from study and experimentation
syn. invention, creation

bring about technological innovation 기술 혁신을 가져오다

1535
literary
[lítərèri]

adj. 문학의, 문필의　of or relating to or characteristic of literature

literary works 문학 작품

1536
ornament
[ɔ́:rnəmənt]

n. 꾸밈, 장식　something used to beautify
syn. accessory, adornment

books are for use, not for ornament 책은 읽으라는 것이지 장식품은 아니다

1537
precious
[préʃəs]

adj. 비싼, 귀중한　held in great esteem for admirable qualities especially of an intrinsic nature
syn. valuable, cherished, treasured

precious works of art 귀중한 예술작품
precious memories 소중한 추억

1538
surgeon
[sə́:rdʒən]

n. 외과 의사   a physician who specializes in surgery

a plastic surgeon 성형외과 의사

1539
hidden
[hídn]

adj. 숨은, 숨겨진   not accessible to view
syn. concealed, covert, unseen

hidden assets 은닉 자산

1540
precise
[prisáis]
-precision n. 정확, 정밀

adj. 정밀한, 정확한   sharply exact or accurate or definite
syn. accurate, exact

precise instructions 정확한 지시

1541
foretell
[fɔːrtél]

v. 예언하다, 예측하다   to make a prediction about
syn. prophesy, predict

foretell the future 장래를 예언하다
foretell the results 결과를 예측하다

1542
concerned
[kənsə́:rnd]

adj. 1 걱정하는 2 관련 있는   worried about something / involved in
syn. 1 anxious, uneasy 2 involved, related

be concerned about the future 미래에 대해 걱정하다
as far as I am concerned 나에 관한 한

1543
inherit
[inhérit]

v. 상속하다, 물려받다   to obtain from someone after their death
syn. bequeath, bestow, endow

inherit an estate 토지를 상속하다

1544
associate
[əsóuʃièit]

v. 연상하다, 연결 짓다   to make a logical connection
syn. tie in, relate, link, link up

associate peace with prosperity 평화와 번영을 연결 지어 생각하다

1545
hypothesis
[haipáθəsis]

n. 가설, 가정   a proposal intended to explain certain facts or observations
syn. theory, assumption, proposition

support the hypothesis 가설을 뒷받침하다
formulate a hypothesis 가설을 세우다

1546

crush

[krʌʃ]

v. 눌러 부수다, 으깨다   to press or squeeze something so hard that it breaks or loses its shape

syn. smash, crumple, press, oppress

crush an aluminum can 알루미늄 캔을 찌그러트리다

1547

knock

[nɑk]

v. 치다, 두드리다   to hit something in a forceful way

syn. knocking, bang, smash, belt

knock on the door 문을 두드리다

1548

consider

[kənsídər]

v. 고려하다, 숙고하다   to think about carefully

syn. see, regard, think

consider a plan overall 종합적으로 계획을 구상하다

1549

bride

[braid]

n. 신부   a woman who has recently been married

a toast to the bride and groom 신랑 신부를 위한 건배

1550

like

[laik]

prep. ~와 닮은, 같은   resembling or similar

syn. similar, alike, same

stars like diamonds 다이아몬드 같은 별

Review

뜻을 써보고 전체 어구의 의미를 생각해 보시오.

01 a wildlife specialist _____ 1515

02 with the limited resources available _____ 1516

03 a conditional contract _____ 1518

04 a blunt refusal _____ 1520

05 in the entire Korea _____ 1525

06 with diligence _____ 1532

07 precious works of art _____ 1537

08 precise instructions _____ 1540

09 a dress of novel design _____ 1501

10 bring about technological innovation _____ 1534

11 buy or sell goods and services _____ 1527

12 go for an outing _____ 1505

13 inherit an estate _____ 1543

14 keep me posted _____ 1509

15 crush an aluminum can _____ 1546

16 beneficial herbs _____ 1529

17 coat the meat with flour _____ 1523

18 a sociable gathering _____ 1511

19 bounce a ball _____ 1521

20 all that old junk in the attic _____ 1513

1551
light
[lait]
-lit -lit

v. 불을 켜다, 점화하다   to make lighter or brighter
syn. light up, illuminate, fire up

light a candle 초에 불을 붙이다

1552
currently
[kə́:rəntli]

adv. 현재   at this time or period
syn. presently

currently they live in Connecticut 그들은 현재 코네티컷 주에 산다

1553
available
[əvéiləbəl]

adj. 이용할 수 있는   obtainable or accessible and ready for use or service
syn. uncommited, usable

available facilities 이용할 수 있는 편의 시설

1554
normal
[nɔ́:rməl]

adj. 정상의, 표준적인   usual or ordinary / not strange
syn. common

a normal condition 정상적인 상황

1555
integral
[íntigrəl]

adj. 완전한, 필수의, 중요한   very important and necessary
syn. entire, essential

an integral part of the social life 사회생활의 필수적인 부분

1556
corn
[kɔ:rn]

n. 곡식, 옥수수   tall annual cereal grass bearing kernels on large ears

a field of corn 곡식을 심어 놓은 들판

1557
method
[méθəd]

n. 방법, 방식   a way of doing something, especially a systematic way
syn. approach, manner

a teaching method 교수법

1558
dilemma
[dilémə]

n. 진퇴양난, 곤궁   state of uncertainty or perplexity
syn. plight, impasse

face a dilemma 딜레마에 봉착하다

1559
potent
[póutənt]

adj. 세력 있는, 힘 있는   having great influence
syn. powerful

potent drugs 강력한 약

1560
curved
[kə:rvd]

adj. 굽은, 곡선 모양의 having or marked by a curve or smoothly rounded bend

a curved ruler 곡선 자

1561
solar
[sóulər]

-sol 홀로

adj. 태양의 relating to or derived from the sun or utilizing the energies of the sun

solar energy 태양에너지

solar eclipse 일식

1562
witness
[wítnis]

v. 목격하다 to see something happen

sys. see, experience, observe

witness many historical events 많은 역사적인 사건들을 목격하다

1563
crowd
[kraud]

n. 군중, 다수 a large number of things or people considered together

syn. throng, multitude

large crowds in the streets 거리의 대규모 군중들

a crowd of papers 많은 서류들

1564
lively
[láivli]

adj. 생기가 넘치는 full of life and energy

syn. energetic, active, alive

lively imagination 왕성한 상상력

1565
post-modern
[póustmɔ́dərn]

adj. 포스트모더니즘의, 최신유행의 of or relating to postmodernism

in a post-modern style 포스트모던 스타일로

1566
crunch
[krʌntʃ]

v. 으드득으드득 씹다, 바삭거리다 to make a crushing noise

syn. crush

the fallen leaves crunch under foot 낙엽들이 밟혀서 바삭거린다

1567
universal
[jù:nəvə́:rsəl]

adj. 전 세계의, 도처에 있는 existing or true at all times or in all places

a universal language 세계어

as universal as the air 공기처럼 어디든지 있는

1568
honest
[ánist]
-honesty n. 정직

adj. 정직한　not hiding the truth about someone or something
syn. sincere, upright

an honest servant 정직한 하인

1569
outward
[áutwərd]

adj. 밖을 향한, 외관의　relating to physical reality rather than with thoughts or the mind
syn. outside, exterior, outer

the outward flow of dollars 달러의 해외 유출
outward beauty 외관상의 아름다움

1570
island
[áilənd]

n. 섬　a land mass that is surrounded by water

desert island 무인도

1571
spectacular
[spektǽkjələr]

adj. 장관을 이루는　sensational in appearance or thrilling in effect
syn. dramatic, sensational, thrilling

a spectacular sight 장관

1572
asthma
[ǽzmə]

n. 천식, 기관지 천식　respiratory disorder characterized by wheezing

suffer from severe asthma 심한 천식을 앓다

1573
corrupt
[kərʌ́pt]
-rupt 망치다

adj. 부패한, 타락한　doing things that are dishonest or illegal in order to make money or to gain or keep power
syn. immoral

a corrupt regime 부패 정권

1574
expedition
[èkspədíʃən]
-ped 발

n. 탐험, 원정　a journey especially by a group of people for a specific purpose
syn. excursion, dispatch

an antarctic expedition 남극 탐험

1575
cost
[kɔːst]

n. 비용　the total spent for goods or services including money and time and labor
syn. price, charge, loss

at all costs 어떤 희생을 치르더라도
cut costs 비용을 절감하다

1576
outcome
[áutkʌm]

n. 결과, 성과　something that happens as a result of an activity or process

syn. result, consequence

predict the outcome of the election 선거의 결과를 예상하다

1577
insurance
[inʃúərəns]

n. 보험, 보험료　promise of reimbursement in the case of loss

insurance for life 종신 보험

1578
swallow
[swάlou]

v. 꿀꺽 삼키다, 참다　to take something into your stomach through your mouth and throat

swallow one's pride 자존심을 억누르다

1579
mixture
[míkstʃər]

n. 혼합, 혼합물　a substance consisting of two or more substances mixed together

a mixture of English and Korean words 영어와 한국어의 혼합

1580
post
[poust]

v. 붙이다, 널리 알리다　to affix in a public place or for public notice

post up a poster 포스터를 붙이다

post the firm as bankrupt 회사가 도난 했다고 발표하다

1581
unusual
[ʌnjúːʒuəl]

adj. 이상한, 유별난　not usual or common or ordinary

syn. strange, weird, extraordinary

experience unusual climate changes 비정상적인 기후변화를 경험하다

1582
fragment
[frǽgmənt]

n. 파편　a piece broken off or cut off of something else

syn. portion, fraction, part, piece

a fragment of rock 돌조각

1583
metabolism
[mətǽbəlìzəm]

n. 신진대사　the organic processes that are necessary for life

body's metabolism 몸의 신진대사

1584
cooperate
[kouápərèit]
-co 함께

v. 협력하다, 협조하다   to work together on a common enterprise of project

syn. collaborate, join forces, get together

cooperate with the police 경찰에 협력하다

1585
insect
[ínsekt]

n. 곤충, 벌레   a small animal that has six legs and a body formed of three parts and that may have wings

a swarm of flying insects 하늘을 나는 곤충 떼

1586
mineral
[mínərəl]

n. 무기물, 미네랄   relating to minerals

be rich in vitamins and minerals 비타민과 미네랄이 풍부하다

1587
copyright
[kápiràit]

n. 판권, 저작권   a document granting exclusive right to publish and sell literary or musical or artistic work

violating copyright laws 저작권법을 위반하는 것

1588
brand-new
[brǽndnjù:]

adj. 신제품의, 새 것의   conspicuously new

syn. up-to-date, latest

ant. stale

a brand-new car 새로 출시된 차

1589
sustain
[səstéin]
-tain 쥐다

v. 떠받치다, 유지하다   to provide what is needed for something or someone to exist, continue, etc.

syn. prop, underpin, support

ant. weaken, defeat

sustain the diplomatic negotiations 외교 협상을 지지하다

1590
guide
[gaid]

v. 안내하다   to determine the direction of travelling

syn. usher, lead, direct

guide explorers 탐험가의 길 안내를 하다

1591
trap
[træp]

n. 덫, 함정   a device in which something can be caught and penned

syn. net, pit, snare

a mouse trap 쥐덫

1592
resent
[rizént]

v. ~에 분개하다   to feel bitter or indignant about

resented being dropped 낙오된 것에 분개했다

1593
appropriate
[əpróuprièit]

adj. 적절한, 어울리는   suitable for a particular person or place or condition, etc.

syn. proper, suitable, fitting

an appropriate example 적절한 예

1594
trash
[træʃ]

n. 쓰레기   worthless material that is to be disposed of

syn. garbage, litter, rubbish

biodegradable trash 썩는 쓰레기
most of his works are trash 그의 작품은 대부분 졸작들이다

1595
boom
[bu:m]

n. 붐, 인기   a sudden increase in the popularity of something

syn. expansion, increase

the aerobics boom of the 1980s 1980년대의 에어로빅 붐

1596
graceful
[gréisfəl]

adj. 우아한   moving in a smooth and attractive way

syn. elegant, refined

the graceful movements of a ballerina 발레리나의 우아한 동작

1597
unlike
[ʌnláik]

prep. 닮지 않은, ~와는 다른   different from something or someone

a landscape unlike any other 다른 어떤 곳과도 다른 풍경

1598
approximately
[əpráksəmitli]

adv. 대략   imprecise but fairly close to correct

syn. nearly, almost, about, around

last approximately an hour 대략 1시간 정도 지속하다

1599
reserve
[rizə́:rv]

n. 비축, 예비   something kept back or saved for future use or a special purpose

keep in reserve 예비로 남겨 두다
the reserve of foreign currency 외화 준비금

1600
grade
[greid]

n. 등급, 성적 a number or letter that indicates how a student performed in a class or on a test

high-grade petrol 고급 휘발유

Review

뜻을 써보고 전체 어구의 의미를 생각해 보시오.

01 witness many historical events   1562

02 lively imagination   1564

03 in a post-modern style   1565

04 the fallen leaves crunch under foot   1566

05 desert island   1570

06 a corrupt regime   1573

07 an antarctic expedition   1574

08 insurance for life   1577

09 a mixture of English and Korean words   1579

10 experience unusual climate changes   1581

11 a fragment of rock   1582

12 cooperate with the police   1584

13 a brand-new car   1588

14 sustain the diplomatic negotiations   1589

15 an appropriate example   1593

16 violating copyright laws   1587

17 a swarm of flying insects   1585

18 a landscape unlike any other   1597

19 the reserve of foreign currency   1599

20 solar eclipse   1561

DAY 33

1601
cooperation
[kouàpəréiʃən]
-co 함께

n. 협력, 협동 joint operation or action
syn. unity, concert, collaboration

economic cooperation 경제협력
in cooperation with the chemical industry 화학업계와 합동으로

1602
gradual
[grǽdʒuəl]

adj. 점진적인, 서서히 일어나는 proceeding by steps or degrees
syn. measured, progressive, step-by-step

a gradual increase in prices 가격의 점진적 상승

1603
nonsense
[nánsens]

n. 말도 안 되는 소리 words or ideas that are foolish or untrue

you talk nonsense all the time 넌 항상 말도 안 되는 말을 해

1604
protect
[prətékt]

v. 보호하다, 지키다 to shield from danger, or damage
syn. guard, shield, defend

protect human rights 인권을 보호하다

1605
wide
[waid]

adj. 폭 넓은, 다양한 having great extent from one side to the other
syn. broad, spacious

win by a wide margin 꽤 큰 차이로 이기다

1606
astronaut
[ǽstrənɔ̀:t]
-astr 별

n. 우주비행사 a person trained to travel in a spacecraft
syn. spaceman, cosmonaut

protect astronauts from Mars' harsh environment
화성의 혹독한 환경으로부터 우주 비행사들을 보호하다

1607
dormant
[dɔ́:rmənt]

adj. 잠자는, 동면의 in a condition of biological rest or suspended animation
syn. hibernating, torpid, inactive

a dormant volcano 휴화산
lie dormant for 200 years or more 200년 이상동안 잠자고 있다

1608
society
[səsáiəti]

n. 사회, 사교 an extended social group having a distinctive cultural and economic organization
syn. social club, guild, company, companionship, fellowship

benefit society as a whole 사회 전체에 이익이 되다

1609
viewer
[vjú:ər]

n. 보는 사람, 구경꾼 someone who looks at something

syn. spectator, witness, watcher, looker

television viewers 텔레비전 시청자들

1610
confirmation
[kùnfərméiʃən]
-con 함께

n. 확정, 확인 proof which shows that something is true or correct

syn. verification, check

lack confirmation 확인되지 않다

1611
hemisphere
[hémisfiər]

n. 반구 half of a sphere / a half of the Earth

the entire Southern Hemisphere 남반구 전역

1612
overhear
[òuvərhíər]

v. 엿듣다, 도청하다 to hear, usually without the knowledge of the speakers

syn. listen in, eavesdrop

overhear a person's talk 남의 말을 엿듣다

1613
worthless
[wə́:rθlis]

adj. 가치 없는, 시시한 lacking in usefulness or value

syn. valueless, useless, futile, unimportant

worthless knowledge 쓸모없는 지식

1614
asset
[æset]

n. 자산, 재산 anything of material value or usefulness that is owned by a person or company

syn. property, wealth, effects

she'll be an asset to the team 그녀는 팀의 자산이 될 것이다

1615
foreign
[fɔ́(:)rin]

adj. 외국의 coming from or belonging to a different place or country

syn. alien, exotic

foreign policy 외교정책

1616
considerate
[kənsídərit]

adj. 사려 깊은, 배려하는 showing concern for the rights and feelings of others

syn. thoughtful, mindful

the most considerate person 가장 배려심 있는 사람

1617

expression

[ikspréʃən]

n. 표현, 표정   the feelings expressed on a person's face

an idiomatic expression 관용적인 표현

a face that lacks expression 표정이 없는 얼굴

1618

constant

[kánstənt]

adj. 거듭되는, 끊임없는   happening all the time or very often over a period of time

syn. changeless, ceaseless

constant interruptions 거듭되는 방해

make constant efforts 끊임없는 노력을 하다

1619

specific

[spisífik]

adj. 특정한, 명확한   special or particular

syn. definite, exact, precise

ant. general, common

specific instructions 명확한 지시

1620

brief

[bri:f]

adj. 짧은, 간결한   of short duration or distance

syn. short, fast, fleeting, concise, compact

a brief stay 짧은 체류

a brief winter vacation 짧은 겨울 방학

1621

infrared

[ìnfrəréd]

adj. 적외선의   producing or using rays of light that cannot be seen and that are longer than rays that produce red light

an infrared film 적외선 필름

1622

pose

[pouz]

v. 자세를 취하다, ~인 체하다   to sit or stand in a particular position in order to be photographed

posed for photographs 사진 찍으려고 포즈를 취했다

1623

conducive

[kəndʒú:siv]

-con 함께

adj. 도움이 되는, 촉진하는   tending to bring about / being partly responsible for

syn. contributing, tending, helping, promoting

exercise is conducive to health 운동은 건강을 돕는다

1624
longevity
[lɑndʒévəti]

n. 장수, 수명   the property of being long-lived

the secret to longevity 장수의 비결

1625
solution
[səljúːʃən]

n. 해결책   something that solves a problem

the solution to the problem 그 문제에 대한 해결책

1626
outburst
[áutbə̀ːrst]

n. 분출, 돌발, 폭발   an unrestrained expression of emotion
syn. eruption, explosion

an outburst of laughter 폭소

1627
conduct
[kɑndʌ́kt]

v. 수행하다, 행동하다   to manage or control
syn. carry on, act, behave, guide, manage

conduct a guest to his room 손님을 방으로 안내하다
conduct a campaign[an orchestra] 캠페인[악단]을 지휘하다

1628
uninterrupted
[ʌ̀nintərʌ́ptid]
-rupt 망치다

adj. 끊임없는, 연속된, 부단한   having undisturbed continuity
syn. continuous

an uninterrupted flight 연속비행

1629
soothe
[suːð]

v. 진정시키다, 달래다   to give moral or emotional strength to
syn. calm, appease, comfort, console, reassure
ant. excite, aggravate, upset

soothe sunburned skin 햇볕에 타서 화끈거리는 피부를 가라앉히다
soothe one's anger 분을 삭이다

1630
confident
[kɑ́nfidənt]

adj. 확신하는, 자신하는   having a feeling or belief that you can do something well
syn. self-assured, self-confident

a confident speaker 자신감 있는 연사

1631
approximation
[əprɑ̀ksəméiʃən]

n. 접근, 근사치   an approximate calculation of quantity
syn. estimate, estimation

an approximation to the truth 진상에 가까운 일

269

1632
direction
[dirékʃən]
-rect 올바름, 인도함

n. 방향, 지시   the course or path on which something is moving or pointing

give directions 지시하다

1633
border
[bɔ́:rdər]

n. 국경선, 경계선   a line that indicates a boundary
syn. edge, margin, verge

a border army 국경 수비대

1634
surmount
[sərmáunt]
-sur 초과하여

v. 오르다, 극복하다   to get on top of / to overcome
syn. conquer, defeat
ant. succumb, descend

surmount difficulties 어려움을 극복하다
surmount an obstacle 장애를 극복하다

1635
aquarium
[əkwέəriəm]

n. 수족관, 유리 수조   a tank or pool or bowl filled with water for keeping live fish and underwater animals
syn. fish tank

the world's smallest aquarium 세계에서 가장 작은 수족관

1636
surplus
[sə́:rplʌs]
-sur 초과하여

n. 나머지, 잔여, 잉여   more than is needed, desired, or required
syn. remainder, residue, excess
ant. shortage

surplus funds 잉여금
a surplus population 과잉 인구

1637
contraction
[kəntrǽkʃən]
-tract 끌다

n. 수축, 단축   the act or process of making something smaller or of becoming smaller
syn. shrinkage, abridgement

the expansion and contraction of the metal 금속의 팽창과 수축

1638
traumatic
[trɔːmǽtik]

adj. 외상(外傷)의, 대단히 충격적인   a very difficult or unpleasant experience that causes someone to have mental problems for a long time
syn. shocking

a traumatic experience 대단히 충격적인 경험

1639
innovative
[ínouvèitiv]
-nov 새로운

adj. 혁신적인 ahead of the times
syn. advanced, forward-looking, modern

change the world with his innovative ideas 혁신적인 생각으로 세상을 바꾸다

1640
bored
[bɔːrd]

adj. 따분한, 지루한 tired of the world
syn. weary, tired

get bored with something 뭔가에 싫증나다

1641
wisdom
[wízdəm]

n. 지혜, 슬기로움 knowledge that is gained by having many experiences in life
syn. judgment, insight, common sense

a young person of great wisdom 매우 지혜로운 젊은이

1642
consult
[kənsʌ́lt]
-con 함께

v. 상담하다, 참고하다 to get or ask advice from
syn. refer, look up

consult a dictionary 사전을 참고하다

1643
live
[laiv]

adj. 살아있는, 생생한 actually being performed at the time of hearing or viewing
syn. alive, lively, resilient

live coverage 생중계

1644
outlet
[áutlet]

n. 배출구, 출구 an opening that permits escape or release
syn. exit, way out

an outlet for one's frustrations 욕구불만의 배출구

1645
sow
[sou]

v. (씨를) 뿌리다 to place seeds in or on the ground for future growth
syn. plant, scatter, seed
ant. harvest, gather

she sowed sunflower seeds 그녀는 해바라기 씨앗을 뿌렸다

1646
interchange
[ìntərtʃéindʒ]

v. 교환하다, 교체하다 to put in the place of another
syn. substitute, replace

interchange opinions freely 의견을 서로 자유로이 교환하다

1647

contain
[kəntéin]
-tain 쥐다

v. 1 ~를 함유하다 2 억누르다   to have as a component / to keep something within limits

syn. 1 include, consist of, embrace 2 restrain, control, hold in

soft drinks usually contain caffeine 탄산음료에는 대개 카페인이 들어 있다

contain one's anger 분노를 억누르다

1648

note
[nout]

n. 1 메모, 쪽지 2 음표   a brief written record / an individual sound in music

leave someone a note 누군가에게 메모를 남기다

played some notes 악보를 보고 연주했다

1649

sparing
[spέəriŋ]

adj. 아끼는, 인색한 avoiding waste

syn. frugal, thrifty

sparing no money 돈을 아끼지 않고

1650

contemporary
[kəntémpərèri]
-con 함께
-tempo 시간

adj. 동시대의, 현대의 characteristic of the present

syn. modern, up-to-date, current

both classical and contemporary music 클래식 음악과 현대 음악 둘 다

Review

뜻을 써보고 전체 어구의 의미를 생각해 보시오.

01 an outlet for one's frustrations _____ 1644

02 a dormant volcano _____ 1607

03 she sowed sunflower seeds _____ 1645

04 a surplus population _____ 1636

05 the solution to the problem _____ 1625

06 an uninterrupted flight _____ 1628

07 a confident speaker _____ 1630

08 economic cooperation _____ 1601

09 an outburst of laughter _____ 1626

10 the world's smallest aquarium _____ 1635

11 a face that lacks expression _____ 1617

12 the most considerate person _____ 1616

13 specific instructions _____ 1619

14 constant interruptions _____ 1618

15 soothe sunburned skin _____ 1629

16 the secret to longevity _____ 1624

17 the entire Southern Hemisphere _____ 1611

18 a brief stay _____ 1620

19 overhear a person's talk _____ 1612

20 worthless knowledge _____ 1613

1651

organic

[ɔ:rgǽnik]

adj. 유기체의 grown or made without the use of artificial chemicals

syn. alive, biotic, living, natural, nonchemical

organic fertilizer 유기 비료

organic farming 유기 농업

1652

horizon

[həráizən]

n. 수평선 the line where the earth or sea seems to meet the sky

above the horizon 수평선 위로

1653

location

[loukéiʃən]

n. 장소, 위치 a place or position

a house in a fine location 자리가 좋은 집

1654

puddle

[pʌ́dl]

n. 웅덩이 a small body of standing water

syn. pool

jump over a puddle 웅덩이를 뛰어넘다

1655

approximate

[əpráksəməit]

adj. 대강의, 가까운 not quite exact or correct

syn. close, near, rough

approximate cost 대략적인 비용

approximate value (수학) 근삿값

1656

except

[iksépt]

-cept 받다

prep. ~을 제외하고 not including someone or something

syn. apart from, aside from, except for

we are all ready except you 너 말고는 우린 모두 준비가 돼 있다

1657

cover

[kʌ́vər]

v. 덮다, 숨기다 to lay or spread something over

syn. hide, conceal

snow covered the highway 간선 도로는 눈으로 덮였다

cover one's feeling 감정을 숨기다

1658

aptitude

[ǽptitù:d]

-apt 적합

n. 소질, 적성 a natural ability to do something or to learn something

syn. leaning, tendency

an aptitude test 적성검사

1659
merge
[məːrdʒ]

v. 합병하다, 합체하다   to become one

syn. blend, integrate, mingle

this company will be merged soon 이 회사 곧 합병할거다

1660
diminish
[dəmíniʃ]
-min 작은, 소형의

v. 줄이다, 감소시키다   to decrease in size, extent, or range

syn. decrease, lessen, fall

rapidly diminishing resources 급속히 줄고 있는 자원

1661
likelihood
[láiklihùd]

n. 있음직한 일, 가능성   the probability of a specified outcome

syn. likeliness, probability

great likelihood 높은 가능성

1662
overestimate
[òuvəréstəmèit]

v. 과대평가하다   to consider something to be better than it really is

syn. overrate, overvalue

overestimate one's abilities 자기의 역량을 과신하다

1663
contrast
[kántræst]
-con 함께

n. 대조, 대비   the opposition or dissimilarity of things that are compared

syn. difference

a sharp contrast 극명한 대조

1664
guilt
[gilt]
-guilty a. 유죄의

n. 죄, 유죄, 죄책감   the state of having committed an offense

syn. shame, wrong, evil

experience regret or guilt 후회와 죄책감을 느끼다

1665
assemble
[əsémbəl]

v. 1 소집하다 2 조립하다   to gather people into one place or group / to create by putting components or members together

syn. 1 gather, congregate, collect, band   2 fit, connect, piece

assemble a committee 위원회를 소집하다
assemble parts into a machine 부품을 기계로 조립하다

1666
consist
[kənsíst]
-con 함께
-sist 서다

v. 구성되다, 이루어지다   to be composed of

the essay consists of 5 chapters 그 에세이는 5장으로 구성된다

1667

notion

[nóuʃən]

n. 관념, 생각   a vague idea in which some confidence is placed

syn. belief, concept, idea

a false notion 잘못된 생각

1668

invaluable

[invǽljuəbəl]

adj. 소중한, 매우 귀중한   having incalculable monetary, intellectual, or spiritual worth

syn. priceless, very valuable

invaluable information 귀중한 정보

1669

morally

[mɔ́(:)rəli]

adv. 도덕상으로, 정신적으로   in a moral manner

act morally 도덕적으로 행동하다

1670

consistent

[kənsístənt]

-con 함께

-sist 서다

adj. 꾸준한, 한결같은   always acting or behaving in the same way

syn. stable, constant, steady

consistent growth 꾸준한 성장

1671

prophetic

[prəfétik]

adj. 예언의, 전조가 되는   foretelling events as if by supernatural intervention

syn. predictive

prophetic writings 예언서

1672

vitamin

[váitəmin]

n. 비타민   any of a group of organic substances essential in small quantities to normal metabolism

this cereal contains essential vitamins 이 시리얼은 필수 비타민을 함유하고 있다

1673

attraction

[ətrǽkʃən]

-tract 끌다

n. 명소, 볼거리   something interesting or enjoyable that people want to visit, see, or do

tourist attractions 관광명소들

1674

formation

[fɔːrméiʃən]

-form 형성하다

n. 형성, 구성   an arrangement of people or things acting as a unit

syn. organization, shaping, constitution

the formation of a Cabinet 내각구성

276

1675
highlight
[háilàit]

v. 강조하다, 눈에 띠게 하다   to move into the foreground to make more visible or prominent

syn. spotlight, play up

highlight one's good point 자신의 장점을 강조하다

1676
minimize
[mínəmàiz]
-min 작은, 소형의

v. 최소로 하다, 얕잡아보다   to make small or insignificant

syn. lessen, understate, downplay

minimize the risk of infection 감염의 위험을 최소화하다

1677
blow
[blou]
-blew -blown

v. 1 (코를) 풀다 2 날리다, 폭파하다   to exhale hard / to destroy by explosion

blow one's nose 코를 풀다

blow the safe open 금고를 폭파시켜 열다

1678
discover
[diskʌ́vər]

v. 발견하다, 밝히다   to see, find, or become aware of something for the first time

syn. detect, find, realize, notice

discover a mistake 실수를 찾아내다

1679
criticize
[krítisàiz]

v. 비난하다, 비평하다   to find fault with

syn. judge, evaluate

criticize freely 자유로이 비평하다

1680
infrastructure
[ínfrəstrʌ̀ktʃər]
-struct 세우다

n. 하부조직, 기반시설   the basic structure or features of a system or organization

syn. substructure, base

an excellent information and communications infrastructure
잘 갖춰진 정보통신 인프라

1681
precisely
[prisáisli]

adv. 정확히   exactly and correctly

syn. sharp

at 2 o'clock precisely 두 시 정각에

1682
prejudice
[prédʒədis]
-pre 이전의

n. 편견, 선입견 a partiality that prevents objective consideration of an issue or situation

syn. bias, preconception

cast away all prejudices 모든 편견을 버리다

1683
stream
[striːm]

n. 개울, 흐름, 동향 a natural body of running water flowing on or under the earth

syn. flow

a stream of traffic 교통의 흐름

1684
rumor
[rúːmər]

n. 소문 gossip passed around by word of mouth

syn. gossip, hearsay

start a rumor 소문을 내다

1685
storm
[stɔːrm]

n. 폭풍우 a violent weather condition with winds, precipitation, thunder and lightning

a storm caught us 폭풍우를 만났다

1686
unpredictable
[ʌnpridíktəbəl]
-dict 말하다
-pre 이전의

adj. 예측할 수 없는 unknown in advance

syn. unforeseeable, uncertain, irregular

unpredictable weather 예측할 수 없는 날씨

1687
stomach
[stʌ́mək]

n. 위, 식욕 the organ in your body where food goes and begins to be digested after you swallow it

syn. abdomen, belly

a pain in the stomach 복통

1688
upgrade
[ʌ́pgrèid]

v. 개선하다, 질을 높이다 to raise in value or esteem

syn. promote, advance

upgrade the quality of life 삶의 질을 높이다

1689
steep
[sti:p]

adj. 가파른, 뾰족한 having a sharp inclination
syn. abrupt, angular
ant. gradual

a steep hill 가파른 언덕

1690
visitor
[vízitər]

n. 방문객 someone who visits
syn. guest, caller, tourist

attract approximately 1 million visitors 대략 1백만 명의 방문객들을 끌어 모으다

1691
stiffen
[stífən]

v. 경직되다 to become stiff or stiffer

stiffen the shirt with starch 풀을 먹여서 셔츠를 빳빳하게 하다

1692
volunteer
[vàləntíər]

v. 자진하여 하다, 지원하다 to offer to do something without being forced to or without getting paid to do it
syn. step forward, offer your services

volunteer to help others 다른 사람들을 돕기를 자청하다

1693
straight
[streit]

adj. 곧은, 솔직한 not having curves, bends, or angles
syn. direct, linear
ant. crooked

a straight talk 솔직한 이야기

1694
woeful
[wóufəl]

adj. 슬픈, 비참한 affected by or full of grief or woe
syn. unfortunate, grievous, distressing

a woeful cry 비통한 외침소리

1695
strategy
[strǽtədʒi]

n. 용병술, 전략 an elaborate and systematic plan of action
syn. approach, design, scheme, tactic

establish a strategy 전략을 짜다

1696
worship
[wə́:rʃip]

v. 예배하다, 숭배하다 to honor or respect someone or something as a god
syn. adore, deify
ant. despise, detest, hate, loathe

worship God 신을 섬기다
worship money 돈을 중히 여기다

1697
widely
[wáidli]

adv. 널리, 크게 to a great degree

syn. broadly, amply

ant. narrowly

use widely 널리 사용하다

a widely-read magazine 널리 읽히는 잡지

1698
stress
[stres]

v. 강조하다 to give special attention to something

syn. emphasize

stressed the need for stricter safety standards
보다 엄격한 안전 규제의 필요성을 강조했다

1699
violence
[váiələns]

n. 폭력, 폭행 the use of physical force to harm someone, to damage property, etc.

syn. force, fierceness, wildness

crimes of violence 폭행죄

1700
strip
[strip]

v. 옷을 벗다 to take off clothes

syn. disrobe, undress, unclothe

He stripped and jumped into the river 그는 옷을 벗고 강으로 뛰어들었다

Review

뜻을 써보고 전체 어구의 의미를 생각해 보시오.

01 rapidly diminishing resources _____ 1660

02 the essay consists of 5 chapters _____ 1666

03 a steep hill _____ 1689

04 volunteer to help others _____ 1692

05 he stripped and jumped into the river _____ 1700

06 consistent growth _____ 1670

07 crimes of violence _____ 1699

08 ① blow one's nose _____ 1677

   ② blow the safe open _____

09 the formation of a Cabinet _____ 1674

10 use widely _____ 1697

11 stressed the need for stricter safety standards _____ 1698

12 stiffen the shirt with starch _____ 1691

13 a straight talk _____ 1693

14 a woeful cry _____ 1694

15 attract approximately 1 million visitors _____ 1690

16 an aptitude test _____ 1658

17 act morally _____ 1669

18 establish a strategy _____ 1695

19 criticize freely _____ 1679

20 cast away all prejudices _____ 1682

DAY 35

1701
overflow
[òuvərflóu]

n. 범람, 홍수   a large flow
syn. flood, overspill

an overflow of population 인구의 과잉

1702
unruly
[ʌ̀nrúːli]

adj. 제멋대로의, 다루기 힘든   noisy and lacking in restraint or discipline
syn. ungovernable, uncontrollable, unmanageable

unruly behavior 제멋대로인 행동
an unruly class 다루기 힘든 학급

1703
dominate
[dámənèit]

v. 지배하다   to be larger in number, quantity, power, status or importance
syn. predominate, rule, prevail

dominated the first half of the match 그 시합 전반전을 지배했다
dominate feelings 감정을 지배하다

1704
exhibition
[èksəbíʃən]

n. 전람회, 전시(회)   the act of exhibiting
syn. showing, presentation

articles on exhibition 진열품

1705
conspicuous
[kənspíkjuəs]

adj. 눈에 잘 띄는, 뚜렷한   obvious to the eye or mind
syn. visible, apparent, noticeable

conspicuous consumption 과시적 소비
a conspicuous star 특히 눈에 띄는 별

1706
architect
[áːrkitèkt]

n. 건축가   a person who designs buildings
syn. designer

a world-famous architect 세계적인 건축기사

1707
constitute
[kánstətjùːt]
-con 함께
-stit 서다

v. 구성하다, 조직하다   to make up or form something
syn. represent, make up, comprise

five players constitute a basketball team 다섯 명의 선수가 농구 팀을 구성한다

1708
hunger
[hʌ́ŋgər]

n. 공복, 굶주림 a physiological need for food

syn. starvation, famine

die of hunger 굶어 죽다

1709
confirmed
[kənfɔ́ːrmd]
-con 함께

adj. 확고부동한, 확립된 not subject to change

syn. established, addicted, chronic

a confirmed disease 만성병

1710
mighty
[máiti]

adj. 대단한, 강력한 having or showing great strength or power

syn. strong, great

the decline of a mighty empire 강력한 제국의 쇠퇴

1711
conflict
[kánflikt]
-con 함께
-flict 치다

n. 갈등, 투쟁 an open clash between two opposing groups

syn. struggle, discord

a conflict of interest 이해 충돌

1712
justice
[dʒʌ́stis]

n. 정의 the quality of being just or fair

syn. fairness, equity, honesty

a sense of justice 정의감

1713
conform
[kənfɔ́ːrm]
-con 함께

v. 순응하다, 일치하다 to adapt or conform oneself to new or different conditions

syn. comply, agree

conform to the rules of the club 클럽 규칙에 따르다

1714
limitless
[límitlis]

adj. 무한의, 무제한의 without limits in extent or size or quantity

syn. infinite, boundless, eternal

a limitless supply of money 무제한적인 돈의 공급

1715
overbearing
[òuvərbɛ́əriŋ]

adj. 고압적인, 남을 지배하려고 하는 trying to control the behavior of other people in an annoying or unwanted way

syn. arrogant, haughty

an overbearing manner 고압적인 태도

1716
sore
[sɔːr]

adj. 아픈, 몸이 아픈   hurting
syn. painful
have a sore throat 목이 아프다

1717
confuse
[kənfjúːz]

v. 혼동하다, 혼란시키다   to mistake one thing for another
syn. perplex, confound, bewilder, puzzle
confuse liberty with license 자유를 방종과 혼동하다

1718
psychologist
[saikálədʒist]

n. 심리학자   a scientist trained in psychology
an educational psychologist 교육 심리학자

1719
unparalleled
[ʌnpǽrəlèld]

adj. 비할 데 없는, 유례없는   never seen or experienced before
syn. alone, unique, unequaled
unparalleled athletic ability 비할 데 없는 운동 능력

1720
forbidden
[fərbídn]

adj. 금지된, 금단의   not permitted or allowed
syn. prohibited, banned, barred
smoking is forbidden in the building 이 건물 안에서 흡연은 금지다

1721
uniform
[júːnəfɔ̀ːrm]

adj. 한결같은, 균일한   always the same
syn. unvarying, consistent, similar, same
vases of uniform size and shape 크기와 모양이 같은 꽃병들

1722
workable
[wə́ːrkəbəl]

adj. 실행 가능한, 운용 가능한   capable of being done with means at hand and circumstances as they are
syn. feasible, practicable
a workable plan 실행 가능한 계획

1723
essence
[ésəns]

n. 본질, 진수   most vital part of some idea or experience
syn. nature, core, heart
the essence of democracy 민주주의의 본질

1724
consume
[kənsúːm]

v. 먹다, 소비하다   to eat or drink / to use fuel, time, resources, etc.

syn. devour, take in, eat up, deplete

consume a bottle of whiskey 위스키 한 병을 다 마셔 버리다

1725
estimation
[èstəméiʃən]

n. 의견, 판단   a document appraising the value of something

syn. opinion, judgement

in the estimation of the law 법률상의 견해로는

1726
annual
[ǽnjuəl]

adj. 일 년마다의   happening once a year

annual average rainfall 연간 평균 강수량

host the annual event 연간 행사를 개최하다

1727
contact
[kántækt]
-con 함께

n. 연락, 접촉   close interaction

syn. connection

direct contact between the two sides 양측의 직접적인 접촉

1728
apparent
[əpǽrənt]

adj. 또렷한, 분명한, 겉치레의   easy to see or understand

syn. evident, manifest, obvious

apparent to the naked eye 육안으로 또렷이 보이는

for no apparent reason 특별한 이유 없이

1729
linger
[líŋgər]

v. 남다, 계속되다   to stay somewhere beyond the usual or expected time

syn. delay, drag, delay

linger awhile after the party 파티가 끝난 후 잠시 남다

1730
contempt
[kəntémpt]

v. 경멸, 모욕   lack of respect accompanied by a feeling of intense dislike

syn. disdain, scorn, disrespect

live in contempt 굴욕을 받으며 살아가다

1731
loan
[loun]

n. 대부금, 대출금   the temporary provision of money

take out a loan 대출을 받다

repay a loan 대출을 갚다

1732

ordinary

[ɔ́:rdənèri]

adj. 보통의, 평범한 normal or usual

syn. average, common

> She seemed perfectly ordinary to me 내가 보기에 그녀는 완전히 평범했다

1733

possession

[pəzéʃən]

-pl. 재산

n. 소유, 소유물 the act of having and controlling property

syn. ownership

> illegal possession of arms 무기의 불법 소지

1734

species

[spí:ʃi(:)z]

n. 종류, 종족 a group of animals or plants that are similar and can produce young animals or plants

> a rare species of beetle 딱정벌레 희귀종

1735

urban

[ə́:rbən]

adj. 도시의 of or relating to cities and the people who live in them

syn. municipal, metropolitan, civic

> build new schools in urban areas 도시지역에 새로운 학교를 세우다

1736

breakthrough

[bréikθrù:]

n. 돌파구, 획기적인 발견 a productive insight / making an important discovery

syn. advance, development

ant. setback

> make a breakthrough 돌파구를 찾다
> a medical breakthrough 의학계의 획기적 발견

1737

conception

[kənsépʃən]

-con 함께

-cept 받다

n. 1 고안 2 임신 the originating of something in the mind / the act of becoming pregnant

syn. 1 idea, plan, design 2 impregnation, insemination

> the conception of a new device 새로운 장비의 고안
> from conception to 24 months after birth 임신부터 출생 후 24개월 동안

1738

upper

[ʌ́pər]

adj. 위쪽의, 높은 located above another or others of the same kind

syn. higher, high

> the upper competition 상급 대회

1739
appetite
[ǽpitàit]

n. 식욕, 입맛, 욕구   a feeling of craving something

syn. hunger, thirst, craving, desire

lose one's appetite 식욕을 잃다

a strong appetite for fame 명성에 대한 강한 욕구

1740
upright
[ʌ́pràit]

adj. 직립한, 곧은   in a vertical position

syn. unsloped, erect, vertical

an upright post 수직 기둥

1741
unnoticed
[ʌ̀nnóutist]

adj. 눈에 띄지 않고   not noticed

syn. unobserved

pass unnoticed 모른 채 넘어가다

1742
vivid
[vívid]
-viv 생명

adj. 생생한   evoking lifelike images within the mind

syn. graphic, lifelike

vivid in one's memory 기억에 생생한

1743
graduate
[grǽdʒuèit]

v. 졸업하다   to earn a degree or diploma from a school, college, or university

syn. qualify, pass, receive a degree

graduate from a school of cookery 요리 학교를 졸업하다

1744
future-oriented
[fjú:tʃərɔ́:riəntid]

adj. 미래지향적인   proceeding for future

a future-oriented, constructive project 미래지향적이고 건설적인 프로젝트

1745
worried
[wə́:rid]

adj. 난처한, 걱정스러운   unhappy because you keep thinking about a problem, or about something bad that might happen

syn. agonized, disturbed, upset

a worried look 걱정스러운 표정

1746
forced
[fɔːrst]

adj. 강요된   forced or compelled

syn. compulsory

forced labor 강제 노동

1747
found
[faund]

v. 설립하다, 건립하다　to start something such as an organization, company, school, or city
syn. establish, set up, launch

found a house on a rock 집을 반석 위에 짓다

1748
cure
[kjuər]

v. 치유하다, 치료하다　to make someone healthy again after an illness
syn. remedy, heal

cure a child's cold 아이의 감기를 고치다

1749
nibble
[níbəl]

v. 조금씩 물어뜯다　to bite off very small pieces
syn. nip, bite, chew

nibble at one's nails 손톱을 물어뜯다

1750
proof
[pru:f]

n. 증거, 입증　any factual evidence that helps to establish the truth of something
syn. evidence

conclusive proof 결정적인 증거

Review

뜻을 써보고 전체 어구의 의미를 생각해 보시오.

01 have a sore throat _____ 1716

02 direct contact between the two sides _____ 1727

03 consume a bottle of whiskey _____ 1724

04 five players constitute a basketball team _____ 1707

05 die of hunger _____ 1708

06 a sense of justice _____ 1712

07 a conflict of interest _____ 1711

08 conform to the rules of the club _____ 1713

09 lose one's appetite _____ 1739

10 a confirmed disease _____ 1709

11 articles on exhibition _____ 1704

12 a future-oriented, constructive project _____ 1744

13 unparalleled athletic ability _____ 1719

14 a conspicuous star _____ 1705

15 a world-famous architect _____ 1706

16 dominate feelings _____ 1703

17 unruly behavior _____ 1702

18 she seemed perfectly ordinary to me _____ 1732

19 build new schools in urban areas _____ 1735

20 vivid in one's memory _____ 1742

1751
sociology
[sòusiáləd3i]

n. 사회학 the study and classification of human societies

minor in sociology 사회학을 부전공하다

1752
research
[risə́:rtʃ]

n. 연구, 조사 systematic investigation to establish facts

syn. analysis, experimentation, inquiry, investigation

research and development 연구와 개발

1753
considerable
[kənsídərəbəl]

adj. 상당한, 중요한, 꽤 많은 large or relatively large in number or amount or extent or degree

syn. sizable, large, ample

considerable expense 상당한 비용

1754
specialty
[spéʃəlti]

n. 특수성, 전문, 특산물 an asset of special worth or utility

syn. career, profession, discipline

specialty dish 특별 요리

1755
instinctive
[instíŋktiv]

adj. 본능적인, 천성의 unthinking / prompted by instinct

syn. innate, inborn, inherent, natural

have an instinctive fear 본능적인 두려움을 갖다

1756
tool
[tu:l]

n. 도구, 공구, 연장 any instrument such as an axe, hammer, or spade for doing special jobs

syn. appliance, device, instrument, utensil

gardener's tools 정원사의 도구들

1757
livestock
[láivstàk]

n. (집합적) 가축 any animals kept for use or profit

syn. stock, farm animal

raise livestock 가축을 기르다

1758
toss
[tɔ:s]

v. 던지다, 뒤척이다, 쫓아내다 to throw or toss with a light motion

syn. fling, launch, sling, throw

toss the newspaper 신문을 툭 던지다

1759
mysterious
[mistíəriəs]

adj. 불가사의한, 원인불명의   not easily understood

syn. inexplicable, puzzling, baffling

a mysterious murder 미궁의 살인 사건

1760
sufficient
[səfíʃənt]

adj. 충분한, 만족한   enough for a particular need or purpose

syn. satisfactory, suitable, enough

ant. deficient, scanty

sufficient time/information 충분한 시간/정보

1761
anthropologist
[æ̀nθrəpálədʒist]

n. 인류학자   a social scientist who specializes in anthropology

employ two anthropologists 두 명의 인류학자를 채용하다

1762
protector
[prətéktər]

n. 보호자, 방어자, 후원자   a person who cares for persons or property

syn. defender, guardian, shielder

regard him as my friend and protector 그를 내 친구이자 보호자로 여기다

1763
confront
[kənfrʌ́nt]
-con 함께

v. 직면하다, 맞서다   to deal with something unpleasant head on

syn. face, face up, present

confront a problem 문제에 직면하다

1764
assumption
[əsʌ́mpʃən]

n. 가정, 추측   a statement that is assumed to be true and from which a conclusion can be drawn

syn. premise, supposition

a precarious assumption 근거 없는 추측

1765
exceed
[iksíːd]

v. 넘다, 도를 넘다   to be greater in scope or size than some standard

syn. transcend, surpass

exceed a budget 예산을 초과하다

1766
merely
[míərli]

adv. 한낱, 그저, 단지   and nothing more

syn. simply, just, only, but

I was merely trying to help. 나는 그저 도와주려던 것이었다.

1767
attachment
[ətǽtʃmənt]

n. 애착, 부착, 첨부   a feeling of affection for a person or an institution
syn. connection, linkage, binding, joining

show a strong attachment to life 삶에 강한 애착을 보이다

1768
literature
[lítərətʃər]
-liter 글자, 문자

n. 문학, 문헌   creative writing of recognized artistic value
syn. writings, books, letters, publications

English literature 영문학

1769
connect
[kənékt]

v. 잇다, 연결하다   to put together two or more pieces
syn. link, tie, link up

You are connected. 연결되었습니다.

1770
outweigh
[àutwéi]

v. ~보다 무겁다, ~보다 가치가 있다   to be heavier than
syn. overshadow, overweigh

outweigh a risk 위험을 무릅쓸만하다

1771
touch
[tʌtʃ]

v. 1 만지다 2 감동시키다   to make physical contact with / to make you feel grateful or sad
syn. 1 feel, finger, graze, handle 2 move

touch the exhibits 진열품에 손대다
have a power to touch people 사람들을 감동시키는 힘이 있다

1772
suggest
[səgdʒést]
-gest 나르다

v. 제안하다, 암시하다   to make a proposal, declare a plan for something
syn. propose, imply, hint

suggest another plan to the committee 위원회에 다른 안을 제출하다

1773
construct
[kənstrʌ́kt]
-struct 세우다

v. 건설하다, 세우다   to build or make something
syn. make, build

construct a theory 이론[학설]을 세우다

1774
trade
[treid]

n. 매매, 거래, 장사, 직업   the commercial exchange of goods and services
syn. exchange, swap, business, job, occupation

Trade was good last year. 작년은 거래가 활발했었다.

1775
construction
[kənstrʌ́kʃən]
-struct 세우다

n. 건설, 구조   the act of constructing something
syn. building, erection, fabrication

under construction 건설 중

1776
herd
[hə:rd]

n. 짐승의 떼, 무리   a group of cattle or sheep or other domestic mammals

a herd of cattle 소떼

1777
hydrogen
[háidrədʒən]

n. 수소   the lightest gas with no color, taste, or smell, that combines with oxygen to form water

hydrogen bomb 수소폭탄

1778
tradition
[trədíʃən]

n. 전설, 전통   an inherited pattern of thought or action
syn. heritage, legacy, convention, custom, practice

keep up the family tradition 집의 전통을 유지하다

1779
unique
[ju:ní:k]
-uni 하나

adj. 독특한, 특별한, 유일한   radically distinctive and without equal
syn. unexampled, single, outstanding

a unique proof 유일한 증거

1780
suitable
[sú:təbəl]

adj. 적당한, 상당한, 적절한   right or acceptable for a particular situation or purpose
syn. appropriate, correct, fit, proper
ant. unfit, irrelevant

a suitable alternative 적절한 대안책

1781
workload
[wə́:rklɔ̀d]

n. 작업부하, 작업량   work that a person is expected to do in a specified time
syn. work load

lighten the workload 일의 부담을 줄이다

1782
voluntary
[váləntèri]

adj. 자발적인, 임의의   done or given because you want to and not because you are forced to
syn. spontaneous, optional, volunteer, unforced

a voluntary contribution 자발적인 기부

1783
utilitarian
[juːtìlətɛ́əriən]

n. 공리적인, 실리적인, 실용적인 having a useful function

syn. practical, pragmatic, functional, realistic

utilitarian education 실용본위의 교육

1784
rule
[ruːl]

n. 규칙 a principle that customarily governs behavior

syn. dictate, edict, regulation, custom

the rules of the club 클럽의 규칙

1785
tune
[tjuːn]

n. 곡, 곡조, 멜로디 a succession of notes forming a distinctive sequence

syn. melody, song, accord, harmony, pitch

whistle a popular tune 휘파람으로 유행가를 부르다

1786
roar
[rɔːr]

v. 으르렁거리다, 외치다, 크게 웃다 to make a loud noise

syn. clamor, shout, storm

ant. whisper

We heard a lion roar. 우리는 사자가 으르렁거리는 소리를 들었다.

1787
futile
[fjúːtl]

adj. 쓸데없는, 무익한 producing no result or effect

syn. vain, useless, unproductive

a futile effort 헛수고

1788
suppose
[səpóuz]

v. 가정하다, 추측하다 to express a supposition

syn. assume, consider, presume, guess

ant. know

Let us suppose the news is really true. 그 뉴스가 사실이라고 가정하자.

1789
trial
[tráiəl]

n. 재판, 공판 the act of testing something

syn. hearing, lawsuit

go to trial 재판에 회부되다

1790
robbery
[rábəri]

n. 강도행위, 약탈 the crime of taking someone else's property

syn. looting

commit robbery 강도질하다

294

1791
conserve
[kənsə́:rv]

v. 보호하다, 절약하다   something safe from being damaged or destroyed

syn. maintain, preserve, reserve, save

ant. waste

conserve natural resources 천연 자원을 보호하다

1792
hence
[hens]

adv. 그러므로, 지금부터   from that fact or reason or as a result

syn. therefore, thus, so

fifty years hence 지금부터 50년 후

1793
position
[pəzíʃən]

n. 위치, 처지, 입장, 자세, 지위   the particular portion of space occupied by something

syn. place, view, posture, attitude

the sleeping position 수면자세

1794
unimaginable
[ʌnimǽdʒənəbəl]

adj. 생각할 수 없는   totally unlikely

syn. impossible, inconceivable

suffer unimaginable hardships 상상할 수 없는 어려움을 겪다

1795
whereas
[hwɛ́ərǽz]

conj. ~임에 반하여, ~인 까닭에   on the other hand

He drives to school, whereas I always walk.
그는 차를 몰고 등교하지만, 나는 언제나 걷는다.

1796
aroma
[əróumə]

n. 향, 냄새   a noticeable and usually pleasant smell

syn. smell, odor

because of the unique aroma and flavor 독특한 향과 맛 때문에

1797
costly
[kɔ́:stli]

adj. 1 값이 비싼 2 희생이 큰   having a high price / entailing great loss or sacrifice

syn. expensive, dear, high-priced, valuable, precious

Costly jewels 값비싼 보석들

a costly victory 희생이 많은 승리

1798
formal
[fɔ́:rməl]

adj. 정식의, 격식을 차린   done according to accepted rules or customs
syn. official, regulated, conventional, correct

sign a formal contract 정식으로 계약을 체결하다

1799
ingredient
[ingrí:diənt]

n. 성분, 원료, 재료   a component of a mixture or compound
syn. component, constituent, element, factor

What is the special ingredient? 특별한 재료는 무엇인가요?

1800
arise
[əráiz]

v. 일어나다, 나타나다, 발생하다   come into existence
syn. originate, stand up, occur, happen

in case a medical dispute arises 의료 분쟁이 생길 경우

296

Review

뜻을 써보고 전체 어구의 의미를 생각해 보시오.

01 **the sleeping** position _____ 1793

02 **a** suitable **alternative** _____ 1780

03 **suffer** unimaginable **hardships** _____ 1794

04 voluntary **works** _____ 1782

05 Trade **was good last year.** _____ 1774

06 **because of its unique** aroma _____ 1796

07 **keep up the family** tradition _____ 1778

08 costly **jewels** _____ 1797

09 **a** precarious **assumption** _____ 1764

10 toss **the newspaper** _____ 1758

11 exceed **a budget** _____ 1765

12 **a** rule **against smoking** _____ 1784

13 suggest **another plan** _____ 1772

14 conserve **natural resources** _____ 1791

15 **show a strong** attachment **to life** _____ 1767

16 **a** futile **effort** _____ 1787

17 **minor in** sociology _____ 1751

18 **raise** livestock _____ 1757

19 **English** literature _____ 1768

20 **have an** instinctive **fear** _____ 1755

DAY 37

1801
whole
[houl]

adj. 전부의, 모든   including all components without exception
syn. entire, complete, full, total

Spend the whole day writing. 온전히 하루를 글을 쓰면서 보내다.

1802
consumer
[kənsú:mər]

n. 소비자, 고객   a person who uses goods or services

consumer demand/choice/rights 소비자의 수요/선택/권리

1803
entrepreneur
[à:ntrəprəné:r]

n. 기업가, 실업가   someone who organizes a business venture and assumes the risk for it
syn. enterpriser

under a deal with an entrepreneur based in the U.S.
미국의 한 기업가와 거래를 하면서
emerging entrepreneur 장래가 유망한 사업가

1804
metaphor
[métəfɔ̀:r]

n. 은유, 암유   a way of describing something by referring to it as something different and suggesting that it has similar qualities to that thing

cancer as a metaphor for death 죽음의 비유로서의 암

1805
sum
[sʌm]

n. 총계, 총액   a quantity of money
syn. total

the sum of 2 and 3 is 5 2+3=5
a sum of five thousand won 일금 오천원정

1806
literal
[lítərəl]
-liter 글자, 문자

adj. 문장의, 글자 그대로의, 정확한   being or reflecting the essential or genuine character of something
syn. matter-of-fact, unimaginative, blunt, factual

literal translation 직역

1807
traditional
[trədíʃənəl]

adj. 전통의, 전통적인   derived from tradition
syn. conventional, typical, customary

a traditional way of life 전통적인 생활양식

1808
sunset
[sʌ́nsèt]

n. 해넘이, 일몰   the time when the sun goes below the horizon in the evening
syn. dusk, nightfall, sundown, twilight
ant. dawn

after sunset 일몰 후에

1809
unjust
[ʌ̀ndʒʌ́st]

adj. 부정한, 불공평한   not fair
syn. wrongful, unfair, partial, biased

an unjust decision 부당한 판결

1810
tragedy
[trǽdʒədi]

n. 비극, 참사, 불행   an event resulting in great loss and misfortune
syn. calamity, catastrophe, disaster
ant. blessing, comedy

aftermath of tragedy 참사의 여파

1811
anthropology
[æ̀nθrəpάlədʒ]

n. 인류학, 인간학   the social science that studies the origins and social relationships of human beings

major in applied anthropology 응용 인류학을 전공하다

1812
consumption
[kənsʌ́mpʃən]

n. 소비, 소모   the act of eating or drinking something
syn. indigestion, using up, expenditure

reduce meat consumption 고기 소비를 줄이다

1813
inhabited
[inhǽbitid]

adj. 사람이 살고 있는   having inhabitants
syn. occupied, populated, dwelled

thickly[sparsely] inhabited 인구가 많은[적은]

1814
migrate
[máigreit]

v. 이주하다, 이동하다   to move from one country or region to another and settle there
syn. move, journey, travel

migrate files 파일을 이동시키다

1815
superior
[səpíəriər]

adj. 우수한, 높은   of high or superior quality or performance
syn. excellent, incomparable
ant. inferior

because of the superior quality and flavor 높은 품질과 맛 때문에

1816

anticipate

[æntísəpèit]

-anti 이전, 앞

v. 예상하다, 기대하다   to regard something as probable or likely

syn. expect, foresee, predict, foretell

anticipate a victory 승리를 예상하다

1817

trail

[treil]

v. 질질 끌다, 뒤쫓다   to lag or linger behind

syn. chase, follow, hunt, pursue

trail one's skirt 스커트를 질질 끌다

1818

roll

[roul]

v. 구르다, 진행하다   to move by turning over and over or from side and side

syn. revolve, rotate

A coin rolled on the floor. 동전이 마룻바닥에 굴렀다.

1819

supernatural

[sù:pərnǽtʃərəl]

adj. 초자연의, 불가사의한   not existing in nature or subject to explanation according to natural laws

syn. magical, mystic, spiritual

possess supernatural powers 초자연적인 힘을 소유하다

1820

container

[kəntéinər]

-tain 쥐다

n. 컨테이너, 용기, 통, 그릇   any object that can be used to hold things

keep food in an airtight container 식품을 밀폐 용기에 담아 두다

1821

antique

[æntíːk]

-anti 이전, 앞

adj. 골동품의, 고대의   made in or typical of earlier times and valued for its age

syn. ancient, age-old

ant. modern, new, recent

an antique dealer 골동품 상인

1822

differ

[dífər]

v. 다르다, 의견이 다르다   to be different / to be of different opinions

syn. disagree, dissent

Tastes differ. 취미는 사람마다 다르다.

1823
military
[mílitèri]

adj. 군의, 군대의 associated with soldiers or the military
syn. martial, soldierly, warlike

military intervention 군사 개입

1824
anxiety
[æŋzáiəti]

n. 불안감, 걱정 a feeling of fear and worry about something uncertain
syn. anxiousness, apprehension, concern, tension

suffer from anxiety and depression 불안감과 우울증으로 고통을 겪다

1825
organism
[ɔ́ːrgənìzəm]

n. 유기체, 생물체 a living thing that has the ability to act or function independently
syn. component, member, part

one of the world's most resilient organisms
세계에서 가장 끈질긴 생명체 중 하나

1826
possibility
[pàsəbíləti]

n. 가능성, 발전 가능성 a future prospect or potential
syn. possibleness, hypothesis, theory

strong possibility 높은 가능성

1827
dig
[dig]

v. 1 파다 2 탐구하다 to break up and move earth / to find something that has been hidden for a long time
syn. 1 dig out, labor 2 understand, grasp

dig a well 우물을 파다
dig for information 정보를 얻으려고 하다

1828
postrevolution
[poustrèvəlúːʃən]

n. 혁명 이후 after revolution

hold a postrevolution rally 혁명 이후 집회를 열다

1829
organize
[ɔ́ːrgənàiz]

v. 조직하다, 편제하다, 구성하다, 준비하다 to create, plan and direct
syn. begin, create, establish

organize a meeting/party/trip 회의/파티/여행을 준비[조직]하다

1830
anxious
[ǽŋkʃəs]

adj. 1 열망하는 2 걱정스러운, 불안한 eagerly desirous / showing anxiety
syn. dying, nervous, uneasy, unquiet

have an anxious wish 간절히 바라는 소원이 하나 있다
feel anxious all day long 하루 종일 불안함을 느끼다

1831
dictate
[díkteit]
-dict 말하다

v. 받아쓰게 하다, 지시하다   to say words for someone else to write down

dictate a letter to the secretary 비서에게 편지를 받아쓰게 하다

1832
superstition
[sùːpərstíʃən]

n. 미신   an irrational belief arising from ignorance or fear

syn. superstitious notion

do away with a superstition 미신을 타파하다

1833
reputation
[rèpjətéiʃən]

n. 명성, 평판, 세평   the state of being held in high esteem and honor

syn. character, fame, name, position, prestige

have a good reputation as a doctor 의사로서의 명망이 높다

1834
train
[trein]

v. 훈련하다, 양성하다   to create by training and teaching

syn. discipline, instruct, teach, prepare

train a dog to obey 개를 말 잘 듣도록 훈련하다

1835
supervision
[sùːpərvíʒən]
-vis 보다

n. 관리, 감독, 지휘, 감시   management by overseeing the performance of a person or group

syn. administration, direction, guidance, management

under the supervision of Dr. Kim 김 박사 감독 하에

1836
diet
[dáiət]

n. 식사, 음식, 식습관   a prescribed selection of foods

have a healthy, balanced diet 건강에 좋은 균형 잡힌 식사를 하다

1837
extracurricular
[èkstrəkəríkjələr]

adj. 정규과목 이외의, 과외의   outside the regular academic curriculum

participate in many extracurricular activities 많은 과외 활동에 참여하다

1838
trait
[treit]

n. 특성, 특징   a distinguishing feature of your personal nature

syn. attribute, characteristic, feature, property

personality traits 성격적 특성

1839
content
[kəntént]

n. 내용물   everything that is included in a collection

syn. contentment

This book has poor contents. 이 책은 내용이 빈약하다

1840
supply
[səplái]

v. 공급하다, 보충하다　to give something useful or necessary to

syn. equip, furnish, give, render

ant. withhold

supply food and blankets 식량과 담요를 보급하다

1841
mutual
[mjú:tʃuəl]

adj. 상호관계가 있는, 공동의　concerning each of two or more persons or things

syn. reciprocal, shared, common, similar

mutual understanding 상호간의 이해

1842
suck
[sʌk]

v. 빨다　to draw into the mouth by using your lips

syn. draw in, sip, swallow, soak up

She was sucking milk through a straw. 그녀는 빨대로 우유를 먹고 있었다.

1843
archaeological
[à:rkiəládʒikəl]

adj. 고고학의　related to or dealing with or devoted to archaeology

syn. archaeologic, archeologic

archeological research 고고학적 연구

1844
subtle
[sʌ́tl]

adj. 감지하기 힘든, 난해한, 미묘한　difficult to detect or grasp by the mind or analyze

syn. elusive, implied, indirect

ant. obvious, undiscerning

subtle colours/flavors/smells 감지하기 힘든 색깔/향/냄새

1845
argue
[á:rgju:]

v. 논쟁하다, 주장하다　to present reasons and arguments

syn. reason, contend, debate

He argued in favor of[against] capital punishment.
그는 사형 찬성론 [반대론]을 주장했다.

1846
stroke
[strouk]

n. 1 한번 치기　2 발작, 뇌졸중　the act of swinging or striking / a sudden illness in part of someone's brain

on the stroke of two 2시를 치면

after she had a stroke 뇌졸중으로 쓰러진 후

1847
boundless
[báundlis]

adj. 무한한, 끝없는 without limits
syn. limitless, endless

his boundless energy 그의 끝없는 정력

1848
strength
[streŋ*k*θ]

n. 힘, 기운 the property of being physically or mentally strong
syn. energy, vigor, vitality
ant. frailty

with all one's strength 온 힘을 다해

1849
breathtaking
[bréθtèikiŋ]

adj. 깜짝 놀랄 만한, 굉장한 tending to cause suspension of regular breathing
syn. exciting, moving, stimulating

a breathtaking beauty 굉장한 미인

1850
arcade
[ɑ:*r*kéid]

n. 아케이드, 상점가, 게임 센터 a covered passageway with shops and stalls on either side
syn. archway, mall, gallery

an underground shopping arcade 지하상가

Review

뜻을 써보고 전체 어구의 의미를 생각해 보시오.

01 migrate file   1814

02 military intervention   1823

03 superior quality and flavor   1815

04 the most resilient organisms   1825

05 anticipate a victory   1816

06 hold a postrevolution rally   1828

07 supernatural powers   1819

08 consumer rights   1802

09 supply food and blankets   1840

10 do away with a superstition   1832

11 emerging entrepreneur   1803

12 tastes differ   1822

13 a breathtaking beauty   1849

14 the boundless energy   1847

15 with all one's strength   1848

16 have a healthy, balanced diet   1836

17 argue in favor of capital punishment   1845

18 subtle colors   1844

19 suck milk through a straw   1842

20 aftermath of tragedy   1810

1851
support
[səpɔ́ːrt]
-port 문

v. 지탱하다, 버티다, 지지하다, 부양하다 to give moral or psychological support, aid, or courage to

syn. bolster, brace, prop, strengthen

support a family 가족을 부양하다

1852
potential
[poʊténʃəl]

adj. 잠재적인 existing in possibility

syn. possible, likely

potential customers 잠재 고객들

1853
require
[rikwáiər]
-quire 찾다, 추구하다

v. 요구하다, 필요로 하다 to need something

syn. lack, need, want, command, compel

ant. have

require attention 주의를 요하다

1854
suppress
[səprés]

v. 억압하다, 진압하다 to put down by force or authority

syn. restrain, repress, silence

suppress a riot 폭동을 진압하다

1855
resemble
[rizémbəl]

v. …와 닮다, …와 공통점이 있다 to be like or similar to

syn. favor, look like, parallel, take after

ant. differ

resemble each other 서로 닮다

1856
extra
[ékstrə]

adj. 추가의, 가외의 more than is needed, desired, or required

syn. excess, redundant, spare, superfluous

at no extra charge 추가 요금 없이

1857
transaction
[trænsǽkʃən]
-trans 가로질러

n. 처리, 취급 the act of transacting within or between groups

syn. arrangement, bargain, deal, exchange

cash transactions 현금 거래

1858
unknown
[ʌnnóun]

adj. 알려지지 않은, 헤아릴 수 없는 not known

syn. unidentified, obscure, strange

an unknown disaster 알려져 있지 않은 대참사

1859
transfer
[trænsfə́:r]
-trans 가로질러

v. 옮기다, 양도하다 to transfer somebody to a different position
syn. move, hand over

transfer property to a person 재산을 남에게 양도하다

1860
isolate
[áisəlèit]
-sol 홀로

v. 고립시키다, 격리시키다 to place or set apart
syn. separate, set apart, detach

a community isolated from civilization 문명으로부터 고립된 사회

1861
hero
[hí:rou]

n. 영웅, 위인 a man distinguished by exceptional courage and nobility and strength
syn. champion, protagonist, star

a war hero 전쟁 영웅

1862
violate
[váiəlèit]

v. 위반하다, 폭행을 가하다 to be in violation of rules or patterns
syn. break, infringe, transgress, trespass

violate social rules 사회의 규칙을 어기다

1863
apology
[əpálədʒi]
-log 말하다

n. 사과, 사죄, 변명 an expression of regret at having caused trouble for someone
syn. confession, acknowledgment, regret, repentance

accepted my apology 사과를 받아들였다

1864
context
[kántekst]
-con 함께

n. 1 전후문맥 2 상황 the words before and after a word or phrase / the situation in which something happens

tell the meaning of this word from its context
문맥 속에서 단어를 의미를 구별하다
the historical context 역사적인 상황

1865
inhibit
[inhíbit]

v. 억제하다, 금하다, 방해하다 to put down by force or authority
syn. suppress, stamp down

inhibit functioning of the brain 뇌의 작용을 방해하다

307

1866
appear
[əpíər]

v. ~처럼 보이다, 나타나다, 나오다   to have a certain outward aspect
syn. look, seem, come out

appear as a substitute 교체선수로 나오다

1867
envious
[énviəs]

adj. ~을 부러워하는   feeling or showing a desire to have what someone else has
syn. covetous, jealous

envious looks 부러운 듯한 표정

1868
digest
[didʒést]
-gest 나르다

v. 1 소화하다[되다]   2 숙고하다   to convert food into absorbable substances / to take into the mind or memory

this food digests well[ill] 이 음식물은 소화가 잘[안] 된다
digest a plan 계획을 짜다

1869
apparently
[əpǽrəntli]

adv. 분명히, 명백히, 외관상으로는   from appearances alone
syn. seemingly, ostensibly, on the face of it, evidently, obviously

apparently frustrated 좌절하는 모습이 역력한

1870
continent
[kántənənt]

n. 대륙, 육지   one of the large landmasses of the earth
syn. mainland

travel on the continent 대륙을 여행하다

1871
multiracial
[mÀltiréiʃəl]

adj. 여러 민족의, 다민족의   made up of or involving or acting on behalf of various races

a multiracial society 다민족 사회

1872
environment
[inváiərənmənt]
-en 내부, 안

n. 환경, 상황   the totality of surrounding conditions
syn. surroundings, ecosystem

a pleasant working/learning environment 쾌적한 작업/학습 환경

1873
appearance
[əpíərəns]

n. 외모, 출현, 겉모습, 출전, 출석   outward or visible aspect of a person or thing
syn. visual aspect, appearing

check one's appearance 외모를 점검하다

1874
equality
[i(:)kwɑ́ləti]

n. 평등, 동등, 공정, 균형 the quality of being the same in quantity or measure or value or status

syn. parity, sameness, similarity

racial equality 인종 평등

1875
blossom
[blɑ́səm]

n. 꽃, 개화기 the flowers of a fruit tree

syn. bloom, flower

the blossom of youth 청춘의 개화기

1876
frontier
[frʌntíər]

n. 국경, 변경 a wilderness at the edge of a settled area of a country

syn. boundary, border, limit, edge

guard the frontier 변방을 지키다

1877
applause
[əplɔ́ːz]

n. 박수갈채, 칭찬 a demonstration of approval by clapping the hands together

syn. hand clapping, clapping

a big round of applause 큰 박수갈채

1878
continuous
[kəntínjuəs]

adj. 연속적인, 지속적인 without interruption

syn. ceaseless, nonstop

despite the continuous efforts 지속적인 노력에도 불구하고

1879
equal
[íːkwəl]

adj. 동등한, 평등한, 같은 having the same quantity, value, or measure as another

syn. identical, same, similar, alike, fair, impartial

fight for equal rights 동등한 권리를 위해 싸우다

1880
digestion
[didʒéstʃən]
-gest 나르다

n. 소화 the process of decomposing organic matter by bacteria

food that is hard[easy] of digestion 소화가 안[잘]되는 음식

1881

broad

[brɔːd]

adj. 넓은, 대강의   having great extent from one side to the other

syn. wide, extensive, comprehensive, general

in a broad sense 넓은 뜻으로

1882

contest

[kántest]

-con 함께

n. 대회, 시합, 콘테스트   an occasion on which a winner is selected from among two or more contestants

syn. match, competition

a beauty contest 미인 콘테스트

1883

forest

[fɔ́(ː)rist]

n. 숲, 산림, 삼림   the trees and other plants in a large densely wooded area

syn. woods, woodland

cut down a forest 산림을 벌채하다

1884

brutal

[brúːtl]

adj. 잔인한, 악랄한, 짐승의   extremely cruel or harsh

syn. cruel, fierce, harsh, tortuous

the most brutal leader in history 역사상 가장 악랄한 지도자

1885

litter

[lítər]

v. 쓰레기를 버리다   to make a place messy by strewing garbage around

syn. scatter, disorder, mess up

people who litter get a $1,000 fine 쓰레기를 버리는 자는 1,000달러의 벌금이 부과 된다

1886

burst

[bəːrst]

v. 1 파열하다, 폭발하다 2 갑자기 들어오다[나가다]   to come open suddenly and violently / to burst outward

syn. 1 split, break open, explode 2 break in

burst into laughter 웃음을 터트리다

burst into the house 집에 침입하다

1887

overlook

[òuvərlúk]

v. 1 ~을 내다보이는 위치에 있다 2 눈감아주다   to have a view of something from above / to forgive a fault or mistake

syn. 1 oversee 2 forgive

overlook the river 강을 내다보다

overlook a fault 과실을 눈감아 주다

1888
contractor
[kəntrǽktər]
-con 함께
-tract 끌다

n. 계약자, 청부업자, 하청업자 someone who contracts to build things
syn. declarer

a building contractor 건설 계약자

1889
predictor
[pridíktər]
-dict 말하다
-pre 이전의

n. 예언자, 예측요인, 지표 someone who makes predictions of the future
syn. forecaster, prognosticator, soothsayer

a key economic predictor 중요한 경제지표

1890
preoccupied
[pri:ákjəpàid]
-pre 이전의

adj. 몰두한, 열중한, 선취한 deeply absorbed in thought
syn. engrossed, engaged, absorbed, deep in thought

preoccupied with an idea 어떤 생각에 골몰한

1891
contrary
[kántreri]
-con 함께

adj. 반대의, 적합하지 않은 very opposed in nature or character or purpose
syn. opposed, opposite, antagonistic, alternate

a contrary current 역류

1892
evolve
[iválv]
-volv 구르다

v. 발전하다, 전개시키다 to develop gradually by a long continuous process
syn. develop

science has evolved over several centuries 과학은 수 세기에 걸쳐 발전해왔다

1893
examination
[igzæmənéiʃən]

n. 시험, 조사, 검사 the act of examining something closely
syn. scrutiny

a physical examination 신체검사

1894
convert
[kənvə́:rt]
-vert 바꾸다

v. 전환하다, 바꾸다 to change from one system to another or to a new plan or policy
syn. alter, change, modify, transform
ant. maintain

converted from 220 to 110 Volt 220볼트에서 110볼트로 바꿨다.

1895
discuss
[diskʌ́s]

v. 논의하다, 토론하다, 상담하다   to speak with others about
syn. talk over, converse, consider, confer with, speak of
discuss our household budget 우리 집 예산에 대해 토론하다

1896
excel
[iksél]

v. 뛰어나다, ~보다 낫다, 탁월하다   to distinguish oneself
syn. stand out, surpass
ant. fail
she excelled in math 그녀는 수학에서 뛰어났다

1897
correction
[kərékʃən]
-rect 올바름, 인도함

n. 정정, 수정, 교정   the act of offering an improvement to replace a mistake
syn. rectification, improvement, amendment
after a brief correction 즉각 수정 후

1898
disharmony
[dishá:rməni]
-dis 멀어짐, 부정

n. 부조화, 불일치   a lack of harmony
syn. inharmoniousness, discord
ant. harmony
create disharmony with the natural environment 자연환경과 부조화를 만들다

1899
discipline
[dísəplin]

n. 기강, 징계, 훈련, 규율   a system of rules of conduct or method of practice
syn. self-control, punishment, reprimand
be under discipline 규율이 엄하다

1900
count
[kaunt]

v. 의지하다, 중요하다, 셈하다   to determine the number or amount of
syn. number, think, consider
every vote counts 모든 표는 중요하다

Review

뜻을 써보고 전체 어구의 의미를 생각해 보시오.

01 at no extra charge   1856

02 cut down a forest   1883

03 the most brutal leader in history 1884

04 create disharmony 1898

05 racial equality 1874

06 discuss our household budget 1895

07 after a brief correction 1897

08 check one's appearance 1873

09 a contrary current 1891

10 accepted my apology 1863

11 violate social rules 1862

12 travel on the continent 1870

13 envious looks 1867

14 appear as a substitute 1866

15 resemble each other 1855

16 the historical context 1864

17 guard the frontier 1876

18 a big round of applause 1877

19 potential customers 1852

20 require attention 1853

DAY 39

1901
punctual
[pʌ́ŋktʃuəl]

adj. 시간을 엄수하는, 어김없는   acting or arriving or performed exactly at the time appointed

syn. prompt, on time, precise

being punctual is important 시간을 잘 지키는 것은 중요하다

1902
spectrum
[spéktrəm]

n. 스펙트럼, 빛띠, 영역   an ordered array of the components of an emission or wave

across the political spectrum 정치적 영역을 뛰어넘어

1903
correlation
[kɔ̀ːrəléiʃən]

-co 함께

n. 상호관계   a reciprocal relation between two or more things

a direct correlation 직접적인 상관관계

1904
crop
[krɑp]

n. 수확, 농작물, 곡물   the yield from plants in a single growing season

syn. harvest

grow[cultivate] crops 작물을 재배하다

1905
work
[wəːrk]

v. 1 일하다, 노력하다 2 효과가 있다   to do a job that you are paid for / to be effective or successful

syn. 1 labor, toil, sweat 2 be effective, function, produce

work hard to improve grades 성적을 올리기 위해 열심히 노력하다
This method doesn't work. 이 방법은 효과가 없다.

1906
dilute
[dilúːt]

v. 1 물을 타다, 희석하다 2 줄이다   to lessen the strength or flavor of a solution or mixture

syn. 1 weaken, thin, water down 2 cut down, reduce

dilute wine with water 포도주에 물을 타다
dilute one's investment 투자를 줄이다

1907
tremble
[trémbəl]

-trem 떨다

v. 떨다, 흔들리다   to move or jerk quickly and involuntarily up and down or sideways

syn. flutter, quake, quiver, shake, shiver, waver

leaves trembling in the breeze 미풍에 흔들리는 나뭇잎들

1908
archaeologist
[ὰːrkiálədʒist]

n. 고고학자 an anthropologist who studies prehistoric people and their culture

syn. archeologist

Archaeologist find the most amazing relics 고고학자들은 가장 놀라운 유물을 찾는다

1909
direct
[dirékt]
-rect 올바름, 인도함

adj. 직접적인, 노골적인 direct in spatial dimensions

syn. straight

direct rays 태양의 직사광선

1910
tremendous
[triméndəs]

adj. 엄청난, 거대한 extraordinarily large in size or extent or amount

syn. colossal, enormous, huge, immense

ant. tiny, ordinary

a tremendous explosion 무시무시한 폭발

1911
prepare
[pripέər]
-pre 이전의

v. 준비하다, 채비하다 to make ready in advance for a particular purpose

syn. fix, set up, ready, cook, set

prepare a lesson 학과 예습을 하다

1912
split
[split]

v. 쪼개다, 나누다 to separate into parts or portions

syn. break, separate, divide

split profits 이익을 나누다

1913
prevalent
[prévələnt]

adj. 일반적인, 널리 알려진 most frequent or common

syn. widespread, pervasive

a prevalent view 일반적인 견해

1914
unwanted
[ὰnwántid]

adj. 원치 않는, 쓸모없는, 불필요한 not wanted / not needed

syn. undesirable, useless, unnecessary

unwanted advice 원치 않는 충고

1915
prior
[práiər]

adj. 앞의, 이전의 earlier in time

syn. antecedent, earlier, former, previous

ant. subsequent

prior to the end of the fiscal year 회계 연도가 끝나기 전에

1916
usually
[júːʒuəli]

adv. 보통, 일반적으로   under normal conditions
syn. normally, commonly, ordinarily
usually I walk home 나는 보통 걸어서 집에 간다

1917
pulse
[pʌls]

n. 맥박, 맥, 고동   the regular movement of blood as the heart pumps it round the body
syn. impulse, heartbeat
a strong/weak pulse 강한/약한 맥

1918
privileged
[prívəlidʒd]

adj. 특권이 있는   blessed with privileges
syn. advantaged, favored, powerful, special
the privileged class 특권 계층

1919
visually
[víʒuəli]
-vis 보다

adv. 시각적으로, 눈에 보이도록   with respect to vision
syn. optically, visibly, clearly
a visually impaired person 시각 장애인

1920
profitable
[práfitəbəl]

adj. 이익이 되는, 유리한, 유익한   yielding material gain or profit
syn. advantageous, lucrative, gainful, money-making
a profitable deal 유리한 거래

1921
wild
[waild]

adj. 야생의, 야만의   in a natural state
syn. untamed
edible wild plants 먹을 수 있는 야생 식물

1922
project
[prɔ́dʒekt]

n. 안, 계획   any piece of work that is undertaken or attempted
syn. plan, undertaking, assignment
carry out a project 계획을 실시하다

1923
awaken
[əwéikən]

v. 깨우다, 눈뜨다   to cause to become awake or conscious
syn. wake, waken
a loud noise awakened her 시끄러운 소음이 그녀를 깨웠다

1924
cottage
[kátidʒ]

n. 시골집, 작은집, 별장   a small house with a single story
syn. bungalow

a cottage on the beach 해변의 작은 별장

1925
proposal
[prəpóuzəl]

n. 신청, 제안   something proposed
syn. suggestion

turn down the proposal 제안을 거절하다

1926
contradict
[kàntrədíkt]
-dict 말하다

v. 부정[부인]하다, 모순되다   to be in contradiction with
syn. deny, disagree

the reports contradict each other 보고서들이 서로 모순된다

1927
countless
[káuntlis]

adj. 셀 수 없는, 무수한   too numerous to be counted
syn. innumerable, infinite

countless people 무수히 많은 사람들

1928
provide
[prəváid]

v. 제공하다, 공급하다   to give someone something that they want or need
syn. supply, furnish

provide energy for the house 집에 에너지를 공급하다

1929
contribute
[kəntríbjut]
-tribute 주다

v. 기여하다, 기부하다, 기고하다   to give money, goods, or your time and effort in order to achieve something
syn. donate, give, supply

contribute to the community chest 공동 모금에 기부하다

1930
courage
[kə́:ridʒ]

n. 용기, 담력, 배짱   a quality of spirit that enables you to face danger or pain without showing fear
syn. bravery, braveness

show courage during a time of crisis 위기의 시기에 용기를 보여주다

1931
treatment
[trí:tmənt]

n. 처리, 치료   care provided to improve a situation
syn. care, approach, handling

the problem of sewage treatment 오수 처리의 문제

1932
rise
[raiz]

v. 일어나다, 치솟다   to move upward
syn. get up, stand, ascend, climb
ant. sit, fall, drop

rise to one's feet 일어서다

1933
tropical
[trάpikəl]

adj. 열대의   relating to or situated in or characteristic of the tropics

tropical plants 열대식물

1934
disappear
[dìsəpíər]
-dis 멀어짐, 부정

v. 사라지다, 실종되다   to die or go away completely
syn. vanish, go away

disappeared without a trace 흔적도 없이 사라졌다

1935
role
[roul]

n. 배역   the actions and activities assigned to a person or group
syn. character, part

a leading role 주역

1936
trek
[trek]

v. 여행하다, 걸어서 가다   to walk usually for a long distance

trekking through the jungles 정글 도보 여행

1937
review
[rivjú:]

n. 재검토, 비평   an act of carefully looking at or examining the quality or condition of something or someone
syn. evaluation, examination, reassessment

the government's review of its education policy 정부의 교육 정책 검토

1938
disappointment
[dìsəpɔ́intmənt]
-dis 멀어짐, 부정

n. 실망, 낙담   a feeling of dissatisfaction
syn. letdown, frustration, failure, dissatisfaction

to one's disappointment 실망스럽게도

1939
trustworthy
[trʌ́stwə̀:rði]

adj. 신뢰할 수 있는, 확실한 worthy of trust or belief
syn. believable, credible
ant. suspicious, disreputable

provide trustworthy news 신뢰할 수 있는 뉴스를 제공하다

1940
revise
[riváiz]

v. 개정하다, 바꾸다 to make changes especially to correct or improve
syn. amend, change, correct

revise one's opinions of a person 아무에 대한 의견을 바꾸다

1941
trend
[trend]

n. 경향, 추세 a general direction in which something tends to move
syn. drift, tendency

set a trend 유행을 창출[결정]하다

1942
restore
[ristɔ́:r]
-re 다시, 역행하여

v. 원 장소에 되돌리다, 되찾다 to return to its original or usable and functioning condition
syn. recondition, reconstruct, repair
ant. damage, destroy

restore order 질서를 회복하다

1943
disastrous
[dizǽstrəs]
-astr 별
-dis 멀어짐, 부정

adj. 처참한, 참단한, 형편없는 having extremely unfortunate or dire consequences
syn. black, calamitous, fatal, fateful

a disastrous harvest/fire/result 형편없는 수확/처참한 화재/처참한 결과

1944
reservoir
[rézərvwà:r]
-re 다시, 역행하여

n. 저장소, 저수지, 매장량 a large or extra supply of something
syn. artificial lake, manmade lake

a reservoir of knowledge 지식의 보고

1945
discount
[dískaunt]

n. 할인, 참작 the act of reducing the selling price of merchandise
syn. price reduction, deduction

large discount chains 대형 할인매장

1946
resist
[rizíst]
-re 다시, 역행하여
-sist 서다

v. 저항하다　to fight against something
syn. struggle against
ant. comply, yield
　resist temptation 유혹에 저항하다

1947
driveway
[dráivwèi]

n. 사유 차도, 진입로　a road leading up to a private house
syn. private road
　pave a driveway 진입로를 포장하다

1948
resource
[rí:sɔ:rs]

n. 자원　available source of wealth
syn. wealth, capital, money
　human resources 인적 자원

1949
equipment
[ikwípmənt]

n. 장비, 설비, 비품　the tools, machines, or other things that you need for a particular job or activity
syn. supplies, gear, apparatus, furnishings
　check[inspect] equipment 장비를 점검하다

1950
respectable
[rispéktəbəl]

adj. 1 존경할 만한, 훌륭한　2 상당한　showing or having standards that society approves of / enough in amount or quality
syn. 1 admirable, worthy, acceptable　2 considerable
　respectable citizens 훌륭한 시민
　a respectable position 상당한 지위

Review

뜻을 써보고 전체 어구의 의미를 생각해 보시오.

01 **turn down the** proposal 1925

02 **a** tremendous **explosion** 1910

03 **a** visually **impaired person** 1919

04 **a** profitable **deal** 1920

05 **a leading** role 1935

06 **show** courage **and determination** 1930

07 **set a** trend 1941

08 countless **people** 1927

09 **across the political** spectrum 1902

10 **a strong** pulse 1917

11 usually **I walk home** 1916

12 **not a direct** correlation 1903

13 respectable **citizens** 1950

14 restore **order** 1942

15 **large** discount **chains** 1945

16 **a** prevalent **view** 1913

17 **pave a** driveway 1947

18 unwanted **advice** 1914

19 contribute **to the community chest** 1929

20 prepare **a lesson** 1911

DAY 40

1951
guard
[gɑ:rd]

v. 보호하다, 경계하다   to keep watch over
syn. watch over, protect, oversee, shield

guard the palace 궁전을 호위하다

1952
steam
[sti:m]

v. 1 (증기를) 분출하다   2 화나게 하다   to cook something by letting steam pass over it / to get angry

This boiler steams well 이 보일러는 증기가 잘 나온다
His critical statement steamed me up 그의 비판적 진술이 나를 화나게 했다

1953
grateful
[gréitfəl]
-grat 기쁨, 감사

adj. 감사하고 있는, 감사의   feeling or showing gratitude
syn. thankful

a grateful heart 감사하는 마음

1954
itch
[itʃ]

v. 가렵다, 근질근질하다   to have an unpleasant feeling that makes you want to scratch it

they were itching to go outside 그들은 외출하고 싶어 근질근질했다

1955
stick
[stik]

v. 찌르다, 박다   to push a pointed object into or through something

stuck the needle into my arm 내 팔에 주사 바늘을 찔렀다

1956
irrigation
[ìrəgéiʃən]

n. 물을 댐, 관개   supplying dry land with water by means of ditches, etc.

lack irrigation systems to keep crops alive
곡물이 자라도록 할 관개시설이 부족하다

1957
item
[áitəm]

n. 품목, 항목   a single thing among a set or on the list
syn. article, entry, detail, unit, element, feature

various items in the pictures 사진 속에 있는 다양한 물건

1958
irritate
[irətèit]

v. 짜증나게 하다   to make angry or excite in an unpleasant way
syn. annoy, bother, vex

his arrogance really irritates me 그의 거만함 때문에 정말 짜증난다

1959
extend
[iksténd]
-tend 뻗다

v. 연장하다, 펼치다   to spread or stretch forth
syn. stretch, prolong, expand

extend both his arms 양 팔을 벌렸다

1960
revenue
[révənjù:]

n. 소득, 수익   the entire amount of income before any deductions are made
syn. gain, gross, income, profits

revenue and expenditure 세입 세출

1961
pressure
[préʃər]
-press 밀다

n. 압력, 압박, 곤란   the force applied to a unit area of surface

the pressure intensified 압력이 심해졌다

1962
reverse
[rivə́:rs]
-re 다시, 역행하여

v. 거꾸로 하다, 바꾸어 놓다   to change something to an opposite state or condition
syn. invert, turn, change

reverse a coat 코트를 뒤집다

1963
workforce
[wə́:rkfɔ̀:rs]

n. 노동자, 노동력   the force of workers available
syn. manpower

the factory's workforce 그 공장의 노동자력

1964
primitive
[prímətiv]
-prim 처음의

adj. 원시의, 원시적인   belonging to an early stage of technical development
syn. crude

primitive cultures 원시문화

1965
archaeology
[à:rkiálədʒi]

n. 고고학   the branch of anthropology that studies prehistoric people and their cultures

a graduate student majoring in archeology 고고학 전공의 한 대학원생

1966
professional
[prəféʃənəl]

n. 전문가, 직업선수   someone who does a job that requires special training, education, or skill
syn. pro, master

you are a professional in this field 당신은 이 분야에서 전문가입니다

1967
drug
[drʌg]

n. 마약, 약   a substance that is used as a medicine or narcotic

he does not smoke or take drugs 그는 담배도 피우지 않고 마약도 하지 않는다

1968
artistry
[áːrtistri]

n. 예술적 기교   a superior skill that you can learn by study and practice and observation

syn. talent, skill

brilliant artistry 뛰어난 예술적 기교

1969
promotion
[prəmóuʃən]

n. 승진, 장려   a move to a higher position

syn. advancement, furtherance

promotion goes by seniority[merit] 승진은 연공[공적]에 의한다

1970
property
[prápərti]

n. 재산, 성질   things, especially valuable things, that are owned by someone / a quality or feature of something

the chemical properties of iron 철의 화학적 성질

1971
avalanche
[ǽvəlæntʃ]

n. 눈[산]사태   a slide of large masses of snow and ice and mud down a mountain

syn. landslide, snowslide

an avalanche-prone slope 산사태가 발생하기 쉬운 경사면

1972
stabilize
[stéibəlàiz]

v. 안정시키다   to make stable and keep from fluctuating or put into an equilibrium

syn. balance, secure, steady

ant. disrupt

stabilize the consumer prices 소비자 가격을 안정시키다

1973
dribble
[dríbəl]

v. (물방울이) 똑똑 떨어지다   to flow in drops or make a liquid flow in this way

syn. drop, carry

water dribbling from the pipe 배관에서 똑똑 떨어지고 있는 물

1974
standard
[stǽndərd]

n. 표준, 기준, 수준　a level of quality, achievement, etc., that is considered acceptable or desirable

syn. criterion

the standard of living 생활수준

1975
dramatic
[drəmǽtik]

adj. 극적인, 인상적인　suitable to or characteristic of drama

syn. theatrical, spectacular, striking

a dramatic event 극적인 사건

1976
drain
[drein]

v. 1 배수하다　2 다 써버리다　to flow off gradually / to deplete of resources

syn. 1 run out, pump out, empty　2 exhaust, use up

this field drains quickly 이 땅은 물이 빨리 빠진다

feel drained of energy 힘이 다 빠진 것처럼 느껴지다

1977
starvation
[stɑːrvéiʃən]

n. 굶주림, 기아　a state of extreme hunger

syn. hunger

struggle with starvation 기아에 허덕이다

1978
crude oil
[krúːd ɔ́il]

n. 원유　a dark oil consisting mainly of hydrocarbons

the ship holds 300,000 tons of crude oil 그 선박은 30만 톤의 원유를 싣고 있다

1979
steadily
[stédili]

adv. 착실하게, 견실하게　at a steady rate or pace

syn. consistently, constantly

sales moved up steadily in August 8월 매출은 지속적 증가세를 보였다

1980
creep
[kriːp]

v. 기다, 포복하다　to move slowly

syn. crawl, wriggle, worm

creep on tiptoe 발끝으로 살금살금 걷다

1981
bow
[bau]

v. 절하다, 인사하다　to bend one's knee or body, or lower one's head

syn. bend, stoop

he bowed before the King 그는 왕 앞에서 절을 했다

1982
drift
[drift]

n. (점진적) 변화   a slow and gradual change from one situation or opinion to another

drift of public opinion 여론의 대세

1983
straightforward
[stréitfɔ́:rwərd]

adj. 간단한, 복잡하지 않은 not complicated or difficult to understand

syn. candid, direct, frank, honest, open, simple

a straightforward process 간단한 절차

1984
due
[dju:]

adj. 1 지급 기일이 된 2 ~할 예정인   payable immediately / scheduled to arrive

syn. 1 payable, owed   2 scheduled

payment is due on October 1 금액 지불은 10월 1일에 해야 한다

her baby is due in May 그녀는 5월에 출산 예정이다

1985
stressful
[strésfəl]

adj. 스트레스가 많은   extremely irritating to the nerves

a stressful job 스트레스가 많은 일

1986
retain
[ritéin]
-re 다시, 역행하여
-tain 쥐다

v. 보유하다, 잊지 않고 있다   to keep or keep possession of something

syn. hold, reserve, conserve, maintain

retain the fact in memory 그 사실을 잊지 않고 있다

1987
stretch
[stretʃ]

v. 뻗치다, 늘이다   to make or become wider or longer

syn. elongate, expand, lengthen

ant. compress

stretch one's trousers 바지의 주름을 펴다

1988
reveal
[rivíːl]

v. 드러내다, 알리다, 나타내다   to make visible

syn. expose, show, uncover, disclose

reveal a secret 비밀을 누설하다

1989
drainage
[dréinidʒ]

n. 배수, 배수방법   a system of pipes of ditches used for draining water or other liquids

drainage work 배수공사

1990
stylish
[stáiliʃ]

adj. 멋진, 우아한   having elegance or taste or refinement in manners or dress
syn. fashionable, vogue

a stylish dinner 격에 맞춘 식사

1991
resolve
[rizálv]
-solv 풀다

v. 해결하다   to bring to an end
syn. decide, determine

resolve one's fears 근심을 해소하다

1992
successive
[səksésiv]

adj. 잇따른, 계속되는   in regular succession without gaps
syn. consecutive, ensuing, succeeding

it rained for five successive days 5일간 계속 비가 왔다

1993
tumble
[tʌ́mbəl]

v. 넘어지다, 뒹굴다   to fall down, as if collapsing
syn. drop, fall, plunge, stumble

tumble down the stairs 계단에서 굴러 떨어지다

1994
responsibility
[rispànsəbíləti]′
-spons 약속

n. 책임, 담당   control over someone or something in your charge
syn. accountability, charge, obligation

a sense of responsibility 책임 의식

1995
sufficiency
[səfíʃənsi]

n. 충분한 상태   sufficient resources to provide comfort and meet obligations

a sufficiency of exercise 충분한 운동

1996
restoration
[rèstəréiʃən]
-re 다시, 역행하여

n. 회복, 되찾음, 복구   the act of restoring something or someone to a satisfactory state
syn. reconstruction

be closed for restoration 복구를 위해 폐쇄되다

1997
isolation
[àisəléiʃən]
-sol 홀로

n. 고립, 격리   a state of separation between persons or groups
syn. separation, solitude

prevent isolation from the public 대중들로부터의 고립되는 것을 막다

1998

extract

[ikstrǽkt]

-tract 끌다

v. 뽑아내다, 발췌하다 to remove, usually with some force or effort

syn. withdraw, remove, uproot, pull out

extract a bad tooth 충치를 뽑다

1999

treat

[triːt]

v. 1 다루다, 취급하다 2 대접하다 to interact in a certain way / to provide with choice or abundant food or drink

syn. 1 deal with, handle 2 buy

treated me as a child 나를 어린애 취급했다

treated me to lunch today 나에게 오늘 점심을 사줬다

2000

routine

[ruːtíːn]

n. 판에 박힌 일 a person's regular way of doing things

syn. pattern, rote, treadmill

daily routine 반복되는 일과

Review

뜻을 써보고 전체 어구의 의미를 생각해 보시오.

01 lack irrigation systems to keep crops alive _____ 1956

02 daily routine _____ 2000

03 stuck the needle into my arm _____ 1955

04 revenue and expenditure _____ 1960

05 ① treated me as a child _____ 1990

   ② treated me to lunch today _____

06 his arrogance really irritates me _____ 1958

07 guard the palace _____ 1951

08 a straightforward process _____ 1983

09 prevent isolation from the public _____ 1997

10 be closed for restoration _____ 1996

11 tumble down the stairs _____ 1993

12 reveal a secret _____ 1988

13 sales moved up steadily in August _____ 1979

14 stabilize the consumer prices _____ 1972

15 you are a professional in this field _____ 1966

16 a graduate student majoring in archeology _____ 1965

17 brilliant artistry _____ 1968

18 reverse a coat _____ 1962

19 a dramatic event _____ 1975

20 ① payment is due on October 1 _____ 1984

   ② her baby is due in May _____

DAY 41

2001
nutritious
[nju:tríʃəs]

adj. 영양이 풍부한   providing nourishment
syn. healthful, nourishing

bananas are very nutritious 바나나는 영양이 풍부하다

2002
mythical
[míθikəl]

adj. 신화의, 신화적인   based on or told of in traditional stories
syn. fabled, fabulous, legendary

a mythical hero 신화의 영웅

2003
orphan
[ɔ́:rfən]

n. 고아 a child who has lost both parents

an orphan asylum 고아원

2004
square
[skwɛər]

adj. 1 정사각형 모양의 2 공정한   having four equal sides and four right
angles or forming a right angle / being honest and fair

a square room 정사각형 모양의 방
a square deal 공정한 거래

2005
unprepared
[ʌnpripɛ́ərd]
-pre 이전의

adj. 준비가 없는, 즉석의   without preparation / not prepared for
syn. not prepared, not ready

be unprepared to give a speech 연설을 할 준비가 되지 않았다

2006
unsuitable
[ʌnsú:təbəl]
-pre 이전의

adj. 부적당한, 적합하지 않은   not meant or adapted for a particular
purpose
syn. unfitting

the movie is unsuitable for children 그 영화는 아이들에게는 적절하지 않다

2007
otherwise
[ʌ́ðərwàiz]

adv. 딴 방법으로, 만약 그렇지 않으면   in other respects or ways
syn. differently

she thought otherwise 그녀는 다르게 생각했다

2008
wireless
[wáiərlis]

adj. 무선의   having no wires

a wireless mouse 무선 마우스

2009
bump
[bʌmp]

v. 부딪치다, 충돌하다   to knock against with force or violence

syn. hit, strike, knock

my car bumped into the tree 내 차는 나무를 들이 받았다

2010
breakdown
[bréikdàun]

n. 고장, 파손, 몰락   a failure in the operation of a machine or system

syn. failure, collapse, downfall, wreck

prevent family breakdown 가정 해체를 막다

2011
outage
[áutidʒ]

n. 정전, 기계의 운전중지   a temporary suspension of operation

syn. power failure

in case of an outage 정전에 대비하여

2012
spread
[spred]

v. 1 벌리다, 펴다   2 (질병 등을) 퍼뜨리다   to open or stretch out / to have an effect on more people

syn. scatter, disperse

spread one's hands 손을 펴다
spread a disease 병을 퍼뜨리다

2013
convenient
[kənvíːnjənt]

adj. 편리한, 형편 좋은   suited to your comfort or purpose or needs

syn. handy

a convenient world 편리한 세상

2014
overcome
[òuvərkʌ́m]

v. 극복하다, 이겨내다   to win a victory over

syn. conquer, master, surmount

overcome the complications 합병증을 극복하다

2015
cooperative
[kouápərèitiv]
-co 함께

adj. 협력적인, 협조적인   involving the joint activity of two or more

syn. concerted, joint, united

maintain a cooperative relationship 협조적인 관계를 유지하다

2016
unresolved
[ʌ̀nrizálvd]
-solv 풀다

adj. 미해결의, 결말이 나지 않은   not solved

syn. uncertain, unsolved

probe the seven unresolved cases 7건의 미결 사건을 조사하다

2017
overshadow
[òuvərʃǽdou]

v. 가리다, 그늘지게 하다   to cast a shadow upon
syn. eclipse

the tall tree overshadowed the house 큰 나무가 집을 가렸다

2018
resistant
[rizístənt]
-sist 서다

adj. 견디는, 내성이 있는   not affected or harmed by something
syn. immune, tolerant

a water-resistant watch 방수시계

2019
stale
[steil]

adj. 상한, 신선미 없는   lacking freshness
syn. rotten, spoiled

stale jokes 진부한 농담

2020
owe
[ou]

v. 빚지고 있다, 신세를 지다   to be obliged to pay or repay
syn. be indebted to

we owe the bank a lot of money 우리는 은행에 많은 빚을 지고 있다

2021
correct
[kərékt]
-rect 올바름, 인도함

v. 바로잡다   to make right or correct
syn. rectify, right

correct errors 실수를 수정하다

2022
countryside
[kʌ́ntrisàid]

n. 시골, 지방   rural regions
syn. rural area

live in the countryside 시골에 살다

2023
prefer
[prifə́:r]
-pre 이전의

v. 선호하다   to like better
syn. favor, choose, opt

prefer beer to wine   포도주보다 맥주를 더 좋아하다

2024
average
[ǽvəridʒ]

adj. 평균의   calculated by adding quantities together and then dividing by the number of quantities

an annual average rainfall 연평균 강수량

2025
convey
[kənvéi]

v. 나르다, 전달하다 to take or carry something from one place to another / to make known to someone
syn. carry, express

struggled to convey his feelings 감정을 전달하려고 애썼다

2026
resort
[ri:sɔ́:rt]

v. 기대다, 의지하다 to turn to something bad or pleasant because you know no other way

resort to violence 폭력에 기대다

2027
spirit
[spírit]
-spir 숨 쉬다

n. 정신, 영혼 the vital principle or animating force within living things
syn. soul, ghost, mood

fighting spirit 투지

2028
boredom
[bɔ́:rdəm]

n. 권태, 지루한 것 the feeling of being bored by something tedious
syn. tedium, monotony, dullness, humdrum

relieve one's boredom 지루함을 달래주다

2029
bunch
[bʌntʃ]

n. 다발, 무리 a grouping of a number of similar things
syn. clump, cluster

a bunch of pink roses 한 다발의 분홍색 장미

2030
splash
[splæʃ]

v. (물·흙탕 등을) 튀기다 to fall or strike against something in small drops
syn. splatter, sprinkle

the car splashed me with mud 자동차가 내게 흙탕을 튀겼다

2031
tribe
[traib]

n. 부족, 종족 a social division of people
syn. bloodline, clan

the Indian tribes of America 아메리카인디언 부족

2032
preliminary
[prilímənèri]
-pre 이전의

adj. 예선의, 예비의 coming before the main part of something
syn. introductory, preparatory

research that is preliminary to the study 연구 사전 조사

2033
disadvantage
[dìsədvǽntidʒ]
-dis 멀어짐, 부정

n. 불리, 불이익, 단점   the quality of having an inferior or less favorable position

syn. drawback, hindrance, handicap

sell goods to disadvantage 물건을 밑지고 팔다

2034
trust
[trʌst]

n. 신뢰, 신용, 책임   something held by one party for the benefit of another

syn. belief, faith

ant. distrust, doubt

fulfill one's trust 책임을 다하다

2035
unsatisfactory
[ʌ̀nsætisfǽktəri]

adj. 불만족스러운   not giving satisfaction

syn. inadequate, insufficient, disappointing

the unsatisfactory reform plan 불만족스러운 개혁안

2036
prefix
[priːfiks]
-pre 이전의

n. 접두사   an affix that is added in front of the word

ant. suffix

added the prefix "re-" 접두사 re-를 붙였다

2037
dirt
[dəːrt]

n. 먼지, 진흙   loose earth or soil

syn. soil, mud, dust

snow may contain harmful dirt 눈은 해로운 먼지를 함유할 수도 있다

2038
craft
[kræft]

n. 솜씨, 공예   a job or trade needing skill, especially with your hands

the jeweller's craft 보석상의 솜씨

2039
trouble
[trʌ́bəl]

n. 불화, 고생   a source of difficulty

syn. difficulty

family troubles 가정불화

2040
preferable
[préfərəbəl]
-pre 이전의

adj. 차라리 나은, 바람직한   more desirable than another

syn. preferred, desirable

poverty is preferable to ill health 가난이 병보다 낫다

2041
residential
[rèzidénʃəl]

adj. 1 주택지의 2 관내 상주를 요하는   a residential area is one in which most of the buildings are houses / involving living at the place where you are working, studying, or being looked after

a residential area 주택가
residential care for children 상주 탁아 시설

2042
avoid
[əvɔ́id]

v. 피하다   to stay clear from
syn. evade, shun, elude, escape

avoid confusion 혼동을 피하다

2043
presence
[prézəns]

n. 존재, 출석   current existence
syn. attendance, occurrence, appearance

your presence is requested 참석해 주세요

2044
distortion
[distɔ́ːrʃən]

n. 왜곡   a change that makes something no longer true or accurate
syn. evasion, deception

a distortion of the facts 사실의 왜곡

2045
disagreement
[dìsəgríːmənt]
-dis 멀어짐, 부정

n. 불일치, 불화   a conflict of people's opinions or actions or characters
syn. dispute, conflict

disagreements between China and the United States
중국과 미국 사이의 의견 불일치

2046
stand
[stænd]

v. 참다, 견디다   to put up with something or somebody unpleasant
syn. endure, tolerate, withstand

stand the pain 고통을 참다

2047
prepay
[priːpéi]
-pre 이전의

v. 선불하다   to pay for something before receiving it
syn. pay in advance

prepay a reply to a telegram 전보의 반신료를 선불하다

2048
reside
[ri:sáid]

v. 살다, 주재하다   to make one's home in a particular place or community

syn. dwell, inhabit, live

He resides here in Seoul 그는 이곳 서울에 살고 있다

2049
browse
[brauz]

v. 여기 저기 구경하다, 살펴보다   to shop around

syn. look through, look round

ant. gaze, stare

browse the want ads 구인 광고를 살펴보다

2050
prelude
[prélju:d]
-pre 이전의

n. 서곡, 전조   something that serves as a preceding event or introduces what follows

syn. preliminary, overture

ant. epilogue

a prelude to one's misfortune 불행의 전조

Review

뜻을 써보고 전체 어구의 의미를 생각해 보시오.

01 a water-resistant watch _____ <small>2018</small>

02 the unsatisfactory reform plan _____ <small>2035</small>

03 research that is preliminary to the study _____ <small>2032</small>

04 a distortion of the facts _____ <small>2044</small>

05 the jeweller's craft _____ <small>2038</small>

06 prepay a reply to a telegram _____ <small>2047</small>

07 avoid confusion _____ <small>2042</small>

08 a convenient world _____ <small>2013</small>

09 the car splashed me with mud _____ <small>2030</small>

10 relieve one's boredom _____ <small>2028</small>

11 an annual average rainfall _____ <small>2024</small>

12 be unprepared to give a speech _____ <small>2005</small>

13 resort to violence _____ <small>2026</small>

14 my car bumped into the tree _____ <small>2009</small>

15 a mythical hero _____ <small>2002</small>

16 prefer beer to wine _____ <small>2023</small>

17 stand the pain _____ <small>2046</small>

18 correct errors _____ <small>2021</small>

19 bananas are very nutritious _____ <small>2001</small>

20 she thought otherwise _____ <small>2007</small>

DAY 42

2051
forest
[fɔ́(:)rist]

n. 숲 the trees and other plants in a large densely wooded area

syn. thicket, woodland

cut down a forest 산림을 벌채하다

2052
wooden
[wúdn]

adj. 1 나무로 만든 2 부자연스러운 consisting of wood / lacking ease or grace

a wooden box 나무로 만든 상자

his performance was wooden 그의 연기는 부자연스러웠다

2053
wiring
[wáiəriŋ]

n. 배선(공사) a circuit of wires for the distribution of electricity

a fault in the wiring 배선의 결함

2054
urgent
[ɔ́:rdʒənt]

adj. 긴급한, 긴박한 compelling immediate action

syn. pressing, compelling, demanding, immediate

some urgent things to take care of first 먼저 처리해야 될 급한 일

2055
rubber
[rʌ́bər]

n. 고무 a strong elastic substance made from the juice of a tropical tree

a rubber ball 고무공

2056
propose
[prəpóuz]

v. 제안하다, 청혼하다 to declare a plan for something / to make a proposal

syn. suggest, advise

propose to abolish the sales tax 판매세를 폐지할 것을 제안하다

2057
prevent
[privént]
-pre 이전의

v. 막다, 예방하다 to keep from happening or arising

syn. keep, stop, block

prevent the cancer from spreading 암이 퍼지는 것을 막다

2058
rough
[rʌf]

adj. 거친, 텁수룩한 caused by an irregular surface

syn. coarse, harsh, rugged

ant. smooth, calm

rough paper 거칠거칠한 종이, 갱지

2059
prophesy
[práfəsài]

v. 예언하다 to predict or reveal through divine inspiration
syn. foretell

prophesy what may happen 무슨 일이 일어날지 예언하다

2060
ritual
[rítʃuəl]

n. 의식, 의례 any customary observance or practice
syn. ceremonial, rite
ant. informality

religious rituals 종교 의식

2061
dirty
[də́ːrti]

adj. 더러운, 지저분한 not clean
syn. unclean, unwashed

dirty hands/clothes 더러운 손/옷

2062
creature
[kríːtʃər]

n. 생물, (특히) 동물, 창조물 a living organism characterized by voluntary movement
syn. animal, animate being

an imaginary creature 상상의 동물

2063
respectively
[rispéktivli]
-spect 보다

adv. 각각의 separately in the order given

Julie and Mark were respectively 17 and 19 years old
줄리와 마크는 각각 17세와 19세였다

2064
fuss
[fʌs]

n. 소란, 말다툼 activity or excitement that is unusual and that often is not wanted or necessary
syn. trouble, bother, hassle

he didn't want to make a fuss 그는 소란 피우는 걸 원치 않았다

2065
frame
[freim]

n. (안경)틀, 액자 the framework for a pair of eyeglasses

a picture frame 사진틀

2066
wise
[waiz]
-wisdom n. 지혜

adj. 현명한, 박식한 having or showing wisdom or knowledge usually from learning or experiencing many things
syn. discerning, insightful, prudent

a wise saying 금언(金言)

2067
blossoming
[blásəm]

n. 꽃핌, 번창   the time and process of budding and unfolding of blossoms

syn. blooming, flowering

with the blossoming of the flower industry 꽃 산업이 번창함에 따라

2068
potentiality
[poutènʃiǽləti]

n. 가능성, 잠재력   the inherent capacity for coming into being

syn. potency

individual potentiality 개인의 잠재력

2069
constructive
[kənstrʌ́ktiv]
-struct 세우다

adj. 건설적인   helping to develop or improve something

syn. positive, helpful, useful

constructive criticism 건설적인 비평

2070
wonder
[wʌ́ndər]

n. 놀라움, 경탄, 불가사의   the feeling aroused by something strange and surprising

syn. miracle, phenomenon, sensation, admiration

show one's wonder 놀라움을 표하다

2071
success
[səksés]

n. 성공, 성취   an event that accomplishes its intended purpose

syn. triumph, victory

ant. failure, defeat

success in life 출세

2072
arena
[ərí:nə]

n. 영역, 무대   a particular environment or walk of life

enter the arena of politics 정계에 들어가다

2073
errand
[érənd]

n. 심부름, 볼일   a short trip that is taken in the performance of a necessary task or mission

syn. mission, assignment, task

run errands for the boss 상사의 잔심부름을 하다

2074
assimilation
[əsìməléiʃən]
-simil 같음

n. 동화(작용), 소화(작용)   the state of being assimilated

syn. absorption

resist assimilation 동화에 저항하다

2075
hide
[haid]

v. 숨기다, 숨다   to prevent from being seen or discovered
syn. conceal, cover, secrete

hide one's feeling 감정을 숨기다

2076
stir
[stəːr]

v. 휘젓다, 움직이다, 선동하다   to move or cause someone or something to move after being still
syn. agitate, mix, whip

stir one's tea 차를 젓다

2077
stem
[stem]

n. 줄기, 대   the main trunk of a plant

fry sweet potato stems 고구마 줄기를 볶다

2078
armrest
[áːrmrèst]

n. 팔걸이   a support for the arm

underneath the armrest 팔걸이 밑에

2079
erase
[iréis]

v. 지우다, 없애다   to remove from memory or existence
syn. remove, eradicate, delete

the ability to erase people's memories 사람의 기억을 지우는 능력

2080
static
[stǽtik]

adj. 정지 상태의, 정적인   not in physical motion
syn. inactive, inert
ant. dynamic, kinetic

hurricane activity is not static 허리케인 활동은 정적이지 않다

2081
assist
[əsíst]
-sist 서다

v. 도와주다, 지원하다   to give help or assistance
syn. help

assist in a campaign 캠페인을 돕다

2082
presentation
[prèzəntéiʃən]

n. 프레젠테이션, 발표   the activity of formally presenting something
syn. showing, introduction

I'm hard at work on my next presentation
다음 발표를 위해 열심히 준비하고 있다

2083
prey
[prei]

n. 먹이, 사냥감 an animal hunted or caught for food

syn. catch, kill, victim

stalk the prey for hours 사냥감을 몇 시간씩 살금살금 따라다니다

2084
rip
[rip]

v. 찢다, 벗겨내다 to tear or be torn violently

syn. tear

rip a letter open 편지를 뜯어 개봉하다

2085
preferred
[prifə́:rd]
-pre 이전의

adj. 선취권이 있는, 바람직한, 우선의 more desirable than another

syn. preferable, favorite, desirable

English speaker preferred 영어사용자 우대

2086
overvalue
[òuvərvǽljuː]

v. 너무 비싸게 보다, 과대평가하다 to place too high a value on something

syn. overestimate

ant. underestimate

overvalue material things 물질적인 것들에 지나치게 가치를 두다

2087
reunion
[riːjúːniən]
-re 다시, 역행하여

n. 재결합, 상봉, 동창회 a party of former associates who have come together again

syn. reunification

college reunions 대학 동창회

2088
overconfident
[òuvərkánfədənt]

adj. 자부심이 강한 excessive confidence

syn. arrogant

grow careless or overconfident 부주의해지거나 자부심이 과하게 되다

2089
architecture
[áːrkətèktʃər]

n. 건축 an architectural product or work

a masterpiece of the classical architecture 고전적인 건축 양식의 걸작

2090
rest
[rest]

n. 1 나머지 2 휴식 something left after other parts have been taken away / a state of inaction

syn. 1 remains, remainder, leftovers 2 pause, break

throw the rest away 나머지는 버리다

take a short rest 잠시 쉬다

2091
hierarchy
[háiərɑ̀ːrki]

n. 체계, 위계질서　a system in which people or things are placed in a series of levels with different importance or status

syn. power structure, pecking order

a rigid hierarchy of social classes 위계질서가 엄격한 사회 계층

2092
norm
[nɔːrm]

n. 기준, 규범, 평균　a standard or model or pattern regarded as typical

syn. standard, model

social norms 사회적 규범

2093
purpose
[pə́ːrpəs]

n. 목적, 용도　an anticipated outcome that is intended

syn. intention, aim, design

serve various purposes 다양한 용도에 쓰이다

2094
arrange
[əréindʒ]

v. 준비하다, 정리하다, 배열하다　to put into a proper or systematic order

syn. organize, plan, prepare

arrange an interview 인터뷰를 준비하다

2095
purchase
[pə́ːrtʃəs]

v. 구매하다　to obtain by purchase

syn. buy

ant. sell

purchase a new car 새 차를 사다

2096
conventional
[kənvénʃənəl]

adj. 전통적인, 인습적인　of a kind that has been around for a long time and is considered to be usual or typical

syn. customary, traditional

conventional wisdom 전통적인 지혜

2097
forever
[fərévər]

adv. 영구히, 끊임없이　for a limitless time

syn. everlastingly, eternally, evermore

no one can live forever 어느 누구도 영원히 살 수는 없다

2098

provoke

[prəvóuk]

-voke 부름, 소리

v. 일으키다, 유발시키다 to cause the occurrence of a feeling or action

syn. **arouse, elicit**

provoke pity 동정을 끌다

2099

disapproval

[dìsəprúːvəl]

-dis 멀어짐, 부정

n. 반감, 못마땅함 a feeling of disliking something or what someone is doing

syn. **disfavor, dislike**

disapproval of his methods 그의 방법에 대한 반감

2100

protein

[próutiːin]

n. 단백질 a substance which is found in foods like meat and eggs, and which helps your body to grow and stay healthy

wonderful sources of protein 훌륭한 단백질 공급원

Review

뜻을 써보고 전체 어구의 의미를 생각해 보시오.

01 **wonderful sources of** protein _____ 2100

02 constructive **criticism** _____ 2069

03 **individual** potentiality _____ 2068

04 **rip** a letter open _____ 2084

05 **social** norms _____ 2092

06 **fry sweet potato** stems _____ 2077

07 conventional **wisdom** _____ 2096

08 **make a** fuss _____ 2064

09 **show one's** wonder _____ 2070

10 prophesy **what may happen** _____ 2059

11 **provoke** pity _____ 2098

12 **an imaginary** creature _____ 2062

13 rough **paper** _____ 2058

14 **a picture** frame _____ 2065

15 **a fault in the** wiring _____ 2053

16 propose **to abolish the sales tax** _____ 2056

17 **resist** assimilation _____ 2074

18 **prevent** the cancer from spreading _____ 2057

19 **throw the** rest **away** _____ 2090

20 **enter the** arena **of politics** _____ 2072

2101
aspect
[金spekt]

n. 양상, 국면   a distinct feature or element in a problem
syn. phase, side, angle, prospect

have many positive aspects 여러 긍정적인 측면을 가지고 있다

2102
installation
[ìnstəléiʃən]
-sta 서다

n. 설치   the act of installing something

telephone installation 전화 설치

2103
discomfort
[diskʌ́mfərt]
-dis 멀어짐, 부정

n. 불쾌, 불안   the state of being tense and feeling pain
syn. uneasiness, annoyance, displeasure

the discomfort level 불쾌지수

2104
assembly
[əsémbli]

n. 1 조립   2 집회, 모임   the act of connecting together the parts of something / a group of people who have gathered together
syn. 1 putting together, joining   2 gathering, group

in our assembly operation 조립공정에서
an assembly of armed men 무장한 사람들의 집회

2105
grant
[grænt]

v. 주다, 수여하다, 부여하다   to let someone have
syn. offer, give

grant a right to him 그에게 권리를 부여하다

2106
instant
[ínstənt]

adj. 즉시의, 당장의   occurring with no delay
syn. immediate, urgent, pressing

instant death 즉사

2107
convince
[kənvíns]

v. 납득시키다   to make someone agree, understand, or realize the truth
syn. persuade

be convinced 납득이 되다

2108
discourage
[diskə́:ridʒ]
-dis 멀어짐, 부정

v. 용기를 잃게 하다, 실망시키다   to take away hope from
syn. deject, dishearten, dispirit, cast down, depress

the children felt discouraged 아이들의 실망감은 컸다

2109
present
[prizént]

v. 제출하다, 선물하다   to give something to someone
syn. give, introduce, show

present a petition 청원서를 제출하다

2110
assign
[əsáin]

v. 할당하다, 지정하다, 정하다   to assign a task to someone
syn. designate, allocate, appoint

assign each of the students a partner 각 학생에게 파트너를 지정하다

2111
graduation
[grǽdʒuéiʃən]

n. 졸업(식), 대학 졸업   the act of receiving a diploma or degree from a school, college, or university

my first job after graduation 졸업 후 잡은 첫 직장

2112
inoffensive
[ìnəfénsiv]

adj. 해가 되지 않는, 악의가 없는   not causing anger or annoyance
syn. unoffending

useful and inoffensive animals 유용하고 해롭지 않은 동물

2113
notice
[nóutis]

n. 주의, 통지   an announcement containing information about an event
syn. heed, attention, glance

without any notice 사전 예고 없이

2114
arrangement
[əréindʒmənt]

n. 준비, 배열, 배치   an organized structure for arranging or classifying
syn. preparation, plan, design

travel arrangements 여행 준비

2115
inquire
[inkwáiər]
-quire 찾다, 추구하다

v. 문의하다, 조사하다   to ask for information
syn. ask, enquire, investigate

difficult matters to inquire into 조사하기 힘든 문제들

2116
disability
[dìsəbíləti]
-dis 멀어짐, 부정

n. 무력, 무능, 신체장애   the condition of being unable to perform as a consequence of physical or mental unfitness
syn. handicap, affliction, ailment

reading disability 읽기 무능력

2117
arrogance
[ǽrəgəns]

n. 오만, 거만 overbearing pride evidenced by a superior manner toward inferiors

syn. conceit, haughtiness

exhibit arrogance 거만한 태도를 보이다

2118
insecure
[ìnsikjúər]

adj. 자신 없는, 불안한 likely to fail or give way

syn. uncertain, unsafe, unstable

he's very insecure about his appearance 그는 자기 외모에 대해 몹시 자신이 없다

2119
error
[érər]

n. 실수, 오류 a wrong action attributable to bad judgment or ignorance or inattention

syn. mistake, fault

correct the errors 오류를 수정하다

2120
artistic
[ɑːrtístik]

adj. 예술의, 예술적인 relating to art or artists

syn. aesthetic, attractive

as a powerful artistic expression 강력한 예술적 표현으로서

2121
essential
[isénʃəl]

adj. 본질적인, 중요한 absolutely necessary

syn. substantial, basic, fundamental

an essential part of our society 우리사회에서 중요한 부분

2122
input
[ínpùt]

n. 입력, 정보, 조언 something put in or given for use by someone or something

syn. remark, comment

provide some valuable input 소중한 조언을 제공하다

2123
mimic
[mímik]

adj. 흉내 내는, 모방의 constituting an imitation

syn. fake, false

ant. genuine, real

a mimic trial 모의재판

2124
inspire
[inspáiər]
-spir 숨 쉬다

v. 고무시키다, 고취시키다   to heighten or intensify
syn. motivate, prompt
inspire patriotism 애국심을 고취시키다

2125
estimate
[éstəmèit]

v. 추정하다, 견적하다   to judge or calculate the value, size or amount of something
syn. calculate, guess, gauge, judge
estimate for the repair of a house 집수리를 위한 견적을 내다

2126
disassemble
[dìsəsémbəl]
-dis 멀어짐, 부정

v. 해체하다, 분해하다   to take apart into its constituent pieces
syn. dismantle, take apart, break up
disassemble a machine 기계를 분해하다

2127
insight
[ínsàit]
-in 내부

n. 간파, 통찰력   clear or deep perception of a situation
syn. perception, understanding
grow an insight for politics 정치에 대한 통찰력을 기르다

2128
born
[bɔ:rn]

adj. 타고난   being talented through inherited qualities
syn. natural, innate
a born poet 타고난 시인

2129
eternal
[itə́:rnəl]

adj. 영원한, 끝없는   continuing forever
syn. everlasting, endless
eternal flames 영원한 불꽃

2130
disaster
[dizǽstər]
-astr 별
-dis 멀어짐, 부정

n. 재난, 재해, 참사   a state of extreme ruin and misfortune
syn. calamity, catastrophe, tragedy
victims of disasters 재앙의 희생자들

2131
disease
[dizí:z]

n. 질병, 병, 질환   a condition of abnormal functioning
syn. illness, sickness, ailment
ways to prevent heart disease 심장병을 막기 위한 방법들

2132
instead
[instéd]

adv. 대신에 as an alternative to something expressed or implied
syn. alternatively, or else, rather

longed instead for a quiet country life 대신에 조용한 시골 생활을 갈망했다

2133
assignment
[əsáinmənt]

n. 과제, 임무 a duty that you are assigned to perform
syn. task, duty, mission, homework

focus on one's assignment 과제에 집중하다

2134
dismiss
[dismís]
-dis 멀어짐, 부정

v. 일축하다, 해고하다 to cease to consider / to discharge from an office or position
syn. ignore, disregard, fire

dismiss the notion of artistic intuition 예술적 직관의 개념을 일축하다

2135
borrow
[bɔ́(:)rou]

v. 빌리다, 차용하다 to get temporarily

May I borrow your lawn mower? 잔디 깎는 기계 좀 빌릴 수 있을까요?

2136
institute
[ínstətʃùːt]
-stit 서다

v. 만들다, 설치하다 to set up or lay the groundwork for
syn. establish, constitute

institute a new course 새 강좌를 개설하다

2137
ethical
[éθikəl]

adj. 윤리적인 relating to the philosophical study of ethics
syn. honorable, moral

ethical codes 윤리강령

2138
disobedient
[dìsəbíːdiənt]
-dis 멀어짐, 부정

adj. 순종치 않는 not obeying or complying with commands of those in authority
syn. insubordinate, unruly

he was disobedient to his mother 그는 엄마의 말을 듣지 않았다

2139
ethnic
[éθnik]

adj. 민족의, 종족의 relating to a particular, racial, or national group
syn. cultural, ethnical

ethnic groups/communities 민족 집단/공동체

2140
institution
[ìnstətʃúːʃən]
-stit 서다

n. 기관, 협회   an organization founded and united for a specific purpose

syn. establishment, foundation

set up another institution 또 다른 기관을 설립하다

2141
instruct
[instrʌ́kt]
-struct 세우다

v. 가르치다, 지시하다   to impart skills or knowledge to someone

syn. teach, inform

instruct students in English 학생들에게 영어로 가르치다

2142
dispute
[dispjúːt]
-dis 멀어짐, 부정

n. 분쟁, 논쟁   a disagreement or argument about something important

syn. difference, conflict

a dispute between the two countries about the border
국경을 두고 벌이는 두 나라 사이의 분쟁

2143
instruction
[instrʌ́kʃən]
-struct 세우다

n. 훈련, 교수, 교육   the activities of educating or instructing

syn. teaching, prescription, guidance

instructions on the packet 포장지에 적힌 설명

2144
assure
[əʃúər]

v. 보증하다, 납득하다   to make something certain

syn. guarantee, ensure, insure

he assured me of his help 그는 반드시 나를 돕겠다고 했다

2145
foe
[fou]

n. 적, 원수, 적대자   an armed adversary

syn. enemy, opposition

friend and foe 아군과 적군

2146
insurer
[inʃúərər]

n. 보험사   a financial institution that sells insurance

syn. insurance firm, insurance underwriter

my insurer is a big company in Boston 내 보험사는 보스턴에 있는 큰 회사다

2147
highly
[háili]

adv. 매우, 고도로   to a high degree or extent

the stone is highly valuable 그 보석은 매우 값어치가 있다

2148
disregard
[dìsrigá:rd]

-dis 멀어짐, 부정

v. 무시하다, 경시하다   to give little or no attention to

syn. ignore, neglect, miss, skip, overlook

disregard any negative effects 부정적 영향을 무시하다

2149
intake
[íntèik]

n. 섭취   the process of taking food into the body through the mouth

syn. consumption, ingestion

minimize the intake of fish 생선 섭취를 최소화하다

2150
astronomer
[əstránəmər]

-astr 별

n. 천문학자   a physicist who studies astronomy

syn. stargazer

he was a mathematician and an astronomer 그는 수학자이자 천문학자였다

Review

뜻을 써보고 전체 어구의 의미를 생각해 보시오.

01 **telephone** installation _____ 2102

02 **friend and** foe _____ 2145

03 **have many positive** aspects _____ 2101

04 **He** assured **me of his help.** _____ 2144

05 **ways to prevent heart** disease _____ 2131

06 **felt** discouraged _____ 2108

07 **a** dispute **between the two countries** _____ 2142

08 **longed** instead **for a quiet country life** _____ 2132

09 inspire **patriotism** _____ 2124

10 **a** mimic **trial** _____ 2123

11 present **a petition** _____ 2109

12 institute **a new course** _____ 2136

13 estimate **for the repair of a house** _____ 2125

14 disregard **any negative effects** _____ 2148

15 ① **in our** assembly **operation** _____ 2104

   ② **an** assembly **of armed men** _____

16 **he was an** astronomer _____ 2150

17 **provide some valuable** input _____ 2122

18 ethnic **groups** _____ 2139

19 **travel** arrangements _____ 2114

20 **without any** notice _____ 2113

2151
evident
[évidənt]

adj. 분명한, 명백한   clearly revealed to the mind or the senses or judgment

syn. apparent, manifest

with evident satisfaction 분명히 만족하여

2152
attentive
[əténtiv]

adj. 주의 깊은, 세심한   giving care or attention

syn. heedful, thoughtful

be attentive to clothes 복장에 주의하다

2153
grind
[graind]
-ground -ground

v. 갈다, 가루로 빻다   to press with a crushing noise

syn. sharpen, crush

grind flour 가루로 빻다

2154
bypass
[báipæs]

v. 우회하다, 회피하다   to avoid something unpleasant or laborious

syn. go around, get around, shun

you cannot bypass these rules 넌 이 규칙들을 피할 수 없다

2155
attitude
[ǽtitjùːd]

n. 태도, 자세   the way you think and feel about someone or something

syn. posture, manner, mood

an optimistic attitude 긍정적인 태도

2156
distort
[distɔ́ːrt]

v. 왜곡하다, 뒤틀다   to change something such as information so that it is no longer true or accurate

syn. falsify, twist

distort the truth 사실을 왜곡하다

2157
homeland
[hóumlæ̀nd]

n. 고국, 모국   the country where you were born

syn. fatherland, motherland

play concerts in the homeland 고국에서 연주회를 열다

2158
broadcasting
[brɔ́ːdkæ̀stiŋ]

n. 방송   the business of making television and radio programmes

a broadcasting station 방송국

2159
distract
[distrǽkt]
-dis 멀어짐, 부정
-tract 끌다

v. 산만하게 하다   to draw someone's attention away from something
syn. divert, turn aside, disturb

distract one's attention 정신을 흐트러뜨리다

2160
grocery
[gróusəri]

n. 1 식료품류   2 잡화점   food and other goods that are sold by a grocer or a supermarket / a marketplace where groceries are sold

change the grocery shopping habits 식료 잡화류 쇼핑 습관을 바꾸다

2161
hinge
[hindʒ]

v. ~에 달려 있다, ~에 의해 정하다   to depend on something
syn. depend, rest

everything hinges on his decision 만사는 그의 결단에 달려 있다

2162
athletic
[æθlétik]

adj. 운동의, 체육의   of or relating to sports, games, or exercises
syn. acrobatic, gymnastic

athletic facilities 운동시설

2163
dissatisfied
[dissǽtisfàid]
-dis 멀어짐, 부정

adj. 불만족한   in a state of sulky dissatisfaction
syn. discontented, frustrated, disappointed

a dissatisfied look 불만족한 표정

2164
evaluate
[ivǽljuèit]

v. 평가하다   to judge how good, useful, or successful something is
syn. measure, valuate, assess

the students' work is evaluated regularly 학생들의 학업은 정기적으로 평가된다

2165
bottom-up
[bátəmʌp]

adj. 상향식의   progressing upward from the lowest levels

bottom-up management   상향식 경영

2166
atmosphere
[ǽtməsfìər]

n. 분위기, 대기   a particular environment or surrounding influence
syn. mood, air

a tense atmosphere 긴장된 분위기

2167
dissent
[disént]
-dis 멀어짐, 부정

v. 의견을 달리하다   to publicly disagree with an official opinion, decision, or set of beliefs

syn. **disagree, differ**

dissent from the opinion 그 의견에 불찬성이다

2168
gravel
[grǽvəl]

n. 자갈   rock fragments and pebbles

syn. **crushed rock**

a gravel road 자갈길

2169
evade
[ivéid]
-vad 가다

v. 피하다, 기피하다   to try to avoid fulfilling, answering, or performing

syn. **circumvent, skirt, dodge**

evade capture 체포를 면하다

2170
attack
[ətǽk]

v. 공격하다, 비난하다   to launch an attack with weapons

syn. **assail, assault**

the enemies attacked at night 적군들이 밤에 공격을 했다

2171
evolution
[èvəlúːʃən]
-volu 구르다

n. 진화, 변화, 전개   a process in which something passes by degrees to a different stage

the theory of evolution 진화론

2172
attorney
[ətə́ːrni]

n. 변호사, 법정대리인 a person whose business is to advise people about laws

syn. **advocate, lawyer, counsel, solicitor**

become an attorney in international law 국제 변호사가 되다

2173
grip
[grip]

n. 1 꽉 쥠 2 파악력   the act of grasping / an intellectual hold or understanding

syn. **1 grasp, clutch   2 understanding**

have a strong grip 악력이 세다
have a good grip on a problem 문제를 잘 파악하고 있다

2174
bubble
[bʌ́bəl]

n. 거품   a tiny, round ball of air or gas inside a liquid
syn. foam

bubbles rose to the water surface 수면 위로 거품이 일었다

2175
auditory
[ɔ́ːditɔ̀ːri]
-aud 듣다

adj. 귀의, 청각의   relating to the process of hearing

auditory hallucinations 환청

2176
distress
[distrés]

n. 고통, 고난   suffering that affects the mind or body
syn. agony, pain

cause psychological distress 심리적인 고통을 유발하다

2177
evoke
[ivóuk]
-voke 부름, 소리

v. (기억, 감정을) 불러일으키다, 자아내다   to bring a memory, feeling, image, etc. into the mind
syn. elicit, inspire, raise

evoke a feeling of love 사랑의 감정을 불러일으키다

2178
burden
[bə́ːrdn]

n. 짐, 부담   something heavy that you have to carry
syn. load, weight

share the burden 부담을 나누다

2179
homely
[hóumli]

adj. 검소한, 못생긴   lacking in physical beauty or proportion
syn. homelike, plain, ugly

a homely meal 검소한 식사

2180
authority
[əθɔ́ːriti]

n. 권위, 당국, 권위자   the power or right to give orders or make decisions
syn. power, specialist

financial authorities 금융당국들

2181
dissolve
[dizάlv]
-solv 풀다

v. 녹다, 녹이다   to mix with a liquid and become part of the liquid
syn. melt

salt dissolves in water 소금은 물에 녹는다
dissolve sugar in water 설탕을 물에 녹이다

2182
attain
[ətéin]
-tain 쥐다

v. 달성하다 to gain with effort

syn. achieve, accomplish

attain one's aims 목표를 달성하다

2183
evaporate
[ivǽpərèit]

v. 증발하다 to change from a liquid into a gas

water can freeze, liquefy, or evaporate 물은 얼도, 액체로 바뀌고, 증발하기도 한다

2184
boundary
[báundəri]

n. 경계 the line or plane indicating the limit or extent of something

syn. bound, limit, edge

set some boundaries 어떤 한계선을 정하다

2185
gravity
[grǽvəti]

n. 중력, 중대함 the force of attraction between all masses in the universe

in a gravity-free state 무중력상태에서

2186
hire
[háiər]

v. 고용하다, 빌려오다, 빌려주다 to engage or hire for work

syn. employ, engage

hire him/her as a model 그/그녀를 모델로 고용하다

2187
honor
[ánər]

n. 명예, 영광, 경의 the state of being honored

syn. respect, regard, glory, homage

give honor to a person 아무에게 경의를 표하다

2188
distance
[dístəns]
-dis 멀어짐, 부정

n. 거리, 먼 곳 the amount of space or time between two points / a point or place that is far away

syn. gap, interval

keep one's distance 거리를 두다

2189
attempt
[ətémpt]

n. 노력, 시도 an effort made to do something

in an attempt to curb violence 폭력을 제한하려는 노력의 일환으로

2190
eventually
[ivéntʃuəli]

adv. 결국, 최종적으로   in the end
syn. finally

Our flight eventually left five hours late. 우리 비행기는 결국 5시간 늦게 떠났다.

2191
brave
[breiv]

adj. 용감한   possessing or displaying courage
syn. courageous, audacious

brave soldiers 용감한 군인들

2192
graze
[greiz]

v. 1 풀을 뜯어 먹다 2 가볍게 스치다   to feed on grass / to scrape gently
syn. 1 pasture, feed   2 skim, touch

cattle grazing in the field 들판에서 풀을 뜯어 먹고 있는 소들
the shot grazed the post 그 슛은 골대를 스치고 지나갔다

2193
distant
[dístənt]
-dis 멀어짐, 부정

adj. (거리가) 먼, 떨어진   separated in space or coming from or going to a distance
syn. far, away

5 miles distant from here 여기서 5마일 떨어진 곳에

2194
historian
[histɔ́ːriən]

n. 역사가   a person who is an authority on history
syn. historiographer, chronicler

a biased historian 편견을 가진 역사가

2195
attend
[əténd]

v. 1 참석하다 2 돌보다   to be present at / to take charge of
syn. 1 go to 2 take care, wait on

attend class 수업에 참여하다
attend the patient 환자를 돌보다

2196
evidence
[évidəns]
-vid 보다

n. 증거, 근거   something which shows that something else exists or is true
syn. grounds

destroy evidence 증거를 없애다

2197
greed
[griːd]

n. 탐욕, 욕심 excessive desire to acquire more than one needs

his actions were motivated by greed 그의 행동들은 탐욕이 동기가 되었다

2198
attention
[əténʃən]

n. 관심, 주목 the act of fixing your mind on something

syn. care, aid

require more human attention 사람의 관심이 더 필요하다

2199
distinguish
[distíŋgwiʃ]
-dis 멀어짐, 부정

v. 구별하다 to mark as different

syn. separate, differentiate

distinguish right from wrong 옳고 그름을 분별하다

2200
bravery
[bréivəri]

n. 용기, 용감성 a quality of spirit that enables you to face danger or pain

syn. courage, fearlessness

praise a fireman for bravery 소방관의 용감성을 칭송하다

Review

뜻을 써보고 전체 어구의 의미를 생각해 보시오.

01 dissent from the opinion   2167

02 have a strong grip   2173

03 the students' work is evaluated regularly   2164

04 grind flour   2153

05 share the burden   2178

06 a dissatisfied look   2163

07 with evident satisfaction   2151

08 cause psychological distress   2176

09 athletic facilities   2162

10 cattle grazing in the field   2192

11 destroy evidence   2196

12 become an attorney in international law   2172

13 require more human attention   2198

14 distract one's attention   2159

15 a biased historian   2194

16 financial authorities   2180

17 keep one's distance   2188

18 be attentive to clothes   2152

19 in an attempt to curb violence   2189

20 an optimistic attitude   2155

2201
intellect
[íntəlèkt]

n. 지력, 지성   knowledge and intellectual ability

syn. mind, intelligence, understanding

a man of intellect 지성 있는 사람

2202
mindful
[máindfəl]

adj. 주의 깊은, 마음에 두는   aware of something that may be important

syn. aware

be mindful of the side effects 부작용을 마음에 두다

2203
crash
[kræʃ]

v. 충돌하다, 추락하다   to fall or come down violently

syn. smash, demolish, shatter

a helicopter crashed 헬리콥터가 추락했다

2204
intelligent
[intélədʒənt]

adj. 지적인, 머리가 좋은   having the capacity for thought and reason especially to a high degree

syn. bright, clever, discerning, keen, knowledgeable

an intelligent young man 머리가 좋은 젊은이

2205
notorious
[noutɔ́:riəs]

adj. 악명 높은   well-known or famous especially for something bad

syn. disreputable, infamous

a notorious rascal 악명 높은 악당

2206
distribute
[distríbjuːt]

-dis 멀어짐, 부정
-tribute 주다

v. 분배하다, 나눠주다   to give out or divide things among several people

syn. dispense, spread

distribute the test materials 시험지를 나눠주다

2207
misconception
[mìskənsépʃən]

-cept 받다

n. 오해, 그릇된 생각   an incorrect conception

syn. misunderstanding

contrary to a common misconception 일반적인 오해와는 달리

2208
evolutionary
[èvəlúːʃənèri]

adj. 진화의, 점진적인   relating to or produced by evolution

syn. progressive, changing

the evolutionary origin of species 진화론적 종의 기원

2209
interference
[ìntərfíərəns]

n. 방해, 간섭 a policy of intervening in the affairs of other countries
syn. intervention

interference in internal affairs 내정 간섭

2210
diverse
[divə́ːrs]

adj. 다양한, 각양각색의 very different
syn. different, distinct, separate, various

culturally diverse environments 문화적으로 다양한 환경

2211
misleading
[mislíːdiŋ]

adj. 호도하는, 판단을 흐리게 하는 designed to deceive or mislead either deliberately or inadvertently
syn. deceptive, delusive

misleading information/advertisements 사람들을 호도하는 정보/광고

2212
examine
[igzǽmin]

v. 조사하다, 검토하다 to inspect closely
syn. analyze, study, test

will be examined in more detail 더 자세히 검토될 것이다

2213
intensive
[inténsiv]

adj. 강한, 집중적인 involving very great effort or work
syn. thorough, strengthened

intensive agriculture 집약농업

2214
nowadays
[náuədèiz]

adv. 현재에는, 오늘날 at the present time
syn. now, today

nowadays there are different types of vegetarianism
오늘날에는 다른 유형의 채식주의자들이 있다.

2215
creative
[kriːéitiv]

adj. 창의적인, 독창적인 having the ability or power to create
syn. productive, inventive, original

creative thinking 창의적인 사고

2216
folk
[fouk]

n. 일반 사람들, 여러분 people in general
syn. common people

ordinary working-class folk 보통 노동자 계층 사람들

2217
dominant
[dάmənənt]

adj. 유력한, 지배적인　exercising influence or control

syn. prevailing, prevalent, predominant

a dominant figure 유력한 인물

2218
executive
[igzékjətiv]

adj. 행정실무의, 경영의　having the power to make and carry out decisions, especially in business

syn. administrative, managerial, supervisory

executive ability 행정실무능력

2219
intention
[inténʃən]

n. 의도, 의향　an anticipated outcome that is intended or that guides your planned actions

syn. purpose, intent, aim

of course there are good intentions 물론 의도는 좋다

2220
exception
[iksépʃən]
-cept 받다

n. 예외, 제외　a deliberate act of omission

syn. exclusion, irregularity

there will be no exceptions to this rule 이 규칙에 예외는 없을 것이다

2221
crazy
[kréizi]

adj. 1 미친 2 열중한, 열광하는　mad or foolish / passionately preoccupied

syn. 1 brainsick, mad 2 enthusiastic, keen, eager

he's crazy to go out in this weather 이런 날씨에 나가는 것을 보니 그는 미쳤다
he's crazy about sports 그는 스포츠에 열광한다

2222
intended
[inténdid]

adj. 1 의도된 2 미래의　in your mind as a purpose or goal

syn. 1 intentional, designed, purposeful 2 future

the intended purpose 소기의 목적
her intended husband 그녀의 장래 남편

2223
exact
[igzǽkt]

adj. 정확한　fully and completely correct or accurate

syn. accurate, precise

hit the exact center of the target 과녁의 정 중앙을 맞추다

2224
miserable
[mízərəbəl]

adj. 불쌍한, 비참한   very unhappy
syn. wretched, poor, piteous, unfortunate

lead a miserable life 비참한 생활을 하다

2225
excuse
[ikskjúːz]

v. 용서하다   to forgive someone for making a mistake, doing something wrong, etc.
syn. forgive, pardon, release

excuse a fault 과실을 눈감아주다

2226
existence
[igzístəns]

n. 존재, 생존   the state or fact of existing
syn. being, reality, living, subsistence

the existence of other worlds 다른 세상의 존재

2227
diversity
[divə́ːrsəti]

n. 다양성   the quality or state of having many different forms, types, ideas, etc.
syn. diverseness, variety

the city is famous for its cultural diversity
그 도시는 문화적 다양성으로 유명하다

2228
nourish
[nə́ːriʃ]

v. 영양분을 공급하다 육성하다   to provide with nourishment
syn. feed, sustain, provide for, furnish

books nourish our mind 책은 마음에 영양분을 준다

2229
exactly
[igzǽktli]

adv. 정확히, 엄밀히 말해서 used to stress that something is accurate, complete, or correct
syn. precisely

meet at exactly five o'clock 정확히 5시에 만나다

2230
intensify
[inténsəfài]
-tens 뻗다

v. 가중시키다, 격렬해지다   to increase in extent or intensity
syn. deepen, heighten, strengthen, increase

intensify the confusion 혼란을 가중시키다

2231
donation
[dounéiʃən]

n. 증여, 기증, 기부　a voluntary gift made to some worthwhile cause

syn. contribution

an organ donation 장기 기증

2232
missing
[mísiŋ]

adj. 실종된, 없는　not able to be found

syn. absent, lost, gone

a book with two pages missing 두 쪽이 없는 책

2233
intentional
[inténʃənəl]

adj. 의도적인, 고의의　done in a way that is planned or intended

syn. deliberate, planned, intended, purposeful

an intentional insult 의도적인 모욕

2234
crime
[kraim]

n. 죄　an act punishable by law

syn. felony, offense, violation

commit a crime 범죄를 저지르다

2235
exhausted
[igzɔ́ːstid]

adj. 다 써버린, 고갈된　drained of energy or effectiveness

syn. tired, dog-tired, fatigued

feel exhausted 기진맥진하다

2236
mistake
[mistéik]

n. 잘못, 틀림　something that is not correct

syn. error, fault

laugh off one's mistakes 자신의 실수를 웃어넘기다

2237
donor
[dóunər]

n. 기증자　a person who makes a gift of something to someone for a good purpose

syn. giver, presenter, bestower

sign up as organ donors 장기 기증자로 서명하다

2238
intently
[inténtli]

adv. 열심히, 일사분란하게　with strained or eager attention

syn. earnestly, attentively

listen intently 열심히 듣다

2239
nuclear
[njú:kliər]

adj. 핵의, 핵무기의　deriving destructive energy from the release of atomic energy

nuclear proliferation 핵 확산

2240
excessive
[iksésiv]
-cess 가다

adj. 과도한, 극단적인　beyond normal limits
syn. undue, unreasonable, extravagant

excessive charges 과도한 요금

2241
interdependent
[ìntərdipéndənt]
-pend 매달다

adj. 서로 의존하는　mutually dependent
syn. mutualist, mutually beneficial

yin and yang are interdependent 음과 양의 상호의존적이다

2242
crucial
[krú:ʃəl]

adj. 결정적인, 중대한　extremely important
syn. critical, final, grave, serious

a crucial issue to the world peace 세계 평화를 결정짓는 중대한 문제

2243
numeral
[njú:mərəl]

adj. 수의, 수를 나타내는　of, relating to, or expressing numbers

the numeral markings 숫자 표기법

2244
excited
[iksáitid]

adj. 흥분한, 활기를 띤　excessively affected by emotion
syn. emotional, activated

an excited buying and selling of stocks 활기를 띤 주식의 매매

2245
interest
[íntərist]

v. ~에 흥미를 갖게 하다　to persuade someone to have, take, or participate in something
syn. absorb, concern, engage, engross
ant. bore

interest boys in science 소년들에게 과학에 흥미를 갖게 하다

2246
distressed
[distrést]

adj. 괴로워하는, 어려운　facing or experiencing financial trouble or difficulty

economically distressed city 경제적으로 어려운 도시

2247
exclude
[iksklú:d]
-clud 닫다

v. 배제하다, 제외하다   to prevent from being included or accepted
syn. except, leave out, leave off, omit

exclude foreign ships from a port 외국 배를 항구에 들이지 않다

2248
interesting
[íntərestiŋ]

adj. 재미있는, 흥미를 일으키는   arousing or holding the attention
syn. absorbing, attractive, appealing

our school has an interesting history 우리 학교는 재미있는 역사를 가지고 있다

2249
dot
[dɑt]

v. 1 점을 찍다   2 흩어져 있다   to mark something with a dot / to have things scattered over an area

forgot to dot the j j에 점 찍는 것을 깜박했다
a lake dotted with boats 보트가 여기 저기 흩어져 있는 호수

2250
misunderstanding
[mìsʌndərstǽndiŋ]

n. 오해   putting the wrong interpretation on something
syn. misinterpretation, misjudge

a gross misunderstanding 심한 오해

Review

뜻을 써보고 전체 어구의 의미를 생각해 보시오.

01 an intelligent young man _____ 2204

02 a notorious rascal _____ 2205

03 contrary to a common misconception _____ 2207

04 interference in internal affairs _____ 2209

05 a book with two pages missing _____ 2232

06 an intentional insult _____ 2233

07 feel exhausted _____ 2235

08 sign up as organ donors _____ 2237

09 intensive agriculture _____ 2213

10 creative thinking _____ 2215

11 a dominant figure _____ 2217

12 ordinary working-class folk _____ 2216

13 there will be no exceptions to this rule _____ 2220

14 meet at exactly five o'clock _____ 2229

15 ① the intended purpose _____ 2222
　　② her intended husband _____

16 misleading information _____ 2211

17 excessive charges _____ 2240

18 nuclear proliferation _____ 2239

19 a man of intellect _____ 2201

20 a gross misunderstanding _____ 2250

2251
hug
[hʌg]

v. 꼭 껴안다, 품다   to squeeze tightly in your arms, usually with fondness

syn. clasp, embrace, hold, grip

hug a person tight 어떤 사람을 꼭 껴안다

2252
expanse
[ikspǽns]

n. 광활한 공간   a large area of something

syn. stretch, vastness

a vast expanse of sand 광활한 모래 지역

2253
interpret
[intə́:rprit]

v. 해석하다, 이해하다, 통역하다   to make sense of / to give an interpretation

syn. define, clarify, explain

interpret one's dreams 꿈을 해석하다

2254
downplay
[dáunplèi]

v. 대수롭지 않게 여기다, 경시하다   to represent as less significant or important

syn. understate, minimize

downplay the public doubts 대중의 의심을 대수롭지 않게 여기다

2255
forget
[fərgét]

v. 잊다, 깜박 잊다   to stop remembering

syn. bury, block, blank out

forget an appointment 약속을 깜박하다

2256
interrelated
[ìntərriléitid]

adj. 서로 밀접한 관계가 있는   reciprocally connected

syn. interconnected

a number of interrelated problems 몇 가지 서로 밀접하게 연관된 문제들

2257
grown
[groun]

a. 성장한, 자라난   fully developed

syn. adult, big, fully grown, grownup

the kids are pretty much all grown up 아이들이 거의 다 자랐다

2258
expect
[ikspékt]

-expected a. 예상된

v. 예상하다, 기대하다   to regard something as probable or likely

syn. anticipate

expect a rise in food prices 식료품 값이 오를 것으로 예상하다

2259
humanity
[hjuːmǽnəti]

n. 인류, 인간성, 인간애   the quality of being humane

syn. mankind, humankind, humaneness

for the benefit of humanity 인류의 이익을 위하여

2260
drop
[drɑp]

n. 1 방울 2 감소, 하락   a shape that is spherical and small / a sudden sharp decrease in some quantity

syn. fall, sink, down

a drop of blood 방울의 피

a drop in prices/temperature 물가/기온의 하락

2261
intense
[inténs]

adj. 극심한, 강렬한   very great in degree

syn. deep, extreme, concentrated

intense heat/cold/pain 극심한 더위/추위/고통

2262
avenge
[əvéndʒ]

v. 원수를 갚다, 복수하다   to harm or punish someone who has harmed you or someone or something that you care about

syn. revenge, retaliate

avenge one's brother 형제의 원수를 갚다

2263
intent
[intént]

n. 의향, 의도, 계획   an anticipated outcome that is intended or that guides your planned actions

syn. purpose, intention, aim, design

with good[evil] intent 선의[악의]로써

2264
double
[dʌ́bəl]

adj. 두 배의, 갑절의   twice as great or many

syn. dual, twofold

skyrocket to almost double 거의 두 배로 급등하다

2265
exit
[égzit]

n. 출구, 퇴장   an opening that permits escape or release

syn. outlet, way out

make a dash for the exit 출구로 돌진하다

371

2266
horrific
[hɔːrífik]

adj. 무서운, 끔찍한   very shocking and unpleasant

syn. awful, hideous, horrid, outrageous

show the most horrific murder scene 가장 무서운 살인 장면을 보여주다

2267
follow
[fálou]

v. 따르다, 지키다   to go after someone

syn. come after, travel along

follow the rules of a game 경기의 규칙을 지키다

2268
exotic
[igzátik]

adj. 외래의, 이국적인   very different, strange, or unusual of a plant or animal

syn. foreign, alien, unfamiliar

exotic plants 외래 식물

2269
ground
[graund]

n. 지면, 땅, 운동장, 기초, 근거   the solid part of the earth's surface / a rational motive for a belief or action

syn. land, earth, dry land, reason

fertile ground 비옥한 땅

2270
fresh
[freʃ]

adj. 새로운, 신선한, 생기 있는   recently made, produced, or harvested

syn. new, brand-new, lively

get some fresh air 신선한 공기를 마시다

2271
experience
[ikspíəriəns]

n. 경험   the accumulation of knowledge or skill that results from direct participation in events or activities

syn. involvement, know-how

experience is the best teacher 경험이 가장 훌륭한 스승이다

2272
internal
[intɔ́ːrnl]

adj. 내부의, 내재적인, 국내의   happening or arising or located within some limits or especially surface

syn. inner, interior, inside

internal organs 내장

2273
doubt
[daut]

n. 의심, 의혹 the state of being unsure of something

syn. uncertainty, doubtfulness

cast doubt upon good qualities 좋은 자질에 대해 의혹을 제기하다

2274
forecast
[fɔ́:rkæst]

v. 예상하다, 예보하다 to predict in advance

syn. foretell, predict

forecast the results 결과를 예측하다

2275
autograph
[ɔ́:təgræf]
-graph 쓰다

n. (유명인의) 서명 the signature of a famous person

syn. John Hancock

ask celebrities for their autographs 유명 인사들에게 사인해달라고 부탁하다

2276
expand
[ikspǽnd]
-ex 바깥, 외부

v. 확대하다, 확장하다, 늘다 to become larger in size, volume, or quantity

syn. spread out, extend

expand investment 투자를 확대하다

2277
forehead
[fɔ́(:)rid]

n. 이마 the part of the face above the eyes

syn. brow

hit me on the forehead 나의 이마를 때렸다

2278
hostile
[hάstil]

adj. 반대하는, 적의의 unfriendly / belonging to an enemy

syn. unfriendly, antagonistic

hostile to reform 개혁에 반대하는

2279
grow
[grou]

v. 1 성장하다 2 ~이 되다 to get bigger by natural development / to become

syn. 1 increase, expand, swell 2 become

rice grows in warm countries 쌀은 따뜻한 지방에서 자란다
she grew angry 그녀는 화가 났다

2280
experiment
[ikspérəmənt]

n. 실험, 시도 the act of conducting a controlled test or investigation

syn. trial, test, experimentation

carry out key experiments 핵심적인 실험을 하다

2281
forgive
[fərgív]

v. 1 용서하다 2 (빚을) 탕감하다 to grant forgiveness / to absolve from payment

syn. 1 excuse, pardon 2 exempt

forgive one's enemies 적을 용서하다
forgive a debt 빚을 탕감하다

2282
intervene
[ìntərvíːn]

v. 사이에 들다, 방해하다, 조정하다 to interrupt something, especially to prevent a bad result

intervene in a dispute 분쟁을 중재하다

2283
dumb
[dʌm]

adj. 멍청한, 벙어리의, 말을 하지 않는 slow to learn or understand

syn. dense, dim, dull, obtuse, slow

What a dumb idea! 무슨 멍청한 생각이야!

2284
frequent
[fríːkwənt]

adj. 자주 일어나는, 빈번한 coming at short intervals or habitually

syn. common, usual, habitual

frequent breaks 잦은 휴식

2285
humble
[hʌ́mbəl]

adj. 비천한, 초라한, 겸손한 low or inferior in station or quality

syn. meek, modest, lowly, unpretending

a humble cottage 초라한 오두막집

2286
expectant
[ikspéktənt]

adj. 흥분하며 기다리는 waiting with excitement

syn. anticipant, anticipative

the expectant crowds outside the palace 궁전 밖에 기다리고 있는 군중들

2287
intuitive
[intʃúːitiv]

adj. 직관적인 having the ability to know or understand things without any proof or evidence

syn. instinctive, spontaneous

intuitive knowledge 직관적 지식

2288
form
[fɔːrm]

n. 형식, 형태, 종류 a shape / a kind or sort

syn. signifier, kind, shape, contour

a church built in the form of a cross 십자가의 형태로 지어진 교회

2289
growth
[grouθ]

n. 성장, 발달   the act or rate of growing and developing

syn. growing, maturation, development, increase

register negative growth 마이너스 성장을 기록하다

2290
expert
[ékspəːrt]

n. 전문가, 달인   a person with special knowledge or ability who performs skillfully

syn. specialist, master, authority

a computer/medical expert 컴퓨터/의학 전문가

2291
intricate
[íntrəkit]

adj. 뒤얽힌, 복잡한, 미묘한   having many complexly arranged elements

syn. complex, complicated, tangled

an intricate machine 복잡한 기계

2292
duration
[djuəréiʃən]

n. 지속, 기간   the period of time during which something continues

syn. continuance, length

for the duration of the war 전쟁 기간 중에

2293
guarantee
[gæ̀rəntíː]

v. 보장하다, 약속하다   to give surety or assume responsibility

syn. certify, vouch for, undertake

guarantee safety 안전을 보장하다

2294
format
[fɔ́ːrmæt]

n. 구성, 형식   the way in which something is arranged or produced

syn. plan, arrangement

a quiz show format 퀴즈 프로의 구성

2295
hungry
[hʌ́ŋgri]

adj. 1 배고픈 2 갈망하는   feeling hunger / extremely desirous

syn. 1 starving, famished, empty, thirsty   2 eager, keen

as hungry as a hunter 몹시 시장하여
be hungry for knowledge 지식을 갈망하다

2296
expense
[ikspéns]

n. 1 지출, 비용 2 희생   cost in money / a sacrifice

syn. 1 cost, price, expenditure   2 sacrifice

spare no expense 비용을 아끼지 않다
at the expense of his/her health 건강을 잃으면서

2297
introduce
[ìntrədjúːs]

v. 소개하다, 도입하다   to cause to come to know personally
syn. present, begin, start

> Can I introduce my wife? 제 아내를 소개할까요?

2298
frenzy
[frénzi]

n. 격앙, 광포, 열광   state of violent mental agitation
syn. craze, agitation, excitement

> drive a person into a frenzy 남을 격분시키다

2299
expensive
[ikspénsiv]

adj. 비싼   high in price or charging high prices
syn. dear, costly, precious

> expensive clothes 비싼 옷

2300
hunting
[hʌ́ntiŋ]

n. 사냥   the pursuit and killing or capture of wild animals regarded as a sport
syn. hunt, search

> go hunting 사냥하러 가다

Review

뜻을 써보고 전체 어구의 의미를 생각해 보시오.

01 for the duration of the war _____ 2292

02 interpret one's dreams _____ 2253

03 frequent breaks _____ 2284

04 hug a person tight _____ 2251

05 a vast expanse of sand _____ 2252

06 a humble cottage _____ 2285

07 a number of interrelated problems _____ 2256

08 go hunting _____ 2300

09 internal organs _____ 2272

10 register negative growth _____ 2289

11 intense heat _____ 2261

12 avenge one's brother _____ 2262

13 expensive clothes _____ 2299

14 make a dash for the exit _____ 2265

15 forget an appointment _____ 2255

16 be hungry for knowledge _____ 2295

17 follow the rules of a game _____ 2267

18 exotic plants _____ 2268

19 a church built in the form of a cross _____ 2288

20 fertile ground _____ 2269

DAY 47

2301
principal
[prínsəpəl]

adj. 주요한, 제 1의   first in importance
syn. chief, main, primary

the principal characters in a play 극중의 주요 등장인물

2302
ashamed
[əʃéimd]

adj. 부끄러이 여겨, 수줍어하여   feeling shame or guilt or embarrassment or remorse
syn. embarrassed, mortified, humiliated

she felt ashamed of me 그녀는 나를 부끄럽게 여겼다

2303
expertise
[èkspərtíːz]

n. 전문가의 의견, 전문기술   the skill or knowledge an expert has
syn. skill, training, know-how

professional/scientific/technical expertise 직업상/과학적/기술적 전문 지식

2304
principle
[prínsəpl]
-prin 처음의

n. 원리, 원칙, 주의   a general truth or rule that ideas or beliefs are based on
syn. rule, law, truth

the principles of democracy 민주주의의 원리

2305
fortune
[fɔ́ːrtʃən]

n. 운, 운명, 재산   luck / a large amount of money
syn. luck, fate, chance

inherit a fortune 재산을 물려받다

2306
steady
[stédi]

adj. 고정된, 확고한, 한결같은   not subject to change or variation especially in behavior
syn. firm, solid, sturdy
ant. shaky, occasional

a steady friend 한결같은 친구

2307
invade
[invéid]
-vad 가다

v. 침략하다   to march aggressively into another's territory by military force
syn. attack, trespass, raid

invaded Manila in the 19th century 19세기에 마닐라를 침략했다

378

2308
private
[práivit]

adj. 민간의, 개인의, 사립의   confined to particular persons or groups
sys. secluded, isolated, personal

private property 사유 재산

2309
former
[fɔ́:rmər]

adj. 전의, 앞의, 전자의   of an earlier time
syn. earlier, prior, previous

a former president of the United States 미국의 전(前) 대통령

2310
expire
[ikspáiər]

v. 1 끝나다, 만기되다 2 숨을 거두다   to lose validity / to pass away
syn. 1 run out   2 die, decease, kick the bucket

My license expires on the first of May. 내 면허증은 5월 1일로 끝난다.
expire peacefully 편안하게 죽다

2311
strange
[streindʒ]

adj. 이상한, 낯선   being definitely out of the ordinary and unexpected
syn. odd, unconventional
ant. ordinary, normal, familiar

feel strange 이상한 기분이 들다

2312
fortunetelling
[fɔ́:rtʃəntèliŋ]

n. 점, 운수판단   the practice of predicting people's futures
syn. forecasting, soothsaying

believe in fortunetelling 점을 믿다

2313
profit
[práfit]

n. 이익, 수익, 이윤   money which is earned by doing business
syn. benefit, gain, advantage, earnings

gross profits 총수익금

2314
invent
[invént]

v. 발명하다   to come up with an idea, plan, explanation, theory, or principle after a mental effort
syn. create, devise, contrive

Who invented jeans? 누가 청바지를 발명했을까?

2315
exploration
[èkspləréiʃən]
-ex 바깥, 외부

n. 탐사, 탐험, 개발   a careful systematic search
syn. expedition, investigation, examination

domestic oil exploration 국내 석유 탐사

2316
profound
[prəfáund]

adj. 깊은, 심오한, 의미심장한   showing intellectual penetration or emotional depth

syn. insightful, penetrating, deep

a profound meaning 심오한 의미

2317
irrational
[iræʃənəl]

adj. 불합리한, 비이성적인   not consistent with or using reason

syn. unreasonable, illogical

irrational behavior 불합리한 행동

2318
fossil
[fásl]

adj. 화석의   preserved from a past geologic age

reduce use of fossil fuel 화석연료의 사용을 줄이다

2319
subconscious
[sʌbkánʃəs]
-sub 아래의

adj. 잠재의식의   just below the level of consciousness

syn. instinctive, intuitive, involuntary

ant. deliberate

subconscious desires 잠재의식적인 욕망

2320
model
[mádl]

v. ~의 모형을 만들다, 설계하다   to plan or create according to models

syn. copy, reproduce, imitate

model a figure in wax 밀랍으로 형을 뜨다

2321
explore
[ikspló:r]
-ex 바깥, 외부

v. 탐험하다, 탐사하다, 탐구하다   to inquire into

syn. travel, tour, examine, investigate

explore new and safe options 새롭고 안전한 선택사항을 탐구하다

2322
investigation
[invèstəgéiʃən]

n. 조사, 연구   an inquiry into unfamiliar or questionable activities

syn. probe, inquiry, search, research

Federal Bureau of Investigation 미연방 조사국(FBI)

2323
local
[lóukəl]

adj. 국내의, 지방의, 현지의   belonging to the place where you live

syn. regional

a local newspaper 지역신문

2324
progressive
[prəgrésiv]

adj. 진보적인, 전진하는   happening or developing gradually over a period of time

syn. advancing, continuing

by making a progressive move 진보적인 움직임으로

2325
freshman
[fréʃmən]

n. 1 고교[대학] 1년생   2 초심자   a first-year undergraduate / any new participant in some activity

syn. fresher, newcomer

high school/college freshmen 고등학교/대학 신입생

a freshman senator 새 상원의원

2326
suffer
[sʌ́fər]

v. (고통 · 변화 등을) 경험하다, 앓다   to undergo or be subjected to

syn. agonize, despair, grieve, lament

suffer from mental illness 정신병을 앓다

2327
export
[ékspɔːrt]
-port 문

n. 수출, 수출품   goods or services sold to a foreign country

syn. exportation, trade commodity

The export of gold is forbidden. 금 수출은 금지다.

2328
fruitful
[frúːtfəl]

adj. 1 열매를 잘 맺는, 비옥한   2 실수입이 많은   producing a good result / very productive

syn. 1 fertile, productive   2 profitable

fruitful soil 비옥한 땅

a fruitful occupation 실수입이 많은 직업

2329
prominent
[prámənənt]

adj. 현저한, 저명한, 탁월한 having a quality that thrusts itself into attention

syn. eminent, outstanding, famous, notable

a prominent writer 저명한 작자

2330
invisible
[invízəbəl]
-vis 보다

adj. 눈에 보이지 않는, 감추어진 impossible or nearly impossible to see

syn. unseeable, concealed, hidden, unseen

invisible differences 눈에 보이지 않는 차이

2331
promise
[prɑ́mis]

v. 약속하다, 약정하다 to make a promise or commitment
syn. pledge, vow, swear, guarantee

as promised 약속한 대로

2332
suitable
[súːtəbəl]

adj. 적당한, 적절한 meant or adapted for an occasion or use
syn. appropriate, correct, fitting, proper
ant. unfit, irrelevant

a suitable alternative 적절한 대안

2333
myth
[miθ]

n. 신화, 미신 a traditional story accepted as history
syn. legend, story, allegory, folk tale

a common myth 일반적 신화

2334
prompt
[prɑmpt]

adj. 1 신속한, 즉각적인 2 정각의 ready and willing or quick to act / arriving at the right time
syn. quick, immediate

a prompt reply 즉각적인 대답
The train is prompt. 기차는 정각에 들어왔다.

2335
expose
[ikspóuz]
-ex 바깥, 외부

v. 드러내다, 노출시키다 to expose or make accessible to some action or influence
syn. show up, uncloak, uncover

expose one's body to the sun 일광욕을 하다

2336
frustration
[frʌstréiʃən]

n. 좌절, 차질, 실패 a feeling of anger or annoyance caused by being unable to do something
syn. defeat

work off your anger and frustration 여러분의 울분과 욕구불만을 풀어버리다

2337
superior
[səpíəriər]

adj. 상사의, 선배의 of higher rank, class, or quality
syn. higher-ranking, senior
ant. inferior, subordinate

He is superior to me at work. 그는 직장에서 나보다 선배이다.

2338
involve
[inválv]
-in 내부

v. 개입하다, 수반하다, 몰두시키다　to connect closely / to engage as a participant

syn. affect, concern, touch

get involved in the exchange market 외환 시장에 개입하다

2339
prone
[proun]

adj. ~하기 쉬운　likely to do, have, or suffer from something

syn. apt, likely, liable

accident-prone　(사람이) 사고를 일으키기 쉬운

2340
express
[iksprés]

v. 표시하다, 표현하다, 발표하다　to talk or write about something that you are thinking or feeling

syn. utter, tell, assert, verbalize, articulate

express dissatisfaction 불만을 표시하다

2341
stiff
[stif]

adj. 뻣뻣한, 경직된　not moving or operating freely

syn. firm, inflexible, rigid, solid

ant. limp, relaxed, natural

a stiff style of writing 딱딱한 문체

2342
formidable
[fɔ́:rmidəbəl]

adj. 가공할, 엄청난, 험악한　extremely impressive in strength or excellence

syn. awesome, impressive, intimidating

a formidable opponent 엄청난 상대

2343
procedure
[prəsí:dʒər]

n. 순서, 절차, 진행　a particular course of action intended to achieve a result

syn. course, operation, process

maintenance procedures 유지 보수 절차

2344
invariably
[invέəriəbli]

adv. 변함없이, 예외 없이　without variation or change, in every case

syn. always, constantly

be almost invariably fatal 거의 예외 없이 치명적이다

2345
explain
[ikspléin]

v. 설명하다, 해석하다   to make plain and comprehensible
syn. clarify, explicate

Let me explain. 제가 설명해 드릴게요.

2346
produce
[prədjúːs]

n. 산출액, 농산물, 제품   fresh fruits and vegetable grown for the market
syn. green goods, green groceries

organic produce 유기농 제품

2347
invasion
[invéiʒən]

n. 침입, 침략   the act of invading
syn. aggression, attack

an invasion of privacy. 사생활 침해

2348
fortunate
[fɔ́ːrtʃənit]

adj. 운이 좋은, 행운의   having unexpected good fortune
syn. lucky, favored, blessed

a fortunate choice 행운의 선택

2349
mobility
[moubíləti]

n. 유동성, 이동성, 기동력   the quality of moving freely

social mobility 사회적 유동[이동]성

2350
productive
[prədʌ́ktiv]

adj. 생산적인, 다산의   producing or capable of producing
syn. generative, fertile

productive dialogues 생산적인 대화

Review

뜻을 써보고 전체 어구의 의미를 생각해 보시오.

01 the principles of democracy   2304

02 a common myth   2333

03 explore new and safe options   2321

04 feel strange   2311

05 accident-prone   2339

06 expose one's body to the sun   2335

07 a formidable opponent   2342

08 work off your anger and frustration   2336

09 get involved in the exchange market   2338

10 inherit a fortune   2305

11 the principal characters in a play   2301

12 a steady friend   2306

13 private property   2308

14 expire peacefully   2310

15 a suitable alternative   2332

16 gross profits   2313

17 a local newspaper   2323

18 irrational behavior   2317

19 a prominent writer   2329

20 suffer from mental illness   2326

2351
modest
[mádist]

adj. 1 약간의, 보통의 2 겸손한   not very large in size or amount / having a humble opinion of yourself

syn. 1 average, intermediate   2 humble, reserved, moderate

modest improvements/reforms 약간의 개선/개혁

he's very modest about his achievements 그는 그의 성과에 매우 겸손하다

2352
output
[áutpùt]

n. 산출, 생산   final product

syn. production, productivity, achievement

This is just the beginning and the output is very small.
아직 시작에 불과해서 결과가 약소합니다.

2353
fun
[fʌn]

n. 즐거운 시간, 장난, 재미   activities that are enjoyable or amusing

syn. diversion, enjoyment, sport

have some fun in nature 자연에서 즐거운 시간을 보내다

2354
irresistible
[ìrizístəbəl]

-re 다시, 역행하여

adj. 저항할 수 없는   impossible to resist especially because of strength or attractiveness

syn. overpowering, formidable, overwhelming

an irresistible force 불가항력

2355
overall
[óuvərɔ́ːl]

adj. 전부의, 종합적인   as a whole / including everything

syn. all-inclusive, comprehensive

ant. isolated

overall inflation 전면적인 인플레이션

2356
guillotine
[ɡílətìːn]

n. 단두대   an instrument used for beheading people

go to the guillotine 단두대에 오르다

2357
function
[fʌ́ŋkʃən]

v. 작용하다, 구실하다   to work or be in action

syn. role, use, activity

Regular exercise improves your brain function.
규칙적인 운동은 뇌 기능을 발달시킵니다.

2358
irritable
[írətəbəl]

adj. 성미가 급한, 애를 태우는   easily irritated or annoyed
syn. impatient, mean, ill-tempered
ant. good-natured

be in an irritable mood 속이 타는 기분이다

2359
mole
[moul]

n. 두더지   a small dark furry animal which is almost blind

moles usually live under the ground 두더지는 보통 땅 속에서 산다

2360
pronunciation
[prənʌ̀nsiéiʃən]

n. 발음   the manner in which someone utters a word
syn. diction, speech, articulation

have good[bad] pronunciation 발음이 좋다[나쁘다]

2361
outdated
[áutdéitid]

adj. 구식의, 기한이 지난   no longer valid or fashionable
syn. out-of-date

an outdated passport 기한이 지난 여권

2362
fueling
[fjú:əliŋ]

n. 연료, 연료공급   the activity of supplying or taking in fuel
syn. refueling

a fueling station 연료 보급소

2363
modern
[mádərn]

adj. 현대의, 근대의   belonging to the modern era
syn. contemporary

modern art 현대미술

2364
outdoors
[áutdɔ́:rz]

adv. 옥외에서, 야외에서   in the outside
syn. outside, out of doors

I'm happiest when I'm outdoors. 나는 야외에 있을 때가 가장 즐겁다.

2365
irrelevant
[iréləvənt]

adj. 부적절한, 상관없는   lacking a logical or causal relation
syn. unrelated, inappropriate

irrelevant remarks 상관없는 발언들

2366
promising
[prámisiŋ]

adj. 전도유망한 showing possibility of achievement or excellence

syn. hopeful, gifted, talented

a promising youth 유망한 청년

2367
fully
[fúli]

adv. 충분히, (수사 앞에서) 꼬박 to the greatest degree or extent

syn. to the full, full, amply

for fully three days 꼬박 3일 동안

2368
guideline
[gáidlàin]

n. 지침서, 정책, 기준 a detailed plan or explanation to guide you in setting standards

syn. specification, description, stipulation

follow corporate guidelines 기업의 지침을 따르다

2369
outlook
[áutlùk]

n. 조망, 전망, 경치 belief about the future

syn. view, scene, vista

have a pleasant outlook 전망이 좋다

2370
promote
[prəmóut]

v. 1 촉진하다, 증진하다 2 승진시키다 to contribute to the progress or growth of / to change the rank or position of someone to a higher or more important one

syn. 1 boost, encourage 2 raise, upgrade, elevate

promote world peace 세계 평화를 촉진시키다

be promoted to senior editor 편집장으로 승진되다

2371
overly
[óuvərli]

adv. 과도하게, 지나치게 exceeding normal or proper limits

syn. excessively, exceedingly

overly explicit 명명백백한

2372
fund
[fʌnd]

n. 자금, 기금 a sum of money set apart for a special purpose

syn. money, stock, capital

fund raising 기금모금

2373
prose
[prouz]

n. 산문   ordinary writing as distinguished from verse

the author's clear elegant prose 그 작가의 명료하고 우아한 산문체

2374
expressive
[iksprésiv]

adj. 표현력이 좋은, 의미심장한   showing emotions and feelings clearly and openly

syn. meaningful, significant, indicative

expressive eyes 표정이 풍부한 눈

2375
molecule
[máləkjùːl]

n. 분자   the simplest structural unit of an element or compound

The molecules in the hot water move at a faster rate.
더운 물에서 분자가 더 빠른 속도로 움직인다.

2376
overtake
[òuvərtéik]

v. 따라잡다, 갑자기 몰려오다   to catch up with and possibly overtake

syn. catch up with

No overtaking! 추월금지!

2377
fundamental
[fʌndəméntl]

adj. 기본의, 근본적인   serving as an essential component

syn. basic, essential, indispensable

make two fundamental mistakes 두 가지 근본적인 실수를 저지르다

2378
numerous
[njúːmərəs]

adj. 다수의, 수많은   amounting to a large indefinite number

syn. many

after starring in numerous popular movies 수많은 영화에서 주연을 맡은 후에

2379
restricted
[ristríktid]

adj. 한정된, 제한된   having a set limit

syn. confined, restrained

a restricted space 제한된 공간

2380
urge
[əːrdʒ]

v. 재촉하다, 주장하다   to force or impel in an indicated direction

syn. press

She urged him to stay. 그녀는 그가 머물도록 설득하려고 했다.

2381
prove
[pru:v]

v. 입증하다　to show the existence, truth of something by using evidence, logic, etc.

syn. demonstrate, establish, validate

She proved to be right. 그녀가 옳다는 것이 드러났다.

2382
extent
[ikstént]

-ex 바깥, 외부

n. 넓이, 정도, 범위　the point or degree to which something extends

syn. reach, span, scope, range

The extent of the damage remains a mystery. 피해의 정도가 아직 미지수다.

2383
monolingual
[mànəlíŋgwəl]

-mono 하나

n. 1개 국어를 사용하는 사람　using or knowing only one language

monolingual speakers 단일 언어 사용자들

2384
resume
[rizú:m]

-re 다시, 역행하여

v. 1 다시 시작하다　2 건강을 회복하다　to take up or begin anew / to recover one's health

syn. 1 reopen, reestablish, take up　2 recover, recommence

resume a story 이야기를 다시 시작하다
resume one's spirits 원기를 회복하다

2385
hybrid
[háibrid]

adj. 잡종의, 혼혈의　produced by crossbreeding

a hybrid of medieval and Renaissance styles 중세와 르네상스의 스타일의 혼합

2386
nursery
[nə́:rsəri]

n. 아이 방, 육아실, 탁아소　a room where children sleep, play, and are sometimes taught

syn. baby's room

use the nursery home at the headquarters
본사에 있는 어린이집을 이용하다

2387
further
[fə́:rðər]

adj. 그 위의, 그 이상의　to a greater degree or extent

syn. farther

For further information, please call at 555-5555.
그 이상의 정보가 필요하시다면 555-5555로 전화주세요.

2388
external
[ikstə́:rnəl]
-ex 바깥, 외부

adj. 외부의, 표면의, 대외적인   located, seen, or used on the outside or surface of something

syn. exterior, outer, outlying

consider external factors 외적 요인을 고려하다

2389
motivate
[móutəvèit]

v. 동기를 부여하다, 자극하다   to give someone a reason for doing something

syn. inspire, drive, stimulate

try to motivate the students 학생들에게 동기부여를 제공하고자 노력하다

2390
ridicule
[rídikjù:l]

n. 조롱, 비웃음   the act of making fun of someone or something in a cruel or harsh way

syn. scorn, mockery, sneering

ant. honor, praise

an object of ridicule 조롱거리

2391
furnish
[fə́:rniʃ]

v. 공급하다, 비치하다   to give something useful or necessary to

syn. supply, provide, render

The sun furnishes heat. 태양은 열을 제공한다.

2392
risk
[risk]

n. 위험, 모험   a source of danger

syn. danger, hazard

ant. security, insure, guarantee

at all risks 어떤 위험을 무릅쓰고라도

2393
provision
[prəvíʒən]

n. 조항, 규정   a stipulated condition

syn. condition, term

renegotiate the provision with the U.S. 미국과 협정 조항을 재교섭하다

2394
nursing
[nə́:rsiŋ]

adj. 양육하는, 간호하는   caring for the sick or injured or infirm

be put in a nursing home 요양원으로 보내지다.

2395
monotonous

[mənátənəs]

-mono 하나

adj. 단조로운, 변함없는 tediously repetitious or lacking in variety

syn. unvaried, tiresome, dull

monotonous occupations / scenery 단조로운 일/경치

2396
extinct

[ikstíŋkt]

adj. 멸종한, 사라진 no longer in existence

syn. extinguished, dead

an extinct species 사라진 종

2397
ripen

[ráipən]

v. 익다, 원숙하다 to become ripe and ready to eat

syn. mature, season, develop

Time will soon ripen. 곧 기회가 무르익는다.

2398
frustrate

[frʌ́streit]

v. 좌절시키다, 실망시키다 to prevent something that someone planned to happen from happening

syn. foil, thwart, defeat

frustrate a plan 계획을 좌절시키다

2399
nutrient

[njú:triənt]

n. 영양분, 영양소 a substance that plants, animals, and people need to live and grow

syn. food, nutriment

a lack of essential nutrients 필수 영양소 결핍

2400
mood

[mu:d]

n. 기분, 마음가짐 the way you feel at a particular time

syn. temper, atmosphere

I'm in the mood for dancing. 전 춤추고 싶어요.

Review

뜻을 써보고 전체 어구의 의미를 생각해 보시오.

01 try to motivate the students   2389

02 a lack of essential nutrients   2399

03 at all risks   2392

04 She urged him to stay.   2380

05 have a pleasant outlook   2369

06 ① modest improvements   2351

　　② he's very modest about his achievements

07 fund raising   2372

08 have some fun in nature   2353

09 the author's clear elegant prose   2373

10 a hybrid of medieval and Renaissance styles   2385

11 in order to use the nursery home   2386

12 a fueling station   2362

13 an extinct species   2396

14 makes two fundamental mistakes   2377

15 an object of ridicule   2390

16 expressive eyes   2374

17 irrelevant remarks   2365

18 follow corporate guidelines   2368

19 a promising youth   2366

20 go to the guillotine   2356

DAY 49

2401
chewy
[tʃuːi]

adj. 질긴, 쫄깃쫄깃한 somewhat firm and sticky
syn. tough

be too chewy 너무 질기다

2402
aircraft
[ɛ́ərkræft]

n. 비행기 a machine that flies through the air
syn. plane, jet, airplane

a company that manufactures aircraft 비행기를 제조하는 회사

2403
outbreak
[áutbrèik]

n. 발발, 발생 a sudden start or increase of fighting or disease
syn. burst, flare, flash

the outbreak of war 전쟁의 발발

2404
sensory
[sénsəri]

adj. 감각의 of or relating to your physical senses

sensory organs 감각 기관

2405
medium
[míːdiəm]
-pl. media
-medi 중간

n. 대중매체 a way of communicating information and news to people

advertising is a powerful medium 광고는 강력한 대중매체이다

2406
flight
[flait]

n. 비행 a trip made by or in an airplane or spacecraft

the airline's flight schedule 그 항공사의 비행 스케줄

2407
shocked
[ʃɑkt]

adj. 충격 받은, 놀란 very surprised and upset by something bad that happens unexpectedly

be deeply shocked 심하게 놀라다

2408
industrial
[indʌ́striəl]

adj. 산업의 relating to industry or the people working in it
syn. manufacturing, business, commercial

rapid post-war industrial development 빠른 전후 산업의 발전

2409
physiology
[fìziálədʒi]

n. 생리학   the science that deals with the way that the bodies of living things operate

the department of physiology 생리학과

2410
sheet
[ʃiːt]

n. (사각으로 납작한) 한 장   a thin flat piece of paper, metal, plastic, glass, etc.

syn. panel, pane

a sheet of steel 철판 한 장

2411
bit
[bit]

n. 일부분, 소량   something small or unimportant of its kind

syn. slice, segment, fragment

wait a bit longer 약간 더 기다리다

2412
mate
[meit]

v. 짝짓기를 하다   if animals mate, they have sex to produce babies

syn. pair, couple, breed

mate dogs 개를 교미시키다

2413
heaven
[hévən]

n. 천국, 천당   the place where God lives and where good people go after they die according to some religions

syn. paradise, sky

ant. hell

prayed to God in Heaven 천국의 신에게 기도했다

2414
pendulum
[péndʒələm]
-pend 매달다

n. 시계추   a stick with a weight at the bottom that swings back and forth inside a clock

attach a pendulum to a timepiece 시계에 추를 달다

2415
geography
[dʒiːágrəfi]

n. 지리학, 지리   an area of study that deals with the location of countries, cities, rivers, mountains, lakes, etc.

the geography of Seoul 서울의 지리

2416
champ
[tʃæmp]

n. 챔피언 champion
syn. victor, winner
ant. loser

a golf champ 골프 우승자

2417
calf
[kæf]

n. 송아지 a young cow

a fat calf 살찐 송아지

2418
ability
[əbíləti]

n. 능력, 재능 the power or skill to do something
syn. capability, competency
ant. disability, inability

a boy of great musical ability 뛰어난 음악적 재능을 가진 소년

2419
recharge
[ri:tʃá:rdʒ]
-re 다시

v. 재충전하다 to refill a battery with electricity
syn. repower, charge up

recharge the battery 배터리를 재충전하다

2420
launder
[lɔ́:ndər]

v. (옷을) 세탁하다 to wash as clothes in water
syn. clean up

a freshly laundered shirt 방금 세탁을 마친 셔츠

2421
jewel
[dʒú:əl]

n. 보석 a valuable stone that has been cut and polished
syn. brilliant, gemstone

precious jewels 귀중한 보석

2422
paw
[pɔ:]

n. (동물의 발톱이 달린) 발 the foot of an animal that has claws

rear paw 뒷발

2423
campaign
[kæmpéin]

n. 군사 작전 a series of military battles, attacks, etc., designed to produce a particular result in a war

bombing campaign 포탄 투하 작전

2424
sake
[seik]

n. 목적　end, purpose

resign for the sake of the party 당의 이익을 위해 사임하다

2425
film
[film]

n. 영화　a series of moving pictures with sound that you can watch at the cinema or at home

syn. movie

watched a film about prison life 감옥 생활에 관한 영화를 봤다

2426
economy
[ikánəmi]

n. 경제　the process or system by which goods and services are produced, sold, and bought in a country or region

the war altered the country's economy 전쟁이 그 나라의 경제를 바꿔놓았다

2427
carbon
[káːrbən]

n. 탄소　a chemical element that forms diamonds and coal and that is found in petroleum and in all living plants and animals

carbon emission 탄소 배출

2428
saw
[sɔː]

v. 톱질하다　to cut or shape wood, metal, etc. with a saw

sawed the boards in half 판자를 반으로 톱질해 잘랐다

2429
latter
[lǽtər]

adj. 후자의, 후반의　(the latter part of a period of time is nearest to the end of it)

the latter half of the year 한 해의 하반기

2430
swell
[swel]
-swelled -swollen

v. 부풀다, 증가하다　to become larger than normal

syn. expand, gain, mount, multiply

ant. contract, decrease, dwindle

the population swelled 인구가 팽창했다

2431
frozen
[fróuzən]

adj. 1 언　2 동결된　subject to long and severe cold / incapable of being changed, moved, or undone

the frozen north 꽁꽁 언 북부

frozen wages 동결된 급여

2432
lament
[ləmént]

v. 한탄하다, 애통해하다　to express sorrow, regret, or unhappiness about something

syn. grieve, mourn, wail

lamented over the loss of her best friend 가장 친한 친구를 잃고 애통해 했다

2433
trivial
[tríviəl]

adj. 사소한, 하찮은　not important

syn. incidental, minor, trifling

ant. major

a trivial sum of money 몇 푼 안 되는 돈
trivial problems 하찮은 문제들

2434
intriguing
[intrí:giŋ]

adj. 흥미를 자아내는　extremely interesting

syn. absorbing, arresting, engaging

ant. boring, dry, dull

an intriguing story 흥미진진한 이야기

2435
deceptive
[diséptiv]

-cept 받다
-de 허락, 부정

adj. 속이는, 현혹시키는　intended to make someone believe something that is not true

syn. false, misleading, delusive

ant. straightforward

new laws against deceptive advertising 사기성 광고를 금하는 새 법률

2436
leisurely
[líːʒərli]

adj. 느긋한　slow and relaxed

syn. sluggish, snaillike, unhurried

ant. bolting, breakneck, breathless

a leisurely pace 느긋한 걸음

2437
shortcut
[ʃɔ́ːrtkʌt]

n. 지름길　a shorter, quicker, or easier way to get to a place

took a shortcut home 지름길로 집에 갔다
a shortcut to success 성공으로 가는 지름길

2438
banish
[bǽniʃ]

v. 추방하다　to force someone to leave a country as punishment

syn. deport, displace, exile

be banished for life 영구 추방당하다

2439
photosynthesis
[fòutousínθəsis]

n. 광합성 the process by which a green plant turns water and carbon dioxide into food when the plant is exposed to light

water is essential for the photosynthesis 물은 광합성에 꼭 필요하다

2440
conversely
[kənvə́:rsli]

adv. 반대로 in a contrary or opposite way
syn. on the other hand

kindness is his strength, and, conversely, his weakness
친절함은 그의 장점인데 역으로 약점이기도 하다

2441
beware
[biwέər]

v. 경계하다, 조심하다 to be careful
syn. look out, watch out, be wary

beware of the dog 개를 조심하다

2442
discernible
[disə́:rnəbəl]

adj. 식별할 수 있는, 구분 되는 able to be seen, noticed, or understood

a discernible improvement 눈에 보이는 개선

2443
fortify
[fɔ́:rtəfài]

v. 강화하다 to make someone or something stronger
syn. brace, forearm, strengthen
ant. weaken

fortify a city against attack 도시를 공습에 대비해 강화하다

2444
fleeting
[flí:tiŋ]

adj. 스쳐가는, 찰나의 lasting for only a short time
syn. brief, momentary
ant. permanent, perpetual, unending

for a fleeting moment 잠깐 순간 동안

2445
gorgeous
[gɔ́:rdʒəs]

adj. 아주 멋진, 화려한 very beautiful or attractive
syn. magnificent, grand, superb

the sunset was gorgeous 일몰이 아름다웠다

2446
rehabilitation
[rì:həbílətéiʃən]
-re 다시

n. 재활 the act or process of rehabilitating

rehabilitation programme 재활 프로그램

399

2447
introspect
[ìntrəspékt]
-spect 보다

v. 내성하다, 자아성찰하다 to examine and analyse one's own thoughts and feelings

introspected **about his mistake** 자기의 실수에 대해 반성했다

2448
anonymous
[ənǽniməs]

adj. 익명의 not named or identified

syn. unidentified, unnamed, unspecified

wish to remain anonymous 익명으로 남기를 희망하다

2449
squad
[skwad]

n. 팀, 분대 a group of people who are involved in a particular activity

syn. army, band, gang

the cleaning squad **arrived** 청소 팀이 도착했다

2450
unsightly
[ʌnsáitli]

adj. 보기 흉한 not pleasant to look at

syn. hideous, homely

ant. attractive, beautiful

the cracks in the ceiling are unsightly 금이 간 천장이 보기 흉하다

Review

뜻을 써보고 전체 어구의 의미를 생각해 보시오.

01 attach a pendulum to a timepiece _____

02 the geography of Seoul _____ 2415

03 bombing campaign _____ 2423

04 recharge the battery _____ 2419

05 watched a film about prison life _____ 2425

06 rear paw _____ 2422

07 carbon emission _____ 2427

08 lamented over the loss of her best friend _____ 2432

09 the airline's flight schedule _____ 2406

10 a discernible improvement _____ 2442

11 a sheet of steel _____ 2410

12 fortify a city against attack _____ 2443

13 the population swelled _____ 2430

14 ① the frozen north _____ 2431
　　② frozen wages _____

15 wish to remain anonymous _____ 2448

16 sensory organs _____ 2404

17 a shortcut to success _____ 2437

18 a freshly laundered shirt _____ 2420

19 water is essential for the photosynthesis _____ 2439

20 the outbreak of war _____ 2403

2451
thrift
[θrift]

n. 절약, 검약   careful use of money so that it is not wasted

syn. frugality

ant. diseconomy, wastefulness

practice thrift 절약을 실천하다

2452
deafen
[défən]

v. 귀를 멀게 하다   to make someone unable to hear

was deafened by the explosion 폭발 때문에 귀가 안 들렸다

2453
dweller
[dwélər]

n. 거주자   someone who lives in a particular type of place

syn. inhabitant, resident

a city/country dweller 도시/시골 거주자

2454
wilderness
[wíldərnis]

n. 황야, 야생   a wild and natural area in which few people live

released the fox back into the wilderness 여우를 다시 야생으로 풀어줬다

2455
underway
[ʌ̀ndərwéi]

adj. 진행 중인   already started or happening

rescue efforts are underway to find the lost hikers
실종된 등산객을 찾기 위한 구조 작업이 진행 중이다

2456
warehouse
[wɛ́ərhàus]

n. 창고   a large building used for storing goods

syn. storehouse

a red brick warehouse 빨간 벽돌로 지어진 창고

2457
vessel
[vésəl]

n. 1 혈관 2 배   a vein in your body / a ship or large boat

a burst blood vessel 파열된 혈관

a passenger vessel 여객선

2458
disorderly
[disɔ́:rdərli]
-dis 멀어짐, 부정

adj. 무질서한   untidy or without any order

syn. untidy, confused, chaotic, messy

ant. orderly

a disorderly pile of clothes 엉망으로 수북한 옷들

2459
microorganism
[màikrouɔ́:rgənìzəm]

n. 미생물　an extremely small living thing that can only be seen with a microscope

some microorganisms cause disease　어떤 미생물들은 병을 유발한다

2460
rationale
[ræ̀ʃənǽl]

n. 이론적 근거　the reason or explanation for something

syn. account, argument, explanation, reason

the rationale for starting the school day an hour later
학교 일과를 한 시간 늦게 시작하는 이유

2461
exaggeration
[igzæ̀dʒəréiʃən]

n. 과장, 허풍　a statement or way of saying something that makes something seem better, larger than it really is

syn. overstatement, inflation, excess, enlargement

a slight exaggeration　약간의 과장

2462
drawback
[drɔ́:bæ̀k]

n. 결점, 문제점　something that causes problems

syn. downside, disadvantage, handicap

ant. advantage, plus

have too many drawbacks　결점이 너무 많다

2463
turbulence
[tə́:rbjələns]

n. 난기류　sudden, violent movements of air or water

syn. tumult, roughness

the plane hit a bit of turbulence during our flight
비행기는 비행 중에 약간의 난기류를 만났다

2464
eligible
[élidʒəbəl]

adj. 자격이 있는　able to be chosen for something

syn. entitled, fit, qualified

be eligible to vote　투표권이 있다

2465
roam
[roum]

v. 배회하다, 어슬렁거리다　to go to different places without having a particular purpose or plan

syn. drift, float, wander

roamed about in search of work　일자리를 찾아 떠돌았다

403

2466
salient
[séiliənt]

adj. 현저한, 두드러진 very important or noticeable

syn. prominent, outstanding, important, marked

the salient points of the article 그 기사의 가장 두드러진 부분들

2467
domesticate
[douméstəkèit]

v. 길들이다, 가축화하다 to train an animal to live with or work for humans

syn. tame

horses have been domesticated to work on farms
말은 농장에서 일하도록 길들여졌다

2468
vendor
[véndər]

n. 행상, 노점상 a person who sells things especially on the street

syn. dealer, merchandiser, seller

the shouts of street vendors 노점 상인들의 함성

2469
pollinate
[pálənèit]

v. 가루받이를 하다 to give a flower or plant pollen so that it can produce seeds

flowers pollinated by bees 벌에 의해 가루받이가 이뤄지는 꽃들

2470
indispensable
[ìndispénsəbəl]

adj. 필수불가결한 extremely important and necessary

syn. critical, essential, vital

ant. dispensable, needless

an indispensable member 핵심 구성원

2471
ventilation
[véntəlèiʃən]

n. 환기, 통풍장치 circulation of air

a room with good ventilation 통풍이 잘 되는 방

2472
obsolete
[àbsəlí:t]

adj. 구식의 no longer used because something newer exists

syn. antiquated, outdated, outmoded

ant. contemporary, current, modern

an obsolete word 고어

an obsolete technology 구시대의 기술

2473
embassy
[émbəsi]

n. 대사관 the building where an ambassador lives and works

protesters gathered outside the American embassy
시위자들이 미국대사관 바깥쪽에 모였다

2474
erroneous
[iróuniəs]

adj. 잘못된, 틀린 not correct
syn. false, inaccurate, incorrect

erroneous assumptions 틀린 가정

2475
vocational
[voukéiʃənəl]

adj. 직업의, 직업과 관련된 relating to the special skills, training, etc.,
that you need for a particular job

a vocational school 직업 훈련 학교

2476
yearn
[jə:rn]

v. 갈망하다, 동경하다 to feel a strong desire or wish for something or
to do something
syn. long, desire, pine, covet

yearn for freedom 자유를 갈망하다

2477
premise
[prémis]
-pre 이전의

n. 전제 a statement or idea that is accepted as being true and that
is used as the basis of an argument
syn. assumption, proposition, hypothesis

the basic premises of the argument 그 주장의 기본 전제

2478
gigantic
[dʒaigǽntik]

adj. 거대한 extremely large
syn. huge, grand, jumbo
ant. micro, tiny

a gigantic skyscraper 거대한 빌딩

2479
intangible
[intǽndʒəbəl]

adj. 만질 수 없는, 무형의 not able to be touched
syn. impalpable
ant. palpable, tangible, touchable

an intangible asset 무형 자산

2480
evacuate
[ivǽkjuèit]

v. 대피시키다, 비우다　to remove someone from a dangerous place
syn. clear, empty, vacate
ant. fill, load

police evacuated the area 경찰은 그 구역의 사람들을 대피시켰다

2481
opaque
[oupéik]

adj. 불투명한　not letting light through
syn. cloudy, clouded, dull, dim
ant. clear, obvious

the opaque water of the muddy river 불투명한 진흙탕의 강물

2482
formulation
[fɔ̀:rmjəléiʃən]

n. (계획 등의) 개발　the development of a plan, system, or proposal

the formulation of new policies 새로운 정책 입안

2483
discriminate
[diskrímənèit]
-dis 멀어짐, 부정

v. 1 차별하다　2 구별하다　to treat someone unfairly because of their religion, race, etc. / to recognize the difference between things

discriminate on the basis of gender 성차별을 하다
discriminate one sound from another 한 소리를 다른 소리와 구별하다

2484
hollow
[hálou]

n. 우묵한 곳　an empty space inside of something
syn. cavity, dent, hole

the birds nested in the hollow of a tree 새들이 나무의 구멍 난 곳에 둥지를 틀었다

2485
reptile
[réptil]

n. 파충류　an animal that has cold blood, that lays eggs, and that has a body covered with scales or hard parts

lizards are reptiles 도마뱀은 파충류다

2486
momentum
[mouméntəm]

n. 힘, 운동량　the strength or force that something has when it is moving
syn. force, power, drive, push, energy

the vehicle gained momentum 그 차는 가속도가 붙었다

2487
nuisance
[njúːsəns]

n. 성가심, 성가신 것 a person, thing, or situation that is annoying or that causes trouble or problems

syn. annoyance, annoyer, bother, gadfly

a public nuisance 사회의 골칫덩이

2488
unattainable
[ʌ̀nətéinəbəl]
-tain 쥐다

adj. 도달하기 어려운 impossible to achieve or obtain

an unattainable goal 이루기 어려운 목표

2489
propel
[prəpél]

v. 나아가게 하다, 추진하다 to push or drive something forward

syn. drive, push, shove, thrust

the train is propelled by steam 그 기차는 증기로 추진력을 얻는다

2490
face-saving
[féissèiviŋ]

adj. 체면을 살리는 done in order to stop people losing respect for you

a face-saving compromise 체면을 살리는 타협

2491
corner
[kɔ́ːrnər]

v. 몰아붙이다 to force a person or animal into a place or position from which escape is very difficult or impossible

a cornered animal can be dangerous 궁지에 몰린 동물은 위험할 수 있다

2492
dementia
[diménʃiə]

n. 치매 a mental illness that causes someone to be unable to think clearly or to understand what is real and what is not real

syn. insanity, derangement, lunacy, madness

a new study on age-related dementias 나이 관련 치매에 관한 새 연구

2493
plummet
[plʌ́mit]

v. 곤두박질치다, 급락하다 to fall suddenly straight down especially from a very high place

syn. drop, plunge, sink

ant. arise, ascend

prices plummeted 가격이 급락했다

2494
third party
[θəːrdpáːrti]

n. 제삼자　a person or organization that is not one of the two main people or organizations involved in a legal agreement or case

third-party insurance 제삼자 손해 배상 보험

2495
overdue
[òuvərdjúː]

adj. 지급기한이 지난, 반납일이 지난　not paid at an expected or required time

syn. delayed, belated, late

overdue library books 반납일이 지난 도서관 책들

2496
endorse
[endɔ́ːrs]

v. 지지하다　to publicly say that you support or approve of someone or something

syn. advocate, back, champion, support

endorse their position 그들의 입장을 지지하다

2497
breakneck
[bréiknèk]

adj. 맹렬한 속도의　dangerously fast

syn. blistering, breathless, brisk, fleet

breakneck speed 무섭도록 빠른 속도

2498
toll
[toul]

n. 사용료　an amount of money that you pay to use a bridge or a road

syn. charge, duty, rate

toll charges 사용료 청구

2499
fling
[fliŋ]
-flung -flung

v. 내던지다　to throw or push something in a sudden and forceful way

syn. cast, chuck, throw, heave

flung their hats into the air 모자를 하늘로 집어던졌다

2500
swiftly
[swíftli]

adv. 재빠르게　with speed

syn. briskly, fleetly, hastily

ant. slowly

he walked swiftly away 그는 재빠르게 걸어가버렸다

Review

뜻을 써보고 전체 어구의 의미를 생각해 보시오.

01 roamed about in search of work _____ 2465

02 have too many drawbacks _____ 2462

03 ① discriminate on the basis of gender _____ 2483

　② discriminate one sound from another _____

04 the shouts of street vendors _____ 2468

05 flung their hats into the air _____ 2499

06 an indispensable member _____ 2470

07 a cornered animal can be dangerous _____ 2491

08 ① a burst blood vessel _____ 2457

　② a passenger vessel _____

09 overdue library books _____ 2495

10 prices plummeted _____ 2493

11 an unattainable goal _____ 2486

12 rescue efforts are underway to find the lost hikers _____ 2455

13 a face-saving compromise _____ 2490

14 lizards are reptiles _____ 2485

15 an obsolete technology _____ 2472

16 a disorderly pile of clothes _____ 2458

17 police evacuated the area _____ 2480

18 an intangible asset _____ 2479

19 was deafened by the explosion _____ 2452

20 a room with good ventilation _____ 2471

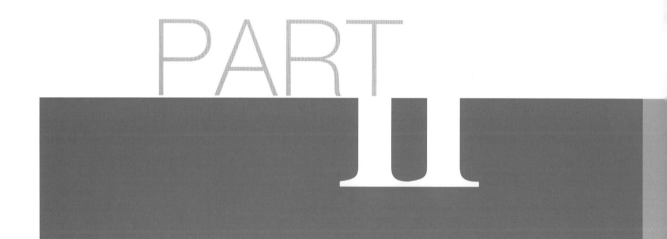

PART II

영어 1등급을 사수하는
고난도 어휘 정복

하 루 5 0 개 씩 학 습 후 리 뷰

2501
barbarous
[báːrbərəs]

adj. 야만스러운, 포악한   very cruel and violent

syn. cruel, brutal

ant. sympathetic, tenderhearted

barbarous crimes 잔인한 범죄

2502
chauffeur
[ʃóufər]

n. 자가용 운전사   a person whose job is to drive people around in a car

a uniformed chauffeur 제복을 입은 자가용 운전사

2503
daybreak
[déibrèik]

n. 새벽, 동틀 녘   the time of day when sunlight first begins to appear

syn. dawn, sunrise

ant. nightfall, sundown, sunset

leave around daybreak 동틀 녘에 떠나다

2504
ubiquitous
[juːbíkwətəs]

adj. 어디에나 있는   seeming to be seen everywhere

syn. ordinary, routine, common, usual

coffee shops are ubiquitous 커피숍은 어디에나 있다

2505
accentuate
[ækséntʃuèit]

v. 강조하다   to make something more noticeable

syn. emphasize, highlight

ant. play down

accentuate the point of a story 이야기의 요점을 강조하다

2506
tableau
[tǽblou]

n. 극적인 장면   a view or sight that looks like a picture

syn. picture, scene, spectacle

made a wonderful tableau 멋진 한 장면이었다

2507
laden
[léidn]

adj. 가득 실은   loaded heavily with something

syn. loaded, burdened

trees heavily laden with fruit 열매가 잔뜩 달린 나무들

2508
wag
[wæg]

v. 좌우로 흔들다   to move something from side to side repeatedly

syn. swish, waggle

a dog wagging its tail 꼬리를 흔들고 있는 개

2509
validate
[vǽlədèit]

v. 입증하다   to officially prove that something is true or correct

syn. support, confirm, verify, vindicate

ant. disprove

validate the hypothesis 가설을 입증하다

2510
rail
[reil]

v. 악담하다, 분노를 표출하다   to express strong anger about something

syn. complain

rail against the way companies fix prices
기업들이 가격을 정하는 방식에 분노를 표하다

2511
petty
[péti]

adj. 작은, 보잘것없는   not very important or serious

syn. trivial, insignificant

a petty argument 사소한 언쟁

2512
weigh
[wei]

v. 숙고하다   to think carefully about something in order to form an opinion or make a decision

syn. consider, contemplate, ponder

took time to weigh his options 시간을 가지고 그의 선택권을 생각해보았다

2513
perverse
[pərvə́:rs]

adj. 괴상한, 비뚤어진   wrong or different in a way that others feel strange or offensive

syn. ill-natured, cross, abnormal

a perverse fascination with death 죽음에 대한 괴상한 환상

2514
perpetuate
[pə(:)rpétʃuèit]

v. 불멸케 하다   to cause something that should be stopped, such as a mistaken idea or a bad situation to continue

syn. eternalize, immortalize

perpetuate a stereotype 편견을 영구화하다

2515
weave
[wi:v]

v. 누비며 나아가다   to move somewhere by going around and between things

syn. zigzag, wind

weaved in and out of traffic 차들을 피해 이리저리 나아갔다

2516
persecution
[pə̀ːrsikjúːʃən]

n. 박해   extremely bad treatment of someone, especially because of their race, religion, or political beliefs

syn. oppression, mistreatment

religious persecution 종교적 박해

2517
water-tight
[wɔ́ːtərtait]

adj. 물샐틈없는   put or fit together so tightly that water cannot enter or pass through

water-tight security 빈틈없는 안보

2518
elicit
[ilísit]

v. 이끌어내다   to get a response, information, etc. from someone

syn. evoke, inspire

elicit no response 아무 반응도 이끌어내지 못하다

2519
genial
[dʒíːnjəl]

adj. 온화한, 부드러운   friendly and kind

syn. pleasant, warm, friendly

genial sunshine 부드러운 햇빛

2520
oath
[ouθ]

n. 맹세   a formal promise, especially one made in a court of law

syn. promise, pledge

an oath of loyalty 충성에 대한 맹세

2521
perish
[périʃ]

v. 사라지다, 소멸하다   to disappear or be destroyed

syn. die, pass away, disappear, vanish

the sailors perished at sea 선원들이 바다에서 사라졌다

2522
adjoining
[ədʒɔ́iniŋ]

adj. 인접한   touching or bounding at a point or line

syn. joining, touching

owners of adjoining properties 인접한 부동산의 주인들

2523
peril
[pérəl]

n. 위험, 유해함   the possibility that you will be hurt or killed or that something unpleasant or bad will happen

syn. hazard, danger

be in peril 위험에 처해있다

414

2524
vanguard
[vǽngɑ̀ːrd]

n. 선봉, 선두   the people who introduce and develop new ways of thinking, new technologies, etc.

syn. forefront, front line, leaders

be in the vanguard 선봉에 서다

2525
pending
[péndiŋ]
-pend 매달다

adj. 임박한, 대기 중인   while waiting for something

syn. amid, undecided, unsettled

the pending case 대기 중인 소송

2526
adept
[ədépt]

adj. 숙련된   very good at doing something that is not easy

syn. skillful, proficient

ant. unseasoned, amateur

be adept in several languages 여러 언어에 능숙하다

2527
hamper
[hǽmpər]

v. 방해하다   to slow the movement, progress, or action of someone

syn. clog, hinder

hamper progress 진행을 방해하다

2528
address
[ədrés]

v. 문제 해결을 고심하다   (if you address a problem, you start trying to solve it)

address the problem of global warming 지구 온난화의 문제 해결을 고심하다

2529
faculty
[fǽkəlti]

n. 교수진, 교사진   all the teachers in a university

syn. teaching staff

a meeting with students and faculty 교사진과 학생들 간의 회의

2530
illusion
[ilúːʒən]

n. 환각, 환상, 착각   something that is false or not real but that seems to be true or real

syn. delusion, dream, fancy

ant. truth

give an illusion 환상을 심어주다

2531
partisan
[páːrtəzən]

adj. 편파적인   showing strong and usually unfair support for one particular person, group, or idea
syn. prejudiced, one-sided, biased

partisan reporting in the paper 편파적인 신문 보도

2532
accusation
[æ̀kjuzéiʃən]

n. 비난, 고소, 혐의   a claim that someone has done something wrong or illegal
syn. charge

denied the accusation 혐의를 부인했다

2533
saturate
[sǽtʃərèit]

v. 포화시키다   to fill something completely with something
syn. drench, drown, soak

saturate the sponge with water 스펀지에 물을 흠뻑 적시다

2534
embroider
[embrɔ́idər]

n. 자수를 놓다   to sew a design on a piece of cloth
syn. decorate, stitch, ornament

a scarf embroidered with tiny flowers 작은 꽃들로 수놓은 스카프

2535
accompaniment
[əkʌ́mpənimənt]

n. 반주   music played to support a person who is singing or playing a musical instrument
syn. backing music

sing without musical accompaniment 악기 반주 없이 노래하다

2536
enlighten
[enláitn]

v. 계몽하다, 이해시키다   to give knowledge or understanding to someone
syn. inform, tell, teach, educate

enlightened us about the problem 그 문제에 대해 우리를 일깨워줬다

2537
enamored
[inǽmərd]

adj. ~에 열광하는   impressed with or enthusiastic about something
syn. captivated, charmed

be enamored with the puzzle 퍼즐에 푹 빠지다

2538
rapture
[rǽptʃər]

n. 황홀, 환희   a state or feeling of great happiness, pleasure, or love
syn. cloud nine, paradise, ecstasy, rhapsody

listened with rapture as the music played 음악의 연주를 황홀경에 빠져서 들었다

2539
obstinate
[ɑ́bstənit]

adj. 완고한   not willing to be reasonable and change your plans, ideas, or behaviour

syn. stubborn, dogged, persistent

my obstinate refusal caused problems 나의 완고한 거절이 문제를 일으켰다

2540
aboriginal
[æ̀bərídʒənəl]

adj. 토착의   of or relating to the people and things that have been in a region from the earliest time

syn. native, born

ant. nonnative

aboriginal races 토착 인종

2541
rack
[ræk]

v. 괴롭히다   to make someone suffer great mental or physical pain

syn. strain, stress, wrench

rack one's brain 머리를 쥐어짜다

2542
abandoned
[əbǽndənd]

adj. 버려진   left by the owner

syn. deserted, forgotten, forsaken

lead a reckless and abandoned life 부주의하고 버림받은 삶을 살다

2543
parasite
[pǽrəsàit]

n. 기생충   an animal or plant that lives in or on another animal or plant and gets food or protection from it

many diseases are caused by parasites 많은 병들은 기생충 때문에 발생한다

2544
sanction
[sǽŋkʃən]

n. 제재, 승인   an official order to stop communication, trade, etc with. a country that has broken international law

syn. ban, restriction, boycott

impose sanctions against the countries 그 나라들에 제재를 가하다

2545
dab
[dæb]

v. 가볍게 두드리다   to lightly touch something usually with quick, small motions

syn. pat, stroke, tap

dab some lotion onto the skin 피부에 로션을 바르다

2546
sage
[seidʒ]

n. 현인 someone who is wise and shows good judgment
syn. wise man, philosopher, guru

the sage Gandhi 성 간디

2547
abound
[əbáund]

v. 풍부하다 to be present in large numbers or in great quantity
syn. brim, overflow
ant. lack, need, want

a region where oil abounds 석유가 풍부한 지역

2548
dangle
[dǽŋgəl]

v. 늘어뜨리다 to hang down loosely especially in a way that makes it possible to swing freely
syn. hang, sling, suspend, swing

dangled my feet in the water 발을 물로 늘어뜨렸다

2549
pang
[pæŋ]

n. (갑작스런) 통증, 가책 a sudden, strong feeling of physical or emotional pain
syn. ache, pain, prick, sting

a pang of guilt 가슴 아픈 죄책감

2550
capricious
[kəpríʃəs]

adj. 변덕스러운 changing often and quickly
syn. changeable, unpredictable, unsettled

a capricious manager 변덕스러운 관리자

Review | 고난도

뜻을 써보고 전체 어구의 의미를 생각해 보시오.

01 perpetuate a stereotype   2514

02 many diseases are caused by parasites   2543

03 made a wonderful tableau   2506

04 an oath of loyalty   2520

05 elicit no response   2518

06 listened with rapture as the music played   2538

07 be in peril   2523

08 a perverse fascination with death   2513

09 a region where oil abounds   2547

10 address the problem of global warming   2528

11 my obstinate refusal caused problems   2539

12 a pang of guilt   2549

13 weaved in and out of traffic   2515

14 a capricious manager   2550

15 accentuate the point of a story   2505

16 the pending case   2525

17 saturate the sponge with water   2533

18 partisan reporting in the paper   2531

19 a petty argument   2511

20 took time to weigh his options   2512

2551
aftermath
[ǽftərmæ̀θ]

n. 여파   the period of time after a bad and usually destructive event

syn. aftereffect

in the aftermath of the war 전쟁의 여파 속에

2552
capsize
[kǽpsaiz]

v. (배가) 뒤집히다   to turn so that the bottom is on top

syn. overturn, turn turtle

the canoe capsized 카누가 뒤집혔다

2553
certified
[sə́:rtəfàid]

adj. 공인된   having met the official requirements that are needed to do particular type of work

ant. unauthentic

a certified gemologist 공인 보석 감정사

2554
celestial
[siléstʃəl]

adj. 하늘의, 천상의   of or relating to heaven

syn. ethereal, heavenly

celestial music 천상의 음악

2555
clatter
[klǽtər]

v. 딸각 소리를 내다   to make a quick series of short loud sounds

syn. clack, rattle

the dishes clattered on the shelf 선반의 그릇들이 딸각거렸다

2556
pivotal
[pívətl]

adj. 중심이 되는, 매우 중요한   very important

syn. critical, key, crucial, vital

ant. minor, trivial, unimportant

a pivotal piece of information 매우 중요한 정보

2557
agitate
[ǽdʒətèit]

v. 동요시키다   to try to get people to support or oppose something

syn. stir, churn

ant. calm, compose, tranquilize

agitate for a strike 파업을 선동하다

2558
plague
[pleig]

n. 전염병   a disease that causes death and that spreads quickly to a large number of people

syn. pest

a plague that swept through the tribe 그 부족을 전멸시켰던 전염병

2559
vex
[veks]

v. 괴롭히다, 짜증나게 하다   to annoy or worry someone

syn. annoy, bother, bug

a headache vexed him all morning 두통이 아침 내내 그를 괴롭혔다

2560
impersonal
[impə́:rsənəl]

adj. 인간미 없는   having or showing no interest in individual people or their feelings

syn. inhuman, cold, remote, bureaucratic

an impersonal, professional attitude 인간미 없는 사무적 태도

2561
entangle
[entǽŋgl]

v. 엉키게 하다   to cause something to get caught in or twisted with something else

syn. interlace, intertwine

ant. disentangle

became entangled in a lawsuit 소송에 휘말리게 되었다

2562
mainstream
[méinstrì:m]

n. 주류, 대세   a prevailing current or direction of activity or influence

the mainstream of modern literature 현대 문학의 주류

2563
combatant
[kəmbǽtənt]

n. 전투원, 전투부대, 참전국   a person, group, or country that takes part in a war

a main combatant in World War II 2차 세계대전의 주요 참전국

2564
pious
[páiəs]

adj. 경건한   devoted to a particular religion

syn. dedicated, devoted

ant. disloyal, faithless

live a quiet, pious life 조용하고 경건한 삶을 살다

2565
demeanor
[dimí:nər]

n. 태도, 처신   the way you look and behave

syn. conduct, behavior

his quiet and reserved demeanour 그의 조용하고 소극적인 태도

2566
ensue
[ensú:]

v. 뒤따르다   to happen after something else, often as a result of it

syn. follow, result

an angry argument ensued 열띤 언쟁이 뒤따랐다

2567
combustion
[kəmbʌ́stʃən]

n. 연소   the act of burning

a combustion chamber 연소실

2568
offspring
[ɔ́(:)fsprìŋ]

n. 자식, 자손   a person's child
syn. descendant

conflicts between parents and offspring 부모와 자식 간의 갈등

2569
flaw
[flɔː]

n. 결점   a mistake or fault in something that makes it useless or less effective
syn. error, mistake, fault, defect

a flaw in the book's plot 그 책의 줄거리상의 결점

2570
alter
[ɔ́:ltər]
-alter 다른

v. 고치다   to change something
syn. make over, modify, revise
ant. fix, freeze, set, stabilize

alter a person's mood 한 사람의 기분을 바꿔놓다

2571
fledgling
[flédʒliŋ]

n. 어린 새, 풋내기   someone or something that is getting started in a new activity
syn. beginner, novice, rookie

a fledgling company 막 출범한 회사

2572
feat
[fiːt]

n. 위업, 뛰어난 솜씨   an act or achievement that shows courage, strength, or skill
syn. accomplishment, achievement

feats of endurance 인내로 이룬 위업

2573
imbricate
[ímbrikit]

adj. 겹쳐 쌓인   lying lapped over each other in regular order

imbricate scales 겹겹이 쌓인 비늘

2574
limb
[lim]

n. 팔[다리]   an arm, or a leg

an artificial limb 의족[의수]

2575

lamentation
[læ̀məntéiʃən]

n. 비탄, 애도 an expression of great sorrow or deep sadness

syn. lament, moan, wail

bitter lamentations for the dead 망자에 대한 비통함

2576

definitive
[difínətiv]

-fin 끝

adj. 결정적인, 확정적인 not able to be argued about or changed

syn. authoritative

ant. inconclusive, indecisive, unclear

a definitive answer to this question 이 질문에 대한 확정적인 답변

2577

variable
[vέəriəbəll]

adj. 변동이 심한, 가변적인 able or likely to change or be changed

syn. changeable, elastic, flexible

ant. established, fixed

a variable interest rate 가변적인 이자율

2578

liken
[láikən]

v. 비교하다 to say that someone or something is similar to another person or thing

syn. compare

liken the two pianists 두 피아니스트를 비교하다

2579

magnitude
[mǽgnətjùːd]

-magni 거대한

n. 규모, 중요성 the size, extent, or importance of something

syn. importance, significance

the magnitude of the issue 그 문제의 중요도

2580

befit
[bifít]

v. 걸맞다 to be suitable to or proper for someone or something

syn. go, serve, suit

dressed as befitted a millionaire 백만장자에 걸맞게 차려입었다

2581

warrant
[wɔ́(ː)rənt]

n. 보증서, 허가증 a document issued by a court that gives the police the power to do something

syn. allowance, authorization, license

an arrest warrant 체포 영장

2582
allocate
[ǽləkèit]

v. 할당하다 to divide and give out for a special reason or to particular people, companies, etc.

syn. allot, distribute

allocate scarce resources 부족한 자원을 할당하다

2583
tack
[tæk]

v. 압정으로 고정하다 to fasten or attach something with tacks

syn. nail, pin, stud

tacked a poster on the wall 벽에 포스터를 압정으로 고정했다

2584
deflect
[diflékt]

-de 하락, 부정
-flec 구부러지다

v. 빗나가게 하다 to cause something that is moving to change direction

syn. turn, divert, veer

try to deflect the blame for the accident 사고에 대한 책임을 피해가려고 애쓰다

2585
maneuver
[mənú:vər]

v. 능숙하게 조종하다 to move someone or something in a situation that needs care or skill

syn. manage, handle, manipulate

maneuvered her car through heavy traffic
혼잡한 교통을 뚫고 능숙하게 운전해 나갔다

2586
ailment
[éilmənt]

n. 가벼운 질병 a sickness or illness

ant. health, wellness

a variety of ailments 각종 질병

2587
improvise
[ímprəvàiz]

v. 즉석에서 지어내다 to speak or perform without preparation

syn. invent offhand, make up, ad-lib

improvised his opening speech 개막 연설을 즉석으로 지어서 했다

2588
embed
[imbéd]

v. 끼워 넣다 to place or set something firmly in something else

syn. implant, ingrain

ant. uproot

fossils embedded in stone 돌에 박혀있는 화석들

2589
offset
[ɔ(:)fsét]

v. 상쇄하다 to create an equal balance between two things

syn. neutralize, compensate for

gains in one area offset losses in another
한 쪽의 이득이 다른 곳의 손실을 상쇄한다

2590
coherent
[kouhíərənt]
-here 달라붙다

adj. 일관성 있는, 논리적인 logical and well-organized

syn. rational, reasonable, sensible

ant. incoherent

a coherent argument 논리적인 주장

2591
acclaim
[əkléim]

n. 찬사를 보내다 to praise in a very strong and enthusiastic way

syn. applaud, cheer, praise

acclaimed her performance 그녀의 공연에 찬사를 보냈다

2592
imperative
[impérətiv]

adj. 의무적인, 중대한 extremely important and urgent

syn. compulsory, forced, mandatory

ant. elective, optional, voluntary

an imperative duty 중대한 의무

2593
coarse
[kɔ:rs]

adj. 조야한, 투박한 a coarse substance or surface feels rough and hard

syn. rough, crude

ant. fine

the coarse outer leaves of the cabbage 양배추의 거친 바깥쪽 잎

2594
belch
[beltʃ]

v. 트림하다 to let out air from the stomach through the mouth very loudly

syn. burp

a noisy car belching out black exhaust 검은 매연을 내뿜는 시끄러운 차

2595
clog
[klɑg]

v. 막다 to slowly form a block in something so that things cannot move through quickly or easily

syn. block, choke

ant. unclog

be clogged by dirt and grease 흙과 기름으로 막혔다

2596
impair
[impέər]

v. 손상시키다   to make something weaker or worse

syn. damage, injure

ant. fix, mend, repair

his health was impaired by overwork 그의 건강은 과로로 손상되었다

2597
adjust
[ədʒʌ́st]
-jus 법, 정의

v. 조정하다   to change something in a minor way so that it works better

syn. adapt

adjusted the car seat 카시트를 조정했다

2598
clumsy
[klʌ́mzi]

adj. 서투른   moving or doing things in a very awkward way and tending to drop or break things

syn. awkward

ant. deft, handy

made a clumsy attempt at a joke 서툴게 농담을 시도했다

2599
affluent
[ǽfluənt]
-flu 흐르다

adj. 풍족한, 부유한   having a large amount of money and owning many expensive things

syn. rich, deep-pocketed

ant. poor, poverty-stricken

an affluent area of Gangnam 강남의 부유한 지역

2600
imminent
[ímənənt]

adj. 임박한   happening very soon

syn. impending, looming, pending

be in imminent danger of extinction 곧 멸종의 위기에 처해있다

Review | 고난도

뜻을 써보고 전체 어구의 의미를 생각해 보시오.

01 the magnitude of the issue _____ 2579

02 liken the two pianists _____ 2578

03 became entangled in a lawsuit _____ 2561

04 bitter lamentations for the dead _____ 2575

05 an impersonal, professional attitude _____ 2560

06 acclaimed her performance _____ 2591

07 an angry argument ensued _____ 2566

08 celestial music _____ 2554

09 a variable interest rate _____ 2577

10 alter a person's mood _____ 2570

11 a coherent argument _____ 2590

12 a main combatant in World War II _____ 2563

13 his health was impaired by overwork _____ 2596

14 tacked a poster on the wall _____ 2593

15 a variety of ailments _____ 2596

16 a headache vexed him all morning _____ 2559

17 be clogged by dirt and grease _____ 2595

18 an artificial limb _____ 2574

19 maneuvered her car through heavy traffic _____ 2585

20 live a quiet, pious life _____ 2564

DAY 53

2601 ambiguous [æmbígjuəs]

adj. 모호한　not clear and therefore capable of being understood in more than one way
syn. mystic, obscure
ant. clear, obvious, plain

an ambiguous smile 모호한 미소

2602 ploy [plɔi]

n. 술책　a clever trick or plan that is used to get someone to do something or to gain an advantage over someone
syn. gambit, gimmick, trick, scheme

a ploy to delay his departure 그가 떠나는 것을 늦추려는 술책

2603 rebellion [ribéljən]
-re 다시, 역행하여

n. 반란　an attempt to remove a government or leader by force
syn. revolt, revolution, rising, uprising

an abortive military rebellion 실패로 돌아간 군사 반란

2604 loft [lɔ:ft]

n. 다락방, 옥탑방　a room or space that is just below the roof of a building and that is often used to store things
syn. attic

live in a converted loft 개조한 옥탑방에 살다

2605 tawny [tɔ́:ni]

adj. 황갈색의　having a brownish-orange color
syn. golden, blond

the tawny coat of a lion 사자의 황갈색 가죽

2606 amass [əmǽs]

v. 축적하다　to gather or collect something, such as a large amount of money especially for yourself
syn. accumulate, gather
ant. scatter

amassed a wealth of information 풍부한 정보를 축적했다

2607 listless [lístlis]

adj. 무기력한　lacking energy or spirit
syn. languid
ant. animated, energetic

made everyone tired and listless 모두를 지치고 무기력하게 만들었다

2608
ambivalent
[æmbívələnt]

adj. 양면가치의, 상반된 감정을 가진   feeling two different things about something at the same time

an ambivalent attitude towards technology 과학기술에 대한 양면적인 태도

2609
harden
[háːrdn]

v. 단단하게 하다   to make hard or harder
ant. soften

hardened his heart 마음을 단단히 먹었다

2610
indulge
[indʌ́ldʒ]

v. 맘껏 충족시키다   to allow to have or do something as a special pleasure
syn. satisfy, fulfil

an opportunity to indulge in reading 맘껏 독서를 할 수 있는 기회

2611
denounce
[dináuns]
-de 하락, 부정

v. 공공연히 비난하다   to publicly state that someone or something is bad or wrong
syn. decry, condemn
ant. bless

denounce the use of violence 폭력 사용을 공공연히 비난하다

2612
bewilder
[biwíldər]

v. 당황하게 하다   to confuse someone very much
syn. baffle, perplex

the change bewildered our customers 그 변화는 우리 고객들을 당황케 했다

2613
gnaw
[nɔː]

v. 갉아먹다   to bite or chew something repeatedly
syn. bite, nibble

a dog gnawing a bone 뼈다귀를 물어뜯고 있는 개

2614
detract
[ditrǽkt]
-de 하락, 부정
-tract 끌다

v. (주의를) 딴 데로 돌리다   to divert
syn. distract
ant. concentrate, focus

detract attention 주의를 딴 데로 돌리다

2615
tangible
[tǽndʒəbəl]

adj. 실체적인   able to be touched or felt
syn. palpable, touchable

a tangible evidence 구체적 증거

2616
hands-on
[hǽndzán]

adj. 실제의, 직접 해 보는 doing something yourself rather than just talking about it or telling other people to do it
syn. firsthand

hands-on experience 직접 해 보는 경험

2617
haunt
[hɔːnt]

v. 오랫동안 괴롭히다 to make someone feel worried and upset for a long time
syn. plague, trouble, obsess, torment

images from the war still haunt him 전쟁의 잔상들이 아직도 그를 괴롭힌다

2618
tentative
[téntətiv]

adj. 잠정적인 still able to be changed
syn. conditional, contingent

tentative plans 잠정적인 계획들

2619
shabby
[ʃǽbi]

adj. 초라한 in poor condition especially because of age or use
syn. dog-eared, moth-eaten
ant. brand-new, fresh

be old and shabby 낡고 허름하다

2620
derive
[diráiv]
-de 하락, 부정

v. 파생하다, ~에서 기원하다 to have something as an origin

this word is derived from Latin 이 단어는 라틴어에서 파생한 것이다

2621
haughty
[hɔ́ːti]

adj. 오만한, 거만한 proud and unfriendly
syn. arrogant
ant. humble, lowly, modest

a haughty expression 거만한 표정

2622
shatter
[ʃǽtər]

v. 산산조각 내다, 부서지다 to break or be broken into many small pieces
syn. pulverize, destroy
ant. build, construct

the rock shattered the window 돌이 창문을 산산조각 냈다

2623
outgrow
[áutgróu]

v. 너무 크게 자라다 to grow too large for someone or something

the plant has outgrown my garden 나무가 내 정원에 비해 너무 크게 자랐다

2624
besiege
[bisí:dʒ]

v. 포위하다 to surround a city or castle with military force until the people inside let you take control

syn. blockade

besieged the castle 성을 포위했다

2625
linear
[líniər]

adj. 선으로 이뤄진, 직선의 consisting of lines or of one straight line

linear perspective 직선 원근법

2626
plausible
[plɔ́:zəbəl]

adj. 그럴 듯한 likely to be true

syn. credible, likely, believable

a plausible explanation 그럴 듯한 설명

2627
reconciliation
[rèkənsìliéiʃən]

n. 화해, 조화 a new and friendly relationship with someone who you argued with or fought with

a reconciliation is unlikely 화해가 이뤄질 것 같지는 않다

2628
infectious
[infékʃəs]

adj. 전염성이 있는 capable of being passed to someone else by germs that enter the body

syn. contagious, spreading

viruses and other infectious agents 바이러스와 다른 전염성 있는 병원균들

2629
throng
[θrɔ(:)ŋ]

n. 군중 a large group of people

syn. mass, mob, crowd

addressed the vast throng 대규모 군중들 앞에서 연설을 했다

2630
refinery
[ri:fáinəri]

-re 다시, 역행하여

n. 정제, 정제공장 a place where the unwanted substances in something such as oil or sugar are removed

an oil refinery 정유 공장

2631
testify
[téstəfài]

v. 증언하다 to make a statement about something that you saw, know, or experienced, usually in a court of law

syn. attest, witness

testify against his drug dealer 마약 상에 대해 반대 증언을 하다

2632
sentiment
[séntəmənt]

n. 감정, 정서 feelings of love, sympathy, kindness, etc.

syn. emotion, passion, feeling

there's no room for sentiment 감정을 위한 공간은 없다

2633
deter
[ditə́:r]

-de 하락, 부정

v. 단념시키다 to cause someone to decide not to do something

syn. discourage, dissuade, inhibit

ant. encourage, persuade

deter people from coming to the game 사람들이 경기를 관람하러 오지 못하게 하다

2634
commodity
[kəmádəti]

n. 상품, 물품 something that can be bought and sold, especially a basic food product or fuel

syn. goods, produce, stock

a farm commodity 농산물

2635
seep
[si:p]

v. 스미다, 배다 to flow or pass slowly through small openings in something

syn. ooze

water seeped in through a crack 물이 틈으로 스며들었다

2636
scrutinize
[skrú:tənàiz]

v. 면밀히 조사하다 to examine something carefully especially in a critical way

syn. review, scan, inspect

scrutinized the document 서류를 면밀히 조사했다

2637
reckless
[réklis]

adj. 무모한 not showing proper concern about the possible bad results of your actions

syn. irresponsible

a wild and reckless young man 거칠고 무모한 청년

2638

indefinite

[indéfənit]

-fin 끝

adj. 무한정의　not certain in amount or length

syn. bottomless, boundless, endless

ant. definite, finite, limited

for an indefinite period of time 정해지지 않은 길이의 시간 동안

2639

seduce

[sidʤúːs]

v. 유혹하다　to persuade someone to do something

syn. lure

seduced him with a better offer 보다 좋은 제안으로 그를 유혹했다

2640

recur

[rikə́ːr]

-re 다시, 역행하여

v. 재발하다　to happen or appear again

syn. happen again, return, come back

the cancer recurred 암이 재발했다

2641

indignant

[indígnənt]

adj. 분개한　feeling or showing anger because of something that is unfair or wrong

syn. angered, steamed up

ant. delighted, pleased

wrote an indignant letter 분노의 편지를 썼다

2642

scant

[skænt]

adj. 미약한, 희박한　very small in size or amount

paid scant attention to the facts 그 사실에 거의 신경을 쓰지 않았다

2643

recount

[rikáunt]

-re 다시, 역행하여

v. (일어난 일을) 말하다　to say what happened

syn. tell, report, detail, describe

recounted his conversation with Jane 제인과의 대화를 말했다

2644

denote

[dinóut]

v. 의미하다　to mean something

syn. mean, express

red flares denoting danger 위험을 의미하는 빨간 불꽃

2645

fluctuate

[flʌ́ktʃuèit]

-flu 흐르다

n. 오르락내리락하다　to change level, strength, or value frequently

syn. change, mutate, shift

ant. stabilize

the temperature fluctuated dramatically 기온이 심하게 오르락내리락했다

2646
commence
[kəméns]

v. 시작하다   to begin

syn. start, kick off

ant. end, terminate

the meeting will commence soon 회의가 곧 시작될 것입니다

2647
opt
[ɑpt]

v. 선택하다   to choose one thing instead of another

syn. choose

opt for low-risk investments 위험이 낮은 투자를 선택하다

2648
flutter
[flʌ́tər]

v. 펄럭이다   to move or flap the wings quickly without flying

syn. flap, wave

the breeze made the curtains flutter 솔바람이 커튼을 펄럭이게 했다

2649
ravage
[rǽvidʒ]

v. 파괴하다   to damage or harm something very badly

syn. destroy, devastate, ruin

a land ravaged by war 전쟁으로 망가진 토지

2650
flicker
[flíkər]

n. 깜빡이다   to burn or glow in an unsteady way

syn. twinkle, shimmer, glimmer

a candle flickering in the window 창가에 깜빡이는 촛불

Review | 고난도

뜻을 써보고 전체 어구의 의미를 생각해 보시오.

01 live in a converted loft   2604

02 a wild and reckless young man   2637

03 the cancer recurred   2640

04 an opportunity to indulge in reading   2610

05 the temperature fluctuated dramatically   2645

06 viruses and other infectious agents   2628

07 be old and shabby   2619

08 wrote an indignant letter   2641

09 scrutinized the document   2636

10 the tawny coat of a lion   2605

11 linear perspective   2625

12 made everyone tired and listless   2607

13 besieged the castle   2624

14 images from the war still haunt him   2617

15 a ploy to delay his departure   2602

16 a dog gnawing a bone   2613

17 deter people from coming to the game   2633

18 an ambiguous smile   2601

19 testify against his drug dealer   2631

20 denounce the use of violence   2611

2651
unbiased
[ʌ̀nbáiəst]

adj. 편견 없는   not having or showing an unfair tendency to believe that some people, ideas, etc., are better than others

syn. nonpartisan, objective, square, fair, unprejudiced

an unbiased opinion 치우치지 않은 의견

2652
deviate
[díːvièit]

v. 빗나가다   to do something that is different or to be different from what is usual or expected

syn. detour, veer

deviated too much from the script 대본에서 너무 많이 벗어났다

2653
relentless
[riléntlis]

adj. 매몰찬, 줄기찬   continuing without becoming weaker, less severe, etc.

syn. determined, dogged, unyielding

relentless criticism 매몰찬 비판

2654
shred
[ʃred]

v. 갈가리 찢다   to cut or tear something into long, thin pieces

syn. rip, tear

shredded the documents 서류를 잘게 찢었다

2655
reign
[rein]

v. 통치하다   to rule as a king, queen, emperor, etc.

syn. rule, govern, be in power

reign over people 국민을 통치하다

2656
insatiable
[inséiʃəbəl]

adj. 만족할 줄 모르는   always wanting more

syn. inappeasable, inextinguishable

an insatiable desire for wealth 끝이 없는 부에 대한 갈망

2657
lure
[luər]

v. 유혹하다, 유인하다   to persuade someone to do something by making it look very attractive

syn. bait, decoy, tempt

lure tourists back to the province 관광객들이 그 지역으로 다시 오도록 유혹하다

2658
shortfall
[ʃɔ́ːrtfɔ̀ːl]

n. 부족분   a lack of something that you need or want, or the amount that you lack

syn. shortage, deficiency, loss

a shortfall in the supply of skilled labour 숙련된 노동력 공급의 부족

2659
shove
[ʃʌv]

v. 밀어 붙이다   to push something with force

syn. drive, propel, push, thrust

shoved the door until it finally opened 문이 열릴 때까지 밀어 붙였다

2660
lopsided
[lápsáidid]

adj. 한쪽으로 기운   having one side that is lower or smaller than the other

syn. tilted, tipping, uneven

ant. even, level, straight

a lopsided vote of 49 to 1 49대 1로 기운 투표

2661
toil
[tɔil]

n. 수고, 노고   difficult and tiring work, especially physical work

syn. hard work, effort, pains

a life of toil 노역의 삶

2662
underlying
[ʌ̀ndərláiiŋ]

adj. 근본적인   concealed but detectable

syn. basic, essential, fundamental

an underlying cause 근본 원인

2663
sob
[sɑb]

v. 흐느끼다   to cry noisily while taking in short, sudden breaths

syn. cry, weep

could not stop sobbing 흐느껴 울기를 멈출 수 없었다

2664
undercut
[ʌ́ndərkʌ̀t]

v. 저가로 공급하다   to offer to sell things or work for a lower cost than another person or company

syn. undersell, underprice

undercut the competing store by 10 percent 경쟁 상점보다 10퍼센트 할인하다

2665
shuffle
[ʃʌfl]

v. 뒤섞다   to move things or people into a different order or into different positions

syn. rearrange, jumble, mix

shuffled the papers on the desk 책상위의 서류를 뒤섞었다

2666
inscription
[inskrípʃən]
-script 쓰다

n. 비문, 새겨진 글   words that are written on or cut into a surface

syn. engraving, lettering

the inscription on a stone monument 비석에 새겨진 문구

2667
token
[tóukən]

n. 징표, 상징   something that is a symbol of a feeling, event, etc.

syn. symbol, mark, sign

a white flag is a token of surrender 흰 깃발은 항복의 상징이다

2668
devalue
[di:vǽlju:]

v. 평가 절하하다   to cause something or someone to seem or to be less valuable or important

syn. depreciate, downgrade, lower

ant. appreciate, enhance, upgrade

devalue a currency 화폐를 평가 절하하다

2669
replicate
[répləkèit]

v. 복제하다   to repeat or copy something exactly

syn. clone, copycat, duplicate

ant. originate

replicated his teacher's writing style 선생님의 문체를 그대로 따라했다

2670
showy
[ʃóui]

adj. 현란한, 눈길을 끄는   having an appearance that attracts attention

syn. brilliant, catchy

a plant with large showy flowers 크고 화려한 꽃이 핀 화초

2671
graffiti
[grəfí:ti]

n. 벽의 낙서   words or pictures drawn on walls in public places

an old building covered with graffiti 낙서로 가득한 낡은 건물

2672
slit
[slit]

n. 갈라진 틈 a long, narrow cut or opening in something

syn. rip, slash, tear

see through the slit in the fence 담장의 갈라진 틈으로 들여다 보다

2673
shorthand
[ʃɔ́:rthæ̀nd]

n. 속기 a method of writing quickly by using symbols or abbreviations for sounds, words, or phrases

typing and shorthand 타자와 속기

2674
residual
[rizídʒuəl]

adj. 잔류성의, 효과가 오래가는 remaining after a process has been completed or something has been removed

syn. remaining

the residual effects of the accident 그 사고의 후유증

2675
solace
[sáləs]
-sol 홀로

n. 위로, 위안 someone or something that gives a feeling of comfort to a person who is sad, depressed, etc.

syn. cheer, relief, comfort

seek solace in religion 종교에서 위안을 찾다

2676
shun
[ʃʌn]

v. 피하다 to deliberately avoid a person, place, or activity

syn. avoid, dodge, duck

shun all forms of luxury 온갖 종류의 사치를 피하다

2677
inhospitable
[inháspitəbəl]
-hosp 대접하다

adj. 불친절한 not generous and friendly to guests or visitors

syn. unfriendly, unsympathetic

be inhospitable in treating 대접이 불친절하다

2678
remnant
[rémnənt]

n. 나머지, 잔여 the part of something that is left when the other parts are gone

syn. leftovers, remains

the last remnants of the famous castle 그 유명한 성의 마지막 남은 흔적들

2679
brethren
[bréðrən]

n. 남자 신도들 the male members of a religious group

syn. comrade, partner, colleague

let us pray, brethren 기도합시다, 신도 여러분

439

2680
siege
[si:dʒ]

n. 포위공격   a situation in which soldiers or police officers surround a city, building, etc., in order to try to take control of it

withstand a siege 포위공격을 견뎌내다

2681
refute
[rifjúːt]
-re 다시, 역행하여

v. 반박하다   to say that something is not true
syn. deny, reject
ant. acknowledge, admit

refuted the testimony of the witness 증인의 증언을 반박했다

2682
scorn
[skɔːɾn]

v. 경멸하다   to show that you think someone or something is not worthy of respect or approval
syn. disdain, disrespect
ant. honor, respect

scorn the use of make-up 화장하는 것을 경멸하다

2683
soluble
[sáljəbəl]

adj. 녹는   capable of being dissolved in a liquid

sugar is soluble in water 설탕은 물에 녹는다

2684
indubitable
[indʒúːbətəbəl]

adj. 의심할 여지없는   not able to be doubted
syn. certain, inarguable, unquestionable

the indubitable fact 의심의 여지없는 사실

2685
luxuriant
[lʌgʒúəriənt]

adj. 번성한, 울창한   having heavy and thick growth
syn. leafy, lush, overgrown
ant. barren, leafless

luxuriant vegetation 울창한 초목

2686
hexagonal
[héksəgànəl]

adj. 육각형의   having six angles and six sides

a hexagonal prism 육각형의 프리즘

2687
slip
[slip]

v. 미끄러지다   if you slip, your feet slide accidentally and you lose your balance or fall over
syn. fall, slide

slip on the wet floor 젖은 바닥에 미끄러지다

440

2688
snarl
[snɑːrl]

v. 으르렁거리다 (if an animal snarls, it makes a low angry sound and shows its teeth)

syn. growl

the dog snarled at me 개가 나를 보고 으르렁거렸다

2689
sight-read
[sáitrìːd]

v. 즉석에서 노래하다[연주하다] to perform written music while reading it for the first time without practicing it

sight-read a simple Schubert song 간단한 슈베르트 음악을 즉석 연주하다

2690
till
[til]

v. 밭을 갈다, 경작하다 to prepare land for putting crops in the ground so that they will grow there

syn. cultivate, tend, farm

the farmers are tilling the soil 농부들이 밭을 갈고 있다

2691
bob
[bɑb]

v. 까딱거리다 to move up and down in a short quick movement

bob the head 고개를 까딱거리다

2692
devour
[diváuər]

v. 집어삼키다 to eat up greedily or ravenously

syn. consume, eat up

devoured everything on his plate 접시에 있던 모든 것을 집어삼켰다

2693
lurk
[ləːrk]

v. 잠복하다 to be in a hidden place

syn. sneak, steal

ant. appear

saw someone lurking around the corner 모퉁이 쪽에 누가 숨어있는 것을 봤다

2694
inherent
[inhíərənt]

adj. 타고난 belonging to the basic nature of someone or something

syn. built-in, natural

risks inherent in the venture 모험에 근본적으로 따르는 위험

2695
lofty
[lɔ́ːfti]

adj. 매우 높은, 고상한 very high and good

syn. high, tall, towering

lofty ideals 고상한 이상

2696
pluck
[plʌk]

v. 잡아 뽑다 to pull something quickly to remove it

syn. pull out, pick

plucked a white hair 흰 머리카락을 잡아 뽑았다

2697
infuse
[infjúːz]
-fus 쏟다, 녹다

v. 주입하다, 불어넣다 to cause a person or thing to be filled with something

syn. imbue

ant. eliminate, remove, take away

infuse the team with confidence 팀에 자신감을 불어넣다

2698
heed
[hiːd]

v. ~에 주의를 기울이다 to pay attention to advice, a warning, etc.

syn. mind, note

ant. disregard, ignore

heed what he says 그가 하는 말에 주의를 기울이다

2699
loiter
[lɔ́itər]

v. 어슬렁거리다 to remain in an area when you do not have a particular reason to be there

syn. dawdle, linger

ant. hurry, speed

don't loiter in this area 이 지역에서 어슬렁거리지 마라

2700
hearten
[hάːrtn]

v. 격려하다, 기쁘게 하다 to cause someone to feel more cheerful or hopeful

syn. cheer up, inspire

ant. discourage, dishearten, dispirit

was heartened by the public's support 대중의 지지에 용기를 내다

442

Review | 고난도

뜻을 써보고 전체 어구의 의미를 생각해 보시오.

01 lure tourists back to the province _____ 2657

02 sight-read a simple Schubert song _____ 2689

03 typing and shorthand _____ 2673

04 heed what he says _____ 2698

05 don't loiter in this area _____ 2699

06 an insatiable desire for wealth _____ 2656

07 devoured everything on his plate _____ 2692

08 luxuriant vegetation _____ 2685

09 saw someone lurking around the corner _____ 2693

10 shredded the documents _____ 2654

11 was heartened by the public's support _____ 2700

12 infuse the team with confidence _____ 2697

13 slip on the wet floor _____ 2687

14 shoved the door until it finally opened _____ 2659

15 lofty ideals _____ 2695

16 the residual effects of the accident _____ 2674

17 an unbiased opinion _____ 2651

18 a plant with large showy flowers _____ 2670

19 shun all forms of luxury _____ 2676

20 the last remnants of the famous castle _____ 2678

DAY 55

2701
withhold
[wiðhóuld]

v. 억제하다, 금하다, 미루다 to refuse to hand over or share
syn. keep back

withhold the disappointment and anger 실망과 분노를 억제하다

2702
anecdote
[ǽnikdòut]

n. 일화 short account of an incident
syn. tale, story, narrative

anecdotes about Abe Lincoln 링컨의 일화

2703
bystander
[báistæ̀ndər]

n. 방관자 a person who is standing near but not taking part in what is happening
syn. onlooker, spectator, passerby

an innocent bystander 단순한 구경꾼

2704
wither
[wíðər]

v. 시들다, 쇠퇴하다 to become dry and weak
syn. shrivel, shrink

the plants withered and died 그 식물들은 시들어 죽었다

2705
viral
[váiərəl]

adj. 바이러스의 relating to or caused by a virus

a viral infection 바이러스 감염

2706
amends
[əméndz]

n. 배상, 벌충 compensation for a loss or injury
syn. atonement, compensation

make amends 배상하다

2707
buckle
[bʌ́kəl]

v. 죄다, 구부리다 to fasten with a buckle or buckles
syn. clasp, warp

buckle one's belt 벨트를 채우다

2708
burrow
[bə́:rou]

v. 굴을 파다 to make a hole or tunnel in the ground by digging
syn. dig, tunnel, excavate

the frogs burrow under the mud 개구리는 진흙 밑으로 굴을 판다

2709
virtuoso
[və:rtʃuóusou]

n. 예술의 거장, 명인   someone who is dazzlingly skilled in any field

a guitar virtuoso 기타의 대가

2710
analogy
[ənǽlədʒi]

n. 비유, 유추, 유사   an inference that if things agree in some respects they probably agree in others

syn. parallel, similarity, resemblance

immature analogy 설익은 비유

2711
antagonize
[æntǽgənàiz]

v. 남에게 적의를 품게 하다   to provoke the hostility of

syn. anger, offend

antagonize her further 더욱 그녀의 적대감을 사다

2712
brokerage
[bróukəridʒ]

n. 중개업   the activities of organizing business deals for other people

a brokerage firm 중개업을 하는 회사

2713
widespread
[wáidspréd]

adj. 만연한, 널리 퍼진   widely circulated or diffused

syn. extensive, prevailing, prevalent

widespread poverty 만연한 빈곤

2714
vulnerable
[vʌ́lnərəbəl]

adj. 취약한, 연약한   susceptible to attack

syn. defenseless, exposed

be vulnerable to criticism 비판받기 쉽다

2715
wilt
[wilt]

v. 시들다, 지치다   to bend over because of not having enough water

syn. droop, shrivel

the plants wilted in the heat 식물들이 열에 시들었다

2716
brood
[bru:d]

v. 곰곰이 생각하다   to think moodily or anxiously about something

syn. consider, deliberate

brood over the trifles 하찮은 일에 신경 쓰다

2717
void
[vɔiv]

adj. 빈, 공허한, 무효의   lacking any legal or binding force

syn. empty, vacant, ineffectual

this bond is null and void 이 증서는 완전히 무효다

2718
hub
[hʌb]

n. 중심지   the central part of a car wheel through which the shaft or axle passes

syn. axis, core, heart

economic and cultural hub 경제와 문화의 중심지

2719
vulgar
[vʌ́lgər]

adj. 저속한, 일반 민중이 사용하는   lacking refinement or cultivation or taste

syn. indecent, obscene

an exceedingly vulgar necktie 너무나 천박한 넥타이

2720
anguish
[ǽŋgwiʃ]

n. 번뇌, 고민   extreme mental distress

syn. pain, agony, torment, torture

in anguish 괴로워서, 괴로운 나머지

2721
vista
[vístə]
-vis 보다

n. 전망, 경치   the visual percept of a region

syn. view, prospect

a beautiful vista of the valley 계곡의 아름다운 경치

2722
holistic
[houlístik]

adj. 전체론의   emphasizing the organic or functional relation between parts and the whole

holistic health 전체적인 건강

2723
forsake
[fərséik]

v. 포기하다, 버리고 돌보지 않다   to leave someone who needs or counts on you

syn. abandon, desert

forsake one's bad habits 나쁜 버릇을 버리다

2724
antibiotics
[æ̀ntibaiátik]
-bio 생명

n. 항생물질, 항생제   a drug that is used to kill harmful bacteria and to cure infections

syn. antibiotic drugs

new bacteria with greater resistance to antibiotics
항생제에 대한 내성이 강한 새로운 박테리아

446

2725
stern
[stəːrn]

adj. 엄격한, 엄중한 of a stern or strict bearing or demeanor
syn. strict, firm, severe
ant. lenient

a stern face 엄한 얼굴

2726
host
[houst]

n. 많은 사람, 떼 a vast multitude
syn. army, horde, swarm

a host of problems 많은 문제들

2727
forthwith
[fɔ̀ːrθwíθ]

adv. 곧, 즉시, 당장 without delay or hesitation
syn. immediately, instantly, straightaway

they were jailed forthwith 그들은 즉시 투옥되었다

2728
grub
[grʌb]

v. 파헤치다, 뿌리를 뽑다 to search about busily

grub for potatoes 흙을 파헤쳐 감자를 캐다

2729
hygiene
[háidʒiːn]

n. 위생 a condition promoting sanitary practices

cannot compromise on food safety and hygiene
식품 안전 및 위생에 대해서는 타협할 수 없다

2730
antipathy
[æntípəθi]

n. 반감 a feeling of intense dislike
syn. aversion, distaste

feel a deep antipathy 강한 반감을 느끼다

2731
brisk
[brisk]

adj. 상쾌한 quick and energetic
syn. invigorating, keen, lively

the brisk autumn days 상쾌한 가을날

2732
compatible
[kəmpǽtəbəl]

adj. 호환이 되는, 양립하는 able to exist and perform in harmonious or
agreeable combination
syn. agreeable, harmonious

employees who are compatible with each other 서로 잘 맞는 직원들

2733
antiseptic
[æntəséptik]

n. 소독제, 방부제　a substance that destroys micro-organisms that carry disease without harming body tissues

syn. disinfectant, sanitary, hygienic

cleanse the wound with antiseptic 상처를 소독제로 세척하라

2734
grudge
[grʌdʒ]

n. 원한, 뒤끝　a resentment strong enough to justify retaliation

syn. grievance, resentment

carry a grudge 원한을 품고 있다

2735
fraud
[frɔːd]

n. 사기, 사기꾼　intentional deception resulting in injury to another person

find evidence of fraud 사기의 관련된 증거를 찾다

2736
applaud
[əplɔ́ːd]

v. 박수갈채를 보내다, 칭찬하다　to clap one's hands or shout after performances to indicate approval

syn. clap, acclaim

applauded the actor 그 배우에게 박수갈채를 보냈다

2737
bribe
[braib]

v. 뇌물로 매수하다　to make illegal payments to in exchange for favors or influence

syn. corrupt, buy, grease one's palms

attempt to bribe a judge 판사를 뇌물로 매수하려 하다

2738
fume
[fjuːm]

v. 씩씩대다　to show or feel anger

syn. be mad, display anger, rage

fumed with anger at the delay 늦는 것에 대해 씩씩댔다

2739
high-profile
[haipróufail]

adj. 세간의 이목을 끄는　attracting much attention and publicity

a high-profile campaign 세간의 이목을 끄는 캠페인

2740
frenetic
[frinétik]

adj. 열광적인, 발광한　excessively agitated

syn. enthusiastic

frenetic screams followed the accident 사고 이후에 황급한 비명소리가 있었다

2741

fortitude

[fɔ́ːrtətjùːd]

n. 용기, 불굴의 의지　strength of mind that enables one to endure adversity with courage

syn. endurance, forbearance, resolution

with fortitude 결연히

2742

compliant

[kəmpláiənt]

adj. 순응하는　disposed or willing to comply

syn. flexible, submissive

a very compliant child 아주 순종적인 아이

2743

apprehension

[æ̀prihénʃən]

n. 걱정, 우려　fearful expectation or anticipation

syn. anxiety, dread, fear

express apprehension 우려를 표명하다

2744

austerity

[ɔːstériti]

n. 긴축, 엄격　a situation in which there is not much money and it is spent only on things that are necessary

syn. abstention

an austerity budget 긴축 예산

2745

communism

[kámjənìzəm]

n. 공산주의　a form of socialism that abolishes private ownership

give up communism 공산주의를 포기하다

2746

composure

[kəmpóuʒər]

n. 평정, 침착　steadiness of mind under stress

syn. dignity, poise, self-control

lose one's composure 마음의 평정을 잃다

2747

hindsight

[háindsàit]

n. 뒤늦은 깨달음　understanding the nature of an event after it has happened

with hindsight, I was wrong 돌이켜보니, 내가 틀렸다

2748

appraise

[əpréiz]

v. 평가하다, 감정하다　to evaluate or estimate the nature, quality, ability, extent, or significance of

syn. measure, evaluate

appraise a person's ability 아무의 능력을 평가하다

2749
guild
[gild]

n. 길드, 상인 조합   a formal association of people with similar interests

syn. association, union

form a guild 조합을 만들다

2750
friction
[frík∫ən]

n. 마찰, 불화   a state of conflict between persons

syn. crashing, rubbing

reduce friction 마찰을 줄이다

Review | 고난도

뜻을 써보고 전체 어구의 의미를 생각해 보시오.

01 buckle **one's belt** _____ 2707

02 **employees who are** compatible **with each other** _____ 2732

03 forsake **one's bad habits** _____ 2723

04 **form a** guild _____ 2749

05 grub **for potatoes** _____ 2728

06 appraise **a person's ability** _____ 2748

07 **find evidence of** fraud _____ 2735

08 **the plants** wilted **in the heat** _____ 2715

09 **an exceedingly** vulgar **necktie** _____ 2719

10 **offer the man in the lobby a** bribe _____ 2737

11 **a** high-profile **campaign** _____ 2739

12 antagonize **her further** _____ 2711

13 applauded **the actor** _____ 2736

14 **a beautiful** vista **of the valley** _____ 2721

15 holistic **health** _____ 2722

16 withhold **the disappointment and anger** _____ 2701

17 **be** vulnerable **to criticism** _____ 2714

18 **a guitar** virtuoso _____ 2709

19 widespread **poverty** _____ 2713

20 **an innocent** bystander _____ 2703

2751
sequential
[sikwénʃəl]
-sequ 뒤따르다

adj. 순차적인 happening in a series or sequence
syn. back-to-back, consecutive

put the cards in sequential order 카드를 순서대로 배열하다

2752
father
[fáːðər]

v. ~을 창안하다[설립하다] to be the founder, producer, or author of

fathered the improvement plan 개선안을 만들었다

2753
altruism
[ǽltruìzəm]

n. 이타심 feelings and behavior that show a desire to help other people and a lack of selfishness
syn. selflessness, generosity, self-sacrifice

volunteered out of altruism 이타심으로 자원했다

2754
figurative
[fíɡjərətiv]

adj. 비유적인, 상징적인 (if you use words in a figurative way, you use them to make a description more interesting or impressive)
syn. metaphoric
ant. literal

its figurative meaning 그것의 비유적인 의미

2755
fleet
[fliːt]

n. 함대, 선단 a group of military ships that are controlled by one leader
syn. armada, caravan

a combined fleet 연합 함대

2756
alienation
[èiljənéiʃən]

n. 멀리함, 이간, 소외 the feeling of not being part of society or a group
syn. estrangement
ant. reconciliation

a sense of alienation from society 사회로부터의 소외감

2757
fertilize
[fɔ́ːrtəlàiz]

v. 기름지게 하다, 거름을 주다 to add a natural or chemical substance to soil in order to help plants grow
syn. enrich, feed, compost

fertilize the lawn every year 해마다 잔디에 거름을 주다

2758
cohesion
[kouhíːʒən]
-co 함께
-hes 달라붙다

n. 응집력   a condition in which people or things are closely united

a lack of cohesion 응집력의 부족

2759
enlist
[enlíst]

v. 입대하다, 참여하다   to sign up for duty in the army, navy, etc.
syn. join, sign up, enroll

enlisted in the navy 해군에 입대했다

2760
leisured
[líːʒərd]

adj. 여유로운   doing things slowly because you feel relaxed and are enjoying yourself

live a leisured life 한가로운 삶을 살다

2761
reflexive
[rifléksiv]
-flex 구부러지다
-re 다시, 역행하여

adj. 반사적인   happening or done without thinking as a reaction to something

reflexive response 반사적 반응

2762
alumnus
[əlʌ́mnəs]
-pl. alumni

n. 동문   someone who was a student at a particular school, college, or university

Cambridge alumni 캠브리지 대학 동문

2763
entity
[éntiti]

n. 실체, 객체   a separate unit that is complete and has its own character
syn. being, individual

become separate entities 개별적 객체가 되다

2764
vault
[vɔːlt]

v. 뛰어 넘다   to leap vigorously
syn. jump, spring, leap

the robber vaulted over the counter 강도가 계산대를 뛰어 넘었다

2765
decree
[dekríː]

n. 명령, 법령   an official order given by a person with power or by a government
syn. command, order

issue a decree 법령을 발표하다

2766
slosh
[slɑʃ]

v. 철벅거리며 걷다   to walk through water, mud, etc., in a forceful and noisy way

syn. plash, splash, swash

sloshed through the big puddle 큰 물 웅덩이를 철벅거리며 건너갔다

2767
sheer
[ʃiər]

adj. 순수한, 순전한   complete and total (used to emphasize the large amount, size, or degree of something)

syn. total, complete, absolute, utter

succeeded through sheer hard work 정말 힘든 일을 겪으며 성공했다

2768
line
[lain]

v. 안감을 대다   to sew a piece of material onto the inside or back of another piece to make it stronger or warmer

a leather coat lined with silk 실크로 안감을 댄 가죽 코트

2769
grandstand
[grǽndstæ̀nd]

n. 정면 특별관람석   a large structure that has many rows of seats where people sit and watch sports competitions, games, or races

grandstand seats 정면 특별관람석의 자리

2770
derivative
[dirívətiv]
-de 하락, 부정

n. 파생물   something that comes from something else

syn. by-product, derivate, offshoot, spin-off

ant. origin

a form of music that is a derivative of jazz 재즈에서 나온 한 음악 형태

2771
stingy
[stíndʒi]

adj. 인색한, 몹시 아끼는   unwilling to spend

syn. miserly, frugal, lean, meager

ant. generous, ample

a stingy person 구두쇠

2772
sloppy
[slɑ́pi]

adj. 단정치 못한   not careful or neat

syn. unkempt, untidy

a sloppy child 단정치 못한 아이

2773
degenerative
[didʒénərèitiv]
-gen 탄생

adj. 퇴화적인, 타락적인 causing the body or part of the body to become weaker or less able to function as time passes

degenerative diseases such as arthritis 관절염과 같은 퇴행성 질병들

2774
shingle
[ʃíŋgəl]

v. 지붕널로 덮다 to cover something with shingles

shingle a roof 널빤지로 지붕을 이다

2775
arbitrary
[áːrbitrèri]

adj. 임의의, 멋대로의 not planned or chosen for a particular reason
syn. impulsive, capricious, erratic

an arbitrary decision made by a leader 지도자의 임의의 결정

2776
asymmetry
[eisímətri]

n. 불균형, 비대칭 a lack of symmetry

there is no asymmetry 균형이 맞지 않는 곳이 없다

2777
dispense
[dispéns]
-dis 멀어짐, 부정

v. 분배하다, 면제하다, 베풀다 to give or provide something
syn. divide, share

dispense food and clothing to the poor 빈민에게 의복과 식량을 베풀다

2778
fondly
[fándli]

adv. 귀엽게, 사랑스럽게 with fondness / with love
syn. lovingly

look fondly backward on the old days 옛날을 그리운 심정으로 상기하다

2779
copious
[kóupiəs]

adj. 막대한, 풍부한 large in number or quantity
syn. abundant, ample, bountiful

a copious harvest 풍작

2780
attune
[ətʃúːn]

v. 조율하다 to bring into harmony with
syn. harmonize

a style attuned to modern taste 현대인의 기호에 맞춘 양식

2781
etch
[etʃ]

v. 아로새기다 to make an etching of
syn. engrave

etched glass 식각 유리

2782
forage
[fɔ́:ridʒ]

v. (먹이 등을) 찾아 돌아다니다 to search for something such as food or supplies

syn. search, hunt, scavenge

foraged for firewood 땔감을 찾아 다녔다

2783
downshift
[dáunʃìft]

v. 저속 기어로 바꾸다 to put the engine of a vehicle into a lower gear

downshifted and turned the steering wheel 저속기어로 바꾸고 핸들을 돌렸다

2784
forlorn
[fərlɔ́:rn]

adj. 고독한, 버림받은 marked by or showing hopelessness

syn. dejected, depressed, miserable

a forlorn child 버림받은 아이

2785
instigate
[ínstəgèit]

v. 부추기다, 조장하다, 선동하다 to provoke or stir up

syn. excite, incite, provoke

instigate anger among the younger generation
젊은 세대의 분노를 부추기다

2786
formative
[fɔ́:rmətiv]
-form 형성하다

adj. (인격) 형성에 중요한, 발달의 capable of forming new cells and tissues

syn. developmental

spent his formative years in New York 그는 성장기를 뉴욕에서 보냈다

2787
exert
[igzə́:rt]

v. 발휘하다, 쓰다 to put to use

syn. apply, employ, exercise, wield

exert every effort 전력을 다하다

2788
intact
[intǽkt]

adj. 손상되지 않은, 원래대로의 constituting the undiminished entirety

syn. unbroken, undamaged, unimpaired

remained intact despite rough handling 함부로 다뤘는데도 깨지지 않았다

2789
extravagant
[ikstrǽvəgənt]

adj. 도가 지나친, 낭비하는 recklessly wasteful

syn. abundant, excessive

an extravagant person 돈을 헤프게 쓰는 사람

2790
evict
[ivíkt]

v. 퇴거시키다, 쫓아내다　to expel or eject without recourse to legal process

syn. dislodge, dismiss, expel, oust

evict a person from a house 사람을 집에서 내쫓다

2791
dire
[daiər]

adj. 대단히 심각한, 비참한　causing great fear or worry

syn. acute, distressing, grievous

dire news 비보(悲報)

2792
ardent
[á:rdənt]

adj. 열렬한, 격렬한　having or showing very strong feelings

syn. eager, fervent

an ardent admirer 열렬한 찬미자

2793
dip
[dip]

v. 살짝 담그다　to put something into a liquid and pull it out again quickly

syn. immerse, submerse

dip the bread in the milk 빵을 우유에 적시다

2794
converge
[kənvə́:rdʒ]
-con 함께

v. 모아지다, 집중되다　to be adjacent or come together

syn. concentrate, focus

all these roads converge on the city 모든 길이 그 도시로 집중해 있다

2795
array
[əréi]

n. 집합체, 배열　an orderly arrangement

syn. arrangement, assortment

an array of flags 쭉 줄지은 깃발들

2796
equate
[ikwéit]

v. 같게 하다, 동일시하다　to consider or describe as similar, equal, or analogous

syn. compare, equal

skills always equate to money in the end 기술은 결국에는 돈과 동일시 된다

2797
artifact
[á:rtəfæ̀kt]

n. 가공품, 유물　a man-made object taken as a whole

hunt for treasures and ancient artifacts 보물과 고대 유물을 쫓다

2798
equilibrium
[ìːkwəlíbriəm]

n. 평형상태, 균형   a state in which opposing forces or actions are balanced so that one is not stronger or greater than the other

syn. balance, stability

a political equilibrium 정치적 균형

2799
exacting
[igzǽktiŋ]

adj. 엄격한, 까다로운   requiring much time, attention, or effort from someone

syn. demanding

an exacting teacher 엄한 선생님

2800
discourse
[dískɔːrs]

n. 담론, 담화   extended verbal expression in speech or writing

syn. lecture, oration, sermon

passionate discourse about new technology 새로운 기술에 대한 열띤 논의

458

Review | 고난도

뜻을 써보고 전체 어구의 의미를 생각해 보시오.

01 remained intact despite rough handling ⎯⎯⎯⎯⎯⎯⎯⎯⎯⎯⎯ 2788

02 grandstand seats ⎯⎯⎯⎯⎯⎯⎯⎯⎯⎯⎯⎯⎯⎯⎯ 2769

03 an extravagant person ⎯⎯⎯⎯⎯⎯⎯⎯⎯⎯⎯⎯ 2789

04 fertilize the lawn every year ⎯⎯⎯⎯⎯⎯⎯⎯⎯⎯ 2757

05 a copious harvest ⎯⎯⎯⎯⎯⎯⎯⎯⎯⎯⎯⎯⎯⎯ 2779

06 exert every effort ⎯⎯⎯⎯⎯⎯⎯⎯⎯⎯⎯⎯⎯⎯ 2797

07 a lack of cohesion ⎯⎯⎯⎯⎯⎯⎯⎯⎯⎯⎯⎯⎯⎯ 2758

08 dire news ⎯⎯⎯⎯⎯⎯⎯⎯⎯⎯⎯⎯⎯⎯⎯⎯⎯ 2791

09 its figurative meaning ⎯⎯⎯⎯⎯⎯⎯⎯⎯⎯⎯⎯ 2754

10 there is no asymmetry ⎯⎯⎯⎯⎯⎯⎯⎯⎯⎯⎯⎯ 2776

11 an array of flags ⎯⎯⎯⎯⎯⎯⎯⎯⎯⎯⎯⎯⎯⎯ 2795

12 shingle a roof ⎯⎯⎯⎯⎯⎯⎯⎯⎯⎯⎯⎯⎯⎯⎯ 2774

13 skills always equate to money in the end ⎯⎯⎯⎯⎯⎯ 2796

14 become separate entities ⎯⎯⎯⎯⎯⎯⎯⎯⎯⎯⎯ 2763

15 put the cards in sequential order ⎯⎯⎯⎯⎯⎯⎯⎯ 2751

16 a stingy person ⎯⎯⎯⎯⎯⎯⎯⎯⎯⎯⎯⎯⎯⎯⎯ 2771

17 reflexive response ⎯⎯⎯⎯⎯⎯⎯⎯⎯⎯⎯⎯⎯⎯ 2761

18 fathered the improvement plan ⎯⎯⎯⎯⎯⎯⎯⎯⎯ 2752

19 degenerative diseases such as arthritis ⎯⎯⎯⎯⎯⎯ 2773

20 volunteered out of altruism ⎯⎯⎯⎯⎯⎯⎯⎯⎯⎯ 2753

2801
dose
[dous]

n. 약의 1회분 a measured portion of medicine taken at any one time

small doses of aspirin 소량의 아스피린

2802
folly
[fáli]

n. 어리석음, 어리석은 행위 the trait of acting stupidly or rashly
syn. foolishness, stupidity

the merest folly 더 없는 어리석음

2803
construe
[kənstrú:]

v. 파악하다, ~의 뜻으로 해석하다 to make sense of / to assign a meaning to
syn. comprehend, infer, interpret

be wrongly construed 잘못 이해되다

2804
aura
[ɔ́:rə]

n. 기운, 분위기, 느낌 an indication of radiant light drawn around the head of a saint
syn. mood, atmosphere, air

an aura of grandeur 숭고함

2805
downright
[dáunràit]

adv. 아주, 완전히 thoroughgoing
syn. completely, thoroughly, utterly

be downright strange 전적으로 이상하다

2806
disperse
[dispə́:rs]
-dis 멀어짐, 부정

v. 해산하다, 흩트리다, 퍼뜨리다 to spread apart
syn. scatter, dispel, dissipate

a book dispersed throughout the world 온 세계에 보급된 책

2807
assertive
[əsə́:rtiv]

adj. 자기주장이 강한, 독단적인 aggressively self-assured
syn. aggressive, domineering, forceful

an assertive foreign policy 독단적인 외교정책

2808
autonomous
[ɔ:tánəməs]

adj. 자율적인, 자치의 not controlled by outside forces
syn. independent, self-sufficient

an autonomous variable 독립 변수

2809
disengage
[dìsengéidʒ]
-dis 멀어짐, 부정

v. 자유롭게 하다, 해방하다   to release from something that holds fast, connects, or entangles

syn. disconnect, separate, uncouple

disengage oneself from one's love affair 연애를 청산하다

2810
domain
[douméin]

n. 영토, 영역   a particular environment or walk of life

syn. kingdom, realm, area

the domain of the polar bear 북극곰의 영역

2811
astounding
[əstáundiŋ]

adj. 몹시 놀라게 하는   so surprisingly impressive as to stun or overwhelm

syn. very surprising

an astounding achievement 놀라운 업적

2812
conspire
[kənspáiər]

v. 공모하다, 작당하다   to engage in plotting or enter into a conspiracy, swear together

syn. conspire, contrive

conspire against the state 국가 반란을 꾀하다

2813
assistive
[əsístiv]
-sist 서다

adj. 도움이 되는   giving assistance

make an assistive device 보조 장치를 만들다

2814
dismount
[dismáunt]
-dis 멀어짐, 부정

v. (자전거 등에서) 내리다   to alight from (a horse)

syn. unhorse, get off, get down

dismount from a bicycle 자전거에서 내리다

2815
distinct
[distíŋkt]
-dis 멀어짐, 부정

adj. 뚜렷한   not alike

syn. different, separate

a distinct culture 독특한 문화

2816
entreat
[entríːt]

v. 간청하다, 원하다, 탄원하다   to ask for or request earnestly
syn. ask, beg

entreat **a person for mercy** 아무에게 간절히 자비를 간청하다

2817
contention
[kənténʃən]

n. 갈등, 언쟁   a point asserted as part of an argument
syn. friction, strife

a bone of contention 불화의 씨

2818
figuratively
[fíɡiurətivli]

adv. 비유적으로, 상징적으로   in a figurative sense
syn. metaphorically, symbolically

figuratively **speaking** 비유적으로 말하자면

2819
exempt
[iɡzémpt]

v. 면제하다   to say that someone does not have to do something that others are required to do
syn. excuse, pardon

commodities exempted **from customs duty** 면세품

2820
dwindle
[dwíndl]

v. 줄다, 작아지다, 축소되다   to become smaller or lose substance
syn. decrease

her savings dwindled **down** 그녀의 저축은 줄어들었다

2821
drench
[drentʃ]

v. 흠뻑 적시다   to make something completely wet
syn. immerse, saturate, soak

be drenched **to the skin** 흠뻑 젖다

2822
authentic
[ɔːθéntik]

adj. 진짜의   conforming to fact and therefore worthy of belief
syn. actual, genuine, legitimate

an authentic **account by an eyewitness** 목격자의 믿을 수 있는 증언

2823
dodge
[dɑdʒ]

v. 피하다, 스치다   to make a sudden movement in a new direction so as to avoid
syn. avoid, elude, evade

managed to dodge **his attack** 가까스로 그의 공격을 피했다

2824
consignment
[kənsáinmənt]

n. 위탁판매   the act or process of sending goods to a person or place to be sold

bought this desk at the consignment shop 이 책상을 중고가게에서 샀다

2825
execute
[éksikjùːt]

v. 1 실행하다 2 사형에 처하다   to carry out or perform an action / to kill as a means of socially sanctioned punishment

syn. 1 administer, enforce 2 put to death, kill

execute an order 주문에 응하다

execute a person for murder 아무를 살인죄로 처형하다

2826
intimacy
[íntəməsi]

n. 친밀함, 상세한 지식   the state of being intimate

syn. privacy, affection, fondness

his intimacy with the history of Korea 한국 역사에 대한 그의 깊은 이해

2827
curb
[kəːrb]

v. 제한하다, 구속하다   to control or limit something

syn. check, harness, inhibit, repress

curb national economic recovery 국가 경제 회복에 지장을 주다

2828
minuscule
[mínʌskjùːl]
-min 작은, 소형의

adj. 아주 작은, 하찮은, 미미한   very small

although the odds are minuscule 가능성은 미미하지만

2829
intolerant
[intálərənt]

adj. 마음이 좁은, 참을 수 없는   unwilling to tolerate difference of opinion

be intolerant of bad manners 무례함을 견딜 수 없다

2830
cordial
[kɔ́ːrdʒəl]
-cord 심장

adj. 충심어린, 충심으로부터의   friendly but quite polite and formal

syn. affable, congenial, friendly

a cordial reception 진심에서 우러나온 환대

2831
congruent
[kángruənt]

adj. 일치하는, 적합한   corresponding in character or kind

syn. congruous

his actions were not congruent with his words 그는 언행이 일치하지 않았다

2832
morale
[mouræl]

n. 사기, 도의 a state of individual psychological well-being based upon a sense of confidence and usefulness and purpose

syn. attitude, spirit, temper

raise morale 사기를 높이다

2833
interlace
[ìntərléis]

v. 얽히게 하다 to join together by crossing them over and under each other

interlace flowers with little branches 꽃과 잔가지를 얽다

2834
congregate
[káŋgrigèit]
–con 함께

v. 모이다, 소집하다 to come together, usually for a purpose

syn. assemble, flock, gather

congregated in the park 공원에 모였다

2835
intrigue
[intríːg]

v. 모의하다, 호기심을 자극하다 to make someone want to know more about something

syn. interest

that old house intrigued me 그 오래된 집이 나의 흥미를 끌었다

2836
mishap
[míshæp]

n. 재난, 불행한 일 an unpredictable outcome that is unfortunate

syn. bad luck, mischance

without mishap 무사히

2837
jostle
[dʒásl]

v. 떠밀다 to push against someone while moving forward in a crowd of people

syn. bounce, bump

jostle one another 서로 밀치다

2838
nauseating
[nɔ́ːrzièitiŋ]

adj. 지겨운, 몹시 싫은 causing disgust

syn. queasy, loathsome

a nauseating story 몹시 불쾌한 이야기

2839
mutation
[mjuːtéiʃən]

n. 돌연변이 an organism that has characteristics resulting from chromosomal alteration

a gene mutation 유전자의 돌연변이

464

2840
myriad
[míriəd]

n. 무수, 1만(萬) a very large number of things
syn. ten thousand

a myriad of stars 무수히 많은 별들

2841
cutthroat
[kʌ́tθròut]

adj. 흉악한, 치열한 ruthless in competition
syn. murderous, fierce

a cutthroat competition 치열한 경기

2842
drastic
[drǽstik]

adj. 강렬한, 과감한 forceful and extreme and rigorous
syn. extreme, radical

drastic measures 과감한 조치

2843
diffuse
[difjúːz]
-fus 쏟다

v. 퍼뜨리다 to spread out
syn. disperse, scatter, spread

diffuse a smell 냄새를 발산하다

2844
coverage
[kʌ́vəridʒ]

n. 범위, 보도 the extent to which something is covered

thanks to the news coverage 뉴스 보도 덕분에

2845
itinerant
[aitínərənt]

adj. 떠돌아다니는 traveling from place to place to work

an itinerant farm hand 뜨내기 농장 노동자

2846
craving
[kréiviŋ]

n. 갈망, 열망 an intense desire for some particular thing
syn. desire, urge, yearning

a craving for chocolate 초콜릿에 대한 갈망

2847
courtesy
[kɔ́ːrtəsi]

n. 공손함, 예의바름, 호의 a courteous or respectful or considerate act
syn. civility, politeness

treated everyone with kindness and courtesy 모두를 친절하고 예의 바르게 대했다

2848
discretion
[diskréʃən]

n. 재량(권), 분별, 신중 freedom to act or judge on one's own
syn. judgment, prudence

act on your own discretion 재량껏 행하다

2849
cyclic
[sáiklik]

adj. 순환하는 happening in cycles

the cyclic recurrence of earthquakes 주기적인 지진의 재발

2850
cult
[kʌlt]

n. 숭배, 숭배자 집단 followers of an exclusive system of religious beliefs and practices

syn. band, faction, group

the cult of nature 자연 숭배

Review | 고난도

뜻을 써보고 전체 어구의 의미를 생각해 보시오.

01 figuratively speaking _____ 2818

02 a cutthroat competition _____ 2841

03 drastic measures _____ 2842

04 diffuse a smell _____ 2843

05 an itinerant farm hand _____ 2845

06 interlace flowers with little branches _____ 2833

07 a craving for chocolate _____ 2846

08 treated everyone with kindness and courtesy _____ 2847

09 curb national economic recovery _____ 2827

10 the cult of nature _____ 2850

11 a nauseating story _____ 2838

12 thanks to the news coverage _____ 2844

13 an assertive foreign policy _____ 2807

14 bought this desk at the consignment shop _____ 2824

15 his intimacy with the history of Korea _____ 2826

16 that old house intrigued me _____ 2835

17 his actions were not congruent with his words _____ 2831

18 a myriad of stars _____ 2840

19 a book dispersed throughout the world _____ 2806

20 conspire against the state _____ 2812

DAY 58

2851
introspection
[ìntrəspékʃən]

n. 자기성찰 the contemplation of your own thoughts and desires and conduct

syn. self-contemplation

encourage introspection 자성을 촉구하다

2852
suspension
[səspénʃən]
-pens 매달다

n. 정학, 정지 a time interval during which there is a temporary cessation of something

one week's suspension from school 일주일의 정학

2853
introvert
[íntrəvə̀:rt]
-vert 바꾸다

n. 내성적인 사람 a person who tends to shrink from social contacts and to become preoccupied with their own thoughts

syn. brooder, loner, thinker

he is an introvert 그는 내성적인 사람이다

2854
prime
[praim]
-prim 처음의

v. 대비시키다, 준비하다 to make something ready for use

syn. prepare, set up

prime a cannon 대포를 준비시키다

2855
restless
[réstlis]

adj. 침착하지 못한, 가만히 못 있는 worried and uneasy

syn. agitated, fidgety, nervous

become restless 안절부절 못하다

2856
sonorous
[sənɔ́:rəs]

adj. 듣기 좋은, 낭랑한 full and loud and deep

syn. resonant, resounding, vibrant

ant. shrill

a sonorous church bell 울려 퍼지는 교회 종소리

2857
tranquil
[trǽŋkwil]

adj. 고요한, 평온한 free from disturbance by heavy waves

syn. calm, pacific, placid

a tranquil sea 고요한 바다

2858
responsive
[rispánsiv]
-spons 약속

adj. 민감하게 반응하는 containing or using responses
syn. sensitive, sympathetic, understanding
ant. cold

   a responsive class 잘 반응하는 학급

2859
pore
[pɔːr]

n. 구멍, 털구멍 any tiny hole admitting passage of a liquid
syn. opening

   sweat from every pore 더워서 땀투성이가 되다

2860
prioritize
[praió:ritàiz]

v. 우선순위를 매기다 to assign a priority to

   prioritize one's tasks 일의 우선순위를 정하다

2861
tract
[trækt]

n. 넓은 지역 an extended area of land
syn. area, region, stretch

   vast tracts of woodland 광활한 숲 지역

2862
vigorous
[vígərəs]

adj. 힘센, 원기 왕성한 healthy and strong
syn. energetic, robust
ant. listless, sluggish

   a vigorous youth 원기 왕성한 청년

2863
submissive
[səbmísiv]
-sub 아래의

adj. 순종적인 always willing to obey someone and never disagreeing
      with them, even if they are unkind to you
syn. compliant, obedient, pliable

   submissive workers 유순한 노동자들

2864
precarious
[prikέəriəs]

adj. 불안정한, 불확실한 likely to change or become dangerous without
      warning
syn. shaky, unstable
ant. secure, well-founded

   a precarious occupation 불안한 직업

2865
resilience
[rizíljəns]
-re 다시, 역행하여

n. 회복력   the ability to become strong, healthy, or successful again after something bad happens

syn. elasticity, adaptability, flexibility

economic resilience 경제적인 탄력성

2866
overt
[óuvə:rt]

adj. 노골적인, 명백한, 공공연한   open and observable / not secret or hidden

syn. conspicuous, obvious, evident

ant. covert, hidden, subtle

overt hostility 노골적인 적대감

2867
modulate
[mάdʒəlèit]

v. 조절하다, 바꾸다   to change or adjust something so that it exists in a balanced or proper amount

syn. adjust, moderate, regulate

modulate radio waves 라디오 무선 주파수를 바꾸다

2868
quagmire
[kwǽgmàiər]

n. 꼼짝할 수 없는 곤경   a situation that is hard to deal with or get out of

sink deeper into a quagmire of violence and lawlessness
폭력과 무법의 수렁으로 더 깊이 빠져들다

2869
noteworthy
[nóutwə̀:rði]

adj. 주목할 만한, 놀라운, 현저한, 눈에 띄는   worthy of notice

syn. outstanding, remarkable

ant. insignificant

a noteworthy feature 주목할 만한 특징

2870
subliminal
[sʌblímənəl]
-sub 아래의

adj. 잠재의식의   below the threshold of conscious perception

syn. instinctive, intuitive, involuntary

ant. deliberate

subliminal advertising 잠재의식하의 광고 (순간적 광고 영상을 주어 잠재의식에 호소함)

2871
sting
[stiŋ]
stung - stung

v. 쏘다, 찌르다   to deliver a sting to

syn. bite, smart, tingle

ant. soothe

a bee stung my arm 벌이 내 팔을 쏘았다

2872
riot
[ráiət]

n. 폭동, 소요, 시위   a public act of violence by an unruly mob

syn. chaos, confusion, tumult, uproar

the riot police 폭동 진압 경찰

2873
populace
[pápjələs]

n. 서민들   the common people

syn. public

support of large sections of the local populace
지역 주민들의 대다수 지역에서의 지지

2874
meddling
[médliŋ]

n. 간섭, 참견   the act of altering something secretly or improperly

syn. tempering

ant. ignoring

needless meddling 쓸데없는 참견

2875
invincible
[invínsəbəl]

adj. 정복할 수 없는, 무적의, 확고한

syn. impossible to defeat or overcome

his invincible stubbornness 그의 꺾이지 않는 완고함

2876
mob
[mɑb]

n. 폭도, 군중   a disorderly crowd of people

syn. swarm, throng

the angry mob smashed store windows 화난 폭도들이 가게 유리창을 부쉈다

2877
menace
[ménəs]

n. 협박, 위협   a threat or the act of threatening

syn. threatening

a menace to world peace 세계 평화에 대한 위협

2878
inward
[ínwərd]

adj. 내부의, 내적인   directed or moving inward or toward a center

syn. inner, inside, internal

inward investment 내부투자

2879
torment
[tɔ́ːrment]

v. 괴롭히다   to make someone suffer a lot, especially mentally

syn. torture, harass

torment a person with harsh noises 귀 따가운 소리로 아무를 괴롭히다

2880
nocturnal
[nɑktə́:rnl]

adj. 야행성의, 야간의   belonging to or active during the night

the bats are nocturnal 박쥐는 야행성이다

2881
suffocate
[sʌ́fəkèit]

v. 질식시키다   to deprive of oxygen and prevent from breathing
syn. smother, stifle, choke

the heat suffocated her 더위에 숨이 막힐 지경이었다

2882
niche
[nitʃ]

n. 틈새시장 구멍, 특정 영역   the situation in which a business's products or services can succeed by being sold to a particular kind or group of people

creating a niche market 틈새시장 개척

2883
outlaw
[áutlɔ̀:]

v. 금지하다, 불법화하다   to make something illegal
syn. ban, forbid, prohibit
ant. legalize, permit

outlaw drunken driving 음주 운전을 금지하다

2884
molten
[móultən]

adj. 용해된   reduced to liquid form by heating
syn. liquified

pour molten lead into a mold 녹은 납을 거푸집에 붓다

2885
poise
[pɔiz]

n. 안정, 침착   a state of being balanced in a stable equilibrium
syn. balance, equilibrium
ant. discomposure

lose one's poise 균형을 잃다

2886
underpin
[ʌ̀ndərpín]

v. 버팀목을 대다, 지지하다   to support from beneath
syn. support

underpin a sagging building 기울어진 건물에 버팀목을 대다

2887
robust
[roubʌ́st]

adj. 튼튼한   sturdy and strong in form, constitution, or construction
syn. energetic, hardy, lively, strong
ant. weak, frail

a robust baby 튼튼한 아기

2888
psyche
[sáiki]

n. 마음, 정신   that which is responsible for one's thoughts and feelings

syn. mind, spirit

the human psyche 인간의 마음

2889
polarity
[poulǽrəti]

n. 양극성, 대립   a relation between two opposite attributes or tendencies

syn. contrariness, oppositeness

ant. identicalness, sameness

polarity between the labor and the management 노사 대립

2890
subsist
[səbsíst]

v. 살아가다, 생명을 보전하다   to support oneself

syn. exist, survive, get on

subsist by begging 구걸하여 살아가다

2891
involuntary
[inváləntèri]

-vol 의지

adj. 비자발적인, 마지못해 하는   not done or made consciously / not done by choice

syn. unintentional

involuntary consent 마음에도 없는 승낙

an involuntary cry of pain 저절로 나오는 고통의 신음소리

2892
overbearing
[òuvərbɛ́əriŋ]

adj. 고압적인, 거만한, 건방진   often trying to control the behavior of other people in an annoying or unwanted way

syn. authoritarian, dictatorial, haughty

an overbearing manner 고압적인 태도

2893
utter
[ʌ́tər]

v. 발언하다   to say something

syn. express, talk, verbalize

utter a groan 신음소리를 내다

2894
supplementary
[sʌ̀pləméntəri]

-ple 채우다

adj. 부가적인, 보충의   provided in addition to what already exists

syn. accessory, additional, extra

supplementary information 추가 정보

2895
swipe
[swaip]

v. 강타하다, 세게 휘두르다   to strike with a swiping motion

syn. smack, strike, hit

The cat swiped at the dog. 고양이가 개를 세게 때렸다.

2896
superficial
[sùːpərfíʃəl]

adj. 피상적인, 표면의   concerned with or comprehending only what is apparent or obvious

syn. cosmetic, sketchy

ant. thorough, substantial

a superficial view of the world 피상적인 세계관

2897
upsell
[ʌpsel]

v. 고객에게 더 비싼 제품을 구매하도록 설득하다   to persuade a customer to buy more of a product or a more expensive product than they had intended

attempt to upsell 고객에게 더 비싼 제품을 구매하도록 설득하려고 시도하다

2898
stall
[stɔːl]

v. 시간을 끌다, 지연시키다   to postpone doing what one should be doing

syn. delay, hold off

ant. accelerate, resume

stall for time 시간을 벌려고 지연시키다

2899
intrusive
[intrúːsiv]

adj. 주제넘게 나서는, 끼어든

syn. annoying, bothersome

an intrusive person 주제넘게 나서는 사람

2900
outmoded
[àutmóudid]

adj. 구식의   out of fashion

syn. obsolete, old-fashioned, out-of-date

outmoded teaching methods 시대에 뒤진 교수법

Review | 고난도

뜻을 써보고 전체 어구의 의미를 생각해 보시오.

01 his invincible stubbornness   2875

02 sweat from every pore   2859

03 torment a person with harsh noises   2879

04 the bats are nocturnal   2880

05 the human psyche   2888

06 polarity between the labor and the management   2889

07 overt hostility   2866

08 outlaw drunken driving   2883

09 pour molten lead into a mold   2884

10 underpin a sagging building   2886

11 a noteworthy feature   2869

12 the heat suffocated her   2881

13 a tranquil sea   2857

14 inward investment   2878

15 a vigorous youth   2862

16 needless meddling   2874

17 a precarious occupation   2864

18 encourage introspection   2851

19 a bee stung my arm   2871

20 he is an introvert   2853

2901
pragmatic
[prǽgmǽtik]

adj. 실용적인   involving or emphasizing practical results rather than theories and ideas

syn. practical, realistic, sensible

ant. romantic

pragmatic philosophy 실용주의 철학

2902
precipitation
[prisìpətéiʃən]

n. 강수량   the quantity of water falling to earth at a specific place within a specified period of time

syn. downfall

annual precipitation 연간 강수량

2903
tuck
[tʌk]

v. 밀어 넣다   to put something in a particular place usually to hide it

syn. cram, insert, shove, stuff

tuck one's shirt in 셔츠 자락을 쑤셔 넣다

2904
posit
[pázit]

v. 사실로 받아들이다[가정하다]   to say that something is true or that something should be accepted as true

posit that each planet moves in a perfect circle
각 행성들이 완전한 원형으로 이동한다고 가정하다

2905
rigorous
[rígərəs]

adj. 엄격한, 엄밀한   rigidly accurate

syn. harsh, strict

ant. lax, careless

rigorous discipline 엄한 규율

2906
solvent
[sálvənt]
-solv 풀다

adj. 지급능력이 있는   able to pay debts

syn. financially sound

stay solvent 채무를 지지 않고 있다

2907
underscore
[ʌ̀ndərskɔ́:r]

v. 강조하다, 밑줄을 긋다   to give extra weight to a communication

syn. underline, emphasize

that is what I wanted to underscore 그것이 바로 내가 강조하고 싶었던 것이다

2908
trapezoid
[trǽpəzɔ̀id]

adj. 사다리꼴의 a four-sided shape that has two sides that are parallel and two sides that are not parallel

a complete trapezoid 완전 사다리꼴

2909
somber
[sámbər]

adj. 어두컴컴한, 침울한 having a dull or dark color / very sad and serious

syn. dark, gloomy, depressing

somber scenery 어두컴컴한 풍경

a somber personality 음침한 성격

2910
tyrant
[táiərənt]

n. 폭군 a cruel and oppressive dictator

syn. dictator, oppressor, totalitarian

humanize the tyrant 폭군을 누그러지게 하다

2911
truce
[tru:s]

n. 휴전, 정전 a state of peace agreed between opponents so they can discuss peace terms

syn. armistice, cease-fire

make a truce 휴전하다

2912
transplant
[trænsplǽnt]
-trans 가로질러

v. 옮겨 심다 to remove a plant from the ground and move it to another place

transplant flowers to a garden 정원에 화초를 옮겨 심다

2913
ruthless
[rú:θlis]

adj. 무자비한, 잔인한 without mercy or pity

syn. brutal, cruel

ant. kind, tender

a ruthless tyrant 무자비한 폭군

2914
stack
[stæk]

n. 무더기, 더미 an orderly pile

syn. heap, hill, mound

ant. scatter

stacks of magazines on the floor 바닥에 놓인 잡지 더미들

2915
run-down
[rʌ́ndáun]

adj. 몹시 황폐한, 지친   very exhausted and tired

syn. tired, exhausted, weary

ant. new, fit

be pretty rundown 몹시 고단하다

2916
procure
[proukjúər]

v. 구하다   to get by special effort

syn. acquire, gain, secure

ant. relinquish

procure the tickets to the concert 콘서트 티켓을 구하다

2917
trappings
[trǽpiŋz]

n. 장식, 치장   outward decoration or dress

syn. furnishing

the trappings of high military rank 고위 장성의 화려한 계급장[훈장]

2918
treason
[tríːzən]

n. 반역(죄), 배신   a crime that undermines the offender's government

syn. betrayal, disloyalty, insurrection, mutiny

be guilty of treason 반역죄가 있다

2919
runaway
[rʌ́nəwèi]

adj. 걷잡을 수 없는, 도주한   (a runaway person has left their home or has escaped from somewhere)

syn. escaped, fugitive, outlaw

a runaway child 도망간 아이

2920
premonition
[prìːməníʃən]
-mon 경고

n. 사전경고, 징후   a feeling or belief that something is going to happen when there is no definite reason to believe it will

syn. forewarning, inkling, omen

have an uneasy premonition 불안한 조짐이 있다

2921
sparse
[spɑːrs]

adj. 드문드문한   not dense

syn. scant, scarce

ant. abundant

a sparse beard 엉성하게 난 턱수염

2922
staple
[stéipəl]

adj. 주요한, 기본적인   necessary or important, especially regarding food or commodities
syn. major, primary
ant. secondary

a staple crop 주요 농작물

2923
stalk
[stɔːk]

v. 몰래 접근하다   to hunt a person or animal by following them without being seen
syn. follow, hunt, pursue

stalked the deer 사슴에게 몰래 접근했다

2924
ruins
[rúːinz]

n. 폐허, 유적   the remains of something destroyed
syn. relics, remains, remnants

the ruins of an ancient temple 고대 사원의 유적

2925
stance
[stæns]

n. 입장, 태도   a rationalized mental attitude

take a detached stance 초연한 태도를 취하다

2926
symmetry
[símətri]

n. 대칭   the fact that something has two halves that are exactly the same
syn. balance, harmony
ant. asymmetry

flowers lacking symmetry 대칭이 잘 안 되는 꽃

2927
stature
[stǽtʃər]

n. 신장, 키   the distance from head to foot
syn. height, size

meet the stature and weight requirements 키와 몸무게 요구조건을 충족시키다

2928
rhetoric
[rétərik]

n. 미사여구, 웅변술   using language effectively to please or persuade

empty rhetoric 공허한 미사여구

2929
synchronize
[síŋkrənàiz]
-chron 시간

v. 동시에 움직이다   to happen at the same time
syn. parallel

synchronized their steps 그들은 보조를 맞췄다

2930
synthetic
[sinθétik]

adj. 합성의, 인조의   not of natural origin / prepared or made artificially
syn. artificial

synthetic vitamin C 합성 비타민 C

2931
spooky
[spúːki]

adj. 섬뜩한, 유령 같은   strange and frightening
syn. eerie, ghostly, scary

a spooky old house 무시무시한 낡은 집

2932
spur
[spəːr]

v. 박차를 가하다   to cause something to happen or to happen more quickly
syn. goad, drive, push

spurred sales growth 매출 증가에 박차를 가했다

2933
ruffled
[rʌfld]

adj. 주름(장식)이 있는, 갈기가 있는   having decorative ruffles or frills
syn. crimped, rippled, frilled

a ruffled blouse 주름 장식을 단 블라우스

2934
transcript
[trǽnskript]
-script 쓰다

n. 1 대본, 사본 2 성적표   something that has been transcribed / an official record of a student's grades

a transcript of a radio program 라디오프로그램 대본
need a copy of my transcript 성적 증명서 한 통이 필요하다

2935
rouse
[rauz]

v. 자극하다, 선동하다   to cause to be agitated, excited, or roused
syn. wake, excite, stir up
ant. sedate, tranquilize

rouse a person's indignation 남을 분개시키다

2936
respondent
[rispándənt]
-spond 약속

n. 응답자   someone who responds
syn. responder, answerer

the majority of respondents 응답자의 대다수

2937
staid
[steid]

adj. 차분한, 고지식한   serious and rather boring
syn. serious, sober, steady, dignified

a staid color 차분한 빛깔

2938
restrain
[riːstréin]

v. 제지하다, 금하다   to keep under control
syn. check, control, curb, repress

restrain one's anger 분노를 억제하다

2939
prom
[prɑm]

n. (학년 말이나 졸업 때 여는) 무도회   a formal ball held for a school class toward the end of the academic year

asked her to the school prom 그녀에게 졸업무도회에 가자고 요청했다

2940
squadron
[skwɑ́drən]

n. 비행 대대   an air force unit larger than a flight and smaller than a group

one Apache helicopter squadron 아파치 헬기 1개 대대

2941
retrieve
[ritríːv]
-re 다시, 역행하여

v. 가져오다, 되찾다   to get or find back
syn. fetch, reclaim, regain

retrieve one's car from the parking lot 주차장에서 자동차를 꺼내오다

2942
protagonist
[proʊtǽgənist]

n. 주연, 주인공   the principal character in a work of fiction
syn. hero
ant. antagonist

female protagonist 여주인공

2943
strident
[stráidənt]

adj. 귀에 거슬리는   sounding harsh and unpleasant
syn. discordant, dissonant

a strident voice 날카로운 목소리

2944
prowess
[práuis]

n. 뛰어난 능력, 용기   a superior skill that you can learn by study and practice and observation
syn. courage, bravery

display prowess 용감함을 보이다

2945
respiratory
[réspərətɔ̀ːri]
-spir 숨 쉬다

adj. 호흡 기관의   relating to the process of breathing air in and out

respiratory ailments 호흡기 질환

2946
prop
[prɑp]

v. 떠받치다, 지지하다   to support by placing against something solid or rigid

syn. support, sustain, truss

prop a ladder against a building 건물에 사닥다리를 기대 세우다

2947
prospect
[prɑ́spekt]
-spect 보다

n. 유력 후보자, 가망이 있는 사람   someone who is considered for something

the prospects for a gold medal 금메달 후보자들

2948
stumble
[stʌ́mbəl]

v. 발을 헛디디다   to miss a step and fall or nearly fall

syn. trip, blunder

stumbled over the tree root 나무 뿌리에 걸려 넘어졌다

2949
pronounced
[prənáunst]

adj. 두드러진, 현저한   very noticeable

syn. marked, noticeable

ant. inconspicuous

a pronounced opinion 두드러진 의견

2950
stringent
[stríndʒənt]

adj. 엄격한   demanding strict attention to rules and procedures

syn. exacting, rigid, rigorous

ant. easy, lenient, weak

carry out stringent inspections 엄격한 검사를 실시하다

Review | 고난도

뜻을 써보고 전체 어구의 의미를 생각해 보시오.

01 **stay** solvent _____ 2906

02 **prop** a ladder against a building _____ 2946

03 the **prospects** for a gold medal _____ 2947

04 **stumbled** over the tree root _____ 2948

05 **somber** scenery _____ 2909

06 carry out **stringent** inspections _____ 2950

07 **respiratory** ailments _____ 2945

08 a **runaway** child _____ 2919

09 a **spooky** old house _____ 2931

10 ① a **transcript** of a radio program _____ 2934

    ② need a copy of my **transcript** _____

11 **retrieve** one's car from the parking lot _____ 2941

12 a complete **trapezoid** _____ 2908

13 be guilty of **treason** _____ 2918

14 a **ruffled** blouse _____ 2933

15 asked her to the school **prom** _____ 2939

16 **synchronized** their steps _____ 2929

17 one Apache helicopter **squadron** _____ 2940

18 **stalked** the deer _____ 2923

19 **rigorous** discipline _____ 2905

20 **empty** rhetoric _____ 2928

2951
civility
[sivíləti]

n. 정중함, 공손함   polite behavior
syn. courtesy, formality, manners
ant. disrespect

exchange civilities 정중한 인사를 교환하다

2952
tenacity
[tənǽsəti]

n. 불굴, 끈기, 집요함   persistent determination
syn. determination, firmness, perseverance

tenacity of purpose 불굴의 의지
lack tenacity 끈기가 부족하다

2953
lubricant
[lú:brəkənt]

n. 윤활유, 미끄럽게 하는 것   a substance which you put on the surfaces
   or parts of something
syn. lube

function as a lubricant 윤활유의 구실을 하다

2954
germinate
[dʒə́:rmənèit]

v. 싹트다, 시작되다, 발아하다   to produce buds, branches
syn. sprout

seeds germinate 씨앗의 싹이 나다

2955
barring
[bá:riŋ]

prep. ~이 없다면, ~을 제외하고   (used to say that something will happen
   unless something else happens)
syn. without, except

barring unforeseen events 뜻밖의 사고만 없다면

2956
anthology
[ænθálədʒi]

n. 작품 선집, 문집   a collection of writings by different writers
syn. collection, compilation

an anthology of poetry 시(詩) 선집

2957
budding
[bʌ́diŋ]

adj. 신진의, 싹이 트는   beginning to develop
syn. blooming, blossoming

a budding author 신진 작가

2958
mingle
[míŋɡəl]

v. 어울리다, 섞이다   to be mixed together

syn. blend, combine, fuse, merge

ant. separate

joy mingled with pain 고통이 뒤섞인 기쁨

2959
policing
[pəlíːsiŋ]

n. 치안유지 활동   activities to protect the community by police officers

the policing of public places 공공장소에 대한 치안유지 활동

2960
protracted
[proutrǽktid]

-tract 끌다

adj. 길어진, 늘어진   continuing for a long time, especially longer than is normal or necessary

syn. lengthy

a protracted legal battle 길어진 법정 싸움

2961
shed
[ʃed]

v. 떨구다, 발산하다   to let something fall off as part of a natural process

syn. drop, spill, scatter

shed tears 눈물을 흘리다

trees shed their leaves each autumn 가을이면 나무들이 잎을 떨군다

2962
refashion
[riːfǽʃən]

-re 다시, 역행하여

v. 개조하다, 고쳐 만들다   to make new

syn. remake, redo, make over

refashion the old building 옛날 건물을 다시 짓다

2963
slurp
[sləːrp]

v. 소리를 내며 먹다   to eat noisily

slurp one's soup 수프를 소리 내며 마시다

2964
enigmatically
[ènigmǽtikəli]

adv. 수수께끼 같이   in a cryptic manner

syn. cryptically

She smiled enigmatically. 그녀는 수수께끼 같은 표정을 지었다.

2965
expatriate
[ekspéitrièit]

-ex 바깥, 외부

n. 국외 거주자   a person who is voluntarily absent from home or country

syn. exile, expat

Korean expatriates in Paris 파리에 거주하는 한국인 거주자들

2966
axle
[ǽksəl]

n. (바퀴의) 차축, 굴대   a shaft on which a wheel rotates

the front/rear axle 앞/뒤 차축

2967
transpire
[trænspáiər]
-spire 숨 쉬다

v. (일이) 일어나다, 발생하다   to come about, happen, or occur

Several important events transpired last week.
지난주에는 몇 가지 중요한 사건들이 일어났다.

2968
revelatory
[rivélətɔ̀:ri]

adj. (모르는 것을) 알게 하는, 계시의   pointing out or revealing clearly

syn. indicative, significative, suggestive

a revelatory insight 새로운 것을 알게 하는 통찰

2969
alias
[éiliəs]

n. 가명, 별명   an additional name that a person sometimes uses

syn. nickname, byname

a fugitive using several aliases 여러 가지 가명을 사용하는 도망자

2970
underdog
[ʌ́ndərdɔ̀(:)g]

n. 약자, 약체   one at a disadvantage and expected to lose

side with the underdog 약자에게 가세하다

2971
ineptitude
[inéptətjùːd]

n. 어설픔, 기량부족   unskillfulness resulting from a lack of training

syn. awkwardness, clumsiness, ineptness

display ineptitude 기술 부족을 드러내다

2972
disconfirm
[dìskənfə́ːrm]
-dis 멀어짐, 부정

v. 반박하다, 부정하다   to deny or refute the validity of

syn. contradict, deny, reject

ant. acknowledge, admit

the article disconfirmed many details of the initial report
그 기사는 최초 보고서의 여러 세부사항을 반박했다

2973
impervious
[impə́ːrviəs]

adj. 영향을 받지 않는, 스며들지 않는   not capable of being affected

syn. impenetrable, inaccessible, airtight

ant. sensitive

impervious to criticism/pain 비판/고통에 휘둘리지 않는

2974
concretize
[kánkrətàiz]

v. 구체화하다, 응집하다 to make something concrete

concretize budget 예산을 구체화하다

2975
anomaly
[ənáməli]

n. 이례적인 것, 변칙 deviation from the normal

syn. deviation, exception, irregularity

many anomalies in the tax system 세제상의 많은 변칙들

2976
enormity
[inɔ́ːrməti]

n. 엄청남, 광대함, 심각함 the quality of being outrageous

syn. outrageousness, immensity

the enormity of the disaster 그 재난의 어마어마함

2977
hull
[hʌl]

n. (배의) 선체, 동체 the frame or body of ship

salvage[refloat] the hull 선체를 인양하다

2978
self-deception
[sélfdisépʃən]

n. 자기기만 a misconception that is favorable to the person who holds it

The opposite of self-deception is facing life as it is.
자기기만의 반대는 인생을 있는 그대로 바라보는 것이다.

2979
nibble
[níbəl]

v. 조금씩 뜯어 먹다 to bite off very small pieces

nibble at one's toast 토스트를 조금씩 뜯어 먹다

2980
gorge
[gɔːrdʒ]

n. 골짜기, 협곡 a deep ravine

The gorge is a National Park and opens at 8.30 a.m.
이 계곡은 국립공원으로 오전 8시30분에 개장합니다.

2981
hypocrisy
[hipákrəsi]

n. 위선 when someone pretends to have certain beliefs or opinions that they do not really have

syn. dishonesty, duplicity, insincerity

ant. sincerity

display hypocrisy 위선적 행위를 하다

2982
extant
[ekstǽnt]

adj. 현존하는   still in existence
syn. existing, living, present, surviving
ant. extinct

extant remains of the ancient wall 그 고대 성벽의 잔존하는 유적

2983
avalanche
[ǽvəlæntʃ]

n. 눈사태   a slide of large masses of snow and ice and mud down a mountain
syn. snow-slide, landslide, landslip

There was an avalanche. 눈사태가 났다.

2984
fetch
[fetʃ]

v. 가서 데려오다   to go and get something
syn. recoup, regain

fetch the children from school 학교에 가서 애들을 데리고 오다

2985
orthopedic
[ɔ̀:rθoupí:dik]

adj. 정형외과의, 정형술의   relating to orthopedics

orthopedic surgery 정형 (외과) 수술

2986
regress
[ri:grés]
-re 다시, 역행하여

v. 퇴보하다, 역행하다   to return to an earlier and usually worse or less developed condition or state
syn. retrogress, return
ant. advance, develop, evolve, progress

regress to a childlike state 어린이 같은 상태로 퇴보하다

2987
dissect
[disékt]

v. 해부하다   to cut open
syn. anatomize, analyze

dissect a human body 인체를 해부하다

2988
superimpose
[sù:pərimpóuz]

v. 덧붙이다, 겹쳐놓다   to place or lay something over something else
syn. superpose, lay over

superimpose one image on another 두 가지 상(像)을 겹치다

2989
mince
[mins]

v. 잘게 썰다   to cut food into very small pieces
syn. chop, hash

minced meat 다진 고기

2990
repulsive
[ripʌ́lsiv]

adj. 혐오감을 일으키는 causing strong dislike or disgust
syn. disgusting, loathsome, nauseating
ant. attractive, beautiful
a repulsive sight 불쾌한 광경

2991
cum laude
[kʌ́m-lɔ́ːdi]

adv. 우등으로 with honor
graduated cum laude 우등으로 졸업했다

2992
expulsion
[ikspʌ́lʃən]
-ex 바깥, 외부

n. 축출, 추방, 제적 the act of forcing someone to leave a place
syn. banishment, dismissal, ejection
ant. invitation
expulsion from school 퇴학

2993
beckon
[békən]

v. 오라고 손짓하다, 매력적으로 보이다 to signal with the hands or nod
syn. gesture, motion, nod, signal, wave
He beckoned me in. 그는 나에게 들어오라고 손짓을 했다.

2994
eclectic
[ekléktik]

adj. 다방면에 걸친, 취사선택하는 selecting what seems best of various styles or ideas
syn. multiple, symbiotic, varied
an eclectic painter 다양한 기법을 사용하는 화가

2995
pundit
[pʌ́ndit]

n. 전문가, 박식한 사람 someone who has been admitted to membership in a scholarly field
syn. initiate, learned person
a political pundit 정치전문가

2996
impasse
[ímpæs]

n. 막다른 골목, 난국, 곤경 a situation in which no progress seems possible
syn. deadlock, halt, stalemate, standoff, standstill, dilemma
arrive at a hopeless impasse 절망적인 난국에 봉착하다

2997
excretion
[ikskríːʃən]

n. 배설작용, 배출 the bodily process of discharging waste matter

syn. body waste, elimination, evacuation, excreting

excretion[excretory] organ 배설기관

2998
mortuary
[mɔ́ːrtjuəri]

n. 영안실 a place in which dead bodies are kept until burial

syn. morgue, funeral parlor

place a dead body in a hospital mortuary 병원 영안실에 시신을 안치하다

2999
hyperbole
[haipɔ́ːrbəlìː]

n. 과장법, 과장적 진술 language that describes something as better or worse than it really is

syn. exaggeration

without hyperbole 과장 없이

3000
fray
[frei]

v. 닳다 to wear out or into shreds

syn. wear thin, rub, wear out

his jeans started to fray 그의 청바지는 닳아지기 시작했다

Review | 고난도

뜻을 써보고 전체 어구의 의미를 생각해 보시오.

01 lack tenacity _____ 2952

02 nibble at one's toast _____ 2979

03 impervious to criticism _____ 2973

04 There was an avalanche. _____ 2983

05 salvage the hull _____ 2977

06 support the underdog _____ 2970

07 a repulsive sight _____ 2990

08 Korean expatriates in Paris _____ 2965

09 an anthology of poetry _____ 2956

10 an eclectic painter _____ 2994

11 excretion organ _____ 2997

12 display ineptitude _____ 2971

13 many anomalies in the tax system _____ 2975

14 place a dead body in a hospital mortuary _____ 2998

15 graduate cum laude _____ 2991

16 Several important events transpired. _____ 2967

17 fetch the children from school _____ 2984

18 slurp one's soup _____ 2963

19 function as a lubricant _____ 2953

20 arrive at a hopeless impasse _____ 2996

PART
III

영어의 초고수가 되는
어근별 단어 정리

바 로 바 로   문 제 로   익 히 는   어 근   학 습

alter: other 다른

alternate 번갈아 하다
[ɔ́ːltərnèit]

She _____ between sadness and happiness.
그녀는 슬픔과 기쁨 사이에서 오락가락했다.

alternative 대안
[ɔːltə́ːrnətiv]

We had to leave since our only other _____ was to wait
in the rain. 다른 유일한 대안이 비를 맞으며 기다리는 것이어서 우리는 떠나야 했다.

anim: life 생명

animation 생기
[æ̀nəméiʃən]

Painting is the only thing that _____ him.
그림 그리는 것만이 그에게 생동감을 줄 수 있다.

animate 생기를 불어 넣다
[ǽnəmèit]

The schoolgirls are talking with _____ .
여학생들이 생기발랄하게 대화를 하고 있다.

ann, enn: year 해, 년

perennial 일 년 내내, 항상
[pərénial]

The rock festival is held _____ in October.
락 축제는 해마다 10월에 열린다.

annual 해마다
[ǽnjuəl]

They celebrated their 10th wedding _____ yesterday.
그들은 어제 결혼 10주년을 축하했다.

anniversary 기념일
[æ̀nəvə́ːrsəri]

I am _____ in debt.
난 항상 빚을 지고 있다.

anti, ante: before 이전, 앞

antique 골동품의
[æntíːk]

The bench is an _____ . 그 벤치는 골동품이다.

The stadium will be completed 2 months earlier than

anticipate 예상하다
[æntísəpèit]

_____ . 경기장은 예상보다 2달 일찍 완성될 것이다.

apt: fit 적합

adapt 적응시키다
[ədǽpt]

aptitude 적성
[ǽptitùːd]

inapt 부적당한
[inǽpt]

I had no _____ for acting and began to hate it.
나는 연기가 적성에 안 맞아 곧 싫어졌다.

Please _____ yourself to my way of doing things.
네가 나의 일 처리 방식에 맞춰주길 바래.

It was very _____ comment. 그건 너무 부적합한 말이었다.

astr: star 별

disaster 재난
[dizǽstər]

asteroid 소행성
[ǽstərɔ̀id]

astronomy 천문학
[əstrɑ́nəmi]

Part of the excitement of _____ is finding things.
천문학의 기쁨 중 하나는 뭔가 발견하는 것에 있다.

The oil spill was a _____ for sea animals.
기름 유출은 해양 동물들에게 재난이었다.

The average _____ is a hundred twenty million miles from
Mars. 보통의 소행성은 화성에서 1억 2천만 마일 떨어져 있다.

aud: hear 듣다

audience 청중
[ɔ́ːdiəns]

audit 회계감사
[ɔ́ːdit]

audible 들리는
[ɔ́ːdəbl]

He danced before an enthusiastic _____ .
그는 열광적인 청중 앞에서 춤을 췄다.

It was a barely _____ whisper.
거의 들리지 않는 속삭임이었다.

The annual _____ was carried out today.
오늘 연간 회계감사가 있었다.

answers ---
alter: alternated / alternative **anim:** animates / animation **ann:** annually / anniversary / perennially **anti:** antique / anticipated
apt: aptitude / adapt / inapt **astr:** astronomy / disaster / asteroid **aud:** audience / audible / audit

bene: good 좋음

benefactor 은인
[bénəfæ̀ktər]

benefit 이익
[bénəfìt]

beneficial 이로운
[bènəfíʃəl]

I hope you'll get maximum _____ from the course.
나는 네가 이 과정으로부터 최대의 혜택을 얻기를 바란다.

Jogging is highly _____ to health.
조깅은 건강에 매우 유익하다.

A rich _____ helped her set up a charity.
돈 많은 기부자가 그녀의 자선단체 설립을 도왔다.

bio: life 생명

symbio**sis** 공생
[sìmbaióusis]

biology 생물학, 생체학
[baiálədʒi]

Researchers are studying the _____ of the rain forest.
과학자들이 우림의 생체환경을 연구하고 있다.

A certain degree of _____ is good for friendship.
어느 정도의 공생 관계는 우정에 좋다.

cap: head 머리

captain 선장, 기장
[kǽptin]

capital 대문자
[kǽpitl]

de**cap**itate 참수하다
[dikǽpətèit]

His handwritten _____ D's look like lowercase b's.
그가 손으로 쓴 대문자 D는 소문자 b처럼 보인다.

The _____ has turned on the "fasten seat belt" sign.
기장은 "안전벨트를 매시오" 신호를 켰다.

He was _____ during the revolution.
혁명 동안 그는 참수되었다.

cede, cess: go, yield 가다, 양보하다

concede 인정[양보]하다
[kənsíːd]

recede 물러가다
[riːsíːd]

predecessor 전임자
[prédisèsər]

precede 앞서다
[priːsíːd]

access 접근
[ǽkses]

Lunch will be _____ by a speech from the principal.
점심 식사 전에 교장선생님 연설이 있겠습니다.

_____ to employees' records is restricted.
사원 기록 열람은 제한됩니다.

He _____ that he had made some mistakes.
그는 몇 가지 실수를 했음을 인정했다.

The pain in his stomach gradually _____ .
배의 통증이 점차 잦아들었다.

She told me how much better my _____ was at everything. 그녀는 내게 전임자가 모든 면에서 나보다 얼마나 탁월했는지 말해줬다.

centr, center: middle 중간

centralize 집중시키다
[séntrəlàiz]

concentration 집중, 집결
[kὰnsəntréiʃən]

eccentric 이상한, 특이한
[ikséntrik]

I lost _____ for a moment and slipped.
나는 잠깐 집중력을 잃고 미끄러졌다.

The company _____ its financial services at its new location. 그 회사는 새 지점에 금융 서비스를 집중시켰다.

The scientist is regarded as being rather _____ .
그 과학자는 약간 특이한 사람으로 여겨진다.

cept, ceive, ceip, cat(t): take 받다

receipt 영수증
[risíːt]

accept 받아들이다
[æksépt]

reception 접수, 환영회
[risépʃən]

deceive 속이다
[disíːv]

perceive 인식하다
[pərsíːv]

They offered him a job, and he _____ without hesitation.
그들은 그에게 일자리를 제의했고 그는 망설임 없이 수락했다.

Let's meet in _____ . 접수대에서 만나자.

Keep your _____ in case you need to return anything.
반품할 경우를 대비해서 영수증을 보관하세요.

Her teacher punished her for trying to _____ him.
그녀의 선생님은 그녀가 그를 속이려 해서 처벌했다.

He is _____ as a future chairman.
그는 미래의 회장으로 인식되고 있다.

chron: time 시간

chronic 만성적인
[kránik]

synchronize
동시에 일어나게 하다
[síŋkrənàiz]

There is a _____ shortage of teachers.
늘 교사가 부족하다.

The dancers practiced until they _____ their movements.
댄서들은 동작이 일치할 때까지 연습했다.

cide: kill 죽이다

suicide 자살
[súːəsàid]

ecocide 생태계 파괴
[íːkousàid]

pesticide 살충제
[péstəsàid]

Many people commit _____ at Christmas.
많은 사람들이 크리스마스에 자살한다.

All _____ act by interfering with the target species'
normal metabolism. 모든 살충제는 목표 종의 정상적 신진대사를 방해함으로써 작용한다.

_____ has now come to overshadow nuclear war as a threat
to global civilization. 생태계 파괴는 핵전쟁을 능가하는 세계 문명의 위험이 되었다.

clud, clus, clos: close 닫다

enclose 둘러싸다
[enklóuz]

conclude 결정하다
kənklú:d]

seclude 격리시키다
[siklú:d]

They _____ that the school should be closed immediately.
그들은 그 학교가 즉시 문을 닫아야 한다고 결론 내렸다.

The patients will be _____ until they are no longer contagious. 환자들은 전염성이 사라질 때까지 격리될 것이다.

Her arms _____ him.
그녀의 팔이 그를 감쌌다.

co, com, con: together, with 함께

cooperation 협력
[kouὰpəréiʃən]

conspire 공모하다
[kənspáiər]

compile 수집하다, 편집하다
[kəmpáil]

companion 동료
[kəmpǽnjən]

community 공동체
[kəmjú:nəti]

compatible 양립할 수 있는
[kəmpǽtəbəl]

compose 구성하다, 작문하다
[kəmpóuz]

He _____ a book of poems.
그는 시집을 한 권 편집했다.

His dog became his closest _____ .
그의 개는 그의 가장 친한 동료가 되었다.

The new library will serve the whole _____ .
새 도서관은 마을 전체에 기여할 것이다.

A study was undertaken in _____ with highschool teachers. 고등학교 선생님들과의 협력으로 한 연구가 수행되었다.

All three men admitted _____ to steal bikes.
세 남자 모두 오토바이를 훔치려고 공모했음을 시인했다.

This software is IBM _____ .
이 프로그램은 아이비엠에 호환된다.

He sat down and _____ a letter of celebration.
그는 앉아서 축하의 글을 작성했다.

answers ---

cept: accepted / reception / receipt / deceive / perceived **chron:** chronic / synchronized **cide:** suicide / pesticides / Ecocide
clud: concluded / secluded / enclosed **co:** compiled / companion / community / cooperation / conspiring / compatible / composed

---

cord: heart 심장, 마음

concord 일치, 조화
[kánkərd]

cordial 진심어린
[kɔ́:rdʒəl]

accord 일치[조화]하다
[əkɔ́:rd]

The newspaper's quote does not _____ with what he actually said. 신문에 인용된 말은 그가 실제로 한 말과 일치하지 않는다.

They are living in _____ with people of different races and religions. 그들은 서로 다른 인종과 종교의 사람들과 조화롭게 살아가고 있다.

They received a _____ greeting from their hostess at the party.
그들은 파티에서 파티 주최자로부터 진심어린 인사를 받았다.

---

corp: body 신체, 몸

corporation 주식회사
[kɔ̀:rpəréiʃən]

corpse 시체
[kɔ:rps]

The _____ was found by children playing in the mountain.
그 시체는 산에서 놀던 아이들에 의해 발견되었다.

He works for a large multinational _____ .
그는 큰 다국적 기업에서 일한다.

---

cracy: government 정부

autocracy 독재정치
[ɔ:tákrəsi]

democracy 민주주의
[dimákrəsi]

aristocracy 귀족정치, 귀족층
[æ̀rəstákrəsi]

The Magna Carta is important because it signified the British rejection of _____ .
마그나카르타는 영국의 독재정치에 대한 거부를 상징하는 점에서 중요하다.

At one time in China only the _____ could own land.
한 때 중국에서는 귀족층만 땅을 소유할 수 있었다.

In a _____ , every citizen should have the right to vote.
민주주의에서 모든 시민은 투표권을 가져야 한다.

cred, creed: believe 믿다

credible 믿을 수 있는
[krédəbəl]

The association only _____ programs that meet its high standards. 그 협회는 협회의 높은 기준에 부합하는 프로그램만 승인한다.

credulous 잘 속는
[krédʒələs]

People of all races, colours, and _____ have to live together. 모든 인종, 피부색, 그리고 신념의 사람들이 공존해야 한다.

credentials 증명서
[kridénʃəlz]

There is no _____ evidence against him. 그에게 불리한 증거들 중 믿을만한 것은 없다.

accredit 인정하다
[əkrédit]

_____ investors were persuaded to part with large sums of money. 귀 얇은 투자자들이 거액을 내놓도록 설득 당했다.

creed 신념
[kri:d]

She had excellent _____ for the job. 그녀는 그 업무에 관련한 훌륭한 자격 사항을 갖췄다.

incredible 믿을 수 없는
[inkrédəbəl]

It's _____ that the baby survived the fall. 아기가 거기서 떨어졌는데 생존하다니 믿을 수 없다.

de: down, not 하락, 부정

degrade 비하하다
[digréid]

I heard their footsteps _____ the stairs. 나는 그들의 발소리가 계단을 내려가는 것을 들었다.

descend 내려가다
[disénd]

I _____ garlic, and wouldn't eat it if you paid me! 나는 마늘이 싫어, 네가 돈을 준다고 해도 먹지 않을 거야!

detest 혐오하다
[ditést]

The movie was criticized because it _____ women. 그 영화는 여성을 비하해서 비판 받았다.

derive 파생하다
[diráiv]

This word is _____ from Latin. 이 단어는 라틴어에서 파생했다.

answers ---

cord: accord / concord / cordial **corp:** corpse / corporation **cracy:** autocracy / aristocracy / democracy
cred: accredits / creeds / credible / Credulous / credentials / incredible **de:** descending / detest / degraded / derived

endemic 그 지방 특유의
[endémik]

demonstrate 시범을 보이다
[démənstrèit]

epidemic 유행병, 대 발생
[èpədémik]

The study _____ that cigarette advertising encourages children to smoke.

그 연구는 담배 광고가 아이들이 담배를 피도록 부치기는 것을 증명하고 있다.

Strikes were _____ to the industry during the 1970s.

1970년대에 파업은 그 산업에서 풍토병과도 같았다.

An _____ of petty crime has hit the area.

경범죄가 그 지역에 급증했다.

indicate 가리키다
[índikèit]

predict 예언하다
[pridíkt]

dictator 독재자
[díkteitər]

contradict 반박하다, 모순되다
[kàntrədíkt]

The country was ruled by a military _____ .

그 나라는 군부 독재자의 통치를 받았다.

Dad just can't bear to be _____ .

아빠는 누가 자신에게 반박하는 것을 못 참는다.

Please _____ your preference on the booking form.

예약 양식에 자신이 선호하는 것을 기입하시오

The forecaster is _____ rain for tomorrow.

일기 예보자는 내일 비가 올 것이라고 말하고 있다.

disperse 흩어지게 하다
[dispə́:rs]

disorder 무질서, 장애
[disɔ́:rdər]

disgrace 불명예
[disgréis]

discard 버리다
[diská:rd]

His actions brought _____ on the family.

그의 행위는 가문에 불명예를 가져왔다.

The dinosaurs _____ millions of years ago.

공룡은 수백만 년 전에 사라졌다.

The identity of the victim has not yet been _____ .

희생자의 신원은 아직 공개되지 않았다.

Sunlight _____ the mist in the morning.

아침에 햇빛이 안개를 흩어지게 했다.

502

disappear 사라지다
[dìsəpíər]

disclose 폭로하다
[disklóuz]

disinterested
사심 없는, 공평한
[disíntəristid]

disdain 멸시하다
[disdéin]

Many suffer from some form of personality _____ .
많은 사람들이 성격 장애를 앓고 있다.

The lawyer provided us with _____ advice.
그 변호사는 우리에게 공평한 충고를 해주었다.

He regarded their proposal with _____ .
그는 그들의 제안을 경멸스럽게 여겼다.

Remove and _____ the withered stems.
시든 줄기들을 잘라서 버려라.

---

em, en: in 내부, 안

embody 구체화하다
[embádi]

entire 완전한, 전체의
[entáiər]

environment 환경
[inváiərənmənt]

This new model _____ many new improvements.
이번 새 모델은 새롭게 개선된 사항들이 녹아 있다.

He grew up in a harsh urban environment.
그는 각박한 도시 환경에서 자랐다.

I can't believe he drunk the _____ bottle!
그가 한 병 다 마셨다니 믿을 수 없다!

answers ---

demo: demonstrates / endemic / epidemic **dic:** dictator / contradicted / indicate / predicting **dis:** disgrace / disappeared / disclosed / dispersed / disorder / disinterested / disdain / discard **em:** embodies / environment / entire

expand 팽창하다
[ikspǽnd]

external 외부의
[ikstə́:rnəl]

explosion 폭발
[iksplóuʒən]

extent 범위, 정도
[ikstént]

expose 노출하다
[ikspóuz]

Several soldiers were injured in a bomb _____ .
여러 군인들이 포탄 폭발에 부상당했다.

I was shocked by the _____ of the damage.
나는 피해 규모에 깜짝 놀랐다.

The universe is _____ . 우주는 팽창하고 있다.

An _____ examiner marked all exam papers.
외부 시험관들이 모든 시험지를 채점했다.

The melting snow _____ the spring flowers.
눈이 녹으면서 봄의 꽃들이 모습을 드러냈다.

---

fin: end 끝

infinite 무한한
[ínfənit]

final 마지막의
[fáinəl]

confine 한정하다
[kənfáin]

definite 한정된, 확실한
[défənit]

The _____ episode will be shown tonight.
마지막 에피소드가 오늘 밤에 방영될 것이다.

Our teacher taught us with _____ patience.
우리 선생님은 무한한 인내심으로 우리를 가르치셨다.

This book will be a _____ hit.
이 책은 분명히 히트할 것이다.

Let's _____ tonight's discussion to the agenda!
오늘 토론은 의제에 한정합시다!

---

flex: bend 구부러지다

flexible 융통성 있는
[fléksəbl]

reflect 반사하다
[riflékt]

Our schedule for this weekend is _____ .
우리의 이번 주말 계획은 융통성이 있다.

The clouds were _____ in the lake.
구름들이 호수에 반영되었다.

afflict 괴롭히다
[əflíkt]

conflict 갈등, 모순
[kάnflikt]

There aren't any _____ between the theories.
그 이론들 사이에는 아무런 모순이 없다.

The disease _____ around two million people every year.
그 질병은 해마다 2백만 명 정도의 사람들에게 고통을 준다.

flu: flow 흐르다

affluent 부유한
[ǽflu(:)ənt]

fluent 유창한
[flú:ənt]

influx 유입
[ínflʌks]

fluctuate 오르내리다
[flʌ́ktʃuèit]

fluid 유연한, 액체
[flú:id]

influence 영향을 미치다
[ínfluəns]

He is a very _____ speaker who always communicates his points well.
그는 언제나 요점을 잘 전달하는 유창한 연사이다.

Seoul is preparing for a large _____ of tourists this summer.
서울은 올해 여름 많은 수의 관광객 유입에 대비하고 있다.

In the desert, the temperature _____ dramatically.
사막에서 기온은 심하게 오르락내리락 한다.

He's _____ and can afford to send his children to the private school. 그는 부유해서 자신의 아이들을 그 사립학교에 보낼 여유가 있다.

_____ leaked from the car's engine.
차 엔진에서 액체가 흘러나왔다.

I was deeply _____ by my mother.
나는 어머니의 영향을 매우 많이 받았다.

form: form 형성하다

transform 변형시키다
[trænsfɔ́:rm]

reform 개선시키다
[ri:fɔ́:rm]

deform 기형으로 만들다
[difɔ́:rm]

Wearing high heels can _____ your feet.
하이힐을 신으면 발이 기형이 될 수 있다.

The abandoned school has been _____ into an art gallery.
폐교가 미술관으로 변모했다.

The laws need to be _____ . 그 법은 개정될 필요가 있다.

answers ---

ex: explosion / extent / expanding / external / exposed **fin:** final / infinite / definite / confine **flex:** flexible / reflected **flict:** conflicts / afflicts **flu:** fluent / influx / fluctuates / affluent / Fluid / influenced **form:** deform / transformed / reformed

DAY 63

fus, fund, fut: pour, melt 쏟다, 녹다

diffuse 흩어지다
[difjúːz]

fusion 융합
[fjúːʒən]

infuse 채우다
[infjúːz]

Her artwork is a _____ of several different styles.
그의 예술작품은 여러 다른 스타일의 융합이다.

Many of his books are _____ with humor and wisdom.
그의 많은 책들은 유머와 지혜로 채워져 있다.

The pollutants _____ into the soil.
오염 물질들이 토양으로 퍼진다.

gen: birth 탄생

ingenuity 영리함
[ìndʒənjúːəti]

generate 발생시키다
[dʒénərèit]

gene 유전자
[dʒiːn]

genesis 기원
[dʒénəsis]

genuine 진짜의
[dʒénjuin]

He believes that shyness is in the _____ .
그는 수줍음은 유전자에 있다고 생각한다.

The _____ of this project was a meeting of experts in 2004.
이 프로젝트의 시작은 2004년의 한 전문가 회의였다.

He showed amazing _____ in finding ways to cut costs.
그는 비용 절감의 방법을 찾는 데 놀라운 영리함을 보여줬다.

We have to _____ some new ideas at the meeting.
우리는 회의에서 새로운 아이디어를 도출해 내야한다.

They showed a _____ interest in our project.
그들은 우리의 프로젝트에 진심으로 관심을 보였다.

gest: carry 나르다

digest 소화하다
[didʒést]

congest 혼잡하게 하다
[kəndʒést]

I have trouble _____ certain foods.
나는 어떤 음식을 잘 소화하지 못한다.

I _____ caution in a situation like this.
저는 이와 같은 상황에서 주의를 제안합니다.

calligraphy 서예
[kəlígrəfi]

diagram 도형, 도해
[dáigræm]

polygraph 거짓말 탐지기
[paligræf]

autobiography 자서전
[ɔːtoubaiágrəfi]

telegraph 전보
[téləgræf]

stenography 속기
[stənágrəfi]

He published his _____ last summer.
그는 작년 여름에 자서전을 발간했다.

I sent the message by _____ . 나는 전보로 그 소식을 전했다.

_____ is one of my hobbies. 서예는 내 취미들 중 하나다.

This _____ shows how the heating system operates.
도해는 보일러가 어떻게 작동하는지 보여준다.

They hooked him up to the _____ and began the test.
그들은 그를 거짓말 탐지기에 연결하고 시험을 시작했다.

Secretaries must be able to do _____ .
비서는 속기를 반드시 할 줄 알아야 한다.

---

grat, gree, grac: pleasing, thankful 기쁨, 감사

grateful 고맙게 여기는
[gréitfəl]

gratitude 감사의 마음
[grǽtətjùːd]

Express your sincere _____ for their help.
그들의 도움에 대한 너의 진심어린 감사의 마음을 전해라.

I'm _____ for the attention.
관심에 감사드립니다.

---

her(e), hes: stick 달라붙다

adhesive 접착제
[ædhíːsiv]

coherent 일관성 있는
[kouhíərənt]

adhere 부착하다
[ædhíər]

The stamp failed to _____ . 우표가 붙지 않았다.

I need a strong _____ to attach the boards.
판자들을 붙일 강력한 접착제가 필요하다.

He gave a _____ account of what had happened.
그는 무슨 일이 있었는지 일관성 있는 설명을 했다.

answers ---

fus: fusion / infused / diffuse **gen:** genes / genesis / ingenuity / generate / genuine **gest:** digesting / suggest
graph(y): autobiography / telegraph / Calligraphy / diagram / polygraph / stenography **grat:** gratitude / grateful
her(e): adhere / adhesive / coherent

hilar: merry 즐거움

hilarious 매우 웃긴
[hilέəriəs]

exhilarating 기운을 돋우는
[igzílərèitiŋ]

Many people don't like his comedy, but I think he's
_____ .
많은 사람들이 그의 코미디를 좋아하지 않지만 난 그가 재미있는 것 같다.

Hang gliding offers the _____ feeling of flying.
행글라이딩은 하늘을 나는 활기찬 기분을 제공한다.

heri: inherit 상속

heredity 유전
[hirédəti]

heritage 유산
[héritidʒ]

inherit 상속하다
[inhérit]

heir 상속인
[εər]

This orchard is my _____ from my father.
이 과수원은 아버지로부터 물려받은 유산이다.

He _____ the family business from his father.
그는 가업을 아버지로부터 물려받았다.

His _____ could inherit millions of dollars.
그의 상속자들은 수백만 달러를 상속받을 수 있다.

_____ plays no part in the disease.
유전은 이 질병과는 상관이 없다.

hosp: treat 대접하다

hospice 여행자 휴식소
[háspis]

hospitable 환대하는
[háspitəbəl]

The people of that village are very _____ .
그 마을 사람들은 매우 친절하다.

He chose to go to a _____ instead of a hospital.
그는 병원보다는 호스피스로 가기로 결정했다.

hum, humili: earth, ground 땅, 바닥

humidity 습기, 습도
[hju:mídəti]

humility 겸손
[hju:míləti]

It's not the heat that will get you — it's the _____ .
당신의 발목을 잡는 것은 열이 아니라 습도일 것이다.

The ordeal taught him _____ .
시련은 그에게 겸손을 가르쳤다.

im, in: in, not 내부, 부정

involve 포함하다
[inválv]

insight 통찰력
[ínsàit]

incurable 불치의
[inkjúərəbəl]

insane 제정신이 아닌
[inséin]

impose 부과하다
[impóuz]

imprison 수감하다
[imprízən]

intact 손상되지 않은
[intǽkt]

income 수입
[ínkʌm]

inevitable 피할 수 없는
[inévitəbəl]

inhabit 거주하다
[inhǽbit]

The government _____ a ban on the sale of ivory.
정부는 상아 판매 금지령을 내렸다.

He was _____ for murder. 그는 살인죄로 수감되었다.

After 50 years, their friendship remained _____ .
50년 후에도 그들의 우정은 금가지 않고 유지되었다.

He earns a good _____ as a writer.
그는 작가로서 많은 수입을 올린다.

He told us a story _____ life on a farm.
그는 농장 생활을 포함한 이야기를 우리에게 들려줬다.

She was _____ with jealousy.
그녀는 질투심으로 제정신이 아니었다.

Getting wet is _____ if you want to give your dog a bath.
당신의 개에게 목욕을 시키고자 한다면 젖는 것은 불가피하다.

Several hundred species of birds _____ the island.
수백 종의 새들이 그 섬에 서식하고 있다.

He is a leader of great _____ .
그는 위대한 통찰력을 가진 지도자이다.

He has a rare, _____ disease.
그는 희귀, 불치병을 가지고 있다.

answers ---
hilar: hilarious / exhilarating **heri:** heritage / inherited / heirs / Heredity **hosp:** hospitable / hospice **hum:** humidity / humility
im: imposed / imprisoned / intact / income / involving / insane / inevitable / inhabit / insight / incurable

ject, jac: throw 던지다

inject 주입하다
[indʒékt]

adjacent 근접한
[ədʒéisnt]

The drug is _____ directly into the base of the spine.
그 약이 척추 하부에 직접 주입되었다.

His house is _____ to a park.
그의 집은 공원에 인접해 있다.

jur, ju, jus: law, right 법, 정의

jury 배심원단
[dʒúəri]

judicial 사법의
[dʒuːdíʃəl]

adjust 맞추다
[ədʒʌ́st]

justify 정당화하다
[dʒʌ́stəfài]

injustice 불공평, 부정
[indʒʌ́stis]

She was selected to serve on a _____ .
그녀는 배심원단으로 활동하도록 선발되었다.

How can we _____ spending so much money on arms?
무기에 쓰는 많은 돈을 어떻게 정당화할 수 있을까?

The book deals with _____ suffered by Native Americans.
그 책은 미국 토착민들이 겪었던 부당함을 다루고 있다.

From a victim's perspective, most _____ systems are biased towards the driver. 피해자의 관점에서 보면 대부분의 사법 시스템은 운전자 편향적이다.

He _____ the car seat so he could reach the pedals.
그는 발이 페달에 닿도록 의자를 조정했다.

lateral: side 측면

multilateral 다자간의
[mʌ̀ltilǽtərəl]

bilateral 양자간의
[bailǽtərəl]

They are worried about _____ trade issues.
그들은 양자 간의 무역 문제를 걱정하고 있다.

Several _____ peace operations were led by the UN.
유엔에 의해 여러 평화 작전이 수행되었다.

collaborate 협력하다
[kəlǽbərèit]

elaborate 상세히 설명하다
[ilǽbərèit]

laborious 수고스러운
[ləbɔ́:riəs]

I'm ready to _____ if you want to hear more.
더 듣고 싶다면 저는 상세히 설명할 준비가 되어 있습니다.

The two companies agreed to _____ .
두 회사는 협력하기로 동의했다.

I spent many _____ hours on the project.
나는 그 프로젝트에 힘들게 몇 시간을 소요했다.

legislate 법률을 제정하다
[lédʒislèit]

legitimate 합법한, 적합한
[lidʒítəmit]

allegiance 충성
[əlí:dʒəns]

legal 적법한
[lí:gəl]

Do you know your _____ rights?
당신의 법적 권리를 알고 있나요?

We must _____ for equal pay.
우리는 동등한 급여에 관한 법을 제정해야 한다.

That's a perfectly _____ question.
그건 딱 적합한 질문이다.

I pledge _____ to the flag of the republic of Korea.
나는 대한민국 국기 앞에 충성을 맹세합니다.

log: speak 말하다

prolog 머리말
[próulag]

monolog 독백
[mánəlɔ̀:g]

The play begins with the main character's _____ .
그 연극은 주인공의 독백으로 시작한다.

She wrote an uplifting _____ for the performance.
그녀는 용기를 북돋우는 그 공연의 서문을 썼다.

liter: letter 글자, 문자

literacy 읽고 쓰는 능력
[lítərəsi]

literature 문학
[lítərətʃər]

Their goal is to achieve basic _____ .
그들의 목표는 기초적인 읽고 쓰는 능력을 익히는 것이다.

He's an expert in Korean _____ .
그는 한국 문학 전문가이다.

luc, lumin: light 빛

illuminate 비추다
[ilú:mənèit]

luminous 빛나는
[lú:mənəs]

The room was _____ with sunlight. 방이 햇빛으로 빛났다.

Candles _____ his face. 촛불들이 그의 얼굴을 비쳤다.

magni, majes: great 거대한, 위대한

majestic 위엄 있는, 웅장한
[mədʒéstik]

magnitude 중대성, 크기
[mǽgnətjù:d]

magnify 확대[과장]하다
[mǽgnəfài]

They didn't seem to appreciate the _____ of the problem.
그들은 문제의 심각성을 인식하지 못하는 것 같았다.

The report _____ the risks involved.
보고서는 관련 위험을 확대했다.

This lovely village is surrounded by _____ mountain scenery. 이 아름다운 마을은 웅장한 산악 풍광으로 둘러싸여 있다.

mand, mend: order 명령하다, 지시하다

command 명령하다
[kəmǽnd]

recommend 추천하다
[rèkəménd]

demand 요구하다
[dimǽnd]

mandate 권한, 신임
[mǽndeit]

He _____ us to leave. 그는 우리에게 떠나라고 명령했다.

The customer _____ a refund. 그 고객은 환불을 요구했다.

The Government claimed to have a _____ for their new legislation. 정부는 새로운 입법에 대한 권한을 가졌다고 주장했다.

I _____ that you buy a more light bicycle.
보다 가벼운 자전거를 살 것을 추천한다.

manu, man: hand 손

mandatory 강제적인
[mǽndətɔ̀:ri]

manual 수동의
[mǽnjuəl]

manuscript 원고, 사본
[mǽnjəskrìpt]

manipulate 능숙하게 처리하다
[mənípjəlèit]

manufacture 제조하다
[mæ̀njəfǽktʃər]

He has a collection of old-fashioned _____ cameras.
그는 구식 수동 카메라를 수집하고 있다.

The tests are _____ for all students wishing to graduate.
그 시험은 졸업하고자 하는 학생들에게는 필수다.

The mechanical arms are _____ by a computer.
로봇 팔은 컴퓨터로 조작된다.

The company _____ men's clothing.
그 회사는 남성 의류를 제조한다.

He sent me a copy of his _____ for proofreading.
그는 교정을 봐 달라고 그의 원고 한 부를 내게 보내줬다.

medi: middle 중간

median 중간의
[míːdiən]

The artist works in two _____ , pencil and watercolor.
그 예술가는 연필과 수채 물감, 두 가지 재료로 작업한다.

mediocre 평범한
[mìːdióukər]

What is the _____ price of homes in this area?
이 지역의 평균 집값이 어떻게 되나요?

medium 매체, 재료
[míːdiəm]

The sculptor did a _____ job.
그 조각가는 평범한 작업을 했다.

intermediate 중급의
[ìntərmíːdiit]

I'm taking _____ English Writing this year.
나는 올해 중급 영작문을 신청할 것이다.

min: small 작은, 소형의

mince 잘게 썰다
[mins]

These drugs _____ blood flow to the brain.
이 약은 뇌로 흐르는 피의 흐름을 감소시킨다.

minimize 축소하다
[mínəmàiz]

Let's _____ the chance of error.
실수의 가능성을 최소화하자.

minority 소수 민족
[minɔ́ːriti]

The recipe says that you should _____ the onions.
조리법에 양파를 잘게 썰어야 한다고 쓰여 있다.

diminish 감소하다
[dəmíniʃ]

The proposal is opposed by a _____ of voters.
그 제안은 소수 투표자들이 반대한다.

mir, mar: wonder, behold 놀라다, 보다

mirror 거울
[mírər]

marvel 놀라다
[máːrvəl]

miracle 기적
[mírəkəl]

mirage 신기루
[miráːʒ]

It would take a _____ for your team to win.
너희 팀이 이기려면 기적이 필요할 것이다.

A peaceful solution proved to be nothing but a _____ .
평화로운 해결은 신기루에 불과했음이 밝혀졌다.

Breaking a _____ is believed to bring seven years of bad luck.
거울을 깨면 7년간 재수가 없다고 믿어진다.

Kids _____ at the magician's skill.
아이들이 마술사의 기술에 놀라워했다.

mit, miss: send 보내다, 전송하다

transmit 전송하다
[trænsmít]

miss 그리워하다
[mis]

submit 제출하다
[səbmít]

emit 발산하다
[imít]

dismiss 해고하다
[dismís]

omit 생략하다
[oumít]

I will _____ you. 네가 그리울 거야.

The technology allows data to be _____ by cellular phones. 그 기술에 의해 자료가 휴대폰을 통해 전송된다.

The factory chimneys are _____ thick, black smoke.
공장 굴뚝들이 짙고 검은 연기를 내뿜고 있다.

Several employees were recently _____ .
여러 직원들이 최근에 해고되었다.

Please don't _____ any details.
세부사항 어느 것도 빼먹지 마세요.

_____ your application by the end of this month.
이달 말까지 지원서를 제출해주세요.

answers ---

medi: media / median / mediocre / intermediate **min:** diminish / minimize / mince / minority **mir:** miracle / mirage / mirror / marveled **mit:** miss / transmitted / emitting / dismissed / omit / Submit

mon: advise, remind 경고, 권고

monitor 감시하다
[mánitər]

summon 소환하다
[sʌ́mən]

monument 기념비
[mánjəmənt]

admonish 충고하다
[ædmániʃ]

Nurses constantly _____ the patient's heart rate.
간호사들이 환자의 심박 수를 지속적으로 확인했다.

They have erected a _____ in his honor.
그들은 그를 기리기 위해 기념비를 세웠다.

My physician _____ me to exercise regularly.
의사는 내게 규칙적으로 운동을 하라고 권고했다.

The king _____ him back to the palace.
왕은 그를 궁전으로 다시 소환했다.

mono: one 하나

monopoly 독점
[mənápəli]

monotonous 단조로운
[mənátənəs]

monarchy 군주 정치
[mánərki]

They supported the idea of _____ as the natural state of things. 그들은 군주 정치의 이념을 사물의 자연스러운 형태로서 지지했다.

The government passed laws intended to break up _____ .
정부는 독점을 와해시키려는 의도의 법안을 통과시켰다.

The rain poured _____ from the dark sky.
어두운 하늘에서 비가 지루하게 내렸다.

not: mark 기록, 표시

notify 통지하다
[nóutəfài]

denote 나타내다
[dinóut]

notable 주목할 만한
[nóutəbəl]

connote 암시하다
[kənóut]

The town is _____ for its busy open-air market.
그 마을은 분주한 야외 시장이 주목할 만하다.

Winners will be _____ as soon as possible.
우승자는 바로 통지가 갈 것입니다.

In the diagram, A _____ amount and T time.
도표에서 A는 amount를, T는 time을 나타낸다.

The adjectives used in the poem all _____ death.
시에 사용된 형용사는 모두 죽음을 암시한다.

nov: new 새로운

renovate 새롭게 고치다
[rénəvèit]

innovation 혁신
[ìnouvéiʃən]

novice 초보자
[návis]

Our company rewards creativity and _____ .
우리 회사는 창의성과 혁신에 대해 보상한다.

Climbing in the Himalayas is not for _____ .
히말라야 등정은 초보자들에게는 맞지 않다.

We _____ the kitchen three years ago.
우리는 부엌을 3년 전에 새롭게 고쳤다.

opt: wish 바라다

adopt 채택하다
[ədápt]

optimism 낙천주의
[áptəmìzəm]

optimum 최적 조건
[áptiməm]

The early sales reports are cause for _____ .
초기 매출 보고서는 낙관의 근거이다.

The substances were mixed in various proportions until an
_____ was reached. 최적의 조합이 나올 때까지 물질들은 다양한 비율로 혼합되었다.

Did he _____ my point of view? 그가 나의 관점을 채택했나요?

answers ---

mon: monitored / monument / admonished / summoned **mono:** monarchy / monopolies / monotonously **not:** notable / notified / denotes / connote **nov:** innovation / novices / renovated **opt:** optimism / optimum / adopt

DAY 65

passi, path: suffer, feel 고생하다, 느끼다

sympathize 공감하다
[símpəθàiz]

compassion 동정
[kəmpǽʃən]

apathy 냉담
[ǽpəθi]

passion 정열
[pǽʃən]

passive 수동적인
[pǽsiv]

pathetic 애처로운
[pəθétik]

Her performance is full of _____ and originality.
그녀의 공연은 정열과 독창성으로 충만하다.

Watching movies is a relatively _____ activity.
영화를 보는 것은 상대적으로 수동적인 활동이다.

She felt _____ for the lost child.
그녀는 실종된 아이에 대해 동정심을 느꼈다.

People have shown surprising _____ toward these important social problems. 사람들은 이렇게 중요한 사회 문제에 놀라운 냉담함을 보였다.

The blind, old dog was a _____ sight.
눈이 먼 늙은 개의 모습은 애처로웠다.

I _____ , but I don't know how to help.
동정심을 느끼지만 어떻게 도울지 모르겠다.

---

ped, patch, pod, pus: foot 발

expedite 촉진하다
[ékspədàit]

pedestrian 보행자
[pədéstriən]

The area is open to cyclists and _____ .
이 지역은 보행자와 자전거 운전자들에게 개방되어 있다.

They tried to _____ the process of returning refugees to their homes. 그들은 난민들의 본국 송환을 앞당기기 위해 노력했다.

---

pel, puls(e): drive 몰다

dispel 쫓아 버리다
[dispél]

pulse 맥박
[pʌls]

compel 강요하다
[kəmpél]

impulse 충동
[ímpʌls]

Illness _____ him to stay in bed.
그는 아파서 침대에 꼼짝없이 묶여 있었다.

He had trouble controlling his _____ .
그는 자신의 충동을 억제하는 데 어려움을 겪었다.

His words _____ our fears. 그의 말에 우리의 공포는 사라졌다.

The nurse took my _____ . 간호사가 내 맥박을 쟀다.

518

pen, pain, pun: punish 처벌하다

impunity 벌을 받지 않음
[impjú:nəti]

Korea could impose _____ tariffs on exports.

한국은 수출 품목에 징벌성의 관세를 부과할 수도 있다.

punitive 형벌의
[pjú:nətiv]

He mistakenly believed that he could insult people with

_____ . 그는 사람들을 모욕하고도 벌을 받지 않을 것이라는 그릇된 생각을 했다.

pend, pens, pond: hang, weigh 매달다

pending 미결의, 곧 일어날
[péndiŋ]

She fastened a gold _____ round her neck.

그녀는 금 펜던트를 그녀의 목에 걸고 조였다.

pendant (목걸이의) 펜던트
[péndənt]

The old couple are living on their _____ .

그 노부부는 연금으로 생활한다.

pension 연금
[pénʃən]

The results of the investigation are _____ .

조사 결과는 곧 나올 것이다.

suspend 매달다
[səspénd]

The town _____ bus service during the storm.

폭풍이 이는 동안 그 마을은 버스 운행을 중단했다.

append 첨부하다
[əpénd]

The results of the survey are _____ to this document.

조사 결과가 이 서류에 첨부되어 있다.

plac: please 기쁘게 하다

complacent 만족해하는
[kəmpléisənt]

The strong economy has made people _____ .

호황의 경제가 사람들을 만족스럽게 했다.

implacable 달랠 수 없는
[implǽkəbəl]

He has an _____ hatred for his political opponents.

그는 반대편 정치 세력에 대한 증오는 끝이 없다.

answers ---

passi: passion / passive / compassion / apathy / pathetic / sympathize **ped:** pedestrians / expedite **pel:** compelled / impulses / dispelled / pulse **pen:** punitive / impunity **pend:** pendant / pensions / pending / suspended / appended **plac:** complacent / implacable

ple: fill 채우다

deplete 고갈시키다
[diplí:t]

You will have _____ time to finish the test.
시험을 마치는 데 충분한 시간이 있습니다.

ample 풍부한
[ǽmpl]

Logging and mining _____ our natural resources.
벌목과 광산 개발은 우리의 천연 자원을 고갈시킨다.

supplement 보충하다
[sʌ́plmənt]

She began _____ her diet with vitamins.
그녀는 식사를 비타민으로 보충하기 시작했다.

plic, ply, plo: fold, weave 접다, 엮다

imply 내포하다
[implái]

Children are being _____ in this factory.
이 공장에서 아이들은 착취당하고 있다.

duplicate 복제하다
[djú:pləkit]

They were given _____ instructions.
그들은 뚜렷한 지시를 받았다.

exploit 개발하다, 착취하다
[éksplɔit]

His silence _____ consent.
그의 침묵은 동의를 의미했다.

explicit 분명한
[iksplísit]

He _____ the video to give to his friends.
그들은 친구들에게 주려고 비디오를 복사했다.

complicate 복잡하게 하다
[kámpləkèit]

Changing jobs now would _____ her life.
지금 직장을 바꾸는 것은 그녀의 삶을 복잡하게 만들 것이다.

port: gate 문

portable 휴대용의
[pɔ́:rtəbl]

They _____ more cars than they imported.
그들은 자동차를 수입한 것보다 많이 수출했다.

transport 운송하다
[trænspɔ́:rt]

He got into Korea with a false _____ .
그는 위조 여권으로 한국에 들어왔다.

import 수입하다
[impɔ́:rt]

Computers become lighter, smaller, and more _____ every year. 컴퓨터는 해마다 가볍고, 작고, 보다 휴대하기 좋아진다.

passport 여권
[pǽspɔ̀:rt]

The watermelons are _____ in large wooden crates.
수박은 큰 나무 상자에 담겨 운송된다.

pre: before 이전의

previous 이전의
[príːviəs]

The teacher _____ the students for the test.
선생님이 학생들에게 시험 준비를 시켰다.

prepare 준비하다
[pripέər]

She seems to have a _____ against fast-food restaurants.
그녀는 패스트푸드 음식점에 편견을 가지고 있는 것 같다.

prevail 우세하다
[privéil]

I _____ this dictionary because of its helpful examples.
나는 유용한 예문들 때문에 이 사전이 더 좋다.

preface 서문
[préfis]

The two characters met in a _____ chapter.
두 인물이 이전 챕터에서 만났다.

prejudice 선입관
[prédʒədis]

Mutual respect _____ among students and teachers here.
이곳에는 학생과 교사간의 상호 존중이 만연하다.

prefer 선호하다
[prifə́ːr]

The book's _____ was written by the editor.
그 책의 머리말은 편집장이 썼다.

press: push 밀다

compress 압축시키다
[kəmprés]

Apply _____ to the wound to stop the bleeding.
상처를 압박해 출혈을 막아라.

depress 위축시키다, 우울하게 하다
[diprés]

The country has long been _____ by a ruthless dictator.
그 나라는 오랫동안 무자비한 독재자의 억압을 받았다.

pressure 압력
[préʃər]

The news seemed to _____ her a little.
그 소식은 그녀를 약간 우울하게 만든 것 같았다.

oppress 짓누르다
[əprés]

Her lips _____ into a frown.
그녀의 입술이 일그러졌다.

impression 인상
[impréʃən]

The applicant made a favorable _____ .
지원자는 호의적인 인상을 남겼다.

primary 근본의
[práimèri]

principle 원리, 원칙
[prínsəpl]

primitive 원시의
[prímətiv]

The technology they used was _____ and outdated.
그들이 사용하는 기술은 원시적이고 시대에 뒤떨어졌다.

The family is the _____ social unit of human life.
가족은 인간 생활의 가장 근본적인 사회 단위이다.

It is our basic _____ that education should be free to everyone. 교육은 모두에게 무료이어야 함은 우리의 기본 원칙이다.

request 부탁하다
[rikwést]

acquire 획득하다
[əkwáiər]

inquire 묻다
[inkwáiər]

The team _____ three new players this year.
그 팀은 올해 선수 세 명을 새로 영입했다.

When I _____ , they told me she was not here.
내가 묻자, 그들은 그녀가 여기에 없다고 했다.

At your _____ , I am enclosing a full refund of your payment.
요청하신대로 결재하신 전체 환불 금액을 동봉합니다.

re: again, back, against 다시, 뒤로, 역행하여

restore 복구하다
[ristɔ́:r]

remarkable 주목할 만한
[rimá:rkəbəl]

replace 대체하다
[ripléis]

reinforce 강화하다
[rìːinfɔ́:rs]

reconcile 화해시키다
[rékənsàil]

revolt 반발하다
[rivóult]

refine 정제하다
[rifáin]

The class will help you _____ your writing style.
이 수업은 너의 문체를 세련되게 하는 데 도움을 줄 것이다.

The film _____ the idea that women should be pretty and dumb. 그 영화는 여자는 예쁘고 둔해야 한다는 생각을 부추기고 있다.

By Saturday, electricity had been _____ .
토요일까지 전기가 복구되었다.

The play has been a _____ success.
그 연극은 주목할 만한 성공이었다.

We have to _____ all the furniture that was damaged in the flood. 홍수로 손상된 가구를 모두 교체해야 한다.

Several players _____ against their new coach.
여러 선수가 새 코치에게 반발했다.

The couple has been making every effort to _____ .
그 부부는 화해하려고 온갖 노력을 기울이고 있다.

DAY 66

rect: right, guide 올바름, 인도함

direct 지도하다
[dirékt]

correct 바로 잡다
[kərékt]

erect 똑바로 세우다
[irékt]

Make sure you use the _____ address.
올바른 주소를 쓰고 있는 지 확인해라.

They are trying to _____ the tent.
그들은 텐트를 세우려고 애쓰고 있다.

We need someone to _____ traffic.
교통정리를 할 사람이 필요하다.

rupt, rout: break 부수다, 망치다

disrupt 혼란시키다
[disrʌ́pt]

abrupt 갑자기 발생한
[əbrʌ́pt]

corrupt 타락한
[kərʌ́pt]

bankrupt 파산한
[bǽŋkrʌpt]

erupt 분출하다
[irʌ́pt]

interrupt 방해하다
[intərʌ́pt]

The lawsuit could leave them _____ .
그 소송은 그들을 파산에 이르게 할 수도 있다.

The volcano _____ with tremendous force.
화산이 엄청난 힘으로 분출했다.

The barking dogs _____ my afternoon nap.
개 짖는 소리가 내 오후 낮잠을 방해했다.

The road came to an _____ end.
도로가 갑자기 끊겼다.

Some _____ cops sell drugs.
일부 타락한 경찰들이 마약을 판다.

It's not polite to _____ .
끼어드는 것은 예의에 어긋난다.

scrib, script: write 쓰다

subscribe 정기 구독하다
[sʌ́bskraib]

describe 묘사하다
[diskráib]

prescribe 처방하다
[priskráib]

_____ today and get your first issue free!
오늘 구독하시면 첫 권은 무료로 받으실 수 있습니다!

This drug should not be _____ to children.
이 약은 아이들에게 처방하면 안 된다.

The witness wasn't able to _____ the robber.
증인은 강도를 묘사하지 못했다.

scend: climb 오르다

descend 내려가다
[disénd]

transcend 초월하다
[trænsénd]

ascend 오르다
[əsénd]

Their balloons slowly _____ into the sky.
그들의 풍선이 하늘로 서서히 올라갔다.

The workers _____ into the hole.
인부들이 구덩이 아래로 내려갔다.

Music _____ cultural boundaries.
음악은 문화적 경계를 넘어선다.

sequ, secut: follow 뒤따르다

consecutive 연속적인
[kənsékjətiv]

subsequent 후속의
[sʌ́bsikwənt]

_____ studies confirmed their findings.
후속 연구는 그들의 발견을 확증했다.

It had snowed for four _____ days.
4일 연속으로 눈이 내렸었다.

answers ---
rect: correct / erect / direct **rupt:** bankrupt / erupted / disrupted / abrupt / corrupt / interrupt **scrib:** Subscribe / prescribed /
describe **scend:** ascended / descended / transcends **sequ:** Subsequent / consecutive

simil, sembl, simul: like, same 같음, 유사함

assimilate 동화하다
[əsíməlèit]

simultaneous
동시 발생적인
[sàiməltéiniəs]

similarity 유사성
[sìməlǽrəti]

The two gunshots were _____ .
두 개의 총성이 동시에 울렸다.

They found it hard to _____ to American society.
그들은 미국 사회에 동화하는 것이 어려움을 알았다.

There's very little _____ between your situation and his.
너의 상황과 그의 상황 사이에는 유사성이 거의 없다.

sist: stand 서다

assist 돕다
[əsíst]

subsist 존재하다
[səbsíst]

consist 이루어지다
[kənsíst]

persist 고집하다
[pəːrsíst]

He _____ my brother with his homework.
그는 내 동생의 숙제를 도와줬다.

The audience _____ mainly of college students.
관객은 주로 대학생들로 이루어졌다.

She _____ in her refusal to admit responsibility.
그녀는 끝까지 책임을 인정하기를 거부했다.

The refugees _____ on a diet of rice and vegetables.
피난민들은 밥과 채소를 먹으면서 근근이 생존하고 있다.

sol: alone 홀로

solitary 고독한, 홀로인
[sɑ́litèri]

console 위로하다
[kənsóul]

solid 고체의, 단단한
[sɑ́lid]

desolate 쓸쓸한, 외로운
[désəlit]

The river was frozen _____ . 강이 꽁꽁 얼었다.

A _____ policeman stood at the gate.
출구에 경찰이 홀로 서 있다.

Nothing could _____ her after his death.
그의 죽음 후에 그 무엇도 그녀를 위로할 수 없었다.

There is a _____ house abandoned years ago in the woods.
숲에 몇 해 전에 버려진 외로운 집 한 채가 있다.

526

solv, solu: loosen 풀다

resolution 해결책, 결심
[rèzəlú:ʃən]

_____ the sugar in one tablespoon of water over a low heat. 약한 불로 한 티스푼의 물에 설탕을 녹여라.

dissolve 용해시키다
[dizálv]

Make a _____ to practice the piano once a week.
한 주에 한 번씩 피아노 연습을 할 결심을 해라.

spect, spec: look 보다

aspect 국면, 양상
[æspekt]

The novel is written from a child's _____ .
그 소설은 아이들의 관점에서 쓰여 졌다.

inspect 조사하다
[inspékt]

I am a shy and _____ person.
나는 수줍고 내성적인 사람이다.

prospective
기대되는, 장래의
[prəspéktiv]

The car has to look good, but without forgetting the safety _____ . 차는 모양이 좋아야하지만 안전의 면모도 잊으면 안 된다.

She bent down to _____ the stain on the rug.
그녀는 양탄자의 얼룩을 자세히 보려고 허리를 숙였다.

circumspect 신중한
[sə́:rkəmspèkt]

perspective 관점
[pə:rspéktiv]

Pay attention to the _____ clients as well.
잠재 고객에도 신경을 써라.

Officials were very _____ about possible causes of the accident. 경찰들은 가능한 사고의 원인에 대해 매우 조심스러웠다.

suspect 의심하다
[səspékt]

Police _____ that he had some connection with the robbery.
경찰은 그가 강도 건과 연관이 있을 것으로 의심했다.

retrospect 회고, 회상
[rétrəspèkt]

In _____ , we should never have allowed that to happen.
돌이켜 보건데, 우리는 그 일이 발생하도록 하지 말았어야 한다.

introspective
내성적인
[ìntrəspéktiv]

answers ---

simil: simultaneous / assimilate / similarity **sist:** assisted / consisted / persisted / subsist **sol:** solid / solitary / console / desolate **solv:** Dissolve / resolution **spect:** perspective / introspective / aspect / inspect / prospective / circumspect / suspected / retrospect

527

spir: breathe 숨 쉬다

inspire 영감을 주다
[inspáiər]

aspire 열망하다
[əspáiər]

expire 만료되다
[ikspáiər]

respire 호흡하다
[rispáiər]

Her courage has _____ us.
그녀의 용기가 우리에게 영감을 줬다.

My driver's license has _____ . 내 면허증은 만료되었다.

Fish use their gills to _____ .
물고기는 호흡하는 데 아가미를 사용한다.

At that time, all artists _____ to go to Rome.
그 당시, 모든 예술가들은 로마로 가기를 열망했다.

spond, spons: promise 약속

respond 응답하다
[rispánd]

sponsor 후원하다
[spánsər]

correspond
통신하다, 일치하다
[kɔ̀:rəspánd]

She hasn't yet _____ to my letter.
그녀는 내 편지에 아직 답장이 없다.

The statistics do not _____ with our own experience.
통계는 우리가 직접 겪은 경험과 일치하지 않는다.

Call now if you are interested in _____ a child.
아동 후원에 관심이 있다면 지금 전화 주세요.

sta, stit: stand 서다

institution 학원
[ìnstətjú:ʃən]

stable 안정적인
[stéibl]

status 지위
[stéitəs]

constitute 형성하다, 제정하다
[kánstətjù:t]

establish 설립하다
[istǽbliʃ]

statue 조각상
[stǽtʃu:]

The street is lined with banks and other financial _____ .
그 거리는 은행과 다른 금융 기관들로 즐비하다.

Eleven players _____ a soccer team.
열 한 명의 선수가 한 축구팀을 구성한다.

The company was _____ in 2010.
그 회사는 2010년에 설립되었다.

The _____ represent peace and war.
그 조각상은 평화와 전쟁을 표현하고 있다.

He wants to improve his _____ in the community.
그는 공동체에서 자신의 지위를 향상시키고 싶어 한다.

Make sure the platform is _____ . 플랫폼이 튼튼한지 확인해라.

struct: build 세우다, 건설하다

instruct 가르치다, 지시하다
[instrʌ́kt]

obstruct 방해하다
[əbstrʌ́kt]

construct 건설하다
[kənstrʌ́kt]

Dad is planning to _____ a barn behind the house.
아버지는 집 뒤에 창고를 지을 계획이시다.

He _____ us that we were to remain in our seats.
그는 우리가 우리의 자리를 지키고 있어야 한다고 지시했다.

A large tree _____ the road.
큰 나무가 길을 가로막았다.

sub: under 아래의

submarine 잠수함
[sʌ́bləmrìːn]

substance 본질, 실체
[sʌ́bstəns]

subside 침전하다
[səbsáid]

There is no _____ to the rumours.
그 소문들은 실체가 없다.

A _____ disappeared into the abyss.
잠수함이 깊은 바다 속으로 사라졌다.

The speaker waited until the laughter _____ .
연사는 웃음소리가 잦아들 때까지 기다렸다.

sur, super: over 초과하여

surplus 과잉
[sə́ːrplʌs]

surpass ~을 능가하다
[sərpǽs]

surface 표면
[sə́ːrfis]

surmount 극복하다
[sərmáunt]

Dry leaves floated on the _____ of the water.
마른 잎들이 물 표면에 떠다녔다.

He _____ immense physical disabilities.
그는 엄청난 신체적 장애를 극복했다.

There is a _____ of workers and not enough jobs.
인력은 넘치고 일자리는 부족하다.

This year, sales _____ 200,000,000 won.
올해, 매출이 2억 원을 초과했다.

answers ---

spir: inspired / expired / respire / aspired **spond:** responded / correspond / sponsoring **sta:** institutions / constitute / established / statues / status / stable **struct:** construct / instructed / obstructed **sub:** substance / submarine / subsided
sur: surface / surmounted / surplus / surpassed

---

tail: cut 자르다

retail 소매
[rí:teil]

detail 세부사항
[dí:teil]

curtail 줄이다
[kə:rtéil]

Every _____ of the performance was carefully planned.
그 공연의 모든 세부사항이 세심하게 계획되었다.

She has a job in _____ . 그녀는 소매업을 한다.

The new law will _____ police powers.
새 법은 경찰의 권한을 축소할 것이다.

---

tain: hold 쥐다

retain 간직하다
[ritéin]

sustain 유지하다
[səstéin]

abstain 삼가다
[æbstéin]

attain 달성하다
[ətéin]

detain 억류하다
[ditéin]

Drivers must _____ from alcohol.
운전자들은 술을 삼가야 한다.

After a year she had _____ her ideal weight.
1년 후 그녀는 이상적인 몸무게를 달성했다.

They were _____ by the police for questioning.
그들은 심문 때문에 경찰에 의해 억류되었다.

They insisted on _____ old customs.
그들은 낡은 관습을 계속 간직하려 했다.

The roof was unable to _____ the weight of snow.
지붕은 눈의 무게를 견딜 수 없었다.

---

tend, tens: stretch, pull 뻗다, 당기다

pretend ~인척하다
[priténd]

extend 늘이다
[iksténd]

intensify 강화하다
[inténsəfài]

An industrial zone _____ along the river.
산업 구역이 강을 따라 늘어서 있다.

It was useless to _____ innocence.
결백한척해도 소용없었다.

They _____ their efforts to increase sales.
그들은 매출을 올리려고 노력을 강화했다.

tempo(r): time 시간

contemporary 현대적인
[kəntémpərèri]

temporary 일시적인
[témpərèri]

The delay is only _____ .
지연은 일시적인 것입니다.

I'm not into _____ arts.
나는 현대 예술에는 관심이 없다.

term: boundary 경계

terminal 종점
[tə́ːrmənəl]

terminate 종결시키다
[tə́ːrmənèit]

Let's meet outside the bus _____ .
버스 종점 바깥에서 만나자.

His contract was _____ last month.
그의 계약은 지난달에 종료되었다.

terr: earth 땅

terrain 지형
[təréin]

territory 영토
[térətɔ̀ːri]

terrestrial 지구의, 육지의
[təréstriəl]

Those islands are in Korean _____ .
그 섬들은 한국 영토에 속해 있다.

We had to drive over some rough _____ .
우리는 험난한 지형으로 운전해서 가야했다.

Scientists haven't even found all the _____ life on our planet. 과학자들은 지구상의 모든 육상동물을 찾아내지도 못했다.

answers ---

tail: detail / retail / curtail **tain:** abstain / attained / detained / retaining / sustain **tend:** extends / pretend / intensified
tempo(r): temporary / comtemporary **term:** terminal / terminated **terr:** territory / terrain / terrestrial

tract, tray: draw 끌다

extract 추출하다, 뽑아내다
[ikstrǽkt]

attract (관심을) 끌다
[ətrǽkt]

portray 묘사하다
[pɔːrtréi]

distract 주의를 딴 곳으로 돌리다
[distrǽkt]

contract 계약서
[kántrækt]

He _____ himself as a victim. 그는 자신을 희생자로 묘사했다.

I was _____ by a loud noise. 나는 시끄러운 소리에 집중력을 잃었다.

I have to have a tooth _____ . 나는 이를 하나 뽑아야 한다.

The scent will _____ certain insects. 그 냄새는 어떤 곤충들을 끌어들일 것이다.

Have you signed the _____ yet? 아직 계약서에 사인 안 했나요?

trem: shake, fear 떨다, 두려워하다

tremor 떨림
[trémər]

tremble 떨다
[trémbəl]

Her lip started to _____ and then she cried.
그녀의 입술이 떨리기 시작하더니 울었다.

I heard a _____ in her voice.
나는 그녀의 목소리에서 떨림을 들었다.

tres, trans: across 가로질러, 넘어

trespass (무단) 침입, 침해
[tréspəs]

transform 변형시키다
[trænsfɔ́ːrm]

transparent 투명한
[trænspɛ́ərənt]

transition 과도기
[trænzíʃən]

He was arrested for _____ .
그는 무단 침입 죄로 체포되었다.

He poured water into a _____ bottle.
그는 투명한 병에 물을 부었다.

Making the _____ from youth to adulthood can be very painful. 청소년에서 성인으로 넘어가는 것은 매우 고통스러울 수 있다.

Increased population has _____ the landscape.
증가한 인구는 그 풍경을 바뀌게 했다.

tribute: give 주다

attribute 속성, 특질
[ətríbjuːt]

contribute 기여[공헌]하다
[kəntríbjut]

distribute 분배하다
[distríbjuːt]

He did not _____ to the project at all.
그는 그 프로젝트에 전혀 기여하지 않았다.

A man is _____ leaflets to passers-by.
한 남자가 행인들에게 전단지를 돌리고 있다.

Both candidates possess the _____ we want in a leader.
후보자 둘 다 우리가 지도자에게 원하는 자질을 갖추고 있다.

uni: one 하나

unique 유일한, 독특한
[juːníːk]

union 연합, 동맹
[júːnjən]

He joined the teachers' _____ .
그는 교직원 협회에 가입했다.

Humans are _____ among mammals in several respects.
인간은 포유류 중에서 여러 측면에서 독특하다

vac: empty 텅 빈

vacuum 진공의
[vǽkjuəm]

evacuate 비우다
[ivǽkjuèit]

vacant 빈, 공허한
[véikənt]

A pump was used to create a _____ inside the bottle.
병 속을 진공상태로 만드는 데 펌프가 사용되었다.

These lockers are all _____ .
사물함이 모두 비었다.

Residents were ordered to _____ the building.
입주자들이 건물 밖으로 나가라는 명령을 받았다.

answers ---
tract: portrayed / distracted / extracted / attract / contract **trem:** tremble / tremor **tres:** trespass / transparent / transition / transformed **tribute:** contribute / distributing / attributes **uni:** union / unique **vac:** vacuum / vacant / evacuate

vad: go 가다

evade 회피하다
[ivéid]

pervade 만연하다
[pərvéid]

invade 침입하다
[invéid]

The island was _____ during the war.
그 섬은 전쟁 중에 침략되었다.

He skilfully _____ reporters' questions.
그는 능숙하게 기자들의 질문을 빠져나갔다.

A strange sour smell _____ the air.
이상하고 시큼한 냄새가 공중에 가득했다.

vert, vers: turn 바꾸다

extrovert 외향적인
[ékstrouvə̀:rt]

convert 전환하다, 개종하다
[kənvə́:rt]

reverse 뒤로 가다
[rivə́:rs]

They _____ the old school into luxury flats.
그들은 폐교를 호화 아파트로 고쳤다.

She _____ into the parking space.
그녀는 주차장으로 후진했다.

My English teacher is a friendly, _____ young
Australian.
우리 영어 선생님은 상냥하고, 외향적인, 젊은 호주 인이다.

vis, vid: look 보다

evidence 증거
[évidəns]

supervise 감독하다
[sú:pərvàiz]

visible 보이는
[vízəbəl]

revise 수정하다
[riváiz]

The outline of the mountains was clearly _____ .
산맥의 윤곽이 또렷하게 보였다.

So far we have no _____ of life on other planets.
현재까지 우리는 다른 행성에 생명체가 있다는 증거가 없다.

He closely _____ the research.
그는 그 연구를 면밀히 감독했다.

We have to _____ our plans because of the delays.
연기되었기 때문에 우리는 계획을 수정해야 한다.

viv, vit: live, life 생명

vital 생명의, 필수적인
[váitl]

vivid 생생한
[vívid]

revive 되살아나다
[riváiv]

Regular exercise is _____ for your health.
규칙적인 운동이 당신의 건강에 필수다.

The economy is beginning to _____ .
경제가 되살아나고 있다.

She had a _____ picture of him in her mind.
그녀의 마음속에는 그의 모습이 생생했다.

voc, voke: call, sound 부름, 소리

evoke 일깨우다
[ivóuk]

advocate 지지하다
[ǽdvəkit]

vocabulary 어휘
[voukǽbjəlèri]

Extremists were openly _____ violence.
극단주의자들이 무력을 공공연히 지지하고 있었다.

Her speech _____ a hostile response.
그녀의 연설은 적대적인 반응을 일깨웠다.

I wish I had a wide _____ .
내가 방대한 어휘력을 보유하고 있다면 좋겠다.

vol: will 의지

malevolent 악의적인
[məlévələnt]

volunteer 자원봉사자
[vàləntíər]

Can I have a _____ to clean the board, please?
누구 자원해서 칠판 지워 줄 사람 있나요?

He gave her a dark, _____ look.
그는 어둡고 악의에 찬 모습을 보였다.

volv, volu: roll 구르다, 돌다

involve 포함하다
[inválv]

I didn't realize publishing a book _____ so much work.
책을 출간하는 것이 그렇게 많은 일을 포함하는지 몰랐다.

evolve 전개[발전]하다
[iválv]

The school has _____ its own style of teaching.
그 학교는 자체 교수법을 발전시켰다.